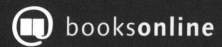 booksonline

Read this book online today:

With SAP PRESS BooksOnline we offer you online access to knowledge from the leading SAP experts. Whether you use it as a beneficial supplement or as an alternative to the printed book, with SAP PRESS BooksOnline you can:

• Access your book anywhere, at any time. All you need is an Internet connection.
• Perform full text searches on your book and on the entire SAP PRESS library.
• Build your own personalized SAP library.

The SAP PRESS customer advantage:

Register this book today at *www.sap-press.com* and obtain exclusive free trial access to its online version. If you like it (and we think you will), you can choose to purchase permanent, unrestricted access to the online edition at a very special price!

Here's how to get started:

1. Visit *www.sap-press.com*.
2. Click on the link for SAP PRESS BooksOnline and login (or create an account).
3. Enter your free trial license key, shown below in the corner of the page.
4. Try out your online book with full, unrestricted access for a limited time!

Your personal free trial **license key**
for this online book is:

8pqr-5tad-f7xj-skw9

Customizing Materials Management Processes in SAP® ERP

SAP PRESS is a joint initiative of SAP and Galileo Press. The know-how offered by SAP specialists combined with the expertise of the Galileo Press publishing house offers the reader expert books in the field. SAP PRESS features first-hand information and expert advice, and provides useful skills for professional decision-making.

SAP PRESS offers a variety of books on technical and business related topics for the SAP user. For further information, please visit our website: *www.sap-press.com*.

Martin Murray
Materials Management with SAP ERP: Functionality and Technical Configuration (3rd Edition)
2011, 666 pp. (hardcover)
ISBN 978-1-59229-358-2

Faisal Mahboob
Integrating Materials Management with Financial Accounting in SAP (2nd Edition)
2013, ~ 500 pp. (hardcover)
ISBN 978-1-59229-426-8

Marc Hoppe et al.
Materials Planning with SAP
2008, 564 pp. (hardcover)
ISBN 978-1-59229-259-2

Jörg Thomas Dickersbach and Gerhard Keller
Production Planning and Control with SAP ERP (2nd Edition)
2011, 338 pp. (hardcover)
ISBN 978-1-59229-360-5

Akash Agrawal

Customizing Materials Management Processes in SAP® ERP

Galileo Press

Bonn • Boston

Galileo Press is named after the Italian physicist, mathematician and philosopher Galileo Galilei (1564–1642). He is known as one of the founders of modern science and an advocate of our contemporary, heliocentric worldview. His words *Eppur si muove* (And yet it moves) have become legendary. The Galileo Press logo depicts Jupiter orbited by the four Galilean moons, which were discovered by Galileo in 1610.

Editor Laura Korslund
Acquisitions Editor Meg Dunkerley
Copyeditor Julie McNamee
Cover Design Graham Geary
Photo Credit iStockphoto.com/adventtr
Layout Design Vera Brauner
Production Graham Geary
Typesetting Publishers' Design and Production Services, Inc.
Printed and bound in the United States of America, on paper from sustainable sources

ISBN 978-1-59229-415-2

© 2012 by Galileo Press Inc., Boston (MA)

2nd edition 2012

Library of Congress Cataloging-in-Publication Data
Agrawal, Akash.
Customizing materials management processes in SAP ERP / Akash Agrawal. —
2nd ed.
p. cm.
ISBN 978-1-59229-415-2 — ISBN 1-59229-415-4 1. Business logistics.
2. Purchasing. 3. Industrial management. 4. SAP ERP. I. Title.
HD38.5.A37 2012
658.70285'53—dc23
2012012439

Contents at a Glance

Dear Reader,

When you speak, we listen! Since the first edition of this book published in 2009, readers like you have been leaving feedback for us and the author, Akash Agrawal. The copies flew off the shelves, and Akash and SAP PRESS decided to team up once again to give you the book you now hold. I'm pleased to present the second edition of *Customizing Materials Management Processes in SAP ERP*, updated for SAP ERP 6.0, enhancement pack 5, and expanded and revised to talk more about the hows and whys of Materials Management in SAP.

Drawing on his years of experience with SAP, Akash has gone to great lengths to make sure this book provides everything you need to know in order to do your job effectively. Throughout the project, I was continually impressed by his dedication to the schedule, detailed attention to achieving the goals of the new book, and seemingly superhuman patience with all of the questions his pesky and demanding editor (me) asked. Now that the result of months of hard work is in, sit back, kick up your feet (unless your company frowns on that), and prepare to learn how to make Materials Management in SAP work best for your business!

We at SAP PRESS are always eager to hear your opinion. What do you think about the second edition of *Customizing Materials Management Processes in SAP ERP*? As your comments and suggestions are our most useful tools to help us make our books the best they can be, we encourage you to visit our website at *www.sap-press.com* and share your feedback.

Thank you for purchasing a book from SAP PRESS!

Laura Korslund
Editor, SAP PRESS

Galileo Press
Boston, MA

laura.korslund@galileo-press.com
www.sap-press.com

Contents

6   Invoice Verification 237

7 Inventory Valuation ... 313

8 Key Configurations in Materials Management in SAP ... 339

Acknowledgments

A book of this proportion would not have been possible without the continuous support of family and friends. I would like to give a very special thanks to all of my family, and especially to my parents for their continuous follow-up to finish this book.

From SAP PRESS, I would like to thank Laura Korslund for her trust and hard work in releasing this book.

In addition, I would like to thank my colleague Prasad Bhat for supporting me during the entire process, and my colleague and senior leader, Ashwin Yardi, for the inspiration to write this book. Furthermore, this book would not have been possible without the help of my friend Yogesh Pampattiwar. Yogesh has extensive experience in procurement and Materials Management, and he has shared his knowledge to make this the best reference book possible.

A special thanks to financial accounting guru Alok Agrawal. Alok is an expert in financial accounting and SAP FI and CO. He helped with writing the text on the various MM–FI integration areas.

Last but not the least, I would like to thank Sanjog Malegaonkar. Sanjog has decades of experience in oil & gas and retail petroleum, as well as vast experience in setting up a large automotive industry plant and operations. He has helped in reviewing the book and he has also suggested many improvement areas.

Akash Agrawal

Preface

First of all, thank you for the overwhelming response for first edition. I would like to thank those readers who sent me various positive responses and let me know which areas could be improved in the second edition.

Now I would like to welcome you to the second edition of *Customizing Materials Management Processes in SAP ERP*, a compilation of business processes and configuration techniques. During my work on various materials management (MM) implementation projects, I always wished for a good resource that could help offer quick solutions and easy-to-follow guidance. That wish has come true with the completion of this reference book. This book will enhance your knowledge of Materials Management in SAP by providing process steps and configuration details for essential business processes.

Who Needs This Book

The main purpose of this book is to explain the various industry best business processes used in MM. As such, it's a reference book for MM consultants to use during their SAP implementation, rollout, and support projects. This book will help consultants find quick solutions for their clients.

This book is also useful if you're an end user who wants to become familiar with common MM functionalities. If you're working on Sales and Distribution (SD) in SAP, for example, this book will help you understand MM-SD integration by covering intercompany stock transfers via SD, inventory management for goods issue to customers, special stock handling, and more. Similarly, if you are working on SAP ERP Financials Financial Accounting, this book will offer you a greater understanding of MM-FI integration. Topics covered in this area include automatic account determination and general ledger account posting during various business transactions.

How to Use This Book

Each chapter in this book focuses on business processes, explaining the business scenario and the step-by-step procedures—supplemented by screenshots—needed to execute the scenario in SAP.

Here's a brief overview of what each chapter covers.

▶ **Chapter 1: Introduction**
This chapter starts with the importance of an ERP system and SAP. It explains the SAP system landscape, which is very important for every SAP professional. It will also give you an overview of how different functional areas of SAP software are integrated.

▶ **Chapter 2: The SAP Organizational Structure**
This chapter explains the various elements of an organizational structure and provides you with in-depth knowledge of all possible organizational structure scenarios.

▶ **Chapter 3: Master Data**
This chapter describes the importance of master data and how different master data such as material master, vendor master, and purchasing info records are maintained at different organization levels. Various important elements of master data, such as material type and vendor account group are covered in detail.

▶ **Chapter 4: Procurement Processes**
This chapter is the heart of the book because it covers various procurement processes across industry verticals. You will obtain in-depth knowledge of procurement processes and their configuration.

▶ **Chapter 5: Inventory Management Processes**
This chapter explains the inventory management functionality. It also explains the inbound and outbound process in inventory management and describes various stock types in inventory management and physical inventory processes.

▶ **Chapter 6: Invoice Verification**
This chapter explains different invoice processing scenarios and the general ledger account postings in each scenario.

▶ **Chapter 7: Inventory Valuation**
This chapter starts by explaining the importance of inventory valuations and then explains various methods of stock valuation. It also describes the functionality of split valuation and how this can be used in different industry scenarios.

- **Chapter 8: Key Configurations in Materials Management in SAP**
  This chapter describes the pricing procedure and automatic account determination functions in SAP. It also explains the step-by-step configuration of these key areas. In addition, this chapter explains the release strategy and version management functionality configuration for various purchasing documents.

- **Chapter 9: Material Classification**
  This chapter explains the importance and use of the classification technique and how this is used for material classification. It also describes the step-by-step process to classify materials.

- **Chapter 10: Batch Management**
  This chapter talks about the usage of batch management, how the batch management process works in SAP, and provides configuration steps.

- **Chapter 11: Material Requirements Planning**
  This chapter explains various types of MRP and how each type of MRP can be used in a real-world scenario. This chapter also explains step-by-step MRP configuration.

- **Chapter 12: Enhancements in Materials Management**
  This chapter is a good starting point for consultants who don't have a technical/programming background. Here, we discuss the various types of development objects in SAP and how they can be used in real time.

- **Chapter 13: Conclusion**
  This final chapter reviews the content covered in each chapter and provides you with lessons learned.

Let's get started. In the next chapter, you'll get an overview of SAP ERP and MM.

Enterprise resource planning applications are no longer optional for enterprises. They play a vital and essential role in business operations, from running day-to-day transactions to providing informative reports and analysis. SAP is the hottest topic in ERP software, and the subject of this chapter.

1 Introduction

Enterprise resource planning (ERP) includes planning, executing, and reporting across multiple business functions or business units. To manage various functional areas within the enterprise, you need to have an appropriate system or application. Different ERP systems (software products) are available from various vendors. The term ERP originally referred to how a large organization planned to use organization-wide resources and, in the past, was only used in reference to larger industrial organizations. Today, however, the concept of ERP is extremely comprehensive and can be applied to any type of business, large or small.

Today's ERP systems can cover a wide range of functions and integrate them into one unified database. Originally, ERP systems were used to control only human resources; supply chain management, customer relations management, financials, manufacturing, and warehouse management were all single, standalone software applications, usually housed with their own database and network. Today, however, they all fit under one umbrella: the ERP system.

In this chapter, we'll provide you with a brief overview of SAP ERP, an introduction to Materials Management (MM) in SAP, and a description of the SAP system environment.

1.1 Overview of SAP ERP

SAP ERP is the world's leading ERP software, developed by SAP AG. SAP ERP is integrated software, which means that all functional areas fall under one umbrella, allowing information to be shared among functional areas.

Figure 1.1 shows some of the functional departments within an enterprise. Each functional department needs information from other departments, which is made possible by an integrated system. For example, the Sales and Distribution department is responsible for marketing and collecting customer orders and therefore generates a demand for finished goods in the Production Planning department. Similarly, raw materials are procured by the Purchasing department based on requirements from the Planning department and kept in inventory and maintained by the Plant Maintenance department. Then, on orders from the Shop Floor Control department, the raw materials are issued to the shop floor. Of course, many of these processes and transactions involve money and must be recorded by the Finance and Controlling department. From just these few examples, you can see how the different departments are dependent on each other and how transaction information flows to multiple departments.

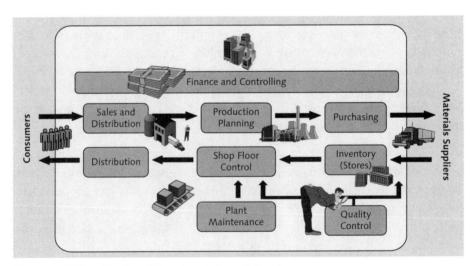

Figure 1.1 Various Functional Departments in an Enterprise

SAP provides an integrated solution for all functional departments of an enterprise by offering a specific component for each. The following are the most commonly used components of SAP ERP:

▶ SAP ERP Financials Financial Accounting (which we'll refer to as Financial Accounting, or FI for short)

▶ Controlling (CO)

- Human Capital Management (HCM; human resources)
- Production Planning (PP)
- Project Systems (PS)
- Sales and Distribution (SD)
- Materials Management (MM)
- Quality Management (QM)
- Plant Maintenance (PM)

SAP has also developed additional products to meet customer requirements. These are also called *new dimensional* products that can be implemented alone or in integration with SAP ERP (or any other ERP) products and include the following:

- SAP Supplier Relationship Management (SAP SRM)
- SAP Supply Chain Management (SAP SCM)
- SAP Customer Relationship Management (SAP CRM)
- SAP NetWeaver Business Warehouse (SAP NetWeaver BW)
- SAP BusinessObjects

Aside from the core components and new dimensional products, SAP also provides industry-specific solutions, including the following:

- **Manufacturing industries**
  - SAP for Aerospace and Defense
  - SAP for Automotive
  - SAP for Consumer Products
  - SAP for Chemicals
  - SAP for Engineering & Construction
  - SAP for High Tech & Electronics
  - SAP for Industrial Machinery & Components
  - SAP for Life Sciences
  - SAP for Mill Products

- ▶ SAP for Mining
- ▶ SAP for Oil and Gas
- ▶ **Services industries**
  - ▶ SAP for Media
  - ▶ SAP for Professional Services
  - ▶ SAP for Telecommunications
  - ▶ SAP for Utilities
  - ▶ SAP for Waste and Recycling
  - ▶ SAP for Travel and Logistics Services
- ▶ **Financial services**
  - ▶ SAP for Banking
  - ▶ SAP for Insurance
- ▶ **Public services**
  - ▶ SAP for Public Sector
  - ▶ SAP for Defense & Security
  - ▶ SAP for Healthcare
  - ▶ SAP for Higher Education & Research
- ▶ **Trading industries**
  - ▶ SAP for Retail
  - ▶ SAP for Wholesale Distribution

SAP software is highly customizable, and it can be altered to meet almost any enterprise requirement. It was originally developed using the ABAP/4 (fourth generation) language, which was used up until the release of SAP 3.1. When SAP 4.0 was introduced, the name of the language was changed to simply ABAP. ABAP is basically the same as ABAP/4 but contains several improvements and features that make it an object-oriented language. In general, you don't need to know ABAP to use SAP software, but SAP does provide the ABAP Development Workbench for customer-specific enhancements. This workbench includes all of the tools necessary to develop and design programs, screens, and more.

1.2 Overview of Materials Management

Materials Management (MM) is a key area within Logistics in SAP. Logistics is the most extensive area of the SAP application and contains the largest number of components: MM, PP, PM, PS, QM, and SD.

MM is a very important component of Logistics because it's tightly integrated with all of the other components of SAP Logistics. MM consists of the following components:

▶ **MM-PUR: Purchasing**
Includes operations such as request for quotation, quotation comparison, outline agreement with vendors, and order monitoring.

▶ **MM-IV: Invoice verification**
Important from an accounting perspective because it allows for vendor payment, and incorrect postings may cause financial loss for the enterprise.

▶ **MM-IM: Inventory management**
Required in every step of supply chain management and is responsible for stock tracking, issuing materials, and receiving materials. Inventory management also verifies the system stock and physical stock at regular intervals and ensures that both records match.

▶ **MM-CBP: Consumption-based planning**
Used to plan the quantity of raw materials to be procured; using CBP is optional.

▶ **MM-EDI: Electronic data interchange**
Required only when you want to send messages—such as purchase orders (POs)—to a vendor in electronic format. Electronic format has many advantages over physical format—such as fax and printouts—because it saves communication time and also the cost of paper and printing.

▶ **MM-IS: Information system**
Contains different reports for management to analyze day-to-day business operations and to help take appropriate strategic decisions. Information systems also provide flexibility to customize reports for customer-specific requirements.

This book deals specifically with MM in SAP ERP operations. However, before we can get to that, you must understand some basic information about the SAP system environment.

1.3 SAP System Environment: Development, Quality, and Production Clients

It's extremely important for everyone involved in SAP implementation, support, rollout, or upgrade projects to understand the SAP system environment. A *system environment* is referred to as a *client*. For example, the development, quality, and production environments are respectively known as the development client, quality client, and production client.

> **Note**
>
> The use of the word "client" here can sometimes cause confusion because the word can also be used to refer to SAP customers.

SAP developed the client concept to use single SAP instances for development, quality testing, and production. Customers can create different clients within the same SAP instance (a single SAP server), for example:

- Client 100: Development
- Client 200: Quality/Testing
- Client 800: Production

Transactional data and master data are differentiated based on a client number, which forms a composite primary key for most of the database tables. When you log on to the SAP system, you enter the client number in the first screen. As shown in Figure 1.2, the client number entered is "800" for production, and the user name and password are entered as well.

When you perform any transaction, the data is saved in a database header table and item table. For example, the header Table EKKO, which is used for PO header data, contains a composite primary key that includes the client number and PO number (see Figure 1.3). The figure shows client 800 and the corresponding PO numbers. If you create a PO for client 800 (the production client), it's saved with a client number and purchase order number and forms a composite primary key. This particular document will only be used for the production client. This is how SAP separates the production, development, and testing data in a single SAP instance. (These tables are also called *client-dependent tables*.)

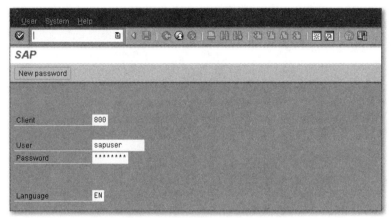

Figure 1.2 SAP Logon Screen: Client Number

Data Browser: Table EKKO Select Entries 200

Check Table...

Table: EKKO
Displayed fields: 20 of 76 Fixed columns: 2 List

Client	Purchasing Doc.	Company Code	Doc. category	Document Type
800	4151504103	1000	F	NB
800	4151504104	1000	F	NB
800	4151504105	1000	F	NB
800	4151504106	1000	F	NB
800	4151504107	1000	F	NB
800	4151504108	1000	F	NB
800	4151504109	1000	F	NB
800	4151504110	1000	F	NB
800	4151504111	1000	F	NB
800	4151504112	1000	F	NB

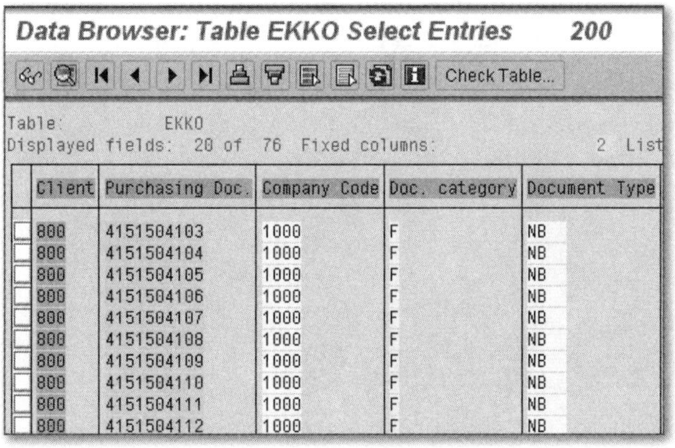

Figure 1.3 Purchase Order Header Table EKKO: Client-Dependent

While configuring the SAP system, you might get a warning stating that a table is *cross-client* (see Figure 1.4). Cross-client tables are client-independent tables, and any changes made in these tables are applicable for all clients.

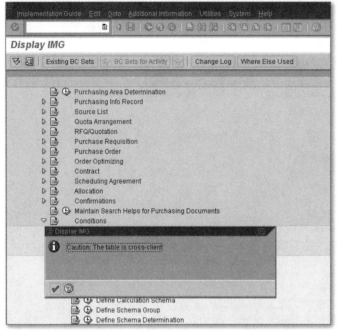

Figure 1.4 Warning Message: Cross-Client Table

Figure 1.5 shows an example of a client-independent table. Table T682 (access sequence table) is a cross-client table; therefore, the client number is not involved in the primary key.

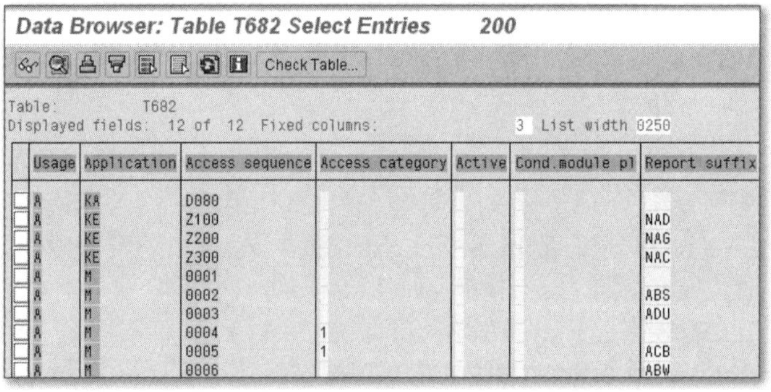

Figure 1.5 Database Table for Access Sequence: Cross-Client Table

The majority of SAP customers use separate servers for each client, which are hosted on separate physical boxes.

Note

Before you start working on any project, it's important to understand the customer's system landscape.

In the following sections, we'll discuss the different types of clients and the process of moving objects from one client to another.

1.3.1 Client Descriptions

Each client is created for a specific purpose, and the system landscape is determined based on customer requirements, complexity, and data safety. The system landscape varies for each customer but will always have a minimum of three clients: development, quality/testing, and production (Figure 1.6).

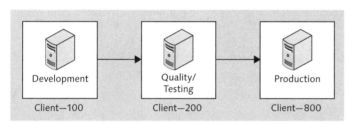

Figure 1.6 System Landscape

The development client is where the customization and development work take place. After the development work is completed, the customization object creates a transport request in the development client, and the object is transported to the quality/testing client. Finally, after it has been tested and found satisfactory, the object is moved to the production client. End users interact with the production client; day-to-day operational transactional data is entered here. Because the production client is used for real-time data, it's very sensitive. Any test transaction posted in the production client is posted in a real-time business transaction of the customer, so you must be careful while working on the production client.

Some SAP customers create two separate clients (a sandbox client and a golden client) instead of one development client. A *sandbox* client is mainly used for configuration ideas and development, and it's also where system design work takes place. When you are comfortable with your configuration solution in the sandbox client, you must reconfigure your solution in the golden client. If the configuration in the sandbox client isn't appropriate, it isn't reconfigured in the golden client. Sandbox clients may contain many additional customizations that haven't been reconfigured in the golden client. The golden client is configured only for approved designs, so it's always a clean system.

The golden client is also known as the configuration client. Ideally, no transactions or testing takes place in the golden client, which means it doesn't have any master data or transactional data. The golden client is used only for configuration and to transport the configuration to the testing/quality and production clients.

1.3.2 Transport Requests

Transport requests are used to move configuration settings from one client to another and are created automatically when you make any changes to configuration tables or programs. When a transport request has been created, it can be moved to another client only if it's released. Basis consultants are responsible for transporting transport request from one client to another.

There are many transaction codes in SAP software to manage transport requests. You can use Transaction SE10 to view and manage transport requests. This transaction allows you to select the request types and statuses you want to display (Figure 1.7).

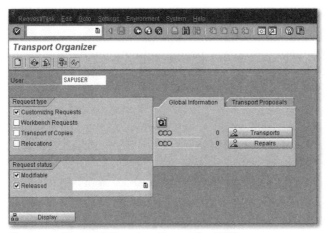

Figure 1.7 Transport Organizer: Transaction SE10

After you click on the DISPLAY button, the system displays the list of transport requests (Figure 1.8). Transport requests with a status of RELEASED can't be changed.

Transport requests with a status of MODIFIABLE can be changed. You can select the same transport request number when saving configuration changes so that the changes are updated in the same transport request. However, if the transport request isn't modifiable, you can't select it for changes; instead, you need to create a new transport request for the changes.

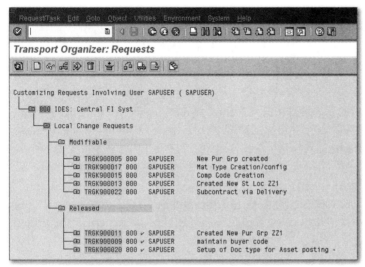

Figure 1.8 Transport Organizer: List of Transport Requests

To release the transport request, select the transport request number and click on the TRANSPORT button (or press F9). First, release the reference Customizing tasks, which you will find under the transport request. Then release the transport request. After a successful release transport, the request is changed to a status of RELEASED and can't be modified.

> **Note**
>
> If you have multiple transport requests for the same Customizing table, you need to ensure that the transport requests are transported in the appropriate sequence. Otherwise, you may miss the configuration settings in the target client properly due to overlapping transport requests (because the last configuration settings can be overwritten by the previous configuration settings).
>
> Now, SAP Solution Manager offers a Change Request Management tool. This tool helps in managing transport requests. It offers storage of documentation for the transport requests, ease of tracking, and auditing changes.

1.4   SAP Enhancement Packages

SAP released its first version SAP R/2 in 1979. Since then, SAP has been continuously working to enhance the functionality and technology to bridge any gaps. In 1991, SAP presented its first application in its SAP R/3 system. With its client-server concept, SAP provided a uniform graphical user interface, dedicated use of relational databases, and support for servers from various manufacturers. In 1992, SAP successfully installed R/3 with selected pilot customers—bringing SAP R/3 to the general public and entering the next level of growth.

SAP has continuously enhanced the technology and added new functionalities, evidenced by releasing various versions such as SAP R/3 3.1h, SAP R/3 4.0B, SAP R/3 4.6B, SAP R/3 4.6C, and SAP R/3 4.7 Enterprise Edition. Existing SAP customers have been upgrading their systems from time to time to new released versions of SAP. After the Enterprise Edition, SAP released SAP ECC 5.0 (Enterprise Central Component) and then released SAP ECC 6.0. After releasing ECC 6.0, SAP has changed its release strategy and decided to release EHPs (enhancement packages) instead of new releases (see Figure 1.9). Enhancement packages are much simpler to deploy as compared to SAP version upgrades. EHP5 is the release at the time of this book's publication, and EHP6 is in process to be released soon.

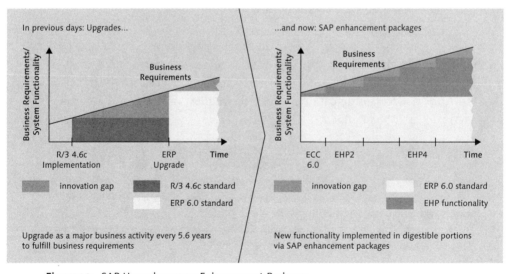

Figure 1.9   SAP Upgrades versus Enhancement Packages

SAP designed the enhancement package for SAP ERP to easily deliver business- and industry-specific functionality, enterprise services bundles, and other functions that enhance and simplify the use of SAP ERP through improvements to the user interface and processes.

You can activate the latest enhancement package via the switch framework, which gives you the flexibility to choose what you want to implement, helps isolate impacted objects, and minimizes testing requirements. This rapid, nonintrusive deployment of selected improvements enables you to benefit from a superior solution fit without risking side effects to other parts of your applications. Figure 1.10 gives you a visual of how the SAP product has evolved and is currently evolving with enhanced technology and applications.

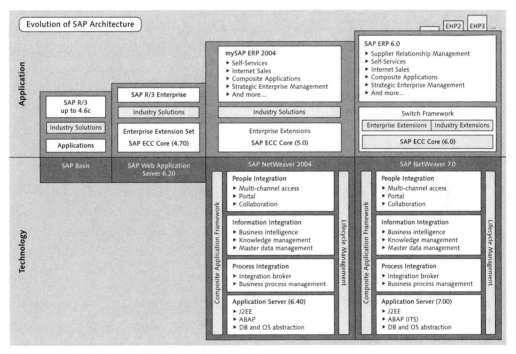

Figure 1.10 Application and Technology Enhancement

37

1.5 SAP Add-Ons and SAP Preconfigured Systems

SAP offers a wide range of add-ons that you can use to enhance your standard SAP system. Similarly, SAP offers preconfigured systems (PCS), which are basically SAP Best Practices for certain industries. To reduce the implementation time, SAP recommends using PCS, where the business processes for an industry are configured and ready to use.

1.5.1 SAP Add-Ons

You can install various add-ons offered by SAP, such as industry solutions, plug-ins, or custom development objects. SAP developed an add-on installation tool—Transaction SAINT—to enable you to install and upgrade these add-ons directly from your standard SAP systems.

Some of the add-ons include the following:

▶ SAP cProject Suite
▶ SAP Catalog Content Management
▶ SAP Learning Solution
▶ SAP Multi Resource Scheduling
▶ SAP Application Interface Framework
▶ SAP Asset Retirement Obligation Management
▶ SAP Asset Lifecycle Accounting

1.5.2 SAP Preconfigured Systems (PCS)

SAP PCS can be installed using the add-on installation tool (Transaction SAINT). A PCS reduces the amount of work needed to install and customize an industry-specific solution.

A PCS consists of the following elements:

▶ Industry-specific solution
▶ Industry-specific SAP client
▶ Industry-specific Customizing data

A PCS also contains test data and industry-specific documentation. You can use this test data to try out examples of processes and scenarios.

1.6   Summary

This chapter provided you with an introduction to SAP ERP and an overview of SAP as a whole. It also outlined the basic components of MM within SAP ERP operations. Most importantly, this chapter described the SAP system landscape and the significance of each system environment: the development, quality, and production clients.

In the next chapter, we'll discuss the organizational structure used in SAP systems.

The organizational structure is the key for a successful SAP implementation. To achieve flawless execution of business processes, it's extremely important that the organizational structure is accurately mapped in the SAP system. This chapter discusses the different types of organizational structures and how to set them up.

2   The SAP Organizational Structure

Configuring an accurate organizational structure is the key to a successful SAP implementation. From a Materials Management (MM) perspective, purchasing organizations, plants, storage locations, and purchasing groups are important elements of an organizational structure. In this chapter, we'll review what organizational structures are and how they're used in SAP systems. We'll also provide the configuration steps for the various possible organizational structures available in the SAP system. You'll learn about many different elements of organizational structures available in industries and how to map these elements into the SAP organizational structure.

2.1   Introduction to Organizational Structures

For any successful implementation project, you must understand your customer's organizational structure and map this organizational structure in a way that meets all of the business process requirements. To do this, you must also understand the essential terminology used in an industry and in the SAP organizational structure.

As shown in Figure 2.1, the different functional departments of an organization are mapped into SAP software using organizational units. *Organizational units* are responsible for a set of business functions. An enterprise or corporate group is mapped into SAP software as a *client*, and different companies or subsidiaries of an enterprise are referred to as the *company code*. Clients and company codes are two types of organizational units that are found at the highest level in the SAP organizational structure.

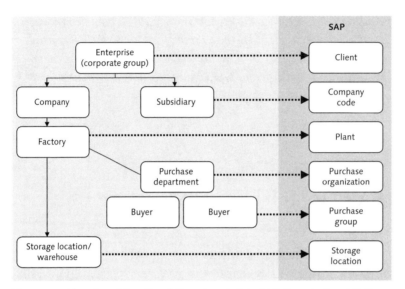

Figure 2.1 Mapping of Functional Departments into SAP Organizational Units

When discussing the levels of the SAP organizational structure, the client is the highest element, but there are many other levels (see Figure 2.2). A client may have one or more company codes assigned to it; each company code may have one or more plants assigned to it; and each plant may have one or more storage locations assigned to it. Furthermore, each company may have a set of purchasing groups. A *purchasing group* is a buyer or group of buyers defined independently of the organizational structure. Therefore, it isn't assigned to a purchasing organization or company code.

Detailed definitions of client, company code, plant, storage locations, and purchasing groups are provided in the following sections.

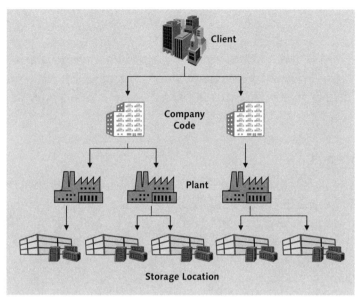

Figure 2.2 The Organizational Structure in SAP Systems

2.1.1   Client/Company

As the highest organizational unit in an SAP system, the client can be a corporate group and can represent a company or a conglomerate of companies. For example, consider a fictional corporate group called ABC Corporation, which has companies such as ABC Steel, ABC FMCG, and ABC Pharmacy. If ABC Corporation wants to implement SAP software for all of its companies in a single instance, then it should be represented as a client. On the other hand, if the different companies install the SAP software individually, then each company will have one SAP instance, and the individual companies will represent the client.

2.1.2   Company Code

The company code is the smallest organizational unit for which you can have an independent accounting department within external accounting. For example, a corporate group (a client) may have one or more independent companies, all of which have their own SAP General Ledger (G/L) account, balance sheet, and profit and loss (P&L) account. Each of these independent business entities needs to be created in the SAP system as separate company codes.

2.1.3   Plant

In industry terminology, a manufacturing facility is called a plant. In an SAP system, however, a plant can be a manufacturing facility, sales office, corporate head office, maintenance plant, or central delivery warehouse. In general, the plant can be any location within a company code that is involved in some activity for the company code.

2.1.4   Storage Location

A storage location is a place within a plant where materials are kept. Inventory management on a quantity basis is carried out at the storage location level in the plant, as is physical inventory. *Physical inventory* is the process of verifying physical stock with the system stock. If any differences exist in stock quantity, system stocks are updated with actual physical stock quantity. Physical inventory is carried out at each storage location level.

2.1.5   Purchasing Organization

In industry terminology, the purchasing department deals with vendors and is responsible for all procurement activities. The purchasing department is mapped as a *purchasing organization* in the SAP system. Purchasing organizations negotiate conditions of purchase with vendors for one or more plants, and they are legally responsible for honoring purchasing contracts.

2.1.6   Purchasing Group

A purchasing group is a term for a buyer or group of buyers responsible for certain purchasing activities. Because a purchase order is a legal document, the purchasing group is represented on a purchase order or contract. The purchasing group can also play an important role in reporting various purchasing transactions. In an SAP system, a purchasing group isn't assigned to purchasing organizations or any other organizational units. Purchasing groups are defined at the client level and can create purchasing documents for any purchasing organization.

Now that you have a good understanding of the various organizational units, let's move on to learn how to create an organizational structure based on business scenarios.

2.2   Business Scenarios and Organizational Structure

The organizational structure needs to be designed and configured in the system based on the different business scenario requirements of the enterprise (client). An SAP system's organizational structure is very flexible, and there are a variety of possible combinations. We'll address these in the following sections.

2.2.1   Scenario 1: Plant-Specific Purchasing

Let's say your customers have separate purchasing departments for each plant, and each purchasing department is responsible for negotiating with vendors, creating contracts, and issuing purchase orders. This scenario is called a *plant-specific purchasing organization*. In this scenario, you need to define a purchasing organization for each plant in the SAP system and then assign these purchasing organizations to their respective plants.

For example, in Figure 2.3, the client has two different company codes, and each company code has plants assigned to it. Company Code-1 has two plants, and Company Code-2 has one plant. Additionally, for each plant, there is a separate purchasing organization. Purchasing Organization 1, Purchasing Organization 2, and Purchasing Organization 3 are assigned to Plant-1, Plant-2, and Plant-3, respectively.

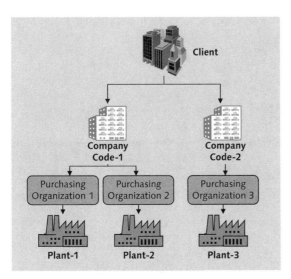

Figure 2.3   Plant-Specific Purchasing Organization

2.2.2 Scenario 2: Cross-Plant Purchasing

Some customers may have a scenario where a single purchasing department is responsible for procurement activities for more than one plant. In this case, you need to create a purchasing organization that's responsible for more than one plant in the same company code.

For example, in Figure 2.4, the client has two different company codes, and each company code has plants assigned to it. Company Code-1 has two plants, and Company Code-2 has one plant. Purchasing Organization 1 is assigned to Plant-1 and Plant-2 because it's responsible for both of the plants in Company Code-1.

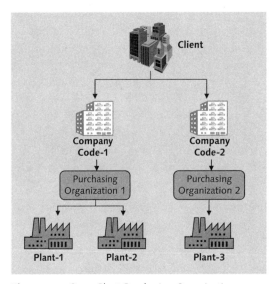

Figure 2.4 Cross-Plant Purchasing Organization

Example

Let's consider a real-world example of a cross-plant purchasing organization. Leading Airlines Company, headquartered in Mumbai, India, has domestic flight services to many cities such as Delhi, Bangalore, and Chennai. The company has created only one purchasing organization, and all of the airports are considered plants. A single purchasing organization is assigned to all of the plants and responsible to procure the goods for all of the airports. Each airport contains storage locations. For customizing details on how to support this business scenario in the SAP system, refer to Sections 2.3.6 and 2.3.7.

2.2.3 Scenario 3: Cross-Company Code/Corporate Group-Wide Purchasing

Some customers have just one purchasing organization for the procurement activities of multiple plants in different company codes. As you can see from Figure 2.5, the client has two different company codes, and each has plants assigned to it. Company Code-1 has two plants, and Company Code-2 has one plant. Purchasing Organization 1 is assigned to Plant-1, Plant-2, and Plant-3 of Company Code-1 and Company Code-2.

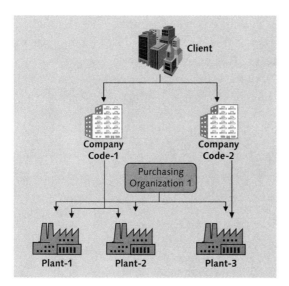

Figure 2.5 Cross-Company Code Purchasing Organization

Example

One of the world's leading producers of printing papers, headquartered in Germany, has more than 15 company codes and 50 plants—and all of the plants are assigned to a single purchasing organization. This was done so that this purchasing organization controls all vendor negotiations, making them responsible for high-volume orders, which increased their negotiation power. Using a single purchasing organization also makes it easier to maintain and track long-term contracts with vendors. For customizing details, go to Sections 2.3.6 and 2.3.7.

> **Note**
>
> In SAP Customizing, you can assign a purchasing organization to a company code and plant. In cross-company code purchasing organizations, you need to assign purchasing organizations to plants only. Don't assign purchasing organizations to company codes. Configuring details are given in Section 2.3.7.

2.2.4   Scenario 4: Reference Purchasing Organization

Some customers may have a scenario where they have one centralized purchasing department at the corporate group level that is responsible for the negotiation and creation of global agreements. These agreements are used by local purchasing organizations to create purchase orders. This business scenario helps companies negotiate better prices due to high-volume purchases. In an SAP system, such a purchasing organization is referred to as a *reference purchasing organization*.

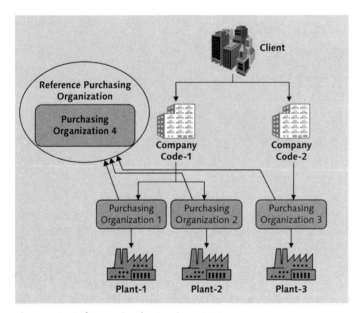

Figure 2.6   Reference Purchasing Organization

For example, in Figure 2.6 the client has two different company codes, and each company code has plants assigned to it. Company Code-1 has two plants, and Company Code-2 has one plant. For each plant, there is a separate purchasing organization: Purchasing Organization 1, Purchasing Organization 2, and Purchasing Organization 3, which are assigned to Plant-1, Plant-2, and Plant-3, respectively. Purchasing Organization 4 is assigned to Purchasing Organization 1, Purchasing Organization 2, and Purchasing Organization 3.

Purchasing Organization 4 is the reference purchasing organization. The reference purchasing organization can negotiate with vendors and create global outline agreements (contracts and scheduling agreements). Plant-specific purchasing organizations (i.e., Purchasing Organization 1, Purchasing Organization 2, and Purchasing Organization 3) can issue purchase orders to vendors with reference to these global agreements.

2.2.5 Scenario 5: Standard Purchasing Organization

SAP also provides a *standard purchasing organization*, which is used to create automatic purchase orders. In the automatic purchase order creation process, the system needs to find the purchasing organization. The system gets the plant code from the purchase requisition and, from the plant code system, determines the standard purchasing organization (because the standard purchasing organization is assigned to the plant). Finally, a purchase order is created.

Now that you have a thorough understanding of the different organizational structure elements and how to apply these elements to different business scenarios, let's move on to the actual steps needed to set up organizational structures.

2.3 Setting Up Organizational Structures in an SAP System

Configuring organizational structures in a sequence with the correct steps is very important. Without the correct configuration, your business transactions will end up posting incorrect entries. In this section, you'll learn the step-by-step procedures to correctly configure an organizational structure.

2.3.1 Creating Company Codes

In general, we recommend that when creating a company code, you copy a company code from an existing company code. In a standard system, company code 0001 is provided by SAP for this purpose. When you copy company codes, the system also copies the parameters specific to the company code. If necessary, you can then change the specific data in the relevant application, which is less time consuming than creating a new company code.

To copy the company code from an existing company code, go to SAP IMG • ENTERPRISE STRUCTURE • DEFINITION • FINANCIAL ACCOUNTING • EDIT, COPY, DELETE, CHECK COMPANY CODE.

Click on the company code COPY option, and then click on the COPY ORGANIZATION OBJECTS button. As shown in Figure 2.7, enter "0001" in the FROM COMPANY CODE field (company code 0001 is SAP AG), and enter the code you want to create into the TO COMPANY CODE field. The company code can be a maximum of four digits long and can be alphanumeric.

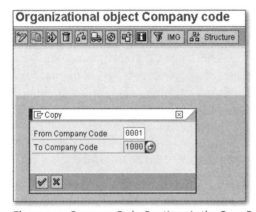

Figure 2.7 Company Code Creation via the Copy Function

Click on the OK button, and a popup window asks whether you want to copy the G/L account company code data. Click YES. When a message appears concerning changing the local currency, select the appropriate currency.

You'll now see a message that outlines the completed activities. From here, you can edit the data in your newly created company code by going to the navigation path SAP IMG • ENTERPRISE STRUCTURE • DEFINITION • FINANCIAL ACCOUNTING • EDIT, COPY, DELETE, CHECK COMPANY CODE • SELECT EDIT COMPANY CODE DATA. By selecting your company code and clicking on the DETAILS button, you can change the company name, city, country, currency, and language.

2.3.2   Defining Valuation Levels

Stock materials can be managed in inventory on the basis of quantity, value, or both. This depends on the material type of the material master record. For each material type, you can configure whether inventory management is on a quantity basis, a value basis, or both. In a standard system, raw material (material type code ROH) is managed on a quantity and value basis. If the stock is managed on a quantity basis, this means that every stock movement such as goods issue or goods receipt is noted in inventory management, and stock quantities are updated. Similarly, if stocks are managed on a value basis, the stock value that is a material value is updated in the financial book of accounts during every goods movement transaction such as goods issue or goods receipt. When you procure valuated materials (managed on a value basis), the stock value is updated into stock G/L accounts. The valuation of stock materials can be done at the plant or company code level. Based on the customer requirements, you need to define the value area for the valuated materials.

To access or define the valuation level, follow the navigation path SAP IMG • ENTERPRISE STRUCTURE • DEFINITION • LOGISTICS-GENERAL • DEFINE VALUATION LEVEL.

Two options are available:

▶ VALUATION AREA IS A PLANT

▶ VALUATION LEVEL IS A COMPANY CODE

Select the required option, and click on SAVE. The valuation area/level is simply the level at which you want to valuate your inventory. If you define valuation at the plant level (recommended), you need to define a separate valuation area for each plant, and stock materials will be valuated separately for each plant.

SAP recommends setting the plant as a valuation area, which is necessary if you are using SAP Production Planning, Costing, or SAP for Retail.

> **Note**
> Once set, you cannot switch the valuation level from plant to company code, or vice versa.

2.3.3   Creating Plants

To create a plant, follow the navigation path SAP IMG • ENTERPRISE STRUCTURE • DEFINITION • LOGISTICS-GENERAL • DEFINE, COPY, DELETE, CHECK PLANT.

You'll see three activity options as shown in Figure 2.8.

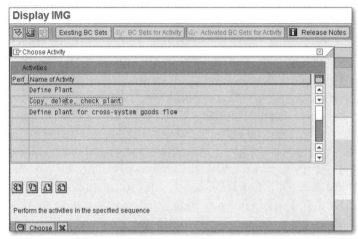

Figure 2.8 Plant Creation

It's best to copy a plant from an existing one, and then make the required changes (just as we discussed with company codes). This copies all of the dependent table entries into Customizing; otherwise, you would need to maintain these manually.

To create a plant via the copy function, follow these steps:

1. Select COPY, DELETE, CHECK PLANT.

2. On the next screen, click on the COPY ORG OBJECT button, and enter the FROM PLANT and TO PLANT codes, as shown in Figure 2.9.

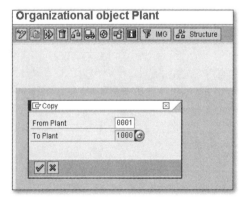

Figure 2.9 Plant Creation by Copying an Existing Plant

3. Finally, click on OK.

4. To see the completed activities, enter the existing plant (from which data will be copied to your new plant) in the FROM PLANT field, and enter the new plant code in the TO PLANT field.

5. Select DEFINE PLANT, select the plant, and either click on DETAILS or press `Ctrl` + `Shift` + `F2` to define the plant's address, factory calendar, telephone numbers, and so on. The language can be set by clicking on the ADDRESS icon.

6. You can maintain a plant's material master data at the plant level for the following views on a material master record in particular: MRP, PURCHASING, STORAGE, WORK SCHEDULING, PRODUCTION RESOURCES/TOOLS, FORECASTING, QUALITY MANAGEMENT, SALES, and COSTING.

> **Note**
>
> If you are working for a U.S.-based customer, you might have to select the the tax jurisdiction code, which is used for determining tax rates in the United States. It actually defines to which tax authority you must pay the taxes. These jurisdiction codes are defined by SAP Finance consultants.

Previously, we mentioned that defining a plant as a valuation area is recommended over a company code. Remember the following important points regarding the key characteristics of a plant:

▸ The plant is assigned to a single company code. A company code can have several plants.

▸ Several storage locations in which material stocks are managed can belong to a plant.

▸ A single business area is assigned to a plant and to a division.

▸ A plant can be assigned to several combinations of sales organization and distribution channels.

▸ A plant can have several shipping points. A shipping point can be assigned to several plants.

▸ A plant can be defined as a maintenance planning plant.

The plant plays an important role in the following areas:

▶ **Material valuation**
If the valuation level is the plant, the material stocks are valuated at plant level, and you can define the material prices for each plant. Each plant can have its own account determination.

▶ **Inventory management**
The material stocks are managed within a plant.

▶ **Material requirements planning (MRP)**
Material requirements are planned for each plant. Each plant has its own MRP data. Analyses for materials planning can be made across plants.

▶ **Costing**
In costing, valuation prices are defined only within a plant.

▶ **Plant maintenance**
If a plant performs plant maintenance planning tasks, it's defined as a maintenance planning plant. A maintenance planning plant can also carry out planning tasks for other plants (maintenance plants).

2.3.4 Assigning Plants to Company Codes

After you've created a company code and plant, you need to assign the plant to the company code. To do this, go to the menu path SAP IMG • ENTERPRISE STRUCTURE • ASSIGNMENT • LOGISTICS-GENERAL • ASSIGN PLANT TO COMPANY CODE, and click on NEW ENTRIES. Enter your company code and plant and click on SAVE, as shown in Figure 2.10. As we discussed earlier, one company code can have multiple plants, so you can assign multiple plants to a company code here. You can also enter multiple company codes and their respective plants and save these settings.

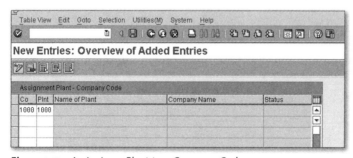

Figure 2.10 Assigning a Plant to a Company Code

2.3.5 Creating Storage Locations for Plants

Storage locations are created under the plant. Because of this, you can reuse the same storage location code for other plants. The menu path for a storage location is SAP IMG • ENTERPRISE STRUCTURE • DEFINITION • MATERIALS MANAGEMENT • MAINTAIN STORAGE LOCATION. Enter the plant number for which you want to create a storage location.

From here, click on the NEW ENTRIES button, and enter the storage location number (SLOc field) and description, as shown in Figure 2.11.

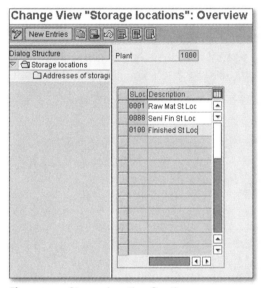

Figure 2.11 Storage Location Creation

Storage locations are always created for a plant. You can also maintain an address for a storage location. To define the address, select the storage location, and click on ADDRESSES OF STORAGE LOCATIONS in the menu on the left. Enter the address data and click SAVE.

Maintain Multiple Addresses

You might be wondering why there is an option to maintain multiple addresses for a storage location. But if you think about it, a storage location can have many entry and exit gates. The postal addresses of these gates could be different from one another. To facilitate this scenario, SAP allows you to maintain multiple addresses for a single storage location, as shown in Figure 2.12. To define multiple addresses, click on ADDRESS in the STORAGE LOCATION section. Enter serial number 01 and address, and then serial number 02 and address and so on. As you can see, there are two address maintained for storage location 1020. By clicking on the NEW button, you can maintain any number of addresses for a storage location.

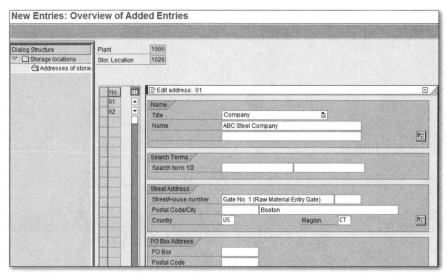

Figure 2.12 Multiple Addresses for a Single Storage Location

A storage location has the following attributes:

▶ There may be one or more storage locations within a plant. For example, your plant in Atlanta may have multiple and separate storage locations, such as for raw materials, semi-finished products, and scrap materials.

▸ A storage location has a description and at least one address.

▸ It's possible to store material data specific to a storage location.

▸ Stocks are managed only on a quantity basis and not on a value basis at the storage location level. (Valuation is either at the plant level or at the company code level.)

▸ Physical inventories are carried out at the storage location level.

▸ A storage location can be assigned to a warehouse number in the Warehouse Management system (WM system). You can assign more than one storage location to the same warehouse number within a plant.

▸ Storage locations are always created for a plant.

2.3.6 Creating Purchasing Organizations

A purchasing organization is responsible for procurement activities, and creating a purchasing organization in the system is important for the purchasing cycle. To create a purchasing organization, follow the menu path SAP IMG • ENTERPRISE STRUCTURE • DEFINITION • MATERIALS MANAGEMENT • MAINTAIN PURCHASING ORGANIZATION. From here, click on NEW ENTRIES and enter the purchasing organization code and description, as shown in Figure 2.13. When finished, save the entries.

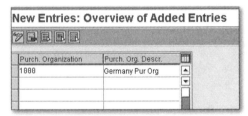

Figure 2.13 Purchase Organization Creation

2.3.7 Assigning Purchasing Organizations to Company Codes and Plants

After you've created the purchasing organization, plants, and company codes, you need to appropriately assign everything to complete the organizational structure. To assign purchasing organizations to company codes or plants, go to SAP IMG • ENTERPRISE STRUCTURE • ASSIGNMENT • MATERIALS MANAGEMENT, as shown in Figure 2.14. Based on your business scenario (refer to Section 2.2), various options are available for assigning purchasing organizations.

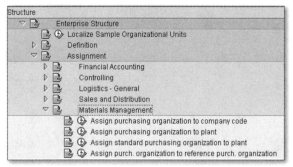

Figure 2.14 Purchasing Organization Assignment Menu Screen

In the following subsections, we'll review the steps for each assignment option and configuration step you've made.

Assigning Purchasing Organizations to Company Codes

To configure the scenario where a purchasing organization is responsible for the plants of one company code only, follow the path SAP IMG • ENTERPRISE STRUCTURE • ASSIGNMENT • MATERIALS MANAGEMENT • ASSIGN PURCHASING ORGANIZATION TO COMPANY CODE. Here you can see all of the purchasing organizations you've created in previous steps and assign the company code to the purchasing organization as shown in Figure 2.15.

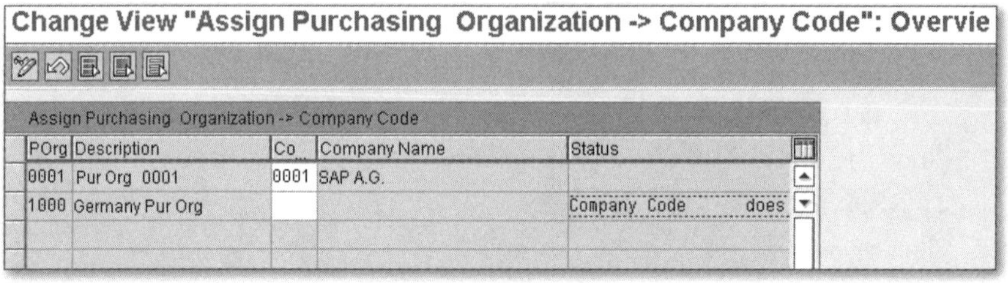

Figure 2.15 Assigning a Purchasing Organization to a Company Code

> **Note**
>
> Assigning a purchasing organization to a company code is required only when you want to create a purchasing organization specific to a certain company code. After you assign a purchasing organization to a company code, you can't assign this purchasing organization to any other company codes or plants.

Remember that in a cross-company code purchasing organization, you don't assign the purchasing organization to a company code. A cross-company code purchasing organization is responsible for procurement activities for plants and those activities belong to different company codes.

Assigning Purchasing Organizations to Plants

Assigning a purchasing organization to a plant is mandatory. If you don't assign a purchasing organization to a plant, you can't create purchase orders for that plant. You can assign one purchasing organization to one or more plants by following the menu path SAP IMG • Enterprise Structure • Assignment • Materials Management • Assign Purchasing Organization to Plant, as shown in Figure 2.16.

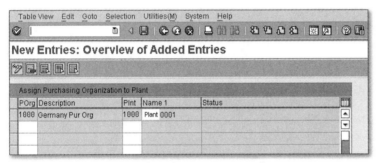

Figure 2.16   Assigning a Purchasing Organization to Plants

As discussed in Section 2.3.2, for the cross-plant purchasing organization scenario, you can assign a purchasing organization to multiple plants with the following options:

▶ One purchasing organization procures for one plant (plant-specific purchasing).

▶ One purchasing organization procures for several plants (cross-plant purchasing).

▶ Several purchasing organizations procure for one plant (a combination of plant-specific purchasing organization, cross-plant purchasing organization, and cross-company code purchasing organization).

2.3.8 Assigning Standard Purchasing Organizations to Plants

If several purchasing organizations procure for a certain plant, you can define one of them as the standard purchasing organization for the pipeline procurement, consignment, and stock transfer scenarios. The standard purchasing organization is used by the system in case of source determination for stock transfers and consignment. In the case of goods issues of pipeline materials, the purchasing information records of the standard purchasing organization are read.

To assign the standard purchasing organization to a plant, use the path SAP IMG • Enterprise Structure • Assignment • Materials Management • Assign Standard Purchasing Organization to Plant. As shown in Figure 2.17, you can define one standard purchasing organization for each plant, and this purchasing organization is automatically proposed and selected by the system while creating automatic purchase orders.

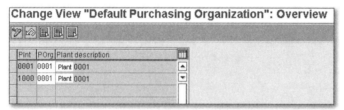

Figure 2.17 Assigning a Standard Purchasing Organization to Plants

2.3.9 Assigning Purchasing Organizations to Reference Purchase Organizations

In an enterprise, you may have a scenario where one purchasing department wants to refer to the purchasing terms and conditions of another purchasing department. In SAP terminology, the referred purchasing department becomes the *reference purchasing organization*. Thus, when a purchasing organization is assigned to a reference purchasing organization, it can make use of the already-negotiated terms of purchases such as rate per unit, discount based on volume, payment terms, and so on.

To set this up, follow the path SAP IMG • Enterprise Structure • Assignment • Materials Management • Assign Purchasing Organization to Ref Purchasing Organization (Figure 2.18).

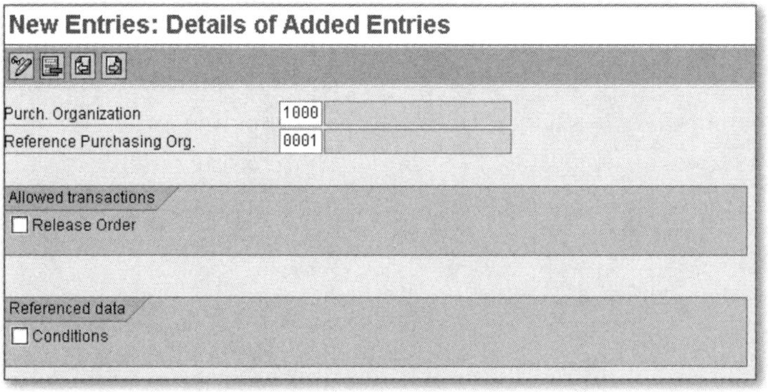

New Entries: Details of Added Entries

Purch. Organization   1000
Reference Purchasing Org.   0001

Allowed transactions
☐ Release Order

Referenced data
☐ Conditions

Figure 2.18 Assigning a Reference Purchasing Organization to a Purchasing Organization

As shown in Figure 2.19 in the following section, in addition to the assignment, the following two settings need to be configured:

▶ ALLOWED TRANSACTIONS — RELEASE ORDER
Check this box when a purchasing organization is allowed to create contract release orders from the contracts of the referenced purchasing organization.

▶ REFERENCED DATA — CONDITIONS
Check this box when a purchasing organization wants to refer only to conditions from the contracts of the reference purchasing organization.

When a purchasing organization wants to refer conditions and create contract release orders from contracts of a referenced purchasing organization, check both boxes.

2.3.10   Creating Purchase Groups

The purchasing group can be an individual or a group of individuals responsible for performing procurement activities such as the creation of purchase orders or contracts.

In an SAP system, the purchasing group is an independent entity, so it isn't assigned to any purchasing organization. To create a purchasing group, follow the path SAP IMG • MATERIALS MANAGEMENT • PURCHASING • CREATE PURCHASING GROUPS. Click on NEW ENTRIES and enter the purchasing group, description, telephone number, and fax number, as shown in Figure 2.19. Save the entries to create the purchasing group.

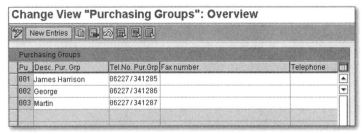

Figure 2.19 Creating and Editing Purchase Groups

2.4 Summary

In this chapter, we've reviewed the basics of organizational structures, including the process of setting them up in an SAP system. Configuring accurate organizational structures is the key to a successful SAP implementation.

You are now able to do the following:

▶ Define an organizational structure based on business processes and operational scenarios in an enterprise.

▶ Understand and configure various units in the SAP organizational structure.

▶ Make assignments based on your knowledge of how the units in MM organizational structures are related to each other.

Let's move on to the next chapter to discuss the different master data used in MM. You'll also learn how to define master data and how to configure various master data elements.

Master data is the source of centrally maintained information that is available for retrieval when required during transactions. This helps maintain consistent information enterprise-wide and eliminates repetitive data entry. We'll discuss the various mater data of Materials Management and also how the data can be customized to meet your customer's requirements.

3   Master Data

In the first part of this chapter, you'll learn how to configure master data and how master data relates to the organizational structure. In the second part of the chapter, you'll learn about the different master data elements required by Materials Management (MM) in SAP ERP and what their advantages and usages are.

Master data refers to a collection of frequently used data records that don't change often; master data is static in nature. The SAP system contains many categories of master data, such as customer master data, vendor master data, and G/L accounts master data. The master data categories specific to MM are:

▶ Vendor master

▶ Material master

▶ Purchasing info records

▶ Source list

▶ Quota arrangement

▶ Service master data

Material master records are the most important of these because they are used in almost all MM transactions, including purchase orders, goods receipts, and invoice receipts. In the following sections, we'll discuss these categories in more detail. Before we get into the individual master data details, however, let's explore how master data is maintained at different organizational levels such as client, company code, plant, purchasing organization, and so on.

Master data is created at the client level, but specific department data (also known as *functional* department data) is maintained at the department level. By creating the material master record at the client level, you ensure that it has a unique material code and that every plant and department doesn't create the same material with a different material code. The department-specific data in the record will then be maintained by various departments such as purchasing, sales, and production.

> **Note**
>
> Data maintained at a higher level is inherited by the lower level of organizational unit. For example, a material number and description maintained at the client level is inherited by the plant and storage location.

3.1 Vendor Master Records

Vendor master records are maintained by both the purchasing and accounting departments, as illustrated in Figure 3.1. As a vendor is crediting business partners in the company, the purchasing department maintains purchase-related data such as payment terms, and the accounting department maintains vendor G/L account information such as bank account details.

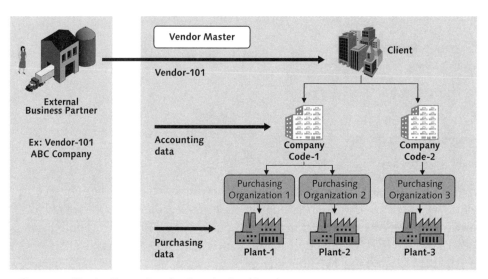

Figure 3.1 Vendor Master Data by Organizational Level

The vendor master record consists of three sections: general data, accounting data, and purchasing data, as follows:

▶ **General data**
General data is maintained at the client level because this data is common for all of the lower-level organizational units. Examples of general data include vendor address, contact phone numbers, and so on.

▶ **Accounting data**
Accounting data is maintained by the accounting department and is created at the company code level. To maintain accounting data, use Transactions FK01, FK02, and FK03.

▶ **Purchasing data**
Purchasing data is maintained by the purchasing department and is created at the purchasing organization level. To maintain purchasing data only, use Transactions MK01, MK02, and MK03.

If you create a vendor centrally, it means you want to maintain accounting data and purchasing data together; in this case, use Transactions XK01, XK02, and XK03.

In the following sections we'll discuss the vendor account group and the four main characteristics this group controls.

3.1.1   Vendor Account Group

The vendor account group plays an important role in vendor master data because it has many controlling functions. It's used to categorize vendors, and vendors similar in nature are grouped together (such as one-time vendors, domestic vendors, overseas vendors, employee vendors, etc.). You create vendor master data in Transaction XK01. You maintain all of the fields on this screen, and also select vendor account groups, as shown in Figure 3.2.

Predefined vendor account groups are available in the SAP system, but you can also create additional account groups based on customer requirements. To configure a new account group, go to SAP IMG • FINANCIAL ACCOUNTING (NEW) • ACCOUNTS RECEIVABLE AND ACCOUNTS PAYABLE • VENDOR ACCOUNTS • MASTER DATA • PREPARATIONS OF CREATING VENDOR MASTER DATA • DEFINE ACCOUNT GROUPS WITH SCREEN LAYOUT (VENDORS). In the screen that displays, you'll see a list of existing account groups. Create a new account group by copying an existing account group and making the required changes in the new account group. You can also create a new account group from scratch, but it's faster to use the copy function.

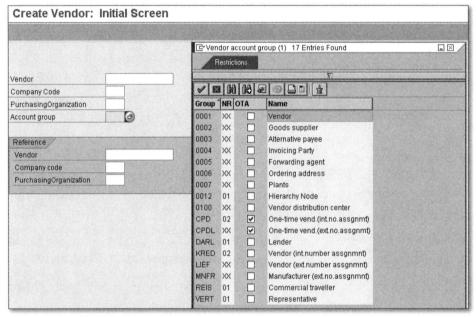

Figure 3.2 Vendor Account Groups

If you're creating an account group for a one-time vendor, select the ONE-TIME ACCOUNT checkbox under GENERAL DATA (Figure 3.3). This functionality is discussed in detail in Section 3.2.4.

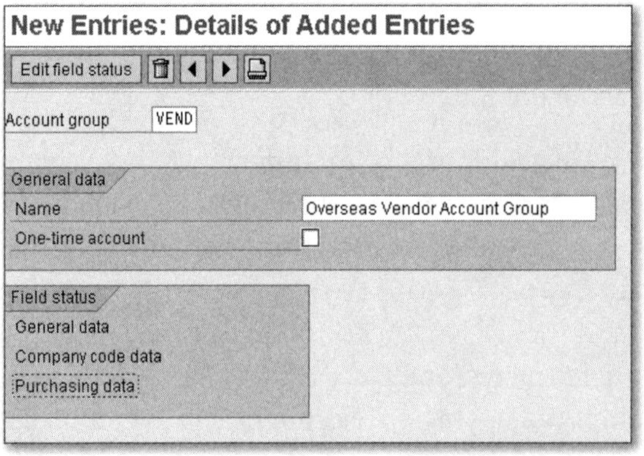

Figure 3.3 Vendor Account Group Creation

The account group controls four specific characteristics:

▶ **Field selection**
Enables you to control the fields in various screens. For example, you can make certain fields required fields and suppress others.

▶ **Number interval**
This can be either an external number range (manually assigned) or an internal number range (system assigned).

▶ **Vendor status**
The account group determines whether the vendor is a one-time vendor.

▶ **Partner schema**
Determines which partner schemas are valid.

We'll discuss these characteristics in more detail in the following sections.

3.1.2   Field Selection

In the GENERAL DATA, COMPANY CODE DATA, and PURCHASING DATA areas of the FIELD STATUS dialog box, you can configure different fields such as SUPPRESS, REQ. ENTRY, OPT. ENTRY, or DISPLAY, as shown in Figure 3.4. The following list describes each of these options:

▶ SUPPRESS
This field won't be displayed when creating vendor master data for your account group.

▶ REQ. ENTRY
This field will be mandatory when creating vendor master records.

▶ OPT. ENTRY
This field will be displayed when creating vendor master data, and you can either enter a value or leave the field blank.

▶ DISPLAY
This field can't be edited when creating vendor master records.

The field status in the vendor master data can be controlled by account group, company code, and activity (transaction code). However, SAP recommends controlling the screen layout via the account group only. In some exceptional cases, you can control field status via activity; for example, if you want to allow entries in the RECONCILIATION ACCOUNT field in create mode (Transaction XK01/FK01) and don't want to allow entry in the RECONCILIATION ACCOUNT field in change mode (Transaction XK02/FK02). In this case, you need to define the field status of the RECONCILIATION field as required by the activity.

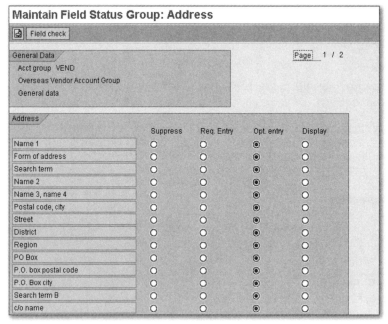

Figure 3.4 Field Status Group Configuration

The following list shows the respective menu paths for the company code and activity methods of control:

▸ **Control by company code**
 If you want to define the screen layout depending on the company code, you can follow the menu path SAP IMG • FINANCIAL ACCOUNTING (NEW) • ACCOUNTS RECEIVABLE AND ACCOUNTS PAYABLE • VENDOR ACCOUNTS • MASTER DATA • PREPARATIONS OF CREATING VENDOR MASTER DATA • DEFINE SCREEN LAYOUT PER COMPANY CODE (VENDORS).

▸ **Control by transaction activity**
 You can also define the screen layout based on the transaction activity—that is, display, create, change for vendor master data, which master record fields are required, optional, or hidden—by following the menu path SAP IMG •

FINANCIAL ACCOUNTING (NEW) • ACCOUNTS RECEIVABLE AND ACCOUNTS PAYABLE •
VENDOR ACCOUNTS • MASTER DATA • PREPARATIONS OF CREATING VENDOR MASTER
DATA • DEFINE SCREEN LAYOUT PER ACTIVITY (VENDORS).

Note

If the field status has been defined in different ways by various modes, the final field status is determined based on the highest priority, as shown in Figure 3.5. The highest priority is SUPPRESS, followed by DISPLAY, REQUIRED, and OPTIONAL.

Priority	Function	Character
1.	Hide	-
2.	Display	*
3.	Required	+
4.	Optional	•

Example with Results

Control Level ↓	Field-1	Field-2	Field-3	Field-4
Account Group	Hide	Required	Required	Optional
Transaction Code	Required	Display	Optional	Optional
Company Code	Display	Optional	Optional	Optional
Result	Hide	Display	Required	Optional

Figure 3.5 Field Selection Priority in the Vendor Master

3.1.3 Number Interval

Each vendor account group will have a type of number assignment—either an *internal number assignment* or an *external number assignment*. Each assignment will also have a *number range* (such as 100000 to 199999). When creating vendor master data based on the type of number assignment and the allowed number range, the vendor code will be generated.

Defining Number Ranges for an Account Group

To create a number range, go to SAP IMG • FINANCIAL ACCOUNTING (NEW) • ACCOUNTS RECEIVABLE AND ACCOUNTS PAYABLE • VENDOR ACCOUNTS • MASTER DATA • PREPARATIONS OF CREATING VENDOR MASTER DATA • CREATE NUMBER RANGES FOR VENDOR ACCOUNTS (Figure 3.6). To create the number ranges for the vendor account, specify the following under a two-character key:

▸ A number interval from which the account number for the vendor accounts should be selected

▸ The type of number assignment (internal or external)

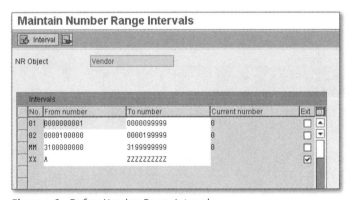

Figure 3.6 Define Number Range Interval

Click on the INTERVAL button and enter the values in the TO NUMBER and FROM NUMBER columns. If you're working with an external number range, select the EXT checkbox; for internal number generations, leave it unchecked.

The next important step is to assign number ranges to the account group.

Assigning Number Ranges to an Account Group

To assign a number range to an account group, go to SAP IMG • FINANCIAL ACCOUNT-ING (NEW) • ACCOUNTS RECEIVABLE AND ACCOUNTS PAYABLE • VENDOR ACCOUNTS • MASTER DATA • PREPARATIONS OF CREATING VENDOR MASTER DATA • ASSIGN NUMBER RANGES TO VENDOR ACCOUNT GROUPS.

In this step, you allocate the number ranges that were created (in the previous step) to the account groups for vendors. You can use one number range for several account groups, as shown in Figure 3.7. Select the number range for your account group and click SAVE.

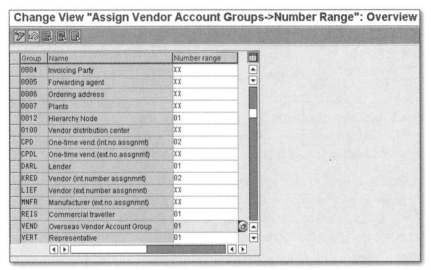

Figure 3.7 Number Range Assignment to Vendor Account Group

3.1.4 Vendor Status (One-Time Vendor)

You can create a vendor master record for one-time vendors with the one-time vendor account group. A *one-time account* records transaction figures for a group of vendors with which you conduct business once or rarely. Certain vendor data (such as address and bank details) aren't entered in the master record but rather in a transactional document (such as a purchase order). This vendor master data will be used in purchasing documents when you're working with a one-time vendor.

In the standard system, the vendor account groups CPD (One-Time Vendor with Internal Number Assignment) and CPDL (One-Time Vendor with External Number Assignment) are preconfigured for one-time vendors. However, you can also create your own vendor account group, if required, as discussed previously in Section 3.1.1. To configure the one-time account group, select the ONE-TIME ACCOUNT checkbox, as previously shown in Figure 3.3.

3.1.5   Reconciliation Accounts for Vendor Master Records

When you create vendor master records, you have to maintain a reconciliation account. The reconciliation account is a G/L account in SAP ERP Financials Financial Accounting (which we'll refer to as Financial Accounting or FI). This is a very important step, as all the financial transactions with the vendor is posted in the G/L account.

Your company or client may have many vendors (perhaps thousands), which increases the size of financial reports and makes it difficult to maintain separate G/L accounts. To resolve this, SAP provides subledger accounting for vendors. A reconciliation account is a G/L account used for multiple vendors, and each vendor will have a subledger account number called the vendor code.

When you create a vendor master record, you need a unique number for the vendor. Depending on the account group, either the system assigns this number automatically, or it's assigned manually. In the case of manual assignment, enter the vendor number. If this vendor number already exists, the system will alert you with an error message. (This vendor number is also used as the subledger account number in FI).

When entering invoices for the vendor, the system uses the reconciliation account from the vendor master records and posts the accounting entries into a reconciliation or G/L account. Because the same reconciliation account can be used for many vendors, it maps a company's liabilities toward several vendors in a single G/L account. For example, as you can see in Figure 3.8, two different vendors (Vendor 1001 and Vendor 1002) have the same reconciliation account. While posting an invoice for each of the vendors, the invoice amount is credited to their subledger account separately, but in FI, it's posted into one G/L account (the reconciliation account).

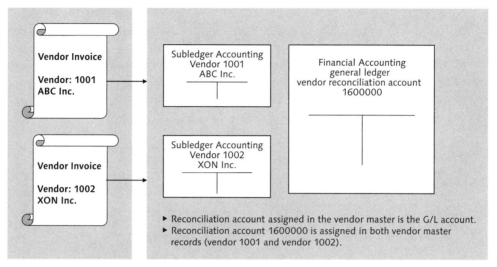

Figure 3.8 Subledger Accounting

3.1.6 Partner Schemas

In purchasing, you have contact with various business partners such as vendors or carriers. For each account group, you can define which roles these business partners may assume. For example, you can specify that certain vendors may function as ordering addresses only and not as invoicing parties. You can use partner roles to define relationships within a corporate group as well as with independent external partners.

Example

Steel Inc. is a corporate group with two companies: South West Steel Inc. and North East Steel Inc. In this scenario, South West Steel Inc., located in California, can be listed as the ordering address, whereas North East Steel Inc., located in New York, can be listed as the goods supplier. Additionally, another enterprise called ABC Carriers can be listed as the goods-delivering partner. These different assignments—ordering address, goods supplier, and goods deliverer—are the roles of the different partners.

Configuring Partners

Let's look at how to configure the partner function.

1. **Define partner roles.**

   The first step in using partner functions is to define the partner role. Go to menu path SAP IMG • MATERIALS MANAGEMENT • PURCHASING • PARTNER DETERMINATION • PARTNER ROLES • DEFINE PARTNER ROLES, as shown in Figure 3.9.

Change View "Definition of Partner Roles": Overview

Funct	Name	NoTpe	Unique	HigherPar.
$$	Area	0	☐	
$1	Created by	US	☐	
01	Shipping point	VS	☐	
1A	Customer hierarchy 1	KU	☐	1B
1B	Customer hierarchy 2	KU	☐	1C
1C	Customer hierarchy 3	KU	☐	1D
1D	Customer hierarchy 4	KU	☐	
2A	Vendor hierarchy 1	LI	☐	2B
2B	Vendor hierarchy 2	LI	☐	2C
2C	Vendor hierarchy 3	LI	☐	2D
2D	Vendor hierarchy 4	LI	☐	
AA	SP Contract rel. ord	KU	☐	
AB	Department resp.	0	☐	
AD	Additionals	LI	☐	
PE	Con.pers.fresh prod.	AP	☐	
SP	Sold-to party	KU	☑	
AI	IS-PAM: Cert. owner	KU	☑	

Figure 3.9 Define Partner Role

For the partner role, enter an alphanumeric key—which may consist of up to two characters—and some descriptive text. After you've entered the partner role, you need to specify the partner type, which is an identifier indicating the kind of partner involved (e.g., a vendor, which is abbreviated as VE).

Note that you can't edit partner types. You can only choose the partner types that are provided by SAP. You can, however, define the higher-level role that's used in purchasing (as of release 4.0) for any partner role.

2. **Maintain language-dependent key reassignments for partner roles.**

   You need to maintain the appropriate language-dependent key reassignment for partner roles. The menu path for this is SAP IMG • MATERIALS MANAGEMENT •

PURCHASING • PARTNER DETERMINATION • PARTNER ROLES • MAINTAIN LANGUAGE-
DEP. KEY REASSIGNMENT FOR PARTNER ROLES, as shown in Figure 3.10.

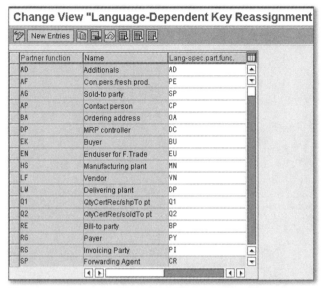

Figure 3.10 Language-Dependent Key Reassignment

In this step, you can change the identifiers for the predefined partner roles to identifiers in your language. For the standard settings, separate identifiers are supplied for all languages, such as the following:

▶ German: Lieferant = LF

▶ English: Vendor = VN

3. **Define permissible partner roles per account group.**
In step 1, you assigned partner roles. Now you need to assign these partner roles to the vendor account group. Only assigned roles will be available for selection when creating the vendor master record. To assign partner roles, go to SAP IMG • MATERIALS MANAGEMENT • PURCHASING • PARTNER DETERMINATION • PARTNER ROLES • DEFINE PERMISSIBLE PARTNER ROLES PER ACCOUNT GROUP, as shown in Figure 3.11.

In this step, you can assign the allowed partner roles for each account group. Vendors created for the account group will be allowed to assume only assigned partner roles. For example, if you've assigned the ordering party partner role to vendor account group 0001, then vendors created for this account group can be ordering parties only, not invoicing parties.

```
Change View "Permissible Partner Roles per Account Group"
```

Funct	Name	Group	Name	
2A	Vendor hierarchy 1	0001	Vendor	
2A	Vendor hierarchy 1	0012	Hierarchy Node	
2B	Vendor hierarchy 2	0001	Vendor	
2B	Vendor hierarchy 2	0012	Hierarchy Node	
2C	Vendor hierarchy 3	0001	Vendor	
2C	Vendor hierarchy 3	0012	Hierarchy Node	
2D	Vendor hierarchy 4	0001	Vendor	
2D	Vendor hierarchy 4	0012	Hierarchy Node	
AD	Additionals	0001	Vendor	
AD	Additionals	KRED	Vendor (int.number assgnmnt)	
AD	Additionals	LIEF	Vendor (ext.number assgnmnt)	
AZ	A.payment recipient	0001	Vendor	
AZ	A.payment recipient	0003	Alternative payee	
AZ	A.payment recipient	0100	Vendor distribution center	
AZ	A.payment recipient	KRED	Vendor (int.number assgnmnt)	
AZ	A.payment recipient	LIEF	Vendor (ext.number assgnmnt)	
OA	Ordering address	0001	Vendor	

Figure 3.11 Permissible Partner Roles per Account Group

Partner Settings

In this section, we'll explain how to define partner determination schemas and assign them to account groups. Partner schemas consist of groups of partner roles that are assigned to vendor account groups at three different levels: purchasing organization, vendor subrange, and plant. While creating the vendor master record, you need to select the account group. Based on the account group and level, the system will determine the partner schema. All of the allowed partner roles of the partner schema will be copied (defaulted) in the vendor master record. Follow these steps:

1. **Define the partner schemas.**
   The first step is to define the partner schemas, which allows you to group various partner roles. You can specify that certain roles in a schema are mandatory (i.e., can't be changed after entry).

Go to the menu path SAP IMG • MATERIALS MANAGEMENT • PURCHASING • PART-
NER DETERMINATION • PARTNER ROLES • DEFINE PARTNER SCHEMAS, as shown in
Figure 3.12 and Figure 3.13.

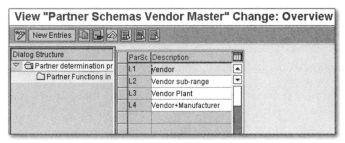

Figure 3.12 Partner Schema—Vendor Master

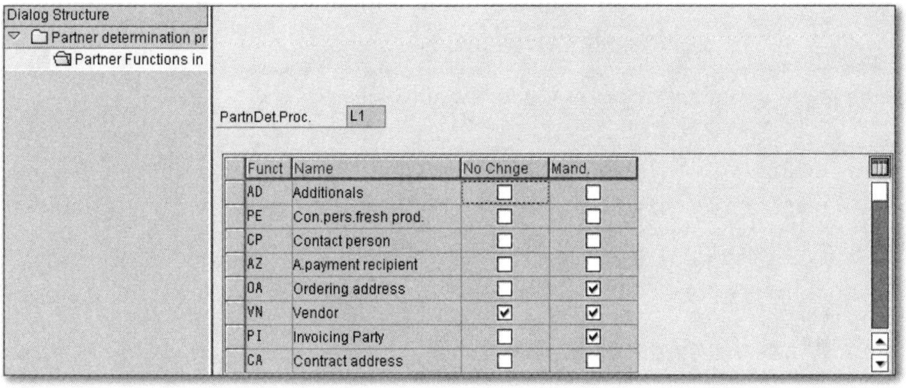

Figure 3.13 Partner Functions in Partner Schema

You can define different partner schemas at different data retention levels within
the vendor master record. For example, you can have a different ordering address
at the purchasing organization level than you do at the plant level.

2. **Assign the partner schemas to account groups.**

   In this step, you assign partner schemas to account groups. Go to SAP IMG •
   MATERIALS MANAGEMENT • PURCHASING • PARTNER DETERMINATION • PARTNER
   ROLES • ASSIGN PARTNER SCHEMAS TO ACCOUNT GROUPS, as shown in Figure 3.14.

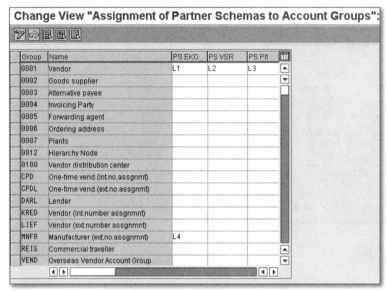

Figure 3.14 Assign Partner Schema to Vendor Account Group

In this section, you've learned about the essential characteristics and functions in vendor master records. In the next section, we'll move on to discuss material master records.

3.2 Material Master Records

Material master records are the key element of MM. In this section, we'll discuss how material master records are created at different organizational levels and how different department-specific data is maintained in different views. We'll also discuss the main controlling elements of material master records such as material type.

Material master records are a company's main source for material-specific data. The transaction codes for material master records are as follows:

▶ Transaction MM01: Create material

▶ Transaction MM02: Change material

▶ Transaction MM03: Display material

Material master data has different views for each department, which are the same as tab pages. For example, the PURCHASING view is used for ordering, the ACCOUNTING view is used for material valuation, and the MRP view is used for planning (Figure 3.15).

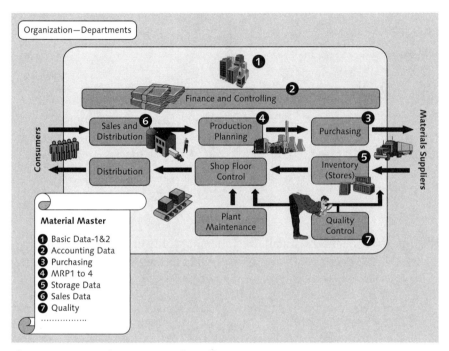

Figure 3.15 Material Master Views for Different Department Data

The material master code is created centrally, and each department can maintain department-specific data in the material master record (just as with the vendor master record). This concept is illustrated in Figure 3.16.

General data that are valid enterprise-wide are stored at the client level, and plant-relevant data is maintained at the plant level. Similarly, data that is valid for a particular storage location is maintained at the storage location level.

Alternatively, storage location data for a material can be created automatically at the time of goods receipt. This is applicable when, for the first time, a material is being received in a storage location for which data isn't maintained in the material master record.

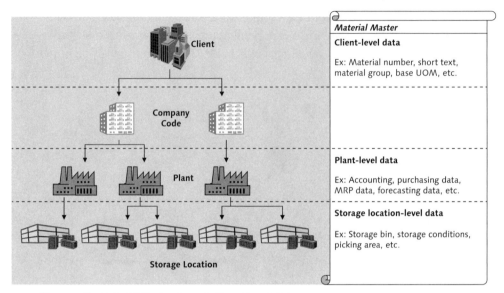

Figure 3.16 Material Master Organizational Level Data

To enable this functionality, maintain the following configuration in Customizing. Go to SAP IMG • MATERIALS MANAGEMENT • INVENTORY MANAGEMENT & PHYSICAL INVENTORY • GOODS RECEIPT • CREATE STORAGE LOCATION AUTOMATICALLY.

Here, you specify whether the automatic creation of storage location data is allowed for goods receipts. We'll go over the following steps to learn how to define this:

1. As shown in Figure 3.17, define which plant and for which movement type you want to enable this functionality.

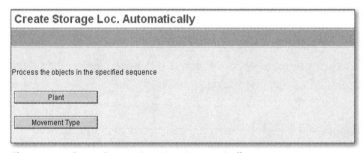

Figure 3.17 Create Storage Location Automatically

2. Click on PLANT, and then select the plant for which you want to enable this functionality; for example, PLANT 0001 and PLANT 1000 are selected for automatic creation of storage location view for a material in Figure 3.18.

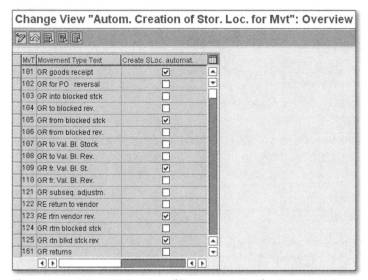

Change View "Autom. Creation of SLoc per Plant": Overview

Plant	Name 1	Create SLoc. automat.	
0001	Werk 0001	☑	
1000	Plant 1	☐	
1010	Plant 3	☐	
1100	Plant 2	☐	
1111	TEST	☐	
2000	Plant 1	☐	
P001	Corp Quality Data Plant	☐	
TES1	Plant 1	☑	

Figure 3.18 Automatic Creation of Storage Location per Plant

3. Define the movement types for which automatic creation of storage location is allowed as shown in Figure 3.19. For this example, select movement types 101, 105, 109, 123, and 125 for this functionality by clicking the checkbox. Whenever you post the goods receipt for a material with movement type 101 and plant 1000, a storage location view will be created automatically for the material.

Change View "Autom. Creation of Stor. Loc. for Mvt": Overview

MvT	Movement Type Text	Create SLoc. automat.	
101	GR goods receipt	☑	
102	GR for PO reversal	☐	
103	GR into blocked stck	☐	
104	GR to blocked rev.	☐	
105	GR from blocked stck	☑	
106	GR from blocked rev.	☐	
107	GR to Val. Bl. Stock	☐	
108	GR to Val. Bl. Rev.	☐	
109	GR fr. Val. Bl. St.	☑	
110	GR fr. Val. Bl. Rev.	☐	
121	GR subseq. adjustm.	☐	
122	RE return to vendor	☐	
123	RE rtrn vendor rev.	☑	
124	GR rtrn blocked stck	☐	
125	GR rtn blkd stck rev	☑	
161	GR returns	☐	

Figure 3.19 Automatic Creation of Storage Location for Movement Type

> **Note**
>
> The storage location data is only created if the quantity is posted to standard storage location stock. It isn't created for receipts into a special stock (e.g., into sales order stock).
>
> The standard system is set in such a way that the storage location data is created automatically for all types of receipts (goods receipt with/without reference, stock transfers, initial entry of stock balances, reversal of goods issues, etc.).

In the following sections, you'll learn about the main attributes and configurations of material master data.

3.2.1 Main Attributes

The main attributes of material master data are the material number, industry sector, and material type, as shown in Figure 3.20.

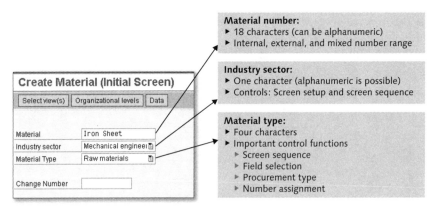

Figure 3.20 Main Attributes of Material Master Data

The *material number* is a unique 18-character field that can be entered manually or can be created automatically by the system, based on the type of number assignment. For an external number assignment, you can enter the material number manually; for an internal number assignment, the system creates the material number automatically when you save the material master record.

The *industry sector* controls the screen setup and screen sequence. The SAP system includes predefined industry sectors, but if any specific requirement doesn't match these predefined sectors, you can create your own.

Material types have many controlling functions, including the following:

- Number assignment
- Number range
- Procurement type
- Screen setup (i.e., allowed views, field selection, and screen sequence)
- Price control
- Account determination
- Quantity and value updating in plants

SAP provides preconfigured material types, but you can also create your own by copying the standard material types and making the required changes. Some of the SAP-provided material types are:

- ROH: Raw material
- HALB: Semi-finished material
- FERT: Finished material

3.2.2 Configuring a New Material Type

To configure a new material type, go to SAP IMG • LOGISTICS-GENERAL • MATERIAL MASTER • BASIC SETTINGS • MATERIAL TYPES • DEFINE ATTRIBUTES OF MATERIAL TYPES (Figure 3.21).

Here, you can either make changes to an SAP-provided material type (such as DIEN, HALB, or FERT), or you can create a new one. To do the latter, click on the NEW ENTRIES button or copy an existing material type and make the required changes.

> **Note**
>
> If you want to create a new material type, we recommend copying an SAP-provided material type and then making changes, instead of starting from scratch. Otherwise, you need to maintain multiple settings and screens, which can be very time consuming.

For additional settings, select the material type from the MTYP column, and click on the DETAILS button. You'll see the details of the selected material type as shown in Figure 3.22.

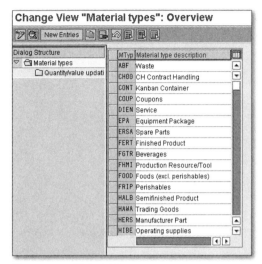

Figure 3.21 Material Types

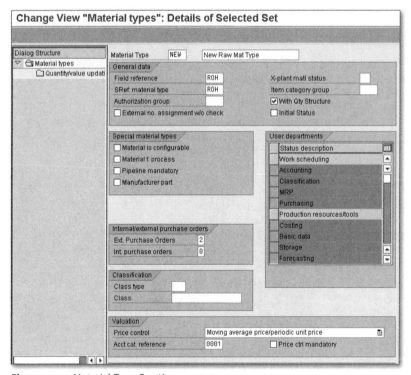

Figure 3.22 Material Type Creation

You need to make the following key settings in material types as shown in Figure 3.22, depending on your business needs:

▶ FIELD REFERENCE (field reference key)
This determines the field status such as required, hidden, display, and optional. In Figure 3.22 you can see ROH is the field reference.

▶ USER DEPARTMENTS (views in the material master)
User departments such as purchasing, sales, and production are referred to as views in the material master. This determines which views can be selected for the material type. For example, a sales view is essential for finished goods because you need to maintain data specific to the sales department to sell the materials.

▶ PIPELINE MANDATORY
This determines whether pipeline handling is possible or mandatory. It also determines whether it's possible to set external and internal purchase orders, as well as quantity and value updates. Pipeline materials are used in continuous process chemical industries, such as oil refinery. Crude petroleum is issued to production for refining via a pipeline.

▶ EXT. PURCHASE ORDERS/INT. PURCHASE ORDERS (type of procurement)
This determines whether internal procurement, external procurement, or both are allowed.

▶ PRICE CONTROL
You can select STANDARD PRICE or MOVING AVERAGE PRICE/PERIODIC UNIT PRICE for a material type, as shown in Figure 3.22. (Price control is discussed in Chapter 7, Section 7.3.) The selected price control is copied (defaulted) when you create a material master record, but you can change the price control from standard price to moving average price and vice versa. If the PRICE CTRL MANDATORY checkbox is activated, the price control method selected in the material type can't be changed while creating a material master record.

After you've selected the material type, click on the QUANTITY/VALUE UPDATING folder (on the left side of the screen). As Figure 3.23 illustrates, you need to select QTY UPDATING and VALUE UPDATE in each valuation area. The significance of these fields is as follows:

▶ QTY UPDATING
Specifies that the material is managed on a quantity basis in the material master record for the relevant valuation area.

▶ VALUE UPDATE

Specifies that the material is managed on a value basis in the material master record for the valuation area concerned. The values are updated in the respective G/L accounts at the same time.

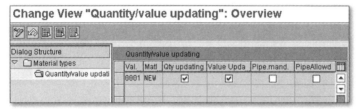

Figure 3.23 Quantity/Value Updating for Material Type and Valuation Area

3.2.3 Defining a Number Range for a Material Type

In this step, you define the type of number assignments and the number of range intervals for material master records. When creating a material master record, you must assign it a unique number. There are two ways of doing this:

▶ **Internal number assignment**
A number within the defined number range is assigned by the SAP system.

▶ **External number assignment**
You can assign a number within the defined number range interval. You can define the intervals for external number assignments numerically as well as alphanumerically.

You can also define both an internal and an external number range interval for the material type.

In real-time scenarios, most companies use internal number assignment when they want numerical number ranges for materials, so that the system automatically assigns the unique material number serially. In cases where they want to define alphanumerical number ranges, they use external number assignment.

To configure a number range for material types, go to the menu path SAP IMG • LOGISTICS-GENERAL • MATERIAL MASTER • BASIC SETTINGS • MATERIAL TYPES • DEFINE NUMBER RANGE FOR EACH MATERIAL TYPE.

Click on MAINTAIN GROUP to maintain a new group for the new number range; you will then see another screen as shown in Figure 3.24. In the top screen menu, go to GROUP • INSERT to open the screen shown in Figure 3.25. Enter the group name in the TEXT field and a new number range in the FROM NUMBER and TO NUMBER fields, and then click SAVE.

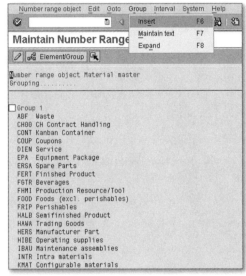

Figure 3.24 Number Range for Material Types

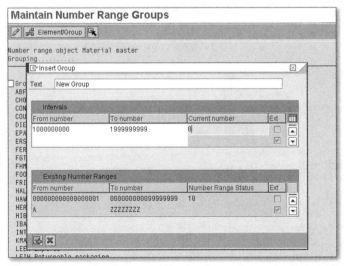

Figure 3.25 Number Range and Number Range Groups for Material Type

3.2.4 Defining Field Selections

The field status of a field in material master data is controlled by the following:

▶ Material type

▶ Transaction code

▶ Industry sector

▶ Plant

▶ Procurement type (internal/external)

Similar fields are organized under different groups called *field selection groups*. For example, FIELD SELECTION GROUP 1 contains two fields, BASE UNIT OF MEASURE and UNIT OF MEASUREMENT TEXT, as shown in Figure 3.26.

A field reference key is assigned to each of the different controlling units such as material types, transaction codes, industry sectors, plants, and procurement types. For example, field reference keys DIEN and MM03 are assigned to the service material type transaction and the display material transaction, respectively.

Maintain the field status for the combination of field selection group and field reference key, as shown in Figure 3.26.

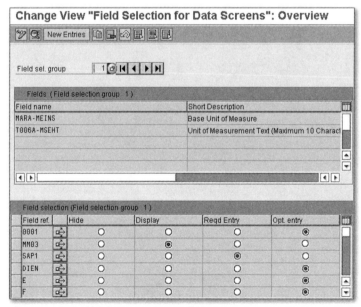

Figure 3.26 Field Selection in Material Master

▸ The field status of a field selection group for the field reference key prefixed with "SAP" must not be changed.

▸ The field reference key for transaction codes and procurement type (E – internal procurement, and F – external procurement) are already configured and can't be changed.

▸ New field reference keys must begin with Y or Z.

▸ New field selection groups, if required, can be taken from those that aren't preconfigured. For example, 206 through 240 are available.

▸ The system determines how the field status should be set, as follows:

  ▸ The field status HIDE has the highest priority, followed by DISPLAY, REQUIRED (MANDATORY), and OPTIONAL, in that order.

  ▸ As shown in Figure 3.26, while in Transaction MM03 (Display Material), all fields in FIELD SELECTION GROUP 1 have a status of DISPLAY.

3.2.5 Defining Material Groups

You can define different material groups to distinguish various materials. For example, an enterprise that manufactures computers can classify computers as desktops, laptops, and servers; each of these would be its own group. To define material groups, go to SAP IMG • LOGISTICS – GENERAL • MATERIAL MASTER • SETTINGS FOR KEY FIELDS • DEFINE MATERIAL GROUPS, as shown in Figure 3.27. You can define the material group by copying the existing material group or by clicking on the NEW ENTRIES button. After clicking on the NEW ENTRIES button, enter the material group code and materials description in their respective fields.

Change View "Material Groups": Overview

Matl Group	Material Group Desc.	Grp.	D	Description 2 for the material group
01	Material group 1			
02	Material group 2			
DESKTOP	Desktop Computer			
LAPTOP	Laptop Computer			
SERVER	Server			

Figure 3.27 Material Groups

The benefits of material groups are in reporting such as spent analysis, distribution of roles and responsibilities in purchasing and inventory departments, and so on. For example, some companies have buyers based on the material group. One buyer is responsible for procuring only materials under material groups Stationery and Repairs. The other buyer is responsible for procuring materials under material group Steel, and so on.

You've now seen how different departments maintain material master data at different organizational levels, and we've gone through the main attributes and configurations of material master data. In the next section, we'll move on to discuss info records.

3.3   Purchasing Info Records

In vendor and material master records, you maintain vendor- and material-specific information. In purchasing info records, you maintain information about the relationships between vendors and their material. For example, each vendor may have specific terms and conditions of purchase for each material—this information is stored in purchasing info records.

As shown in Figure 3.28, purchasing info records contain the information for material and vendor combinations. This information is defaulted (copied) during the purchase order creation.

You can maintain the following data in purchasing info records:

▶ Current and future prices and conditions (gross price, freight, and discounts)

▶ Delivery data (planned delivery time and tolerances)

▶ Vendor data (vendor material number, vendor material group, etc.)

▶ Texts

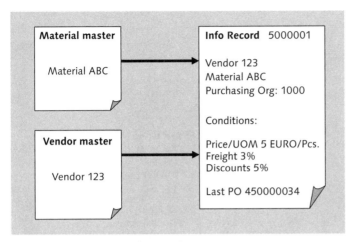

Figure 3.28 Purchasing Info Records

In the standard system, two types of text are available. First, there is internal info memo record text, which is used for internal comments only. Internal comments will be copied into purchase orders (POs) but shouldn't be copied to output such as print, fax, or email. Second, there is the PO text, which is used to describe PO items or materials copied into the PO *and* to the output. In addition to these standard types of text, any other type can be configured as well.

Because the system populates this data automatically while creating POs, purchasing info records save time and provide consistent data.

3.3.1 Structure

Info records are maintained at different organizational levels, as shown in Figure 3.29. Examples include client level, purchasing organization level, and plant level.

As shown in Figure 3.29, purchasing info records have general data, purchasing organization data, and plant data. It's common for general data to be maintained at the client level for all purchasing organizations and plants.

When you create a PO, the system searches for the valid info record for the purchasing organization/plant combination. If there are no such info records, the system searches for the purchasing organization only.

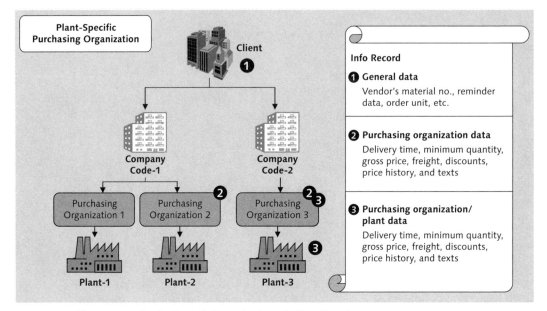

Figure 3.29 Purchasing Info Record—Organizational Levels

In addition, purchasing info records are created for a type of procurement, also called *info category*. When you create an info record using Transaction ME11, you need to select the info category, as shown in Figure 3.30. You need to create separate info records for each type of info category.

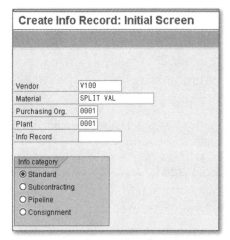

Figure 3.30 Info Record—Info Type

There are four info records categories in the INFO CATEGORY section:

▶ STANDARD
Standard info record for a standard procurement type.

▶ SUBCONTRACTING
Subcontracting info record for a subcontracting procurement type.

▶ PIPELINE
Pipeline info record for a pipeline procurement type.

▶ CONSIGNMENT
Consignment info record for a consignment procurement type.

In a special scenario of consumables materials with no material number, purchasing info records are created based on the material group.

Regular Vendor

The regular vendor is used by the system during source determination. This is a vendor from whom you regularly buy a particular material. You can set the REGULAR VENDOR indicator in the general data of a purchasing info record, as shown in Figure 3.31. This can be set for only one purchasing info record for each material. If the use of a regular vendor is permitted and is configured for a specific plant in Customizing, the regular vendor will always be suggested during source determination.

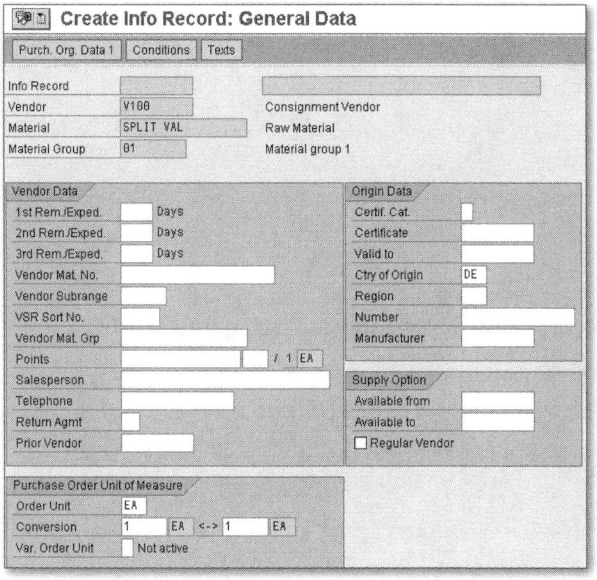

Figure 3.31 Info Record—Regular Vendor

3.3.2 Creating an Info Record

Purchasing info records can be created manually, or they can be created automatically when you create POs or outline agreements (Figure 3.32).

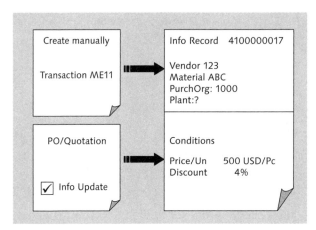

Figure 3.32 Info Record Creation—Manual or Automatic

Manual Creation

Purchasing info records can be created manually for a purchasing organization and/or plant via Transaction ME11. Transaction ME12 can be used for updating already-created purchasing info records.

Automatic Creation

Purchasing info records can be created or updated automatically by setting the INFO UPDATE indicator while maintaining a quotation, PO, or outline agreement. Furthermore, the type of purchasing document determines what updates are triggered by the info update indicator, as follows:

▶ **Quotation**
Time-dependent conditions are copied into the purchasing info record.

▶ **Purchase order/contract release order/scheduling agreement**
Conditions are never created or updated. The purchasing info record is updated with the document number in the last document number field.

▶ **Contract**
If purchasing info records already exist, they aren't updated. If purchasing info

records don't exist, they're created with time-dependent conditions from the contract.

Let's move on to the configuration settings required for purchasing info records.

3.3.3 Configuration

You can define how prices are stored in purchasing info records for each plant. Let's go through the configuration settings for condition control in purchasing info records.

Condition Control at the Plant Level

For each plant, you can define how prices and conditions are stored. To do this, go to SAP IMG • MATERIALS MANAGEMENT • PURCHASING • CONDITIONS • DEFINE CONDITION CONTROL AT PLANT LEVEL, as shown in Figure 3.33.

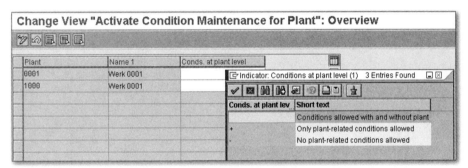

Figure 3.33 Configuration for Condition Control at the Plant Level

For each plant, you can select any of the following options:

▶ CONDITIONS ALLOWED WITH AND WITHOUT PLANT
You can create purchasing info records either at the plant level or at the purchasing organization level.

▶ ONLY PLANT-RELATED CONDITIONS ALLOWED
You must create purchasing info records and contract items at the plant level. Therefore, centrally agreed contracts can't be created.

▶ NO PLANT-RELATED CONDITIONS ALLOWED
You may not create any purchasing info records or contract items at the plant level.

Activate Regular Vendor per Plant

For each plant, you can define whether using the regular vendor is permitted (for scenarios, refer to Section 3.1.1). To do so, go to SAP IMG • MATERIALS MANAGEMENT • PURCHASING • SOURCE DETERMINATION • DEFINE REGULAR VENDOR. Select the REG.VENDOR checkbox, as shown in Figure 3.34.

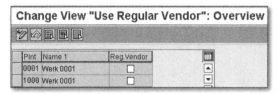

Figure 3.34 Regular Vendor

3.4 Source List

The source list is a type of master data that contains a list of allowed sources of supply for a material in a specific plant and for a certain period of time.

You can define the vendors with whom you procure a material, along with the validity period. The source list helps ensure that purchase orders aren't issued to the vendors who aren't authorized to supply a particular material.

3.4.1 Structure

The source list is used for the following:

▸ Maintaining a fixed source of supply

▸ Limiting the selection of sources of supply during the source-determination process

▸ Blocking a source of supply

A source list contains the following information for a material-plant combination, as shown in Figure 3.35:

▸ **Validity period**
   The VALID FROM and VALID TO fields provide the period during which the source of supply is valid.

▶ **Sources of supply**

These can be purchasing info records, supplying plants, or contract and scheduling agreements.

▶ **Blocked indicator**

If you wish to block a particular source of supply, you can set the blocked checkbox (BLK) in the source list. If you want to exclude material from external procurement, enter the validity period only. Don't enter a source of supply and set the BLK checkbox.

▶ **Fixed indicator**

If you want to set a certain source of supply as the default, set the fixed source of supply checkbox (FIX) in the source list. However, note that the FIX box is ignored during the planning run.

▶ **MRP indicator**

If you want a particular source of supply to be considered during the planning run, set the MRP indicator to "1." This will allow the system to understand that it's relevant for MRP. If you want to generate schedule lines during the planning run, the indicator has to be set to "2."

	Maintain Source List: Overview Screen

| Material | CONSG MAT | Consignment Material |
| Plant | 0001 | Werk 0001 |

Source List Records

Valid from	Valid to	Vendor	POrg	PPl	OUn	Agmt	Item	Fix	Blk	MRP	MRP Area
01.01.2009	31.12.2009	V100	0001					☐	☐		
01.01.2009	31.12.2009		0001			5600000452	10	☐	☐		

Figure 3.35 Source List Overview

3.4.2 Creating the Source List

You can create the source list manually or have it generated automatically. To create a source list manually, use Transaction ME01, as shown previously in Figure 3.35. A source list can also be created from a purchasing info record and an outline agreement.

In a purchasing info record, select Extras • Source List. The source list will be generated for all of the plants for which the purchasing organization is responsible. You can limit the plants by selecting Goto • Plant.

In an outline agreement, select Item • Maintain Source List. If a plant isn't maintained for this item, one has to be entered in the source list. In material group contracts, the material-specific source list can be created in a similar fashion. Here, you can also either include entered materials or exclude them from the subject contract.

Alternatively, a source list can be generated for a material or group of materials in a plant via Transaction ME05. However, note that this is a mass-generation program and should be used judiciously.

3.4.3 Configuration

If you want to make a source list mandatory for a material, you can set the Source List Required indicator in the material master record of that material. If you want to make the source list mandatory for all materials in a plant, go to SAP IMG • Materials Management • Source List • Define Source List Requirement at Plant Level, as shown in Figure 3.36. Click on the checkbox for the plant for which you want to make it mandatory.

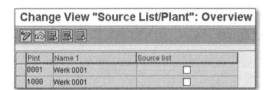

Figure 3.36 Defining the Source List Requirement at the Plant Level

You now know the purpose of source lists and the various settings associated with them. Let's move on to the subject of quota arrangement to discuss how the different sources of supply can be used in purchasing.

3.5 Quota Arrangement

An enterprise may have different sources of supply for the same material. If you want to distribute POs among these sources of supply in a systematic manner, you can use the quota arrangement function of MM with SAP ERP.

If a quota arrangement exists for a material, it has the highest priority during source determination.

3.5.1 Elements

Quota arrangement consists of various elements. Let's discuss the meaning of each of these elements before we see how to configure the quota arrangement in the system:

▶ **Validity period**
Quota arrangement for a material is maintained for a specified time period.

▶ **Procurement type**
This can be either internal or external procurement.

▶ **Special procurement type**
This can be consignment, subcontracting, or third-party procurements.

▶ **Procurement plant**
This can be a supplying plant that acts as a vendor.

▶ **Quota**
This is the number that specifies which portion of a requirement should be procured from a given source of supply. For example, if there are three sources of supply for a material and you want requirements to be evenly distributed among all three sources, enter "1" as the quota. The quota per vendor will be automatically converted to 33%.

▶ **Quota base quantity**
This is treated as an additional quota-allocated quantity. You can use this to regulate the quota arrangement without actually changing the quota if, for example, a new source of supply is included in the arrangement. Otherwise, if not set manually, let the system determine this quantity.

▶ **Quota allocated quantity**
This is the total quantity from all purchasing documents such as requisitions, orders, contract release orders, and planned orders. The quota-allocated quantity is updated automatically for each order proposal to which the quota arrangement is applied.

▶ **Quota rating**

This is used by the system to determine the source of supply. The system calculates the quota rating as follows:

quota rating = (quota – allocated qty + quota base qty) / quota

You can maintain the quota arrangement via Transaction MEQ1, as shown in Figure 3.37.

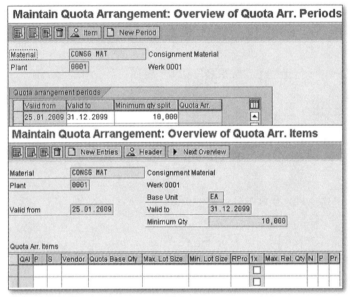

Figure 3.37 Quota Arrangement Maintenance

Example

Let's say that you include a new vendor in an already-existing quota arrangement. The existing quota arrangement consists of two vendors, who are each assigned 50% of the material requirements that arise. Each of these vendors has a high quota-allocated quantity because your company has already ordered a lot of material from them during the validity period of the quota arrangement.

The new vendor is to be assigned the same share of forthcoming requirements as the other two. However, according to the formula for calculating the quota rating, all requirements will be allocated to the new vendor until such time as his quota rating exceeds that of one of the other two vendors.

If the purchase requisitions are to be assigned evenly with immediate effect, as if the new vendor had been a party to the quota arrangement from the start, you must enter the quota base quantity for the new vendor appropriately, or have it determined by the system.

The system provides the following procedures for calculating the quota base quantity:

▸ **Individual calculation**
Calculates the quota base quantity for the selected quota arrangement items. Select the items whose quota base quantity is to be recalculated, and choose EDIT • BASE QUANTITIES • INDIVIDUAL CALCULATION.

▸ **Collective calculation**
Calculates the quota base quantity for *all* quota arrangement items. Use this procedure if you want to set the quota rating to the same value for each source. Choose EDIT • BASE QUANTITIES • COLLECTIVE CALCULATION.

▸ **Calculation of quota rating**
For example, you create a purchase requisition for a material (100 pc) for which the source determination process in the requisition is regulated on the basis of a quota arrangement. Table 3.1 shows the current situation with regard to the quota arrangement at the time of source determination.

Vendor	Quota	Quota-Allocated Quantity	Quota Base Quantity
A	3	780	0
B	2	380	0
C	1	0	260

Table 3.1 Example of Quota Arrangement

In accordance with the formula *Quota rating = (quota allocated qty + quota base qty) / quota*, the quota ratings for vendors A, B, and C are as follows in Table 3.2.

Vendor	Quota Rating
A	(780 + 0) / 3 = 260
B	(380 + 0) / 2 = 190
C	(0 + 260) / 1 = 260

Table 3.2 Example of Quota Arrangement—Quota Ratings

This means that the source representing vendor B will be assigned to the next requisition item because this vendor has the lowest quota rating.

> **Note**
>
> If a quota arrangement applies, this doesn't mean that the quantity of a single manually created purchase requisition is automatically apportioned among different sources. That is, the entire requested quantity of a purchase requisition item is assigned fully to one source in accordance with the quota arrangement. You can only divide up a single requirement according to the quota in the planning run.

After the purchase requisition (Transaction ME51N) for a quantity of 100 has been saved, the situation regarding the quota arrangement is as shown in Table 3.3.

Vendor	Quota	Quota-Allocated Quantity	Quota Base Quantity
A	3	780	0
B	2	480	0
C	1	0	260

Table 3.3 Example of Quota Arrangement—Quota Quantities

In accordance with the formula *quota rating = (quota allocated qty + quota base qty) / quota*, the quota ratings for vendors A, B, and C are as shown in Table 3.4.

Vendor	Quota Rating
A	(780 + 0) / 3 = 260
B	(480 + 0) / 2 = 240
C	(0 + 260) / 1 = 260

Table 3.4 Example of Quota Arrangement—Quota Ratings

If several sources of supply have the same quota rating, the system assigns to the requirement the source with the lowest quota arrangement item in the overview of the quota arrangement.

You can also simulate source determination using the quota arrangement. To do this, go to maintenance for quota arrangement, and choose the menu path Extras • Simulation • Quota Arrangement or Extras • Simulation • Source of Supply. If you choose the first menu path, only the quota arrangement is checked. If you choose the second menu path, outline agreements, info records, and source lists are included too.

3.5.2 Master Data and Configuration

To enable the quota arrangement functionality, you need to maintain the material master data as detailed here, and you need to define the quota arrangement usage indicator in Customizing. The steps are outlined in the following subsections.

Step 1: Material Master Settings

If you want to use quota arrangement for a material, it must be set in the purchasing view of a material master record, as shown in Figure 3.38.

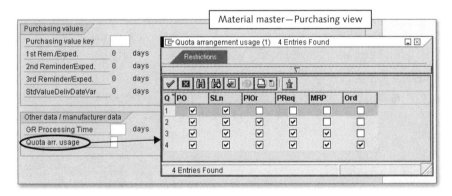

Figure 3.38 Quota Arrangement Usage Indicator in a Material Master Record

An entry in this field determines the areas in which the source determination facility finds the appropriate source on the basis of the quota arrangement. The quota-allocated quantity of the relevant quota arrangement item is updated from the areas specified via this indicator. The following areas can be taken into consideration:

- ▶ **Purchase requisitions**
  The source determination process is controlled via the quota arrangement, and the quantity requested for a material is included in the quota-allocated quantity.

- ▶ **Purchase orders**
  The quantity of the material ordered during the validity period is included in the quota-allocated quantity, provided the purchase order was not generated with reference to a requisition for which the quota arrangement was already used.

- ▶ **Scheduling agreement**
  The total quantity of the scheduling agreement delivery schedule lines for this material goes into the quota-allocated quantity.

- ▶ **Planned orders**
  The total quantity of all relevant assigned planned orders for this material goes into the quota-allocated quantity. If the planned order is converted to a requisition, however, the quantity-allocated quantity isn't updated again.

- ▶ **Materials planning**
  Source determination on the basis of quota arrangements can also be used in material requirements planning (MRP). Planned orders and purchase requisitions generated in the planning run have a source assigned on a quota basis, and the quota-allocated quantity is updated.

- ▶ **Production order**
  The total quantity from all production orders for this material goes into the quota-allocated quantity of a relevant quota arrangement item for in-house production.

Step 2: Configuration

You can use quota arrangements in connection with the following transactions:

- ▶ Purchase orders
- ▶ Scheduling agreement delivery schedules
- ▶ Planned orders
- ▶ Purchase requisitions
- ▶ MRP
- ▶ Invoices

In this step, you can specify which quota arrangement rule is allowed for each material master record. You can group the usage combinations you've chosen under keys. You need to select these keys at plant level in the material master record.

To do so, go to SAP IMG • MATERIALS MANAGEMENT • PURCHASING • QUOTA ARRANGEMENT • DEFINE QUOTA ARRANGEMENT USAGE. Click on the NEW ENTRIES button, enter the key, and select the checkbox for the transactions you want to use in quota arrangements. As shown in Figure 3.39, QUOTA ARR.USAGE 1 has PURCHASE ORDER and SA SCHEDULE LINE selected.

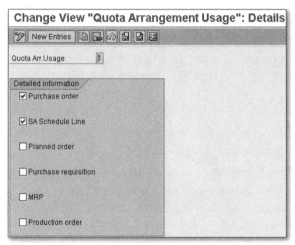

Figure 3.39 Quota Arrangement Usage Configuration

Note

Service master records are used only for the procurement of services, as discussed in Chapter 4, Section 4.6.2.

3.6 Catalogs in SAP ERP

As of SAP ECC 6.0 (SAP_APPL 600), you can use web-based catalogs in Purchasing via an Open Catalog Interface (OCI). It's possible to both upload purchasing data from the system into a catalog and download catalog data into material items of purchasing documents (requisitions with Transaction ME51N and purchase orders with Transaction ME21N). You make the technical settings for both uploads and downloads of catalog data in Customizing for Purchasing. Catalogs are more user friendly, as they provide various search criteria to search for a specific material. Different categories of materials may have different catalogues, and the search functionality really helps users search and select the required material.

Using Transaction MECCM (Send Purchasing Data to Catalog), you can transfer data from the items of purchase contracts and purchasing info records to a linked SAP Catalog Content Management system (SAP CCM) via SAP NetWeaver Process Integration (SAP NetWeaver PI). You can select the data to be transferred by material, vendor, purchasing organization, and receiving plant.

Note

The component for creating and managing electronic catalogs, SAP MDM Catalog, is part of the delivery scope of both SAP SRM and SAP ERP 6.0.

3.7   Summary

In this chapter, we reviewed how to configure master data with your business processes in mind. You should now understand the significance of the various organizational levels in master data and be able to decipher the different types of master data required in MM. We've also reviewed how to configure master data based on various business scenarios.

Let's now move on to the next chapter to discuss the application of various types of master data in procurement processes.

Procurement processes are an extremely important part of Materials Management, and learning about the various elements and aspects involved in these processes is an essential part of effectively using this application. How you customize the procurement processes is the key to a successful implementation.

4 Procurement Processes

Procurement processes are important functions within an enterprise. In response to a need for a system of best practices, SAP created a set of predefined procurement processes that can be customized to suit specific customer requirements.

The procurement cycle typically starts with the requirement of a material or a service, and ends with processing payment to the supplier. In industry terminology, this is called the *procure to pay* (P2P) cycle. In this chapter, we'll discuss the following:

- ▶ Direct material procurement
- ▶ Indirect material procurement
- ▶ Services procurement
- ▶ Consignment procurement
- ▶ Subcontracting procurement
- ▶ Third-party procurement
- ▶ Outline agreements
- ▶ Stock transfers
- ▶ Intercompany procurement

All of the procurement processes are similar in nature in that they start with a requirement and close with payment processing. However, depending on what and how you're procuring, they can be distinguished from one another. The SAP system uses the item category to determine what can be procured and how procurement can be carried out. Therefore, before we move on to describe each business process and its customizing steps in detail, you need to understand the concept of item category.

4.1   Item Category

In SAP procurement, a very important basic concept common to all procurement processes is the *item category*. The SAP system uses the item category to determine what can be procured and how procurement can be carried out. It determines the type of procurement process and is defined in the procurement documents. The item categories provided by SAP, such as STANDARD, LIMIT, CONSIGNMENT, and so on, are illustrated in Figure 4.1.

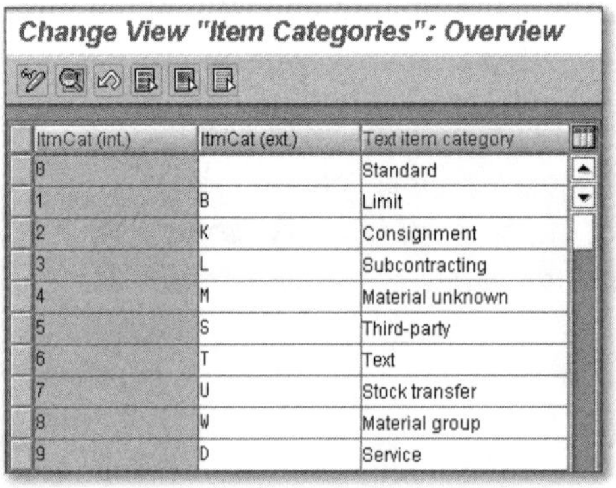

Change View "Item Categories": Overview		
ItmCat (int.)	ItmCat (ext.)	Text item category
0		Standard
1	B	Limit
2	K	Consignment
3	L	Subcontracting
4	M	Material unknown
5	S	Third-party
6	T	Text
7	U	Stock transfer
8	W	Material group
9	D	Service

Figure 4.1   Item Categories

You select the appropriate item category in a purchasing document based on the type of procurement, and the item category available depends on the document type. For example, if you select the document type "FO" (framework order), you'll get only three item categories to select — STANDARD, LIMIT, and SERVICES — because a framework order can't be created for other item categories such as SUBCONTRACTING, and so on. For each document type, the allowed item category can be configured; this topic will be covered in Chapter 8.

As shown in Figure 4.1, item categories are defined from 0 to 9. They can't be changed or modified; however, their external representation and text can be changed if needed. For example, ITMCAT (INT.) 2 is represented externally by K in the ITMCAT (EXT.) column, and its description is CONSIGNMENT. You can change the external representation K to C (or any other letter that's not used by another item category), and you can also change the description, if required.

> **Note**
>
> Item categories are predefined by SAP and you can't change the internal representation of an item category between 0 and 9. The only aspects of item categories that you can edit are their descriptions and external representations. To do so, the menu path is SAP IMG • MATERIALS MANAGEMENT • PURCHASING • DEFINE EXTERNAL REPRESENTATION OF ITEM CATEGORIES.

As illustrated in Figure 4.2, the item category controls the account assignment (CONTROL: ACCT. ASSGT), goods receipt (CONTROL: GOODS RECEIPT), and invoice receipt (CONTROL: INVOICE RECEIPT).

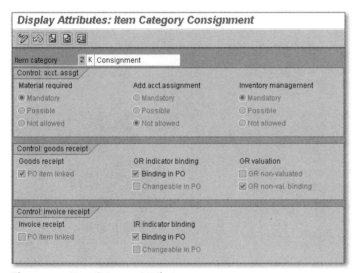

Figure 4.2 Item Category Attributes

For example, ITEM CATEGORY K represents the consignment procurement process, entailing that material and inventory management, among many other controls, are mandatory. We'll discuss each item category control when covering the different procurement processes.

Now that you understand the concept of item categories, we can go into more detail about the P2P cycle. We'll begin with an introduction to P2P and then discuss each of the procurement processes, covering the process steps and configuration involved in each.

4.2 Procure to Pay

Procure to pay (P2P) is used widely across different industry verticals and is the most common and important procurement process. Figure 4.3 shows the complete P2P cycle. It starts with the generation of a purchase requisition, which is converted into a purchase order (PO) and sent to the supplier. The supplier then dispatches the goods based on the quantity and delivery date specified in that PO. Upon receiving the supplied materials, the goods receipt is posted, and the supplier invoice is verified and posted. After that, the invoice posting payment is processed. This last step completes the P2P cycle (Figure 4.3).

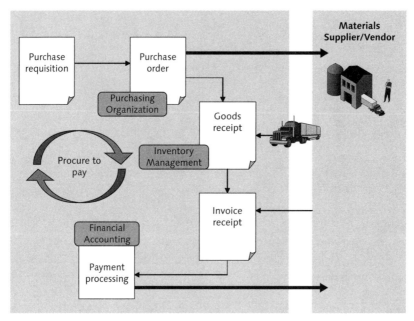

Figure 4.3 Procure to Pay Business Scenario

4.2.1   Business Scenario

To explain the P2P process in more detail, let's use a specific business scenario as an example. An enterprise engaged in the manufacturing of mountain bicycles requires many components (such as tires and suspension systems) that are procured externally and then assembled to form a complete bicycle. To manage the external procurement process, the planning department uses sales forecasts to generate purchase requirements. Once determined, these requirements — including the quantity and delivery date of materials — are passed on to the purchasing department. The purchasing department then identifies the supplier and issues the PO. The store's department ensures that the goods are received on arrival and that the goods receipt note is issued. Finally, the finance department verifies the invoice and processes payment to the supplier.

Now that we've discussed the general steps involved in the P2P process, let's look at each element of the process in detail.

4.2.2   P2P Documents

In the P2P process, various documents are used such as purchase requisitions, request for quotations, quotations, POs, goods receipts, and invoice receipts. Some of these documents are internal documents, and some are external documents. Documents that are required to capture information for the internal use of an enterprise are called *internal documents*. For example, purchase requisitions are internal documents used by various department of an enterprise to request the purchasing department to procure materials or services.

In real-time scenarios, the production department creates the purchase requisition for the raw materials required for production either manually or automatically through a materials requirements planning (MRP) run. External documents are the documents used to send information to external business partners such as vendors. For example, a PO is an external document. POs are sent outside the enterprise to vendors.

We'll now discuss the various documents involved in the P2P cycle.

Purchase Requisition

A *purchase requisition* (PR) is an internal document used to request procurement of a material or service. As shown in Figure 4.4, it can be created either manually via Transaction ME51N or automatically in MRP. To create purchase requisitions automatically from MRP, the option to create auto purchase requisitions needs to be selected. The purchase requisition contains many fields—such as MATERIAL or SERVICE, QUANTITY, DELIVERY DATE, and SOURCE OF SUPPLY—but these fields vary depending on the type of procurement. SAP has provided predefined document types for various procurement types. For example, document type NB is used for standard procurement, and UB is used for stock transfer procurement.

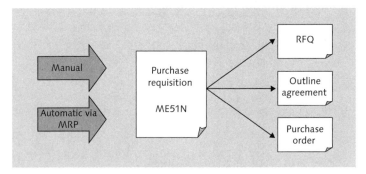

Figure 4.4 Creation of a Purchase Requisition

Preceding documents such as a request for quotation (RFQ), outline agreement, or PO can be created with reference to a specific purchase requisition.

RFQ/Quotation

An RFQ is an external document used by a purchasing department to identify a supplier. It can be created automatically with reference to a purchase requisition or manually, as shown in Figure 4.5. SAP provides an RFQ predefined document type called AN, which can be customized to suit customer requirements through document types configuration, which is discussed in Chapter 8. An RFQ typically consists of many fields, such as MATERIAL DESCRIPTION or SERVICE DESCRIPTION, QUANTITY, and REQUIRED-BY DATE. Once received, supplier responses are updated on the respective RFQ, and the purchasing department can send the POs to the selected vendors. If vendor prices or conditions aren't acceptable to the purchasing department, it can also send rejection letters to vendors.

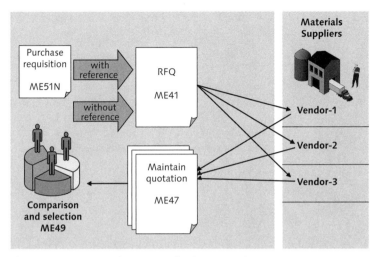

Figure 4.5 Creation of an RFQ and a Quotation Comparison

You can link several RFQs that belong together using a collective number. Enter the collective number in the header data of the RFQ. When analyzing RFQs and quotations, you can use the collective number as a selection criterion in Transaction ME49 (Quotation Comparison).

Preceding documents such as POs or contracts can be created with reference to quotations.

Purchase Order

A *purchase order* (PO) is a request to a supplier to supply certain goods or services under stated conditions. POs are external documents, sent outside your company to the supplier (Figure 4.6). They can be created with or without reference to purchase requisitions, RFQs, and contracts. SAP offers different ways of automatically converting purchase requisitions into POs; one example of this is Transaction ME59.

When you create a PO, most of the information is default data from master records. Similar to purchase requisitions, SAP provides predefined document types for creating POs; for example, FO is provided for the blanket/limit/framework type of procurement.

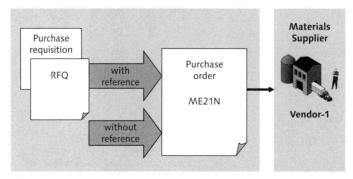

Figure 4.6 Different Ways to Create a PO

Order Acknowledgment

An order acknowledgment is the confirmation sent by vendor for a particular PO that shows the vendor is acknowledging that the terms and conditions of the PO (i.e., ordered item, quantity, price, delivery schedule, etc.) are agreed. The most important use of the order acknowledgment process is the confirmation of delivery schedule by the vendor. This helps in MRP to ensure you'll have materials available on the required dates.

You can enter vendor acknowledgments for POs or scheduling agreement delivery schedule lines. You can manually enter confirmations that you receive or have them processed automatically when you receive them via EDI (Figure 4.7)

To use the confirmations, select the confirmation control key in the PO line item of the CONFIRMATIONS tab. When you receive the order acknowledgment of the vendor, you change your PO by entering the confirmation data (date, time, quantity, and number of order acknowledgment) in the PO in the CONFIRMATIONS tab.

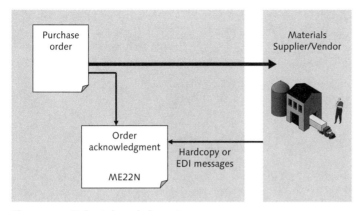

Figure 4.7 Order Acknowledgment

Goods Receipt

A *goods receipt* is an acknowledgment for a receipt of goods (Figure 4.8) and updates both inventory status and PO history. It also generates two documents in the system: a material document and an accounting document. The material document updates the stock in inventory, and the accounting document updates the G/L accounts in Financial Accounting (FI).

When a goods receipt is made with reference to a PO, the system supplies the open PO items and quantity. At the time of the goods receipt, the system also checks the underdelivery and overdelivery tolerances from the PO.

Invoice Verification

To process payments to suppliers, you need to post an invoice. The invoice can be posted with or without reference to a PO. A typical invoice verification and posting procedure is illustrated in Figure 4.9.

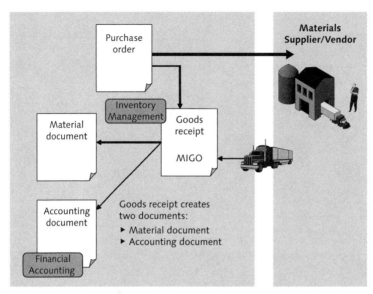

Figure 4.8 Goods Receipt Flow

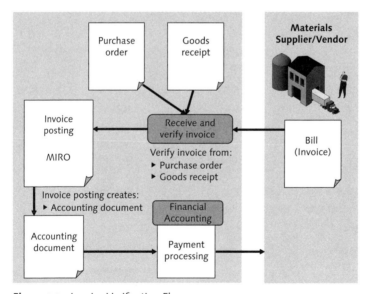

Figure 4.9 Invoice Verification Flow

When you enter an invoice with reference to a PO, the system automatically supplies the information provided in that PO, such as the material, quantity, terms of payment, and amount. After the invoice is posted, it's processed for payment by the finance department. Invoice posting also updates the PO history.

As shown in Figure 4.10, the P2P cycle can be applied in the procurement of stock/ direct material or consumable/indirect material. In the next sections, we'll discuss these procurement processes in detail.

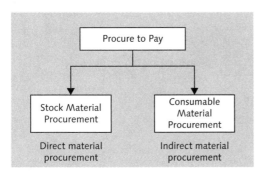

Figure 4.10 The P2P Process

4.3 Direct Material Procurement

The direct material procurement process is used for stock materials. You'll now learn about the business scenario, process steps, and configuration of direct material procurement in the system.

4.3.1 Business Scenario

Consider an enterprise engaged in the manufacturing of mobile handsets. This enterprise needs to procure some of the parts for the handsets—such as batteries and key pads—which are later used during production. These parts are examples of *direct materials*, which are materials required for production (i.e., raw materials). Direct materials are purchased, kept in inventory, and issued to the production department on a needs basis. Stock is maintained in inventory levels on a quantity and value basis.

As we've already discussed, a goods receipt transaction creates two documents: a material document and an accounting document (Figure 4.11). The material document updates the stock quantity in the storage location, and the accounting document updates the G/L account in FI. Goods receipts for stock materials are relevant for stock valuation.

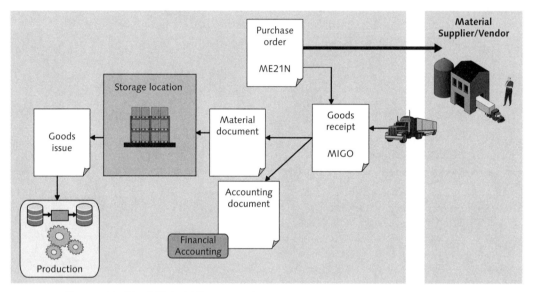

Figure 4.11 Direct Material Procurement

4.3.2 Process Steps

The direct materials procurement process starts with the creation of a purchase requisition and ends with processing payments to the supplier. The steps are as follows:

1. **Create the purchase requisition.**
   Create the purchase requisition via Transaction ME51N, and select document type NB (the document used for standard purchase requisitions). Enter the material, quantity, UOM, delivery date, and plant. Select BLANK as the item category, which is the standard item category. You can also assign the source of supply via the source determination process.

2. **Create the PO.**

   Create a PO via Transaction ME21N, with reference to the purchase requisition. Select the NB document type and the BLANK item category. If the source isn't assigned in the purchase requisition, enter the vendor and price.

3. **Post the goods receipt.**

   Upon receipt of the material, post the goods receipt via Transaction MIGO, with reference to the PO. All of the details in the goods receipt are copied from the PO.

4. **Post the invoice.**

   Upon receipt of the invoice from the vendor, post the invoice in the system via Transaction MIRO. Enter the document date, posting date, and PO number. The PO will copy the item, quantity, amount, and price. Before saving, you can check the account posting via the SIMULATE button.

> **Note**
>
> The source determination process can be triggered in the purchase requisition by either checking the SOURCE DETERMINATION checkbox when in create mode or by assigning sources of supply when in change mode.

4.3.3   Configuration Steps

If required, the direct material procurement process can be customized with the help of document types. Document types control many factors such as field selection and number ranges. This is discussed in more detail in Chapter 8.

Now that you understand direct material procurement, let's move on to the topic of indirect material procurement.

4.4   Indirect Material Procurement

Indirect materials are consumable materials such as office supplies and spare parts. Spare parts are parts of a machine that are required whenever the part life is over or it's damaged. We'll now discuss the business scenario, process steps, and configuration steps for indirect material procurement.

4.4.1 Business Scenario

An enterprise that manufactures mobile handsets requires indirect materials such as stationery, printers, and computers for their staff to carry out day-to-day business activities. Out of these materials, office supplies are kept in stock, but computers are procured on an as-needed basis. These items are procured directly for a cost center, and the costs of the materials are posted into the cost centers consumption G/L accounts as an expense. In this case, these items aren't managed on a value basis in inventory management because the material costs are directly posted into the consumption accounts.

When a material is procured directly for consumption, a material master record isn't necessary. The following are different examples of consumable materials:

▸ Consumable material without a material master record. For example, if your office stationery includes several small items, you may not want to complicate the process by creating a material master; rather, you want to enter the text for the materials such as clips, pen, pencil, sharpener and so on.

▸ Consumable material with a material master record that isn't subject to inventory management (not a quantity or a value basis).

▸ Consumable material with a material master record that is subject to inventory management on a quantity basis but not a value basis. This scenario is applicable when you want to track the consumables quantity in your inventory, and each issue and receipt needs to be tracked, however, the materials valuation isn't posted to the stock account at the time of goods receipt.

Because indirect materials aren't managed on a value basis, they won't update the stock valuation. The materials are procured for a cost center, and the material value is posted into consumption accounts (Figure 4.12).

Because indirect materials are procured for direct consumption, it becomes essential to assign a type of consumption category in the PO. This assignment is facilitated through the account assignment category in the SAP system, which specifies whether accounting for an item is affected via an auxiliary account such as a cost center, project, or sales order. The account assignment category further determines which cost elements are necessary for the particular category. For example, account assignment category C, which represents the sales order, requires the sales order number and the G/L account.

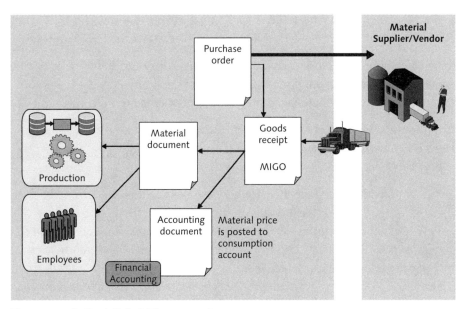

Figure 4.12 Indirect Material Procurement

The SAP system includes several predefined account assignment categories such as A (Asset), K (Cost Center), and P (Project), as shown in Figure 4.13.

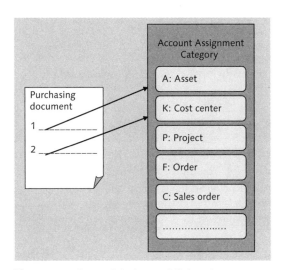

Figure 4.13 Account Assignment Categories

If any customer-specific requirement isn't met through the predefined account assignment categories, you can create your own, as discussed earlier in Section 4.3.3.

You can specify one or more account assignments for an item. If you specify a multiple account assignment, you must also specify how the PO quantity is to be distributed among the individual account assignment objects.

Distribution can be on a quantity or a percentage basis. If you enter a multiple account assignment for an item, the NON-VALUATED GR indicator is automatically set for this item. (You can see this indicator in the DELIVERY tab of the PO item details.)

In addition, you must specify in the item how the costs are to be distributed if only part of the ordered quantity is initially delivered and invoiced. (You can see this field in the ACCOUNT ASSIGNMENT tab of the PO item details. After you click on the MULTIPLE ACCOUNT ASSIGNMENT button, you can see the field PARTIAL INVOICING. From the dropdown, you can select DISTRIBUTE PROPORTIONALLY or DISTRIBUTE in sequence). Following are the two methods of cost distribution for a partial invoice:

▶ The partial invoice amount can be distributed among the account assignment items of a PO item proportionally (in accordance with the distribution ratio).

▶ The partial invoice amount can be distributed among the account assignment items of a PO item on a progressive fill-up basis (step-by-step). In this procedure, account assignment item 1 is completed first, then account assignment item 2, and so on, until the invoice value is reached.

The partial invoice indicator can also be derived automatically from the account assignment category if a partial invoice indicator is specified in Customizing for the account assignment category.

> **Note**
>
> Since the release of SAP ERP 6.0 EHP4, a valuated goods receipt can also be posted for PO items with multiple account assignment. To do this, you must activate the business function LOG_MM_MAA_1 via the Switch Framework (Transaction SFW5) as shown in Figure 4.14. You can use this business function to post a valuated goods receipt for multiple account assignment and to choose to manage the distribution based on quantity, percentage, and value (new).

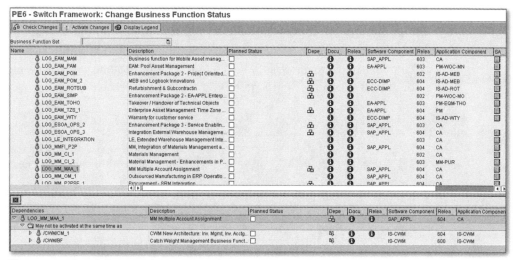

Figure 4.14 Switch Framework to Activate the Business Function

4.4.2 Process Steps

The process steps for indirect material procurement are similar to those in direct material procurement, except for the addition of the account assignment category.

1. **Create the purchase requisition.**
   Create the purchase requisition via Transaction ME51N, and select document type NB (standard purchase requisition). Enter the material, quantity, UOM, delivery date, plant, and any one of the account assignment categories such as cost center, asset, sales order, and so on.

2. **Create the PO.**
   Create the PO via Transaction ME21N, with reference to the purchase requisition. Based on the account assignment category selected, you need to enter the cost elements such as the G/L account number for consumption posting.

3. **Post the goods receipt.**
   On receipt of the material, post the goods receipt via Transaction MIGO, with reference to the PO. All of the details in the goods receipt are copied from the PO such as open PO quantity, plant, and so on. The storage location field isn't required as materials are directly consumed.

4. **Post the invoice.**

On receipt of the invoice from the vendor, post the invoice in the system via Transaction MIRO. Enter the document date, posting date, and PO number. The PO will copy the item, quantity, amount, and price. Before saving, you can check the account posting via the SIMULATE button.

> **Note**
>
> A scenario may exist where you need to procure direct materials for a project or a sales order. You can do this by designating the account assignment category in the purchasing documents. In this case, materials aren't subject to stock valuation.

4.4.3 Configuration Steps

The indirect material process can also be customized via the account assignment category and material type, as discussed in the following sections.

Let's look at a real-world example to show when you might need to customize the account assignment category to meet your business requirements.

Business Example

A leading multinational company headquartered in the United States produces edible oils. This company has one purchasing department dedicated to indirect materials/consumables procurement operating on a shared services model. This purchasing department gets requests from multiple departments but at times for the same product or service. For example, the factory, corporate office, regional office, depot, and so on requires laptops, computer peripherals, stationery, and infrastructure support. All such similar requests are combined together and then procured to get the benefit of volume discounts, better service, and faster deliveries and also to maintain standardization across the company. When such products or services are ordered, the POs are account assigned, and respective department's cost centers are charged.

The purchasing department started using the multiple account assignment option. This produced all of the goods receipts but without any accounting documents. The accounting documents were posted only when invoices are posted. This is because per standard SAP operations, when you use the multiple account assignment option, it automatically sets the GR NON-VALUATED indicator for that line item of the PO.

The auditors of the company notified the company's management and pointed out that per US GAAP reporting requirements, financial documentation should be updated at the time of goods receipt.

Considering this requirement, it became necessary to stop the use of multiple account assignment for the account assignment category K (cost center). This leads to customization of an account assignment category K.

The solution was to create custom account assignment category, say Z, by copying standard account assignment category K (cost center). The multiple account assignment option is then disabled/unchecked in account assignment category Z.

Now, with account assignment category Z, the purchase department has to create a PO with several lines for the same product or service for each cost center. Although this led to some operational inefficiency, it met the legal requirements.

The next section describes how you can create the custom account assignment category.

Account Assignment Category

To create new account assignment categories, go to SAP IMG • MATERIALS MANAGEMENT • PURCHASING • ACCOUNT ASSIGNMENT • MAINTAIN ACCOUNT ASSIGNMENT CATEGORIES. Click on NEW ENTRIES, or copy the SAP-provided account assignment category, as shown in Figure 4.15.

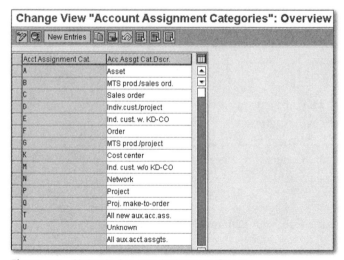

Figure 4.15 Maintain Account Assignment Category

You can define various controlling options for the account assignment category. For example, the GOODS RECEIPT indicator defines whether a goods receipt is required, the GR NON-VALUATED indicator defines whether the goods receipt should be non-valuated, and the INVOICE RECEIPT indicator defines whether an invoice is required (Figure 4.16). You can also define different fields to be mandatory, optional, displayed, or hidden.

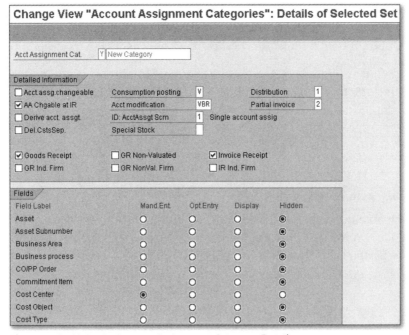

Figure 4.16 Maintain Account Assignment Category: Details

Material Type

Indirect materials may or may not have material master records. Indirect material master records are created with material type UNBW (non-valuated materials) or NLAG (non-stock materials) because these materials aren't valuated. The material type plays an important role in deciding whether materials will be maintained in inventory on a quantity basis, value basis, or both, as follows:

▸ **ROH**
  Raw material is maintained on both a quantity and value basis.

▶ **NLAG**

Non-stock material is material that isn't stored and isn't maintained on a quantity or value basis (Figure 4.17).

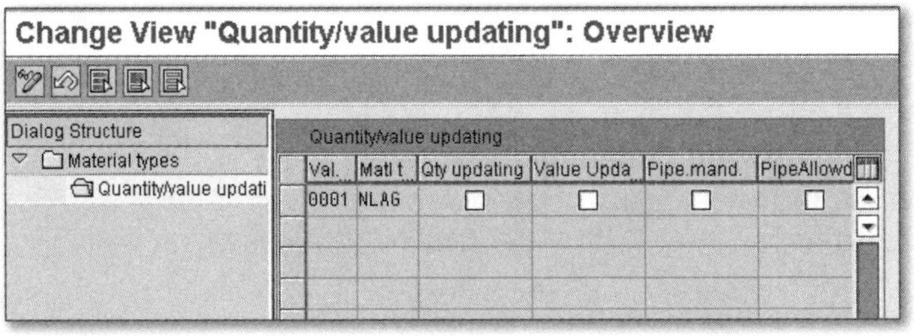

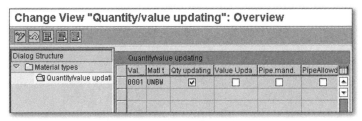

Figure 4.17 Material Type NLAG—Configuration Settings

▶ **UNBW**

Non-valuated material is material that's stored in a storage location, but not valuated (Figure 4.18).

Figure 4.18 Material Type UNBW—Configuration Settings

To check the configuration for standard material types provided by SAP, go to SAP IMG • Logistics General • Basic Settings • Material Type • Define Attributes of Material Types.

If you have customer-specific requirements, you can create your own material type for consumable materials. (See the configuration steps necessary to create a new material type in Chapter 3, Section 3.2.2.)

4.5 Blanket Purchase Orders for Consumable Materials

Blanket POs are often appropriate for low-value materials and are used to procure consumable materials and services that are frequently ordered from the same supplier. Blanket POs are valid for a longer term—such as for a year or two—and with a value limit. Let's explore when a business will want to use blanket POs and then discuss how to create them in Section 4.5.3.

4.5.1 Business Scenario

Consider, for example, a business that supplies their offices with general cleaning and janitorial supplies, ordered on a bi-weekly or monthly basis. This company should use a blanket PO rather than creating a separate PO each time they need supplies. When the material is consumed or services are performed, an invoice is posted in the system with reference to the PO, and no goods receipts are posted in the system. You can directly post invoices for the materials procured, as shown in Figure 4.19.

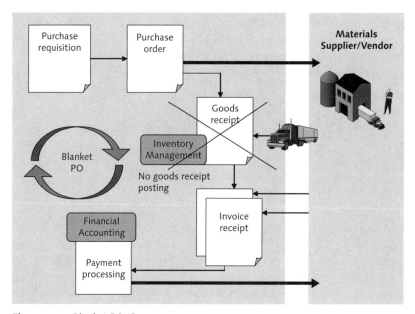

Figure 4.19   Blanket PO: Process

Process costs are often in total contrast to a comparatively low requirement value and don't bear any sort of relation to the value of materials or services procured. You can reduce these process costs, which may be very high in the case of procurement costs, by using a blanket PO instead of a standard PO. Such a single long-term PO can be used to procure a variety of materials or services whose modest value does not justify the high processing cost of issuing a series of individual POs.

The blanket PO process has several business advantages that result in lower transaction costs, as follows:

▶ Blanket POs are valid for the long term; therefore, you don't need to create them every time you reorder supplies.

▶ A goods receipt isn't required.

▶ Material master records aren't required.

4.5.2 Process Steps

The process steps in a blanket PO are similar to those in the indirect material procurement process, but there is no goods receipt posting. Proceed as follows:

1. **Create the purchase requisition.**
   Create the purchase requisition via Transaction ME51N, and select document type FO (framework order). Enter the item category as "B – limit", and then enter the quantity, UOM, plant, material group, overall limit, and any one of the account assignment categories, such as cost center.

2. **Create the PO.**
   Create the PO via Transaction ME21N, with reference to the purchase requisition. Enter the vendor, validity start date, and end date. Note the following important characteristics of a blanket PO:

   ▶ Order type FO (framework order)
     – Validity period in the header of the PO (field selection)

   ▶ Item category B (limit)
     – Limit in the item
     – No material number
     – Account assignment category U (unknown) allowed
     – No goods receipt or service entry

If the account assignment was specified in the PO, this data is proposed in the invoices, and additional or multiple account assignment is possible in invoice verification.

3. **Post the invoice.**

   On receipt of the invoice from the vendor, post the invoice in the system via Transaction MIRO. Enter the document date, posting date, and PO number. The PO will copy the item and quantity. Enter the amount, and save. Before saving, you can check the account posting via the SIMULATE button.

4.5.3 Configuration Steps

The FO document type provided by SAP is used to create blanket POs. This document type enables you to enter a validity period at the PO header level, and use item category B (limit item) for POs, as shown in Figure 4.20.

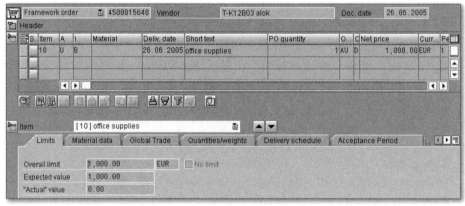

Figure 4.20 Blanket PO

If required, you can create new document types for blanket POs. Document type configuration is discussed in Chapter 8.

4.6 Service Procurement

Service procurement takes place when a company hires a vendor for external services, which are tasks carried out by an external contractor. Let's go through the business scenario, process steps, and configuration steps next.

4.6.1 Business Scenario

Consider, for example, a business that needs to hire a company to paint an office building or repair electric fittings. These are external services. External service procurement is similar to consumable materials procurement because services are also procured for consumption. First, you create and send a service PO to the vendor, and then the vendor performs the services for you. There are no goods receipts in service procurement; instead, you need to maintain a service entry sheet for the work completed by the vendor, as shown in Figure 4.21.

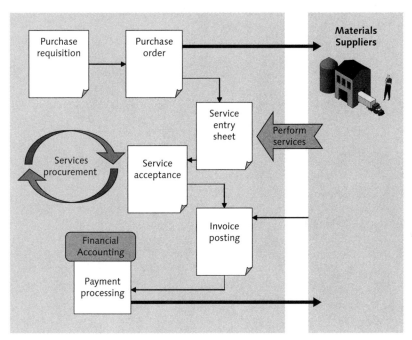

Figure 4.21 The Service Procurement Process

You can create a service master record for service procurement. In the next subsections, we'll discuss the service master record and the various documents involved in service procurement.

4.6.2 Service Master Record

For service procurement, a service master record can be created via Transaction AC03. A service master record contains a service description and a unit of measure, as shown in Figure 4.22. For example, for painting the office and factory premises, you can create a service master for painting, and you can specify the unit of measure as a square foot because services performed are measured in terms of the area of wall painted. Via the conditions, you can assign a price to each service master record. In the next sections, we'll discuss the different documents involved in service procurement.

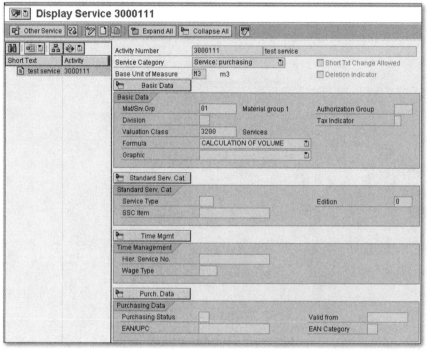

Figure 4.22 Service Master

Service master records can be used by other departments within the organization besides Purchasing, such as Project System, Plant Maintenance, and Customer Service for their business processes, including services for plant equipment, services for customer repairs, and returns.

4.6.3 Documents and Price Conditions in Service Procurement

Service procurement is slightly different from material procurement because the service entry sheet is used instead of a goods receipt. Performed services are entered in service entry sheets, and after it's signed off, the system will allow you to post the invoice. Let's discuss the service entry sheet and invoice verification in detail.

Service Entry Sheet

All of the performed services need to be entered into service entry sheets. After the service entry sheet is signed off, account postings are made. The service entry sheet can be entered and signed off in one transaction or in two steps.

Invoice Verification for Services

Invoice verification is carried out with reference to POs. All services that are signed off for a particular PO are suggested for invoice verification.

Defining Prices via Master Conditions

There are several ways of storing long-term prices for services in the form of service conditions. Prices stored in service conditions will automatically be proposed at the time of the PO creation. The following list details the ways to store long-term prices as service conditions:

1. **Maintain the master conditions at the service level.**
   Prices can be maintained for services, as shown in Figure 4.23. Use Transaction ML45 to add, Transaction ML46 to change, and Transaction ML47 to display service conditions at the service level.

Create Total Price Condition (PRS) : Fast Entry

Service Conditions (Own Estimate)

Service	Description	Amount	Unit	per	U...	C.	S.	Valid on	Valid to	Tax...	Wt...
T-LM211	Delivering of new fluores...	100.00	EUR	1	PC	C		26.06.2005	31.12.9999		

Figure 4.23 Conditions for Services at the Service Level

2. **Maintain the master conditions at the service and vendor level.**
   Select the vendor, and enter prices for the different services for the vendor, as shown in Figure 4.24. Use Transaction ML39 to add, Transaction ML40 to change, and Transaction ML41 to display master conditions.

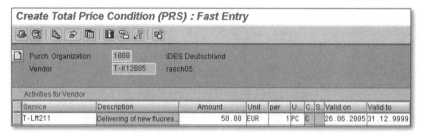

Figure 4.24 Conditions for Services at the Service and Vendor Level

3. **Maintain master conditions at the service, vendor, and plant level.**
   Select the vendor and plant combination, and maintain the prices for services, as shown in Figure 4.25. Use Transaction ML33 to add, Transaction ML34 to change, and Transaction ML35 to display the master conditions.

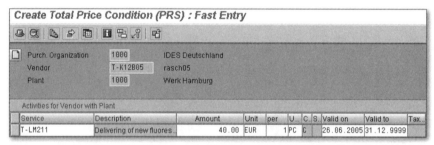

Figure 4.25 Conditions for Services at the Purchasing Organization and Plant Level

4.6.4 Process Steps

Follow these process steps for services procurement:

1. **Create the PO.**
   Create the PO via Transaction ME21N. Use item category D (services), and account assignment category K (cost center), or U (unknown). In the item details, enter the service master number. The quantity and prices will be picked up from condition records (provided they have been maintained), as shown in Figure 4.26.

2. **Maintain and accept the service entry sheet.**
   In service procurement, instead of a goods receipt, a service entry sheet is maintained for the work performed. You maintain and accept the service entry sheet via Transaction ML81N. If account assignment category U was selected in the

PO, while entering the service entry sheet, you need to change this to any other account assignment category, such as cost center or project, as shown in Figure 4.27.

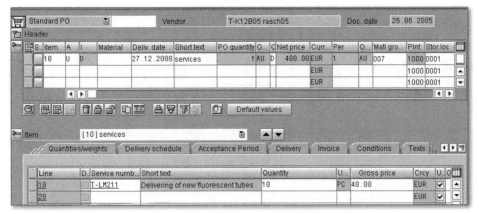

Figure 4.26 A Service PO

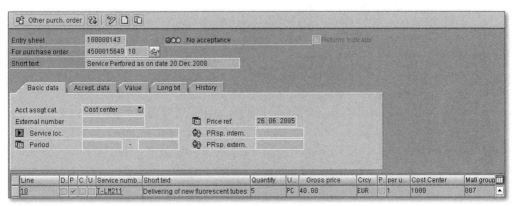

Figure 4.27 Service Entry Sheet

After you accept the service entry sheet by clicking ACCEPT—or by pressing `Ctrl` + `F1`—and clicking on SAVE, the system will automatically generate the material and accounting documents.

3. **Verify the invoice.**
   You can post the invoice via Transaction MIRO, with reference to the service PO. The system will propose the accepted services quantity that hasn't yet been invoiced.

4.6.5 Configuration Steps

In the following subsections, we'll discuss the various configuration steps for service procurement.

Defining the Organizational Status for Service Categories

The SAP system enables you to assign service master records administered in your company to different groups, according to their usage. These groups are called *service categories*. In this step, you maintain the organizational status of the service categories.

> **Example**
>
> Service categories are defined based on the usage of the services by different departments such as purchasing, sales, and production. For example, painting services for internal plants are executed by internal resources. In this case, you aren't procuring the services from an external vendor; hence, MM-related data isn't required. But because this has cost implications and you want to post these expenses to the cost center associated to the plant, you would need to maintain the Controlling (CO) data. In this scenario, an organization service category with basic data and CO data needs to be created.

To characterize service categories in more detail, they're assigned an organizational status. The *organizational status* indicates the areas in which service master records are used. Examples include basic data, CO or cost accounting data, purchasing data, and sales data. SAP recommends working with the standard SAP-supplied organizational status for service categories, as shown in Figure 4.28.

To define the organizational status for service categories, go to SAP IMG • MATERIALS MANAGEMENT • EXTERNAL SERVICES MANAGEMENT • SERVICE MASTER • DEFINE ORGANIZATIONAL STATUS FOR SERVICE CATEGORIES. Transactions AS01, AS02, and AS03 are defined by SAP, as shown in Figure 4.28.

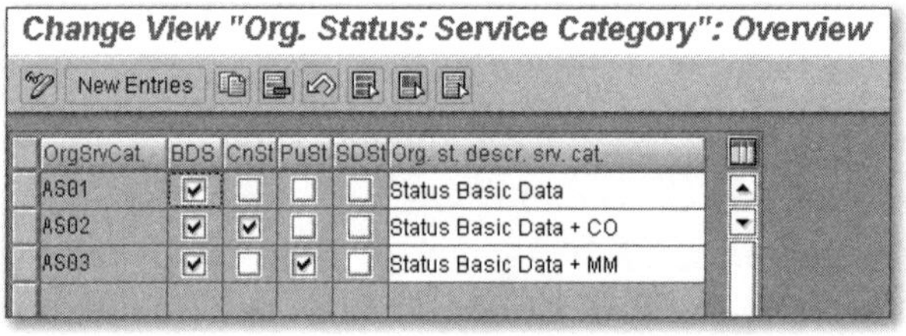

Figure 4.28 Organizational Service Category

The following organizational statuses can be maintained for service categories:

▶ BDS (Basic data status)
Click this indicator to store basic data in a service master record.

▶ CnSt (Controlling status)
Click this indicator to store controlling/cost accounting data in a service master record.

▶ PuSt (Purchasing data status)
Click this indicator to store purchasing data in a service master record.

▶ SDSt (Sales and Distribution status)
Click this indicator to store Sales and Distribution (SD) data in a service master record.

Defining the Service Category

In this step, you define the service category. The *service category* is most important for structuring service master records and providing a default value for the valuation classes.

> **Example**
>
> A manufacturing company involved in manufacturing has a huge plant and several buildings. The company's internal painting department takes care of painting services requirements. However, any repair-related services are procured from external vendors. The company wants to track and account separately for these two different types of services—internal and external services—by customizing two service categories.

Service master records can be assigned to number ranges on the basis of the service category. To define a new service category, go to SAP IMG • MATERIALS MANAGEMENT • EXTERNAL SERVICES MANAGEMENT • SERVICE MASTER • DEFINE SERVICE CATEGORIES.

To define a new service category, select NEW ENTRIES and enter the service category code in the SERV. CAT column. Next, select the organization status service category (ORGSRVCAT.) and account category reference (AREF), as shown in Figure 4.29. The account category reference is used for valuation classes, and each account category reference has a set of valuation classes assigned to it.

Change View "Service Category": Overview

New Entries

Serv. cat.	OrgSrvCat.	Ext	ARef	Service category descr.
ALL	AS02	☐	0006	Complete service
BULD	AS03	☑	0006	Construction
GRND	AS01	☐	0006	Basis service
INST	AS03	☐	0006	Plant maintenance
MINI	AS03	☐	0006	
SERV	AS03	☑	0006	Service: purchasing
SRV1	AS01	☐	0006	General Services
SRV2	AS01	☐	0006	Hardware Services
SRV3	AS01	☐	0006	Software Services
SRV4	AS01	☐	0006	Train.&Consult. Services
SRV5	AS01	☐	0006	Technical Services
SRV6	AS01	☐	0006	Contract Services

Figure 4.29 Service Category

Assigning a Number Range to the Service Category

In this step, you assign an internal or external number range to the service categories. To do so, go to SAP IMG • Materials Management • External Services Management • Service Master • Assign Number Range. Create the number range for the number range groups, and assign the service category to the number range groups, as shown in Figure 4.30.

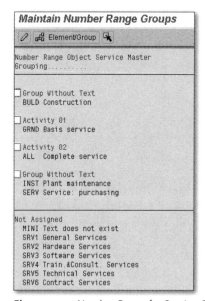

Maintain Number Range Groups

Element/Group

Number Range Object Service Master
Grouping.........

☐Group Without Text
  BULD Construction

☐Activity 01
  GRND Basis service

☐Activity 02
  ALL Complete service

☐Group Without Text
  INST Plant maintenance
  SERV Service: purchasing

Not Assigned
  MINI Text does not exist
  SRV1 General Services
  SRV2 Hardware Services
  SRV3 Software Services
  SRV4 Train.&Consult. Services
  SRV5 Technical Services
  SRV6 Contract Services

Figure 4.30 Number Range for Service Categories

Defining and Assigning the Number Range for the Service Entry Sheet

Next, you need to define the number range for the service entry sheet and for the service specification. To do so, go to SAP IMG • MATERIALS MANAGEMENT • EXTERNAL SERVICES MANAGEMENT • NUMBER RANGE (Figure 4.31).

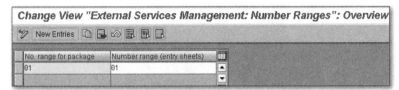

Figure 4.31   Number Range Interval for the Service Entry Sheet

Source Determination and Default Values

In this step, you set up the source determination and various default values at the client or purchasing organization level. If you've created settings at the purchasing organization level, these settings get priority over the client level. If the settings aren't created at the purchasing organization level, the system uses the general settings created at the client level. To define various default values, go to SAP IMG • MATERIALS MANAGEMENT • EXTERNAL SERVICES MANAGEMENT • SOURCE DETERMINATION AND DEFAULT VALUES. As shown in Figure 4.32, you can define default settings such as LINE NO. INCREMENT IN SERV. SPECIFICATIONS, DEFAULT MATERIAL GROUP AT ITEM LEVEL, and UNIT OF MEASURE AT ITEM LEVEL.

You can also specify whether the conditions you've maintained for services in the master record should be updated by the data in purchasing documents. To configure this, check the SET CONDITION UPDATE INDICATOR AS DEFAULT IN PURCHASE ORDER checkbox, as shown in Figure 4.32. Users can deactivate the default indicator for individual service lines in the relevant purchasing document, and the conditions in the master records of these services will remain unchanged.

Source Determination

For the system to suggest a source when services are procured, you must create a setting in the SOURCE DETERMINATION area. If you don't create a setting, no search for suitable sources will take place.

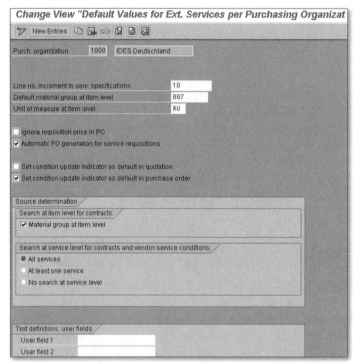

Figure 4.32 Source Determination and Default Values Configuration

You can use one or both of the two options for having sources suggested:

▶ SEARCH AT ITEM LEVEL FOR CONTRACTS
For services belonging to a material group, the source-determination process is set at the item level. This means that contract items with the same material group are suggested as sources for a requisition item. (Whether or not the specific individual service requested is included in the contract in question is immaterial.)

▶ SEARCH AT SERVICE LEVEL FOR CONTRACTS AND VENDOR-SERVICE CONDITIONS
The following options are available:

  ▶ ALL SERVICES
  In the process of determining suitable sources, the system suggests the contracts that contain all services requested in the purchase requisition.

  ▶ AT LEAST ONE SERVICE
  In the process of determining suitable sources, the system suggests the contracts that contain at least one of the services requested in the purchase requisition.

► No search at service level

Source determination isn't carried out at the service line level.

4.7 Consignment Procurement

Consignment procurement takes place when you have an arrangement with a vendor that allows the vendor to keep its materials on your premises. When the material is issued to your production or stock, you must pay the vendor. In the SAP system, you can settle your consignment liabilities with the vendor on a monthly basis.

4.7.1 Business Scenario

Consider a car-manufacturing enterprise that procures tires from a supplier but keeps the stock of tires at the manufacturing plant. In this case, the manufacturing enterprise is liable for payment only when the tires are issued to production. Until then, the stock is owned by the supplier. The vendor is informed of material withdrawals on a regular basis, and the quantity withdrawn is invoiced at certain time intervals. The consignment-procurement process is illustrated in Figure 4.33.

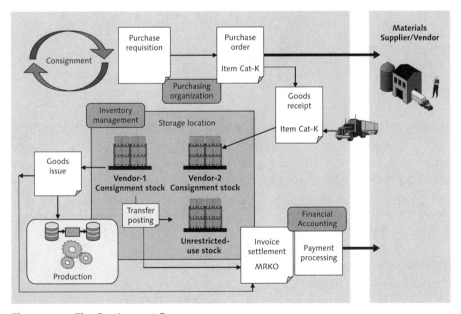

Figure 4.33 The Consignment Process

For consignment procurement, you need to define consignment info records to pick the consignment material price and conditions during invoice settlement. In a consignment PO, prices aren't maintained. At the time of consignment settlement, the prices and conditions are picked up from the consignment info records. This is because invoices are settled periodically and not posted with reference to a PO.

Consignment Info Record

Info records for consignments are different from info records for stock material procurement. While creating a consignment info record, you need to select the info record category CONSIGNMENT, as shown in Figure 4.34.

Figure 4.34 Consignment Info Record

The consignment price, which can be defined periodically, is stored in the consignment info record. You can manage consignment prices in foreign currencies; the PO currency of the vendor is used for consignment withdrawals. You can also use conditions in purchasing, as well as definitions of discounts and price/quantity scales. A vendor consignment price for a material is valid plant-wide.

Consignment stocks from a vendor are managed at the storage location level, as shown in Figure 4.35. Consignment stock can be stored with different stock types, such as unrestricted use stock, quality stock, and blocked stock. Transfer postings are possible to change the stock type. If your company has both its own stock and consignment stock of the same material, the two are managed separately.

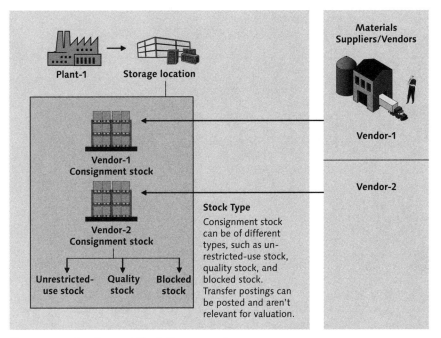

Figure 4.35 Consignment Stock Management

4.7.2 Process Steps

Follow these process steps for consignment procurement:

1. **Create a consignment PO.**

   Create a consignment PO via Transaction ME21N. Select item category K (Consignment), and enter the material, quantity, plant, and storage location, as shown in Figure 4.36.

   In consignment POs, price and conditions aren't maintained. The consignment PO history isn't updated with the invoice.

2. **Post the goods receipt.**

   You can post the goods receipt via Transaction MIGO. When you post a goods receipt for a consignment PO, it will create only a material document, and the movement type will be 101 K, as shown in Figure 4.37. K is a special stock indicator for consignment material.

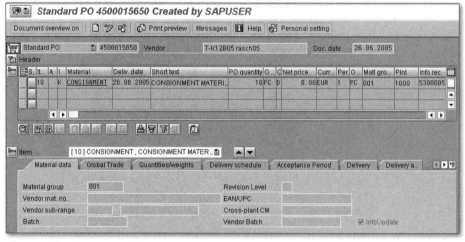

Figure 4.36 Consignment PO

Note

An accounting document won't be created at the time of the goods receipt because the received material is still owned by the vendor, and no payment is due.

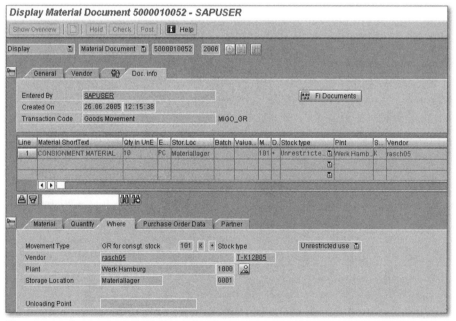

Figure 4.37 Consignment Stock Goods Receipt

You can check the vendor's consignment stock overview via Transaction MMBE, as shown in Figure 4.38.

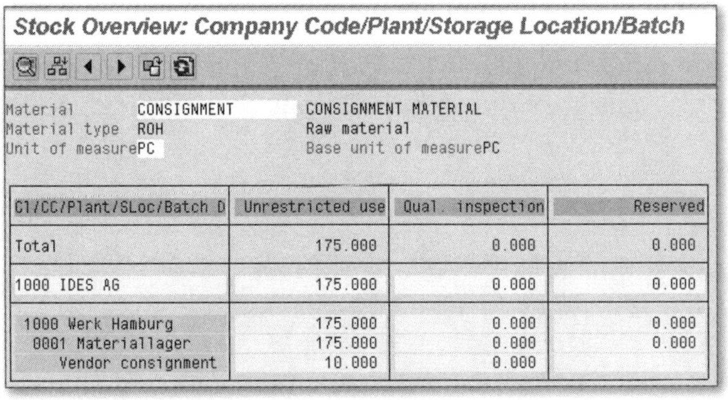

Stock Overview: Company Code/Plant/Storage Location/Batch

Material	CONSIGNMENT	CONSIGNMENT MATERIAL	
Material type	ROH	Raw material	
Unit of measure	PC	Base unit of measure	PC

Cl/CC/Plant/SLoc/Batch D	Unrestricted use	Qual. inspection	Reserved
Total	175.000	0.000	0.000
1000 IDES AG	175.000	0.000	0.000
1000 Werk Hamburg	175.000	0.000	0.000
0001 Materiallager	175.000	0.000	0.000
Vendor consignment	10.000	0.000	

Figure 4.38 Stock Overview Report

Consignment stocks can be managed as unrestricted use stock, quality inspection stock, and blocked stock. Any of the stock types are irrelevant for valuation because the stock is owned by the vendor.

3. **Post goods issue from the consignment stock.**
   In this step, you issue the goods to production or transfer the goods from a consignment stock to your own stock. These processes work as follows:
   - **Transfer material from consignment stock to your own stock**
     You can transfer goods from consignment stock to your own unrestricted use stock via Transaction MIGO_TR. To do so, select movement type 411 K, and enter the vendor code, quantity, and storage location. This transfer posting will create material and accounting documents. When transferring goods from consignment stock into your own stock, liability is generated. Accounts payable will be credited, and the stock account will be debited.
   - **Goods issue from consignment stock to production**
     You can issue goods to production from consignment stock via Transaction MIGO_GI. Select movement type 201 K, and enter the vendor code, quantity, storage location, cost center, and G/L account for consumption posting. This transaction will create material and accounting documents. When issuing goods to production from consignment stock, liability is generated. Accounts payable will be credited, and the consumption account will be debited.

4. **Settle the consignment liabilities.**

   You can settle consignment withdrawals online, as well as on a batch basis. Enter the invoices for consignment liabilities without reference to a PO.

   Transaction MRKO is used to settle consignment liabilities. Select the company code, vendor, and plant combination for invoice settlement, and select the processing option as SETTLE. Figure 4.39 shows the list of material documents pending for settlement.

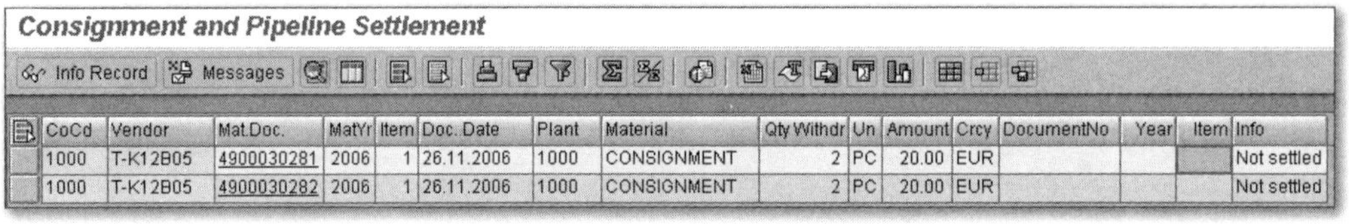

Consignment and Pipeline Settlement

CoCd	Vendor	Mat.Doc.	MatYr	Item	Doc. Date	Plant	Material	Qty Withdr	Un	Amount	Crcy	DocumentNo	Year	Item	Info
1000	T-K12B05	4900030281	2006	1	26.11.2006	1000	CONSIGNMENT	2	PC	20.00	EUR				Not settled
1000	T-K12B05	4900030282	2006	1	26.11.2006	1000	CONSIGNMENT	2	PC	20.00	EUR				Not settled

Figure 4.39 Consignment Settlement: Before Invoice Processing

Figure 4.40 shows the list of material documents and invoice documents after the consignment liability has been processed. The vendor account will be credited, and accounts payable will be debited.

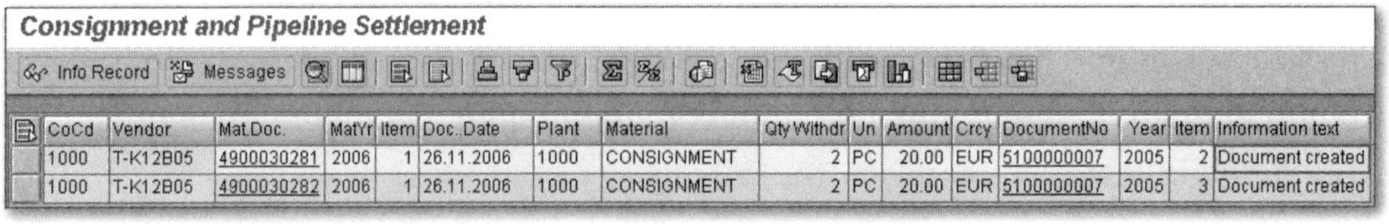

Consignment and Pipeline Settlement

CoCd	Vendor	Mat.Doc.	MatYr	Item	Doc..Date	Plant	Material	Qty Withdr	Un	Amount	Crcy	DocumentNo	Year	Item	Information text
1000	T-K12B05	4900030281	2006	1	26.11.2006	1000	CONSIGNMENT	2	PC	20.00	EUR	5100000007	2005	2	Document created
1000	T-K12B05	4900030282	2006	1	26.11.2006	1000	CONSIGNMENT	2	PC	20.00	EUR	5100000007	2005	3	Document created

Figure 4.40 Consignment Settlement: After Invoice Processing

> **Note**
>
> The price and conditions are picked up from the consignment info records.

Now that you have a good understanding of the consignment process steps, let's move on to the configuration steps.

4.7.3 Configuration Steps

If your client requires it, you can configure the automatic settlement of consignment liabilities. In this case, the system will automatically settle the consignment liability by executing Transaction MRKO. For example, a car manufacturing company obtains tires by consignment procurement from its vendor, and the company wants to run an automatic settlement program for the tires being issued to production on a daily basis.

You can also settle consignment liabilities via a batch job by using Transaction SM36 and Program RMVKON00, with the required variant.

4.8   Subcontract Procurement

The subcontract procurement process is different from the other material procurement processes we've discussed so far. It involves an agreement where you issue raw materials to a vendor, and the vendor makes finished or semi-finished products from the raw materials. These finished or semi-finished products are then supplied back to you, as shown in Figure 4.41 in the following section. Let's now discuss a business scenario and the process steps.

4.8.1   Business Scenario

An enterprise is engaged in car manufacturing and procures components such as ring gears, pinions, and axle shafts from a supplier. With subcontract procurement, the car-manufacturing enterprise issues the raw materials (such as steel sheets) to the supplier, who then manufactures the components. The supplier produces components per the design and quality standards given by the manufacturing company and sends back these components to the manufacturing company. The supplier is paid for the labor charges. These components are used by the manufacturing company to assemble the cars.

The subcontract scenario process flow is shown in Figure 4.41, where the purchase requisition is converted to a PO and sent to the vendor, and then the raw materials are issued via a goods issue. Upon arrival of the semi-finished or finished components, a goods receipt is posted in the system. The vendor invoice is then posted, and payment is processed by the finance department.

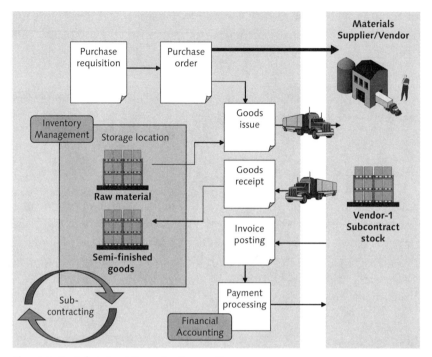

Figure 4.41 Subcontract Scenario: Process Flow

When you issue goods to subcontractors, there is no G/L account posting because you still own the stock (Figure 4.42). Stock issued to the subcontractor is valuated in stock valuation and is also shown in stock overview reports until you post the goods receipt of the ordered material. When you post the goods receipt, the system creates the material and accounting documents.

After the goods receipt is posted, the vendor's invoice is entered with reference to the PO, and a subsequent adjustment for overconsumption or underconsumption of the components can be made at the same time.

For the subcontract process, the bill of material (BOM) and subcontract info records can be defined. The BOM is a list of materials—quantity included—required to manufacture a component. You must create a BOM for the material you want a subcontract vendor to produce or assemble for you (Figure 4.43). Use Transaction CS01 and select BOM USAGE 1 (Production BOM). Then define all of the materials, with their quantities, that are required to make one unit of subcontract material.

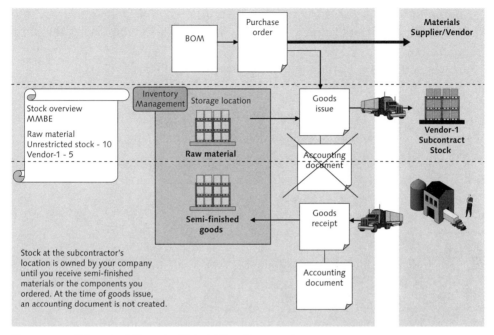

Figure 4.42 Subcontract Scenario: Material Handling

You may have a scenario where co-products are produced while manufacturing the end product. (Co-products are the products that are produced along with the production of the main product.) You can define these products in the BOM with a minus sign as shown in ITEM 0040, COMPONENT T-T401, in Figure 4.43.

Material	T-B111		Casing							
Plant	1000	Werk Hamburg								
Alternative BOM	1									

Material | Document | General

	Item	ICt	Component	Component description	Quantity		Un	A...	Sis	Valid From	Valid To
	0010	L	T-T101	Slug for spiral casing	1		PC			23.04.2006	31.12.9999
	0020	L	T-T201	Flat gasket	1		PC			23.04.2006	31.12.9999
	0030	L	T-T301	Hexagon head screw M10	8		PC			23.04.2006	31.12.9999
	0040	L	T-T401	Slug for Shaft	2 -		PC			27.06.2007	31.12.9999

Figure 4.43 Bill of Material

Subcontract info records for subcontract procurement are different from info records for stock material procurement. When creating an info record, select the info records category SUBCONTRACTING, as shown in Figure 4.44. The conditions defined in the info records are then copied into the subcontract PO.

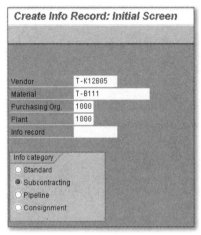

Figure 4.44 Subcontracting Info Records

4.8.2 Process Steps

The following are the process steps for subcontracting procurement:

1. **Create a subcontract PO.**

    The subcontract PO is created with item category L, as shown in Figure 4.45. Each item contains the components that should be provided to the vendor, and these components can be entered manually or can be determined using a BOM explosion. The PO price is the vendor's service price for the labor. Conditions for subcontract orders can be stored in subcontract info records.

    Create a subcontract PO via Transaction ME21N, and select item category L. Enter the material, quantity, delivery date, plant, and supplier.

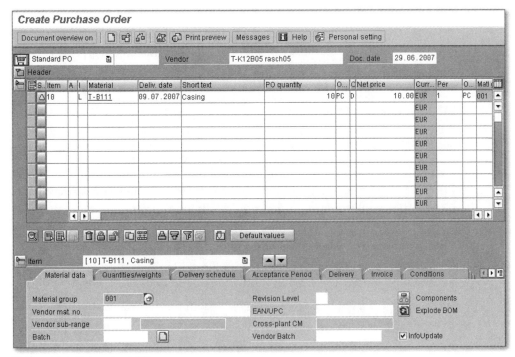

Figure 4.45 Subcontract PO

2. **Post the goods issue.**

   After the subcontract PO is issued, you need to issue materials to the subcontractor. You can check this component requirement via Transaction ME2O, which provides the SC Stock Monitoring for Vendor report (Figure 4.46).

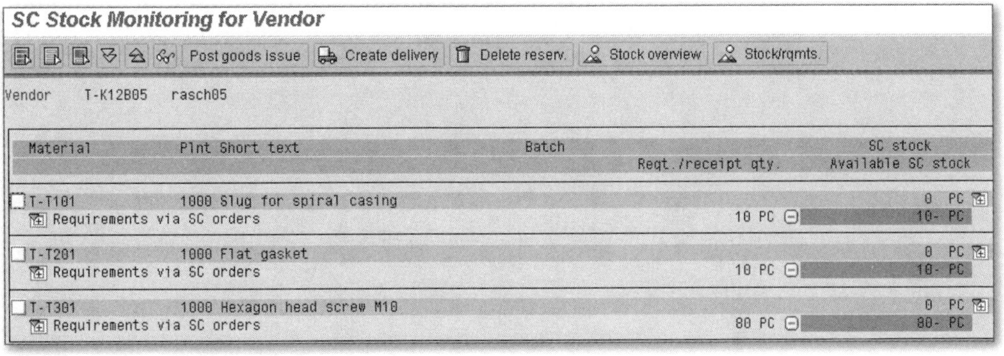

Figure 4.46 Subcontract Stock Overview Report

You can post a goods issue from the report by selecting the item and clicking on the POST GOODS ISSUE button. This will issue goods to the subcontractor. You can also issue goods via Transaction MIGO_TR, with movement type 541. Enter the PO number, and the system will use the PO to determine the materials and quantity that should be issued to the vendor.

When you issue goods to a subcontractor, the SAP system will create only a material document. An accounting document isn't necessary because this material is still owned by your company.

3. **Post the goods receipt.**

Based on your subcontract PO, the subcontractor produces the material and supplies it to you. When you receive the goods, you need to post a goods receipt transaction with reference to the appropriate PO. This will update your stock quantity and will also post the consumption of components you've issued to the subcontractor. Post the goods receipt via Transaction MIGO and enter the PO number, and the system will supply the open PO quantity (Figure 4.47).

When you post a goods receipt, the system will receive the final material with movement type 101. All of the components required to manufacture the final material are posted with movement Type 543, and co-products are posted with movement type 545. The DIRECTION column in the goods receipt screen shows plus and minus (+/-) signs based on receipt and consumption, as shown in Figure 4.47.

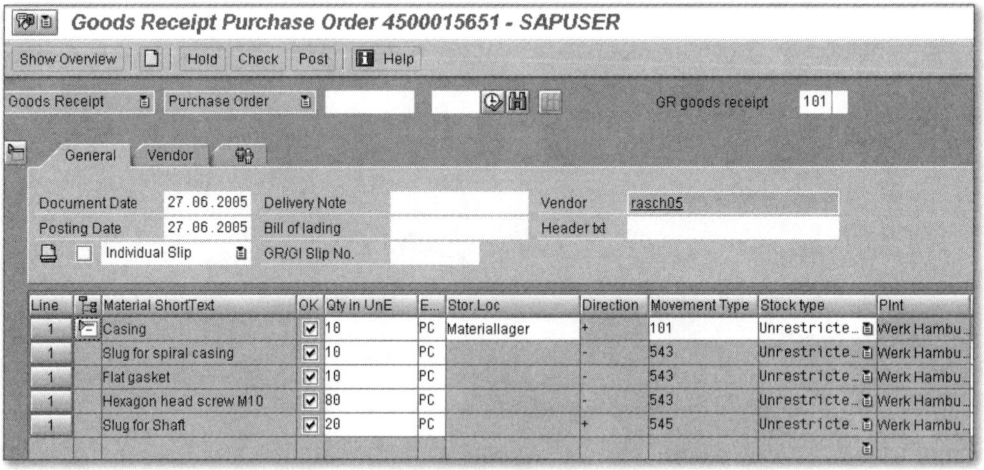

Figure 4.47 Goods Receipt: Subcontract Material

The subcontracting goods receipt will create an accounting document, and a minimum of six G/L accounts will be posted (Figure 4.48). These accounts are as follows:

▶ **Raw materials price**

When you receive semi-finished goods from a subcontractor, the raw materials have been consumed. Therefore, the SAP system will post the raw material price to the following accounts:

– Raw material stock account: credit

– Consumption account: debit

▶ **Semi-finished materials price**

When you receive semi-finished materials, their valuation price will be a total of the raw material price and labor charges. Therefore, the SAP system will post to the following accounts:

– Semi-finished material stock account: debit

– Cost of goods manufactured: credit

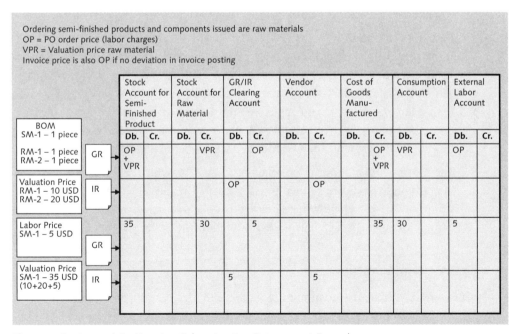

Figure 4.48 Account Postings in a Subcontracting Procurement Example

▶ **External labor price**
Labor charges will be posted into intermediate accounts (i.e., GR/IR accounts) because vendor liability will be created only when you post an invoice.

– GR/IR account: credit

– External labor account expense: debit

You have a BOM for a semi-finished product, and you issue a PO to your vendor for one piece. One piece each of material RM-1 and RM-2 is required to manufacture semi-finished good SM-1. RM-1's valuation price is $10, RM-2's valuation price is $20, and the labor charge is $5. Figure 4.48 shows the G/L accounts that will be posted at the time of the goods receipt.

4. **Post the invoice.**
Upon receipt of the invoice from the vendor, post the invoice in the SAP system via Transaction MIRO. Enter the document date, posting date, and PO number. The PO will supply the item, quantity, amount, and price. Before saving, you can check the account posting via the SIMULATE button.

5. **Post the settlement.**
If the vendor informs you of overconsumption or underconsumption after the goods receipt has been posted, you must make an adjustment. In this case, settlement is entered with reference to the PO. Transaction MIGO_GS is used for underconsumption and overconsumption adjustments. After you post an underconsumption, this material will be listed in the stock to be received from the subcontractor, and the vendor should return the material to you.

The movement type for underconsumption is 544, which will increase the stock quantity in the available subcontractor stock. The movement type for overconsumption is 543, which will decrease the stock quantity from the available subcontractor stock. You can also use Transaction MB04 for overconsumption.

4.8.3 Configuration Steps

If required, you can use document types to customize the subcontract procurement process. Document types control many factors, such as field selection and number ranges. This is discussed in more detail in Chapter 8. You might be wondering why we're suggesting that you use item category L for subcontracting process.

Attributes of item category L (as shown in Figure 4.49) determine that subcontracting components have to be provided for the manufacture of a material that is to be ordered.

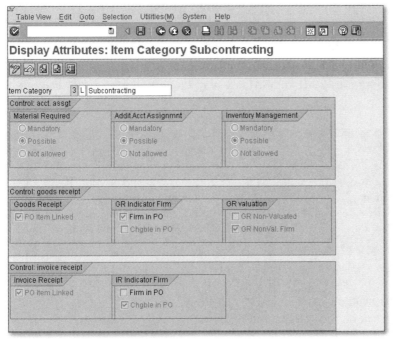

Figure 4.49 Attributes of Item Category L

The use of item category L has the following effects on a PO item:

▶ The PO item can be created with or without a material master record. If a PO item is created with a material number, specifying an account assignment category is optional.

▶ The indicators for goods receipt and invoice receipt are set as PO ITEM LINKED, which means PO requires goods receipt and invoice receipts.

▶ The GR REQUIRED indicator can't be changed in the PO. This means the goods receipt must be posted against the PO. However, the IR indicator can be unchecked in the PO, and, in this case, the invoice will be optional with reference to the PO. The indicator for non-valuated goods receipt isn't proposed; neither can it be set manually in the PO. It means the goods receipt must be valuated and will post an accounting document.

4.8.4 Enhancements in Subcontracting Since SAP ERP 6.0 EHP4

Since the release of SAP EHP4 for SAP ERP 6.0 (SAP_APPL 604), you can use the outsourced manufacturing business function (LOG_MM_CI_1). This business function enables you to structure your subcontracting processes more efficiently.

In particular, brand manufacturers use subcontractors to produce their products. This SAP solution supports all of the essential aspects of the subcontracting process. Process steps are clearly represented through the integration of SAP Supply Network Collaboration (SNC) and SAP ERP Production Planning (PP), making it easier to monitor your production process.

> **Real-World Example of Outsourced Manufacturing**
>
> Unilever, the world's renowned FMCG (fast-moving consumer goods) products company, has many vendors who are responsible for producing goods for the company. During production planning, all of these outsourced manufacturing locations are considered, production orders are generated, and the same information is sent to vendors to produce the goods. All of the raw materials are issued by Unilever. The vendor is supposed to follow the recipe for each product given by Unilever.

To use the outsourced manufacturing process, turn on the business function LOG_MM_CI_1 by using Transaction SWF5 as shown in Figure 4.50. Select the business function, click on the SYSTEMS setting in the menu, and then activate or press Ctrl + F3.

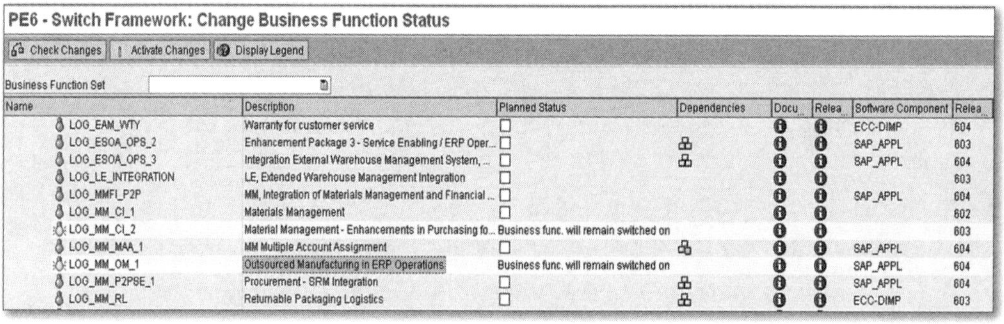

Figure 4.50 Switch Framework—Activate Business Function

After you activate the outsourced manufacturing business function LOG_MM_CI_1, the following functionalities will be activated in the system:

- Subcontracting Cockpit
- Stock in transfer for subcontractor and customer consignment
- One-step stock transfer for subcontracting
- Scrap report for subcontract order
- Subcontract orders and production orders in CO
- New fields for data transfer from SAP ERP to SAP SNC
- Transfer data from the approved manufacturer parts list (AMPL) to SAP SNC using the Core Interface (CIF)

We'll only discuss the subcontracting-related functionality and how you can configure and use these functions. The other functionalities aren't within the scope of MM in SAP.

4.8.5   New Transactions in Subcontracting

You'll get three new transactions in the SAP Easy Access menu (see Figure 4.51).

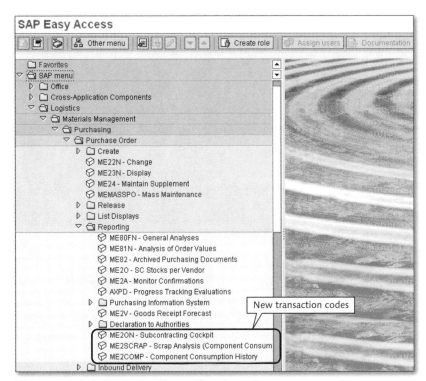

Figure 4.51   SAP Easy Access Menu—New Transactions

Let's quickly go over each of these:

▶ **Transaction ME2ON: Subcontracting Cockpit**
The Subcontracting Cockpit user interface is clearly laid out, and makes it easier for you to control and monitor the subcontracting process. This single screen provides direct access to the subcontracting processes.

You can process the following documents in the Subcontracting Cockpit:

- ▶ Purchase orders
- ▶ Purchase requisitions
- ▶ Outbound deliveries with open goods issues
- ▶ Reservations
- ▶ External deliveries (subcontracting components that are prepared by a third party)

▶ **Transaction ME2SCRAP: Scrap Analysis (Component Consumption)**
This report also provides the average scrap for a vendor within a specified time. You can select the following criteria for the scrap analysis:

- ▶ Purchase order
- ▶ Vendor
- ▶ Plant
- ▶ Time periods

▶ **Transaction ME2COMP: Component Consumption History**
In this report, you can analyze the component consumption planned versus current consumption.

4.8.6 Two-Step Stock Transfer and Subcontracting Cockpit

Now let's discuss the two-step stock transfers to the subcontractor, using the Subcontracting Cockpit, and the new movement types introduced by SAP.

In a real-world scenario, often the subcontractor plant is far away from the manufacturing plant, and it takes two days transit time to deliver the goods by road transport. In such a scenario, you can use two-step stock transfers. In the first step, you issue the goods, which appears as stock in transit. After the material reaches the subcontractor premises, you need to post putaway transaction. Following is the entire process step by step:

1. **Create a subcontract PO.**

   Create a subcontract PO via Transaction ME21N as discussed earlier in the sub-contract process steps.

2. **Execute the Subcontracting Cockpit.**

   Go to Transaction ME2ON, and select the vendor and material for which you've created the PO in the first step. Execute the transaction, and you'll get a report as shown in Figure 4.52. The requirements of components are listed in Figure 4.52 as GEAR BOX ASSEMBLY-101 requiring a quantity of 20, and GEAR BOX-102 requiring a quantity of 10.

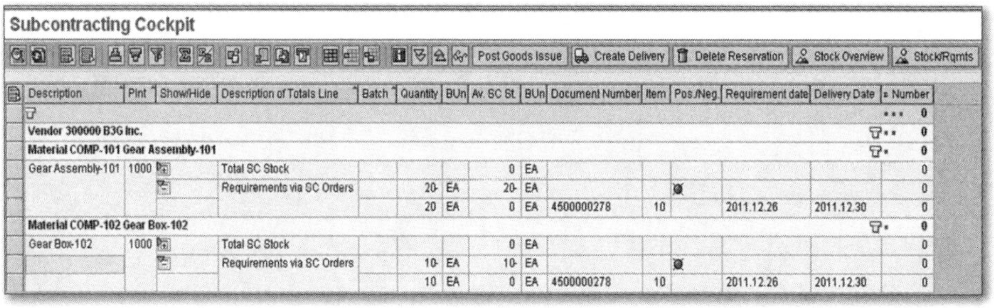

Figure 4.52 Subcontracting Cockpit

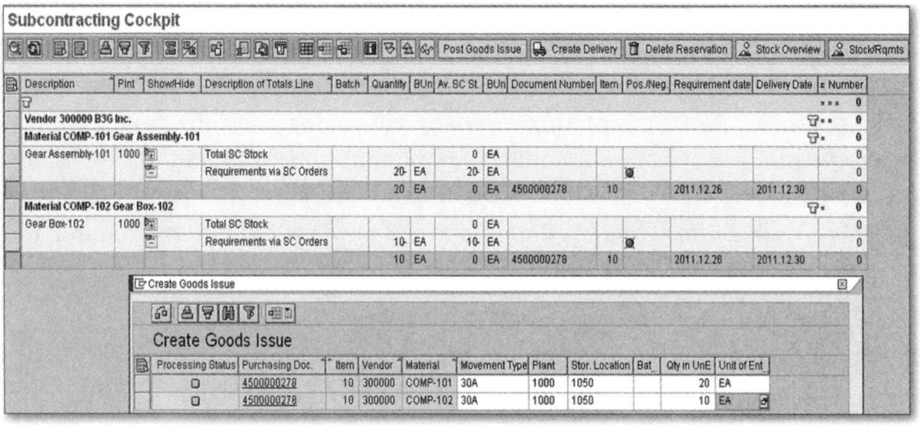

Figure 4.53 Goods Issue from the Subcontracting Cockpit

3. **Issue the goods to the subcontractor.**

   From the Subcontracting Cockpit, issue the material to the subcontracted vendor. Select the PO line from the report, and click on the POST GOODS ISSUE button. A new popup screen appears as shown in Figure 4.53. You can check the quantity, plant, storage location, and so on. If you want to transfer stock in one step, choose MOVEMENT TYPE 541. Per this new scenario, you can issue the material in two steps by using MOVEMENT TYPE 30A.

In a two-step transfer, the material is issued and is in transit in the first step. You can see this in the stock overview report by using Transaction MMBE as shown in Figure 4.54. You can see that stock material with a quantity of 20 is in transit for the subcontractor.

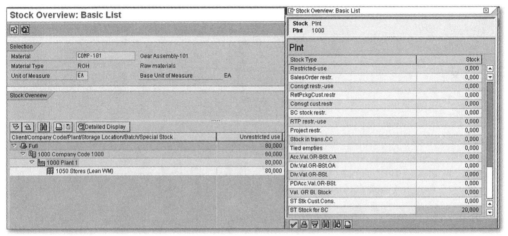

Figure 4.54 Stock Overview Report

After the material reaches the subcontractor, you need to post the putaway transaction by using MOVEMENT TYPE 30C as shown in Figure 4.55. Go to Transaction MIGO (Goods Receipt), select the transfer posting, and enter the material, quantity, plant, and subcontract vendor. Enter "30C" in the MOVEMENT TYPE column and post the transaction.

New Movement Types

Following are the new movement types since the release of EHP4:

▶ **Movement Type 30A: Transfer of unrestricted-use stock to subcontracting stock in two steps—stock removal**

  ▶ The transferred quantity is posted from the unrestricted-use stock in the issuing plant to the stock in transfer for the subcontractor.

  ▶ The reversal movement type is 30B.

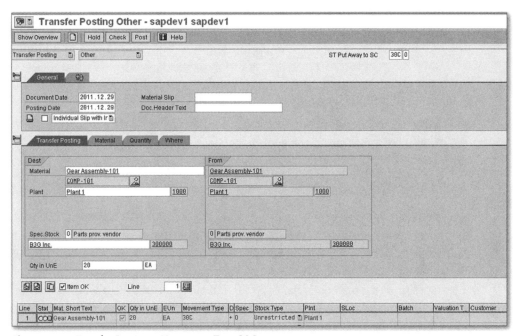

Figure 4.55 Transfer Posting—Movement Type 30C

▸ **Movement Type 30C: Transfer of unrestricted-use stock to subcontracting stock in two steps—putaway**

  ▸ The transferred quantity is posted from the stock in transfer for the receiving subcontractor to the unrestricted-use subcontracting stock. This movement isn't valuated.

  ▸ The special stock indicator is O.

  ▸ The reversal movement type is 30D.

4.8.7 Stock Transfer Direct to Subcontractor

Now let's discuss the new functionality that allows you to perform a stock transfer from the issuing plant to the subcontractor of the receiving plant. We'll discuss in detail the various types of stock transfer in SAP later in Section 4.11.

Consider the following example to help understand this functionality: you have two plants named Plant A and Plant B. Plant A has issued a subcontract order to a vendor to manufacture a material, but Plant A doesn't have raw materials available in stock. Per the planning run, Plant B has sufficient stock that can be transferred to Plant A. You can do this in one of two ways:

- ▶ Transfer the material to Plant A from Plant B and then issue the material to the subcontract vendor by goods issue.

- ▶ Transfer the material directly from Plant B to the subcontract vendor and make the automatic postings in the system.

The second option is more cost-effective because you can save transaction cost, loading/unloading cost, and transportation time.

You can transfer the material from one plant to the other plant's subcontract vendor directly as shown in Figure 4.56. In the DELIVERY ADDRESS tab, enter the vendor code and check the SC VEND (subcontract vendor) checkbox. Create the PO by using Transaction ME21N, select the transaction type as STOCK TRANSP. ORDER, and enter the supplying plant, material, quantity, item category "U", and all other details. Then click on the DELIVERY ADDRESS tab of the item details, enter the subcontract vendor, and check the SC VEND checkbox as shown in Figure 4.56. Finally, post the PO.

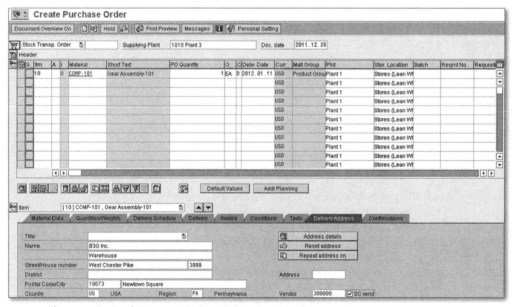

Figure 4.56 Stock Transport Order—Subcontract Vendor

4.9   Third-Party Procurement

Third-party procurement takes place when you order goods from a vendor, and the vendor ships the goods to a third party (usually your customer or subcontract vendor). In this case, the vendor sends you an invoice, and you make the payment, as shown in Figure 4.57. This process is advantageous because it reduces transportation, loading, and unloading costs, as well as delivery time.

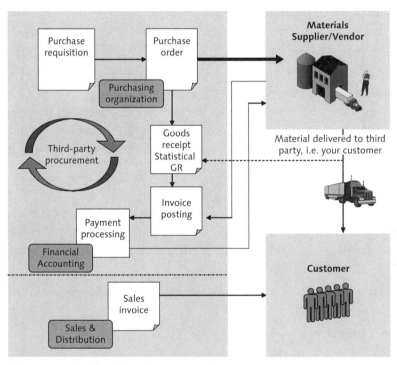

Figure 4.57   The Third-Party Procurement Process

4.9.1   Business Scenario

Consider an enterprise selling and distributing cement to a customer constructing a bridge. This enterprise procures cement from a cement manufacturing company, and then asks this company to ship the cement to the customer involved in the bridge construction.

When you place an order to your vendor in the third-party procurement scenario, the delivery address will be the address of the business partner to whom you want to ship the goods. In this case, you post a statistical goods receipt in your system for the confirmation of the goods shipped to the third party. The invoice is posted and paid using the normal procurement process.

4.9.2 Process Steps

The following steps are for the third-party procurement process with respect to two separate scenarios: third-party procurement for a subcontract vendor and third-party procurement for a customer.

Scenario 1: Third-Party Procurement for a Subcontract Vendor

Let's say you have a subcontractor who requires multiple components to make an assembly for you, and you buy some of these components from a vendor. In such a scenario, you may ask your vendor to ship the goods directly to your subcontractor so that delivery time is fast, and materials transportation and loading and unloading costs are saved. Let's see how to run the scenario in the system with the following steps:

1. **Create the PO.**
   Create a PO for the vendor from whom you want to purchase goods via Transaction ME21N. In the item details, go to the DELIVERY ADDRESS tab, and enter the subcontracting vendor code. Select the SC VEND checkbox, as shown in Figure 4.58.

   After you enter your subcontracting vendor, the system will supply the delivery address from the vendor master record.

2. **Post the goods receipt.**
   Post the goods receipt with reference to the PO. The SAP system will create material and accounting documents. Because goods are shipped directly to subcontracting vendors, you can see this stock via Transaction ME2O. Movement type 101 O is used in the goods receipt.

3. **Post the invoice.**
   Upon receipt of the invoice from the vendor, post the invoice in the system via Transaction MIRO. Enter the document date, posting date, and PO number. The PO will supply the item, quantity, amount, and price. Before saving, you can check the account posting via the SIMULATE button.

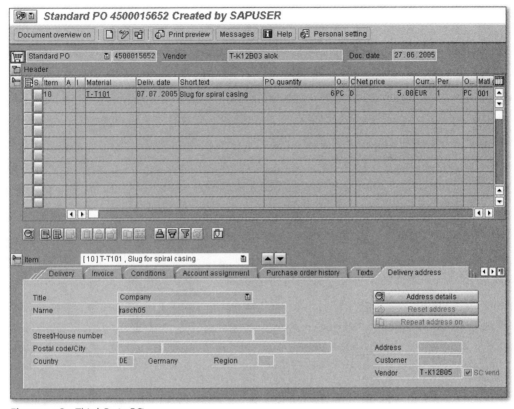

Figure 4.58 Third-Party PO

Scenario 2: Third-Party Procurement for a Customer

This scenario is used when you're involved in trading, and you want the vendor to ship the goods to your customer directly. Let's say your customer has ordered some materials, and you actually don't manufacture these materials; rather you purchase from a vendor and sell to your customer. In this scenario, it makes sense to create a PO with the delivery address of the customer so that materials are directly shipped to the customer, which saves transportation and loading/unloading costs.

To do this, you use the steps we listed in the previous scenario with a few amendments we'll describe here. Settle your invoice with the vendor, and issue sales billing documents to your customer. When creating the PO, select ITEM CATEGORY S (third party) and ACCT ASSIGNMENT CAT. 1 (third party). After you select ITEM CATEGORY

S, you can see the CUSTOMER field on the PO ITEM DETAILS DELIVERY ADDRESS tab. Enter the customer number to whom the vendor should send the materials. After the PO is sent, you can post a goods receipt for it. This goods receipt will generate material and accounting documents.

In this scenario, the consumption raw material account will be debited, and the GR/IR account will be credited.

4.9.3 Configuration Steps

If required, document types can be used to customize the third-party procurement process. Document types control many factors, such as field selection and number ranges. This is discussed in more detail in Chapter 8.

4.10 Outline Agreements

An *outline agreement* is a longer-term purchase arrangement with a vendor. It concerns the supply of materials or the performance of services according to predetermined conditions. These conditions are valid for a certain period of time and cover a predefined total purchase quantity or value. Delivery dates aren't specific in outline agreements. Instead, this information is provided separately in release orders or rolling delivery schedules, depending on the type of agreement. As shown in Figure 4.59, there are two types of outline agreements: contract and scheduling agreements.

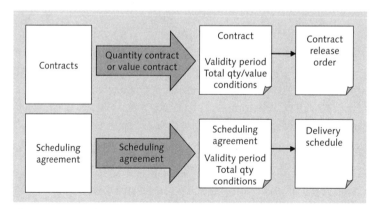

Figure 4.59 Outline Agreement Flow

4.10.1 Contract Agreements

Contract agreements are outline agreements with a vendor concerning the supply of material or performance of services. They don't contain details of the delivery dates for each of the items. Rather, delivery dates are imposed on the vendor via release orders. Contract agreements are created for long periods—for example, one year—and POs, with reference to the contract, are created on a needs basis release (Figure 4.60). The prices and conditions are copied from the contract to the PO, goods are received against the PO, and the invoice is posted with reference to the PO.

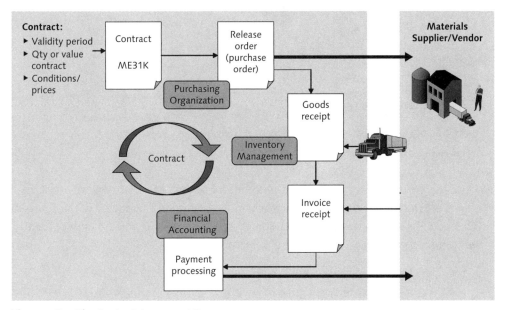

Figure 4.60 The Contract Agreement Process

Business Scenario

As an example, consider an enterprise engaged in paper manufacturing that has a one-year contract (including negotiated rates, terms, and conditions) with a chemical supplier. Each time this enterprise requires chemicals, the paper manufacturing company issues a PO with reference to the contract.

The two types of contracts are quantity contracts and value contracts (Figure 4.61), as described here:

▶ **Quantity contract**

This contract is based on quantity and is fulfilled when the total agreed-upon quantity is supplied by the vendor.

▶ **Value contract**

This contract is based on total value and is fulfilled when the total agreed-upon value is supplied by the vendor.

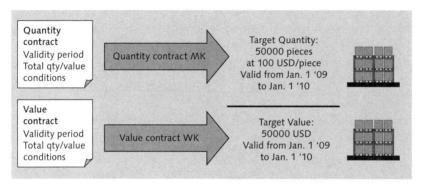

Figure 4.61 Quantity and Value Contracts

You can create contracts manually, with reference to other contracts, purchase requisitions, and RFQs or quotations. The validity period is mandatory in the contract header. For each item in a quantity contract, you need to define the target quantity and item conditions.

Item categories M (material unknown) and W (material group) are used for contracts (Figure 4.62). Item category M is recommended for materials that have the same price but different material numbers. In the contract, enter the material group, quantity, and unit of measure, but no material number. The material number is entered at the time of release orders. Item category W is recommended for materials that belong to the same material group but have different prices. In the contract, enter the material group, but not a price. Item category W can only be used for value contracts.

Contracts can be created for a plant or for multiple plants belonging to the same purchasing organization. This is known as a *centrally agreed* contract. All of the plants that are assigned to a purchasing organization can order against a centrally agreed contract (Figure 4.63). A centrally agreed contract gives more negotiation power to an enterprise. Using the plant conditions function, the centrally agreed contract allows you to stipulate separate prices and conditions for each receiving plant.

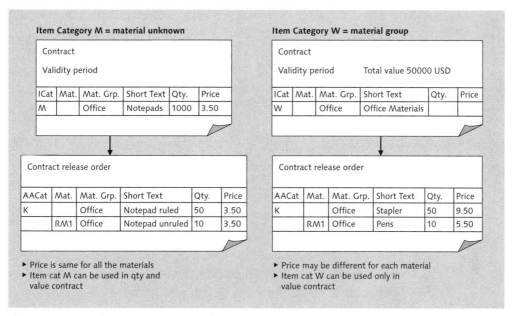

Figure 4.62 Special Item Categories M and W

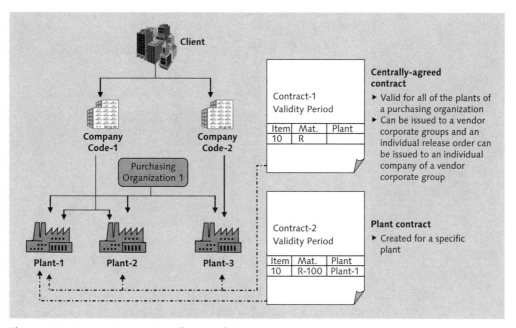

Figure 4.63 Contract Types: Centrally-Agreed Contract

In the following sections, we'll discuss the process steps and configuration involved in contract agreements.

Process Steps

Follow these steps for contract processing:

1. **Create the contract.**

   The following transaction codes are used to create, change, and display contracts:

   ▶ Transaction ME31K: Create contract

   ▶ Transaction ME32K: Change contract

   ▶ Transaction ME33K: Display contract

   During the creation of a contract, select agreement type MK for a quantity contract, and WK for a value contract. When you create a contract for a purchasing organization, the prices (i.e., conditions) are valid for all of the plants within this purchasing organization. However, you can also define plant-specific conditions in contracts.

   To enter a plant-specific condition, select the appropriate line, and from the top menu, select EDIT • PLANT CONDITIONS • OVERVIEW. Enter the plant and press Enter, which will bring up a price screen where you can define plant-specific prices. In Figure 4.64, you can see that plant-specific conditions are defined for CONDITIONS PLANT 1000.

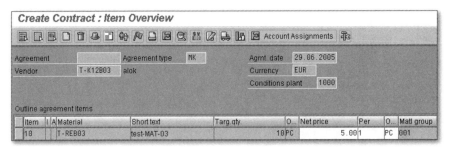

Figure 4.64 Contract: Plant-Specific Conditions

2. **Create the release orders.**

   Release orders are POs you create with reference to the contract via Transaction ME21N. Select the contract and choose ADOPT. You then need to enter the quantity, plant, and delivery date. The plant prices will be picked up from the contract.

The goods receipt and invoice receipt steps are the same as those in the direct material procurement process in Section 4.3.2.

Configuration Steps

You can define number ranges and document types in contracts. To define a number range, go to SAP IMG • Materials Management • Purchasing • Contract • Define Number Range. Click on Change Intervals, and then click on Insert Interval. You need to enter the From Number and To Number (Figure 4.65). Then click Save.

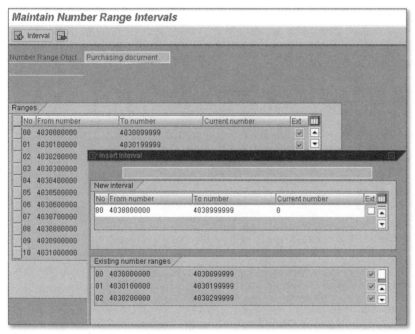

Figure 4.65 Define the Number Range

To create new document types, go to SAP IMG • Materials Management • Purchasing • Contract • Define Document Type. In this screen, you must assign different characteristics such as item interval, allowed item categories, field selection reference key, allowed follow-on document types, and number range (Figure 4.66).

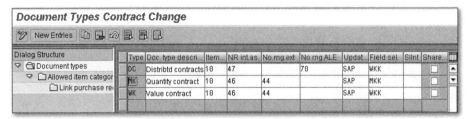

Figure 4.66 Document Type for Contracts

4.10.2 Invoices for Contracts

As of SAP ERP 6.0 EHP5 (SAP_APPL 605), you can use the Materials Management—Enhancements in Procurement (LOG_MM_CI_3) business function to post invoices with reference to contracts in the following ways:

▶ Invoice with a direct reference to an SAP ERP contract or SAP SRM central contract.

▶ Invoice with reference to a limit PO item, which contains a reference to a contract.

▶ Invoice with a reference to a limit PO item without a contract reference with the option to reference a contract during invoice verification.

Next we'll discuss how to process invoices with reference to a contract.

Process Step

Follow these steps to process invoices with reference to a contract:

1. **Create the contract.**
   Go to Transaction ME31K and create a contract.

2. **Post the invoice.**
   Go to Transaction MIRO, click on the CONTRACT REFERENCE tab, and enter the contract number as shown in Figure 4.67. Enter the amount and click on the ACCOUNT ASSIGNMENT button in the line item details. Next, enter the amount and quantity there, and post the invoice.

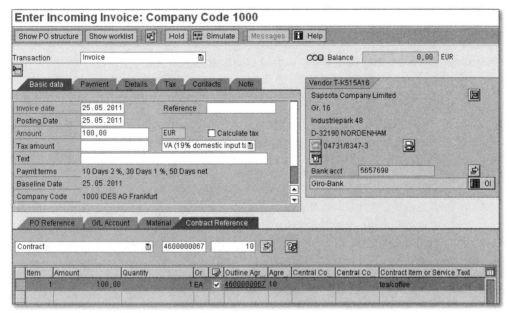

Figure 4.67 Invoice with Reference to Contract

3. After the invoice is posted, check that your changes have been made in the CONTRACT HISTORY tab as shown in Figure 4.68.

Figure 4.68 Contract History Tab

Customizing

To enable users to post invoices directly to contracts, you must activate direct posting to contracts in the Customizing activity. Go to SAP IMG • MATERIALS MANAGEMENT • LOGISTICS INVOICE VERIFICATION • INCOMING INVOICE • ACTIVATE DIRECT POSTING TO CONTRACTS. Select the CONTRACT TAB ACTIVE checkbox.

Now that we've discussed contract agreements, let's move on to scheduling agreements.

4.10.3 Scheduling Agreements

A scheduling agreement is an outline agreement where a vendor supplies the materials according to predetermined conditions.

Business Scenario

As an example, consider a car manufacturing business. The company plans its production on a monthly and daily basis. Based on the daily production schedule, the supplier needs to deliver specific components (e.g., material required for horn assembly).

In this case, delivery dates and quantities are communicated to the vendor in the form of schedule lines. Schedule lines can also be generated manually or by using MRP. Schedule lines don't constitute separate documents; rather, they are part of the scheduling agreement.

Schedule lines are generated automatically based on the release type selected in the scheduling agreement. There are two types of scheduling agreement releases:

▶ Forecast (FRC) delivery schedules are used to give the vendor a medium-term overview of your requirement. They're based on the forecast demand.

▶ Just-in-time (JIT) delivery schedules are used to inform your vendor of a near-future requirement. Such schedules may comprise a daily or hourly breakdown of your requirements over the next few days or weeks.

Process Steps

Follow these process steps for scheduling agreements:

1. **Create the scheduling agreement.**
   The following transaction codes are used to create, change, and display scheduling agreements:

   ▶ Transaction ME31L: Create scheduling agreements

   ▶ Transaction ME32L: Change scheduling agreements

   ▶ Transaction ME33L: Display scheduling agreements

   Create a scheduling agreement with DOCUMENT TYPE LPA, and enter the validity date and target quantity. In the additional data screen, you can check to make sure that the release creation profile has copied from the vendor master record.

To generate FRC and JIT delivery schedules under a scheduling agreement, you must first define the necessary prerequisite in the material master and vendor master records, as follows:

▶ **Set the prerequisite in the material master.**
On the PURCHASING tab of the material master record, set the JIT SCHED. INDICATOR to 1 (Figure 4.69).

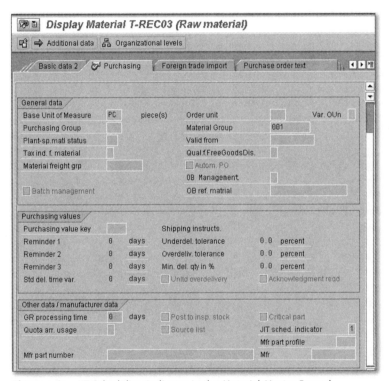

Figure 4.69 JIT Scheduling Indicator in the Material Master Record

▶ **Set the prerequisite in the vendor master.**
Assign a creation profile in the vendor master in the plant-specific purchasing data, as shown in Figure 4.70. To do so, use Transaction XK02.

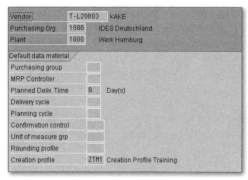

Figure 4.70 Creation Profile in the Vendor Master

2. **Maintain the delivery schedule.**

   Maintain the delivery schedule via Transaction ME38. Select the appropriate line item and go to ITEM • DELIVERY SCHEDULE (Figure 4.71).

| | Maintain Sch. Agmt. Schedule : Delivery Schedule for Item 00010 | | | | | | | | | | |

Agreement	5500000124			Quantity			830	PC			
Material	T-REC03			test-MAT-03							
Cum. rec. qty.		0		Old qty.			0				

C	Delivery date	Scheduled quantity	Time	F	C	Stat.d.dte	Purch.req.	Item	Cum. schd. qty.	Prev. cum. qty.	Sc...
D	29.06.2005	50	10:00		R	29.06.2005			50		1
D	29.06.2005	60	14:00		R	29.06.2005			110		2
D	30.06.2005	80	10:00		R	30.06.2005			190		3
D	30.06.2005	40	14:00		R	30.06.2005			230		4
D	02.07.2005	60	10:00		R	02.07.2005			290		5
D	02.07.2005	80	14:00		R	02.07.2005			370		6
D	06.07.2005	50	10:00		R	06.07.2005			420		7
D	06.07.2005	60	14:00		R	06.07.2005			480		8
D	13.07.2005	150			R	13.07.2005			630		9
D	20.07.2005	200			R	20.07.2005			830		10

Figure 4.71 Scheduling Agreement: Delivery Schedule

The goods receipt and invoice receipt steps are the same as those in the direct material procurement process.

Configuration Steps

You need to configure the number range and document types for scheduling agreements. To define the number range, go to SAP IMG • MATERIALS MANAGEMENT • PURCHASING • SCHEDULING AGREEMENT • DEFINE NUMBER RANGE. Click on CHANGE

INTERVALS, and then click on INSERT INTERVAL. Enter the FROM NUMBER and TO NUMBER (Figure 4.72). Then click SAVE.

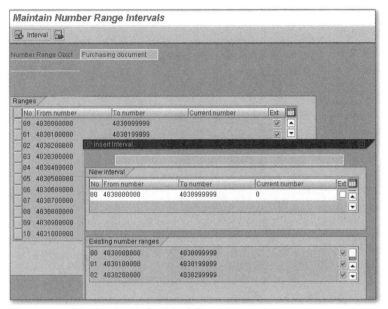

Figure 4.72 Number Range for Scheduling Agreement

The SAP system includes preconfigured document types, such as LP and LPA. However, you can also create new document types by going to SAP IMG • MATERIALS MANAGEMENT • PURCHASING • SCHEDULING AGREEMENT • DEFINE DOCUMENT TYPE. In this screen, define characteristics such as item interval, allowed item categories, field selection reference key, allowed follow-on document types, and number range (Figure 4.73).

Document Types Scheduling agreement Change

Dialog Structure	Type	Doc. type descript.	Item...	NR int.as.	No.rng.ext	Updat...	Field sel.	Cont...	Slint	
▽ 🗀 Document types	LP	Scheduling agreement	10	55	56	SAP	LPL			
▽ 🗀 Allowed item categor	LPA	Scheduling agreement	10	55	56	SAP	LPL			
🗀 Link purchase rei	LU	Transp. sched. agmt.	10	55	56	SAP	LUL	T		
	Z1	TDSA		ZA	00	SAP	LPL			

Figure 4.73 Document Type for Scheduling Agreements

4.11   Stock Transfer

You can transfer the stock from one storage location to another, from one plant to another, or from one company code to another. Figure 4.74 shows the different stock transfer scenarios.

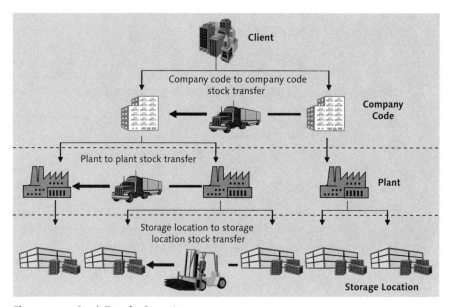

Figure 4.74   Stock Transfer Scenarios

Stock transfers can be carried out at three different levels:

▶ Stock transfer from one company code to another

▶ Stock transfer from one plant to another

▶ Stock transfer from one storage location to another

4.11.1   Business Scenario

A business engaged in car manufacturing has two manufacturing plants, and during production, the company transfers many of the components from one plant to the other plant, based on the requirement and available quantity, to reduce the inventory carrying cost.

There are two different ways to transfer stock:

▶ One-step stock transfer

▶ Two-step stock transfer

We'll discuss both of these processes in the following sections.

4.11.2 One-Step Stock Transfer

The one-step stock transfer process transfers the stock from one location to another in a single step; therefore, a single transaction posts results in goods issue (from the issuing location) and goods receipt (into the receiving location).

The one-step stock transfer is used to transfer stock from one storage location to another storage location within one plant. Because materials are transferred within the same plant, the stock valuation won't be changed. Therefore, no accounting document is created.

The one-step stock transfer can also be used to transfer stock from one plant to another plant. This procedure doesn't involve stock in transit, and materials are posted directly to unrestricted-use stock in the receiving plant. If the valuation area is at the plant level, the stock transfer from one plant to another will create an accounting document.

Stock transfer takes place in one transaction, as shown in Figure 4.75.

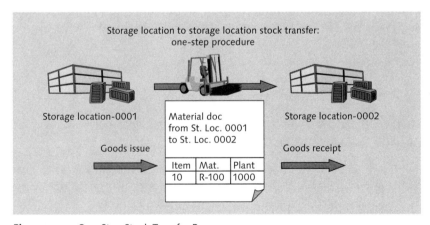

Figure 4.75 One-Step Stock Transfer Process

Process Steps

To carry out a stock transfer from one storage location to another within the same plant, you can use Transaction MIGO_TR. Enter the material and FROM and DEST (destination) storage locations. Enter movement type "311" in the TF TFR. WITHIN PLANT field to transfer goods from one storage location to another in the same plant, as shown in Figure 4.76.

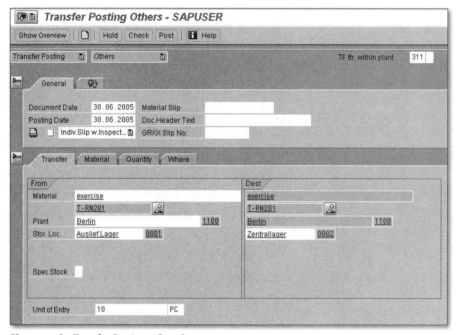

Figure 4.76 Transfer Posting—One-Step

When you post the transaction, the stock is transferred. You can check the stock quantities via Transaction MMBE (Stock Overview Report).

The stock transfer transaction won't create any accounting documents because the valuation area (i.e., plant) is the same.

On the other hand, you may want to transfer stock from one plant to another. You can do so using the one-step stock transfer procedure. Go to Transaction MIGO_TR and enter the material, from plant and storage location, and to plant and storage location. Enter movement type "301" and save the transaction. The system will transfer the stock quantities to the destination storage location/plant. You can check this via Transaction MMBE.

A stock transfer between two different plants will create an accounting document if the valuation area is at the plant level.

4.11.3 Two-Step Stock Transfer

In a two-step stock transfer, goods are issued from one issuing point. The stock will remain in transit until the goods are received at the receiving point.

The two-step procedure is used for transferring stock between two different plants in different locations. Stock valuation takes place if the valuation area is at the plant level.

> **Note**
>
> The goods receiving plant will be responsible for any damage of goods during transit.

As shown in Figure 4.77, Plant 1000 located in Los Angeles posts the goods issue transaction. The stock is then transported to Plant 2000 located in Atlanta. The goods will remain in transit for several days. When they arrive at the Atlanta plant, this plant needs to post a goods receipt transaction in the system. This will update the stock quantity in the storage location.

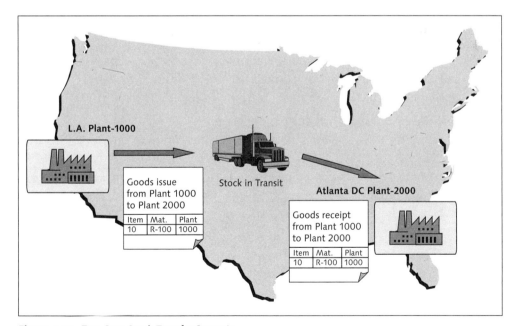

Figure 4.77 Two-Step Stock Transfer Scenario

Process Steps

To transfer stock via the two-step procedure, use Transaction MIGO_TR; fill in the fields for MATERIAL, QUANTITY, FROM PLANT, and TO PLANT; and enter movement type "303" (plant to plant transfer stock removal). After you post this transaction, stock is removed from the issuing plant and will show as stock in transit. If the valuation area is at the plant level, the SAP system will create an accounting document.

After the material is received in the receiving storage location/plant, you need to post the transaction with movement type 305 (transfer posting plant to plant—place in storage location).

4.11.4   Stock Transport Orders

You can use stock transport orders to transfer goods from one plant to another. Stock transport orders are used to define delivery costs, and they're created via Transaction ME21N (Create PO).

You can use the one-step or two-step procedures with stock transport orders.

Process Steps

Follow these process steps for stock transport orders:

1. **Create the stock transport order.**
   Create the stock transport order via Transaction ME21N, and select document type UB (stock transport order). Enter the supplying plant, material, quantity, and receiving plant. You can also maintain conditions such as delivery cost. Item category U should be used for stock transport orders, as shown in Figure 4.78.

2. **Post the goods issue from the issuing plant.**
   To post the goods issue from the issuing plant, use Transaction MIGO_GI. Enter movement type "351" and the stock transport order number. After you save this transaction, the stock will be removed from the issuing plant and will remain in transit until the receiving plant makes a goods receipt entry. The SAP system will create the accounting document.

3. **Post the goods receipt into the receiving plant.**
   To post the goods receipt into the receiving plant, use Transaction MIGO_GR. Enter the stock transport order number and movement type "101"; then save. The system will update the stock into the receiving plant and storage location.

The system won't create an accounting document because account postings are already made at the time of goods issue.

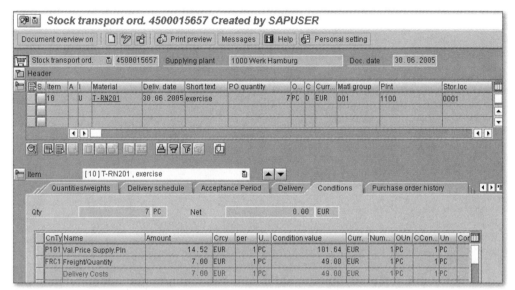

Figure 4.78 A Stock Transport Order

4.11.5 Stock Transfer from One Company Code Plant to Another Company Code Plant

You can transfer stock from one company code to another via stock transport orders without the involvement of the sales and distribution department.

This process is similar to a stock transfer between two plants of the same company code.

Process Steps

Follow these process steps to transfer stock from one company code to another:

1. **Create the stock transport order.**
   Create the stock transport order via Transaction ME21N. Select document type UB and item category U. Enter the supplying plant, receiving plant, material, quantity, delivery dates, and condition for transportation cost.

In the next few steps, we'll use an example where the supplying plant is plant 1000 of company code 1000, and the receiving plant is plant 1001 of company code 1001.

2. **Post the goods issue.**
Post the goods issue from supplying plant 1000 via Transaction MIGO_GI, and enter movement type "351".

3. **Post the goods receipt.**
Post the goods receipt into receiving plant 1001 via Transaction MIGO_GI, and enter movement type "101".

4.12   Intercompany Purchases

A corporate group may have multiple company codes within an SAP system. In this case, one company in the corporate group can procure goods from another company in the group.

4.12.1   Business Scenario

Your business might need to purchase goods from one company code to another. Let's look at a real-world example, where a large telecom company involved in setting up radio base stations for mobile communication has operations worldwide. The company has a manufacturing plant in Sweden where the components required for the radio base station are manufactured. The company has a legal company code in each country. Whenever it sets up a radio base station in any country other than Sweden, the company procures these components from a Swedish legal entity (company code). To make this happen, the company has an intercompany purchase scenario configured in the system. This can be done via normal sales and purchasing processes because both company codes are independent legal accounting entities. In these cases, you need to post all of the sales transactions for the issuing company code and all of the purchase transactions for the receiving company code.

However, SAP provides intercompany stock transfer via the SD component, which is simpler and more user-friendly than using the normal sales and purchasing cycle. An intercompany stock transfer via the SD process is shown in Figure 4.79 in the following section.

There are two ways to set up intercompany stock transfers via the SD component:

▸ Stock transport order with delivery via shipping

▸ Stock transport order with delivery and billing document

We'll discuss both of these options in the following subsections.

4.12.2 Stock Transport Order with Delivery via Shipping

Stock transport orders with delivery via shipping use purchasing, shipping, and inventory functions. The stock transport order is created by the plant of the receiving company code, and the issuing company code creates a delivery document and issues goods. After the material is received, the receiving plant posts a goods receipt (Figure 4.79).

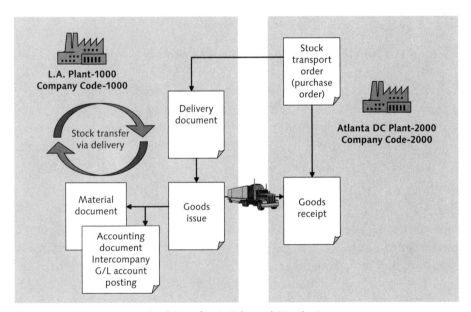

Figure 4.79 Intercompany Stock Transfer via Sales and Distribution

Delivery costs can be entered in the stock transport order. In this case, the system creates two accounting documents when the goods issue is posted. The stock posting is offset against a company code clearing account.

Follow these process steps for intercompany stock transfers via the delivery process:

1. **Create a stock transport order at the receiving plant.**
   As an example, let's say that plant A wants to order materials from plant B. Plant

A enters a stock transfer order via Transaction ME21N. The stock transfer is then used to plan the movement.

2. **Post a delivery at the issuing plant.**
Plant B supplies the goods to plant A. Plant B enters a replenishment delivery in shipping. The goods are then posted to the stock in transit of the receiving plant. Post the goods issue with movement type 641.

3. **Post the goods receipt at the receiving plant.**
After the goods arrive at the receiving plant, the plant posts a goods receipt for the delivery. The stock in transit is therefore reduced, and the unrestricted-use stock is increased.

4.12.3 Stock Transport Order with Delivery and Billing Document/ Invoice

Stock transport orders with delivery and billing use the purchasing, shipping, sales billing, inventory management, and invoice verification functions. The stock transport order is created by the plant of the receiving company code. The issuing company code creates a delivery document and issues the goods. After the material is received, the receiving plant posts a goods receipt (Figure 4.80). The issuing company code generates the billing document via the SD billing transaction, and the receiving company code posts the invoice via the MM invoice posting transaction.

With this type of stock transfer, the transfer posting isn't valuated at the valuation price of the material in the issuing plant. Instead, it's defined—using conditions—in both the issuing and receiving plants. The price determination is carried out in both Purchasing and SD. In Purchasing, the price of the material is determined in the usual manner (e.g., from the info record). In SD, the pricing is also carried out as it normally is during the billing process. The goods movements are valuated at the price determined in each case. Accounting documents are created for the goods issue, the goods receipt, billing, and the invoice receipt.

Follow these process steps for intercompany stock transfers via the delivery and billing process:

1. **Create the stock transport order at the receiving plant.**
Create the stock transfer order via Transaction ME21N. Select document type NB, and enter the vendor (which must have the supplying plant assigned in the vendor master record), material, quantity, and delivery dates. Save the document.

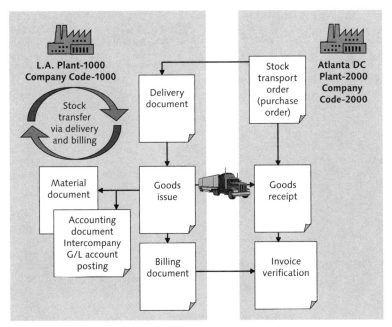

Figure 4.80 Intercompany Stock Transfer via Delivery and Billing

2. **Post the delivery at the issuing plant.**
   The issuing plant enters a replenishment delivery in SD. Unlike a stock transfer without a billing document, no stock in transit is created. Post the goods issue with movement type 643.

3. **Create the billing document at the issuing plant.**
   The issuing plant creates the billing document for the delivery.

4. **Post the goods receipt at the receiving plant.**
   The receiving plant posts the goods receipt for the delivery. The goods are posted to unrestricted-use stock. For proper document flow, we recommend posting the goods receipt with reference to the delivery document.

5. **Post the invoice at the receiving plant.**
   The invoice referring to the billing document is entered at the receiving plant.

4.12.4 Configuration Steps

Follow the configuration steps to define cross-company stock transport with delivery via shipping, with or without billing.

Defining Shipping Data for Plants

To define shipping data, go to SAP IMG • MATERIALS MANAGEMENT • PURCHASING • PURCHASE ORDER • SETUP STOCK TRANSPORT ORDER • DEFINE SHIPPING DATA FOR PLANTS. In this step, you maintain the shipping data for plants for stock transfer processing, as shown in Figure 4.81.

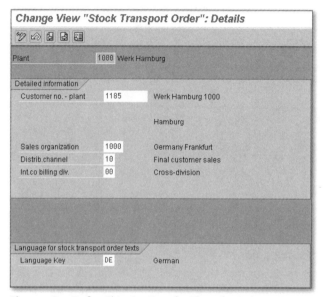

Figure 4.81 Define Shipping Data for Plants for Delivery Document

You also maintain the customer number of the receiving plant. If a custom provision has been made for a stock transfer to be carried out with an SD delivery, this customer number is used in the SD shipping process to identify the goods recipient (ship-to party).

You can also define the sales organization, distribution channel, and division for the supplying plant. With this data, the system determines the shipping information for the material to be transferred (e.g., the shipping point).

Creating Checking Rules

In this step, you create rules for the availability check for stock transport orders, as shown in Figure 4.82. This check lets you find out whether the quantity requested is available in the supplying plant, for example, in the case of materials that will be transferred over longer distances from one site to another. To create a checking rule, go to SAP IMG • MATERIALS MANAGEMENT • PURCHASING • PURCHASE ORDER • SETUP STOCK TRANSPORT ORDER • CREATE CHECKING RULE.

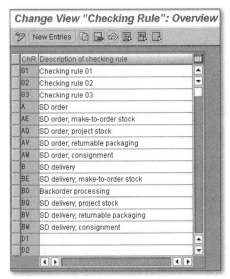

Figure 4.82   Define Checking Rule

Defining Checking Rules

To define a checking rule, go to SAP IMG • MATERIALS MANAGEMENT • PURCHASING • PURCHASE ORDER • SETUP STOCK TRANSPORT ORDER • DEFINE CHECKING RULE. In this step, you specify which requirements and stocks should be taken into account before the stock transfer takes place (Figure 4.83). For materials that should be transferred from one site to another, you can carry out an availability check to find out whether the requested quantity is actually available at the supplying plant.

Assigning Delivery Types and Checking Rules

To assign a delivery type and checking rule, go to SAP IMG • MATERIALS MANAGEMENT • PURCHASING • PURCHASE ORDER • SETUP STOCK TRANSPORT ORDER • ASSIGN DELIVERY TYPE AND CHECKING RULE. In this step, you specify whether an SD delivery should be created for a certain combination of supplying plant and document type. You can also specify which delivery type should be used, as shown in Figure 4.84. The delivery type in SD determines how a delivery is handled.

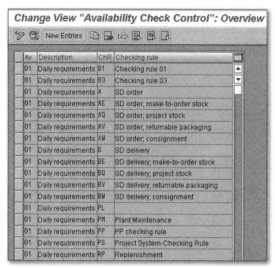

Figure 4.83 Define Checking Rule for Availability Check

Change View "Stock Transfer Data": Overview

New Entries

Type	QTyp.descr	SPlt	Name 1	DlvTy	Description	C...	Description o...	S...	R...	Del...	Del...	DT...
NB	Standard PO	1000	Werk Hamburg	NL	Replenishme...	B	SD delivery	☐	☐			
NB	Standard PO	1111	Werk Hamburg	NL	Replenishme...	B	SD delivery	☐	☐			
NB	Standard PO	1200	Dresden	NLCC	Replen.Cross...	B	SD delivery	☑	☐			
NB	Standard PO	1400	Stuttgart	NLCC	Replen.Cross...	B	SD delivery	☑	☐			
NB	Standard PO	2000	Heathrow / Ha...	NLCC	Replen.Cross...	B	SD delivery	☑	☐			
NB	Standard PO	2010	DC London	NLCC	Replen.Cross...	B	SD delivery	☑	☐			
NB	Standard PO	2200	Paris	NLCC	Replen.Cross...	B	SD delivery	☑	☐			
NB	Standard PO	2300	Barcelona	NL	Replenishme...	B	SD delivery	☐	☐			
NB	Standard PO	2400	Milano Distrib...					☐	☐			
NB	Standard PO	2500	Rotterdam Dis...					☐	☐			
NB	Standard PO	3000	New York					☐	☐			
NB	Standard PO	3100	Chicago	NLCC	Replen.Cross...	B	SD delivery	☐	☐			
NB	Standard PO	3200	Atlanta					☐	☐			
NB	Standard PO	3800	Denver Distrib...					☐	☐			
NB	Standard PO	4000	Toronto	NLCC	Replen.Cross...	B	SD delivery	☑	☐			

Figure 4.84 Assign a Delivery Type to a Document Type and Supplying Plant

Assigning Document Types, One-Step Procedures, and Underdelivery Tolerances

To assign a document type for the supplying plant and issuing plant combination, go to SAP IMG • MATERIALS MANAGEMENT • PURCHASING • PURCHASE ORDER • SETUP STOCK TRANSPORT ORDER • ASSIGN DOCUMENT TYPE, ONE STEP PROCEDURE, UNDERDELIVERY TOLERANCE. In this step, you define which document type should be used for a certain combination of supplying and receiving plants (Figure 4.85).

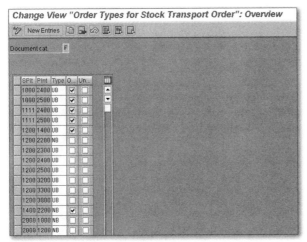

Figure 4.85 Assign a Document Type to a Supplying and Receiving Plant Combination

Aside from the previously mentioned configuration, you also need to ensure that the vendor master record is created for the supplying plant. To do so, use Transaction XK01, and create the supplying plant as a vendor at the receiving plant. Then, in the PURCHASING view, assign the supplying plant to this vendor master record by going to EXTRAS • ADDL PURCHASING DATA.

4.13 Summary

You should now have a good understanding of the various transactions and documents involved in procurement processes. This will enable you to suggest the business process that will best meet the requirements of your customer and configure the required procurement processes.

In the next chapter, we'll discuss various inventory management processes.

Inventory management involves the procedures and techniques used to manage stock materials on a quantity and value basis. We'll show you how to work with inventory management processes to meet your business requirements.

5 Inventory Management Processes

Companies store and manage materials (such as raw materials, semi-finished goods, and finished goods) in storage locations. Frequently, for various reasons, materials must be moved in and out of these storage locations. If a storage location *receives* goods, the stock quantity is updated with a goods receipt entry (in this case, the quantity will have increased). If a storage location *issues* goods, the quantity is updated with a goods issue entry (in this case, the quantity will have decreased). For every goods movement transaction, whether it's a goods issue or a goods receipt, the SAP system creates a material document. If materials and transactions are subjected to stock valuation, the SAP system also creates an accounting document. The process of overseeing the movement of materials between storage locations is known as *inventory management*. See Figure 5.1 for an illustration of the inventory management process.

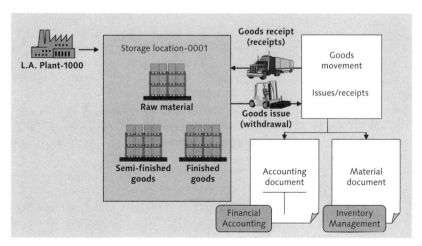

Figure 5.1 Inventory Management Scenario

As shown in Figure 5.2, you can view the stock quantity available for each material at the storage location, plant, company code, and client (also known as the corporate group) level. Stock overview reports can be generated via Transaction MMBE.

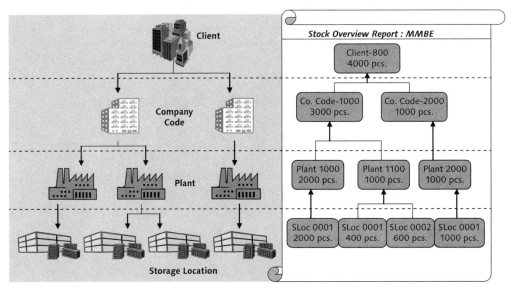

Figure 5.2 Stock Overview Report at Different Organizational Levels

In this chapter, we'll discuss the five different areas of inventory management processes and customization:

▶ Inbound processes

▶ Outbound processes

▶ Internal inventory management processes

▶ Physical inventory management processes

▶ Vendor returns processes

We'll also discuss the different types of stock that can be involved in these processes. However, before we get into specifics, we must cover an essential concept involved in all of these processes: movement types.

5.1 Movement Types

One of the key concepts in inventory management is the idea of a *movement type*. The SAP system uses movement type numbers to distinguish between various types of goods movement such as a goods receipt against a PO, vendor return, or cost center return; or, alternatively, the system uses a goods issue against a cost center issue, customer issue, and so on.

The movement type is a three-digit number (also known as a movement type key). As illustrated in Figure 5.3, different receipts and different issues are differentiated by movement type. As such movement types have important control functions in inventory management, and play a central role in automatic account determination. Together with other influencing factors, the movement type determines which stock or consumption accounts are updated in Financial Accounting (FI).

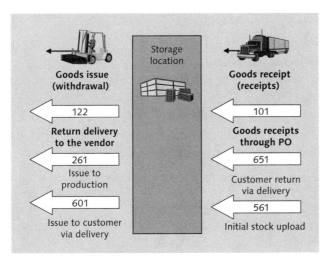

Figure 5.3 Movement Types

There are SAP-defined movement types, but you can also create your own to meet specific client requirements.

5.1.1 Business Scenario

A large distributor in Germany who uses SAP software buys its goods from the FMCG manufacturer and sells these goods to retailers in Germany. The FMCG manufacturer is using a non-SAP ERP system, which is integrated with the distributor's SAP system. Documents are posted automatically via the interface.

The FMCG manufacturer dispatches goods to the distributor, and via the interface, the goods receipt is posted in the SAP system with movement type 101.

At times, the distributor company gets bulk orders from retailers, and it wants the manufacturing company to supply these materials directly to retailers (F2R, factory to retail scenario). In this case, the interface also will post the goods receipt in the SAP system, but to differentiate both the processes, the company has created new movement type 901 by copying standard movement type 101.

This has solved the issue of stock updates at the inventory level and also helped in the reporting requirements.

5.1.2 Configuration Steps

Let's discuss the configuration steps used to create movement types:

1. **Record the reason for the goods movement.**
   When returning goods to the vendor, select the appropriate reason key, and the reason for the movement will be stored in the material document. In inventory management, you can use a report to evaluate the material documents in which a reason for movement was specified. Display a list of material documents that have been posted for a particular reason via Transaction MBGR.

   For example, consider a scenario where you're required to define a reason whenever you're returning materials to a vendor. You can define the reason keys, with the descriptions as follows:

   ▶ 0001: Poor quality

   ▶ 0002: Damaged materials

   In this step, you record the reason for the goods movement by following the menu path SAP IMG • Materials Management • Inventory Management and Physical Inventory • Movement Types • Record Reason for Goods Movement.

   Next, click on the Control Reason button, and specify whether the reason entry is optional, mandatory, or suppressed for each movement (Figure 5.4). For example, for movement type 101, the Reas. field is suppressed. This means that during goods receipt entry for movement type 101, the Reason field won't be displayed in the document.

Change View "Control: Reason for Movement": Overview

MvT	Movement Type Text	Reas.	Control reason
101	GR goods receipt	-	Field is suppressed.
102	Reversal of GR	.	Entry in this field is optional.
103	GR into blocked stck	.	Entry in this field is optional.
104	Rev. GR to blocked	-	Field is suppressed.
105	GR from blocked stck	-	Field is suppressed.
106	Rev.GR from blocked	-	Field is suppressed.
121	GR subseq. adjustm.	.	Entry in this field is optional.
122	RE return to vendor	+	Entry in this field is required.
123	RE rtrn vendor rev.	-	Field is suppressed.
124	GR rtrn blocked stck	+	Entry in this field is required.
125	GR rtn blkd stck rev	-	Field is suppressed.
131	Goods receipt	-	Field is suppressed.
132	Goods receipt	-	Field is suppressed.
141	GR G subseq. adjustm	-	Field is suppressed.
142	GR G subseq. adjustm	-	Field is suppressed.
161	GR returns	.	Entry in this field is optional.

Figure 5.4 Control: Reason for Movement Types

Now, click on the REASON FOR MOVEMENT button, and you'll get a list of SAP-defined reasons for different movement types (see Figure 5.5). Choose one of these, or click on the NEW ENTRIES button and enter the reason key and description of the reason for movement. After you save your entry, the reason code you define in this step can be selected during materials movement.

Change View "Reason for Movement": Overview

MvT	Movement Type Text	Reason	Reason for movement
103	GR into blocked stck	103	Spoiled
122	RE return to vendor	1	Poor quality
122	RE return to vendor	2	Incomplete
122	RE return to vendor	3	Damaged
261	GI for order	261	Unplanned use
262	RE for order	262	Reversal Reason
543	GI issue sls.ord.st.	543	Damage in transport
544	GI receipt sls.or.st	544	Damage in ret.transp
551	GI scrapping	1	Shrinkage
551	GI scrapping	2	Spoiled
552	RE scrapping	1	Shrinkage
552	RE scrapping	2	Spoiled
922	RE return to vendor	1	Poor quality
922	RE return to vendor	2	Incomplete
922	RE return to vendor	3	Damaged
943	GI issue sls.ord.st.	543	Damage in transport

Figure 5.5 Reasons for Goods Movements

2. **Copy or change the movement type.**

In this step, you can define a new movement type or change the setting of an existing movement type. To define or change existing movement types, go to SAP IMG • MATERIALS MANAGEMENT • INVENTORY MANAGEMENT AND PHYSICAL INVENTORY • MOVEMENT TYPES • COPY, CHANGE MOVEMENT TYPES.

A pop-up window for field selection will appear. Check the CLIENT AND MOVEMENT TYPE checkbox, and enter the client number and movement type in the FROM and To fields. This will result in a list of movement types, as shown in Figure 5.6.

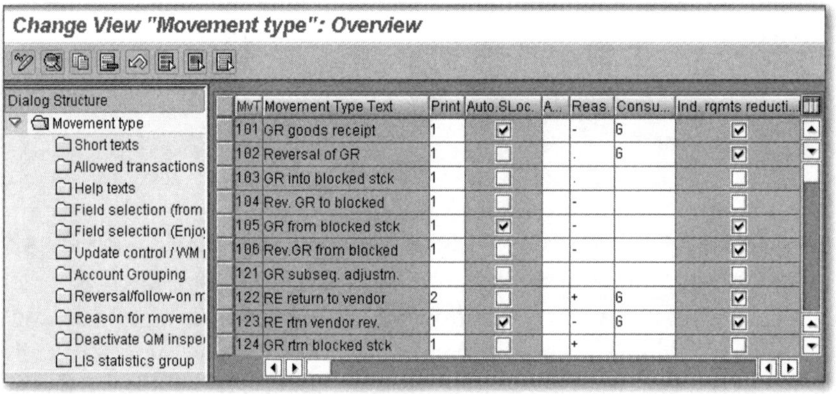

Figure 5.6 Movement Type: Change View

To change an existing movement type, select the movement type, and use the tree menu in the left side of the screen to make the required changes. To create a new movement type, click on COPY, enter the new movement type key, and press ⌷Enter⌷. The system will then ask you whether you want to copy everything or only copy a specific entry. If you select COPY ALL, the system will copy all of the dependent settings also.

As shown in Figure 5.7, you can set many controlling parameters for a movement type. For example, under ENTRY CONTROL, you can define whether printing the material document is allowed, whether the G/L account field is displayed, and more. You can also define the UPDATING CONTROL settings for the movement type, for example, whether automatic storage location creation (CREATE SLOC. AUTOMAT) and automatic purchase orders (AUTOMATIC PO) are allowed at the time of goods receipt.

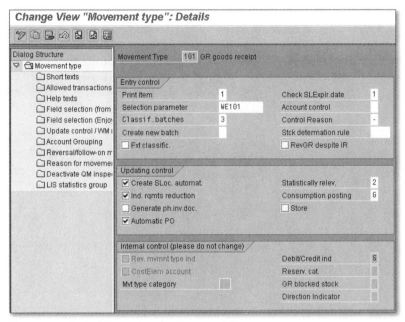

Figure 5.7 Control Parameters for Movement Type

From the tree menu on the left side of the screen, you can also define other control fields; for example: SHORT TEXTS, ALLOWED TRANSACTIONS, FIELD SELECTION, REASON FOR MOVEMENT, DEACTIVATE QM INSPECTION, and ACCOUNT GROUPING.

> **Note**
>
> The ACCOUNT GROUPING field is required for automatic account determination.

Now that we've explained the concept and configuration of movement types, let's move on to the topic of inbound and outbound processes in inventory management.

5.2 Unit of Measurement for Goods Movement

SAP allows you to maintain the multiple unit of measurement (UOM) for a material. Stock quantity is managed in the base unit of measure. So when you buy or sell a material in a different UOM, the system will calculate the quantity per the base UOM and post the issue or receipt accordingly. You can maintain the alternative

UOM in the materials master under additional data, by clicking on the UNITS OF MEASURE tab and entering the alternative UOMs as shown in Figure 5.8.

For example, in the sales for a FMCG products manufacturing company, the washing soap is counted in pieces (base UOM of piece), but it also has an alternate UOM such as box, which consists of 60 pieces.

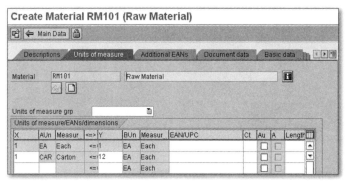

Figure 5.8 Alternative UOM in Material Master

SAP also provides the following various types of UOM settings:

▶ BASE UNIT OF MEASURE
Base UOM is a unit of measure in which stocks of the material are managed. The system converts all of the quantities you enter in other UOMs to the base UOM. This is maintained in the BASIC DATA 1 view while creating the material master as shown in Figure 5.9.

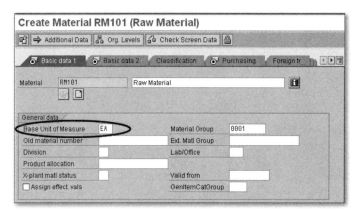

Figure 5.9 Base UOM in the Material Master

▶ UNIT OF ENTRY

UOM in which a goods movement is entered. The unit of entry can be different from the stock keeping unit.

▶ ORDER UNIT

Located in the PURCHASING tab, this field specifies the UOM in which the material is ordered. Enter a value in this field only if you want to use a UOM different from the base UOM as shown in Figure 5.10. If the field does not contain an entry, the system will assume that the UOM is the base UOM.

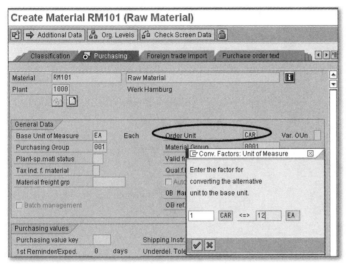

Figure 5.10 Order Unit in Material Master

▶ SALES UNIT

UOM in which you want to sell the material. This can be maintained in the SALES: SALES ORG 1 view (Figure 5.11).

▶ UNIT OF ISSUE

Unit in which the material is issued from the storage location or warehouse. In inventory management, the system proposes the unit of issue for goods issues, transfer postings, other goods receipts, and reservations. For example, if your BASE UNIT OF MEASURE setting is each (EA), you want to issue this material in a box, and each box contains 100 pieces, you can maintain the unit of issue as BOX, as shown in Figure 5.12.

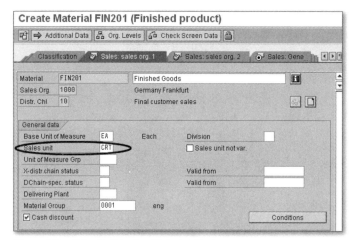

Figure 5.11   Sales Unit in the Material Master

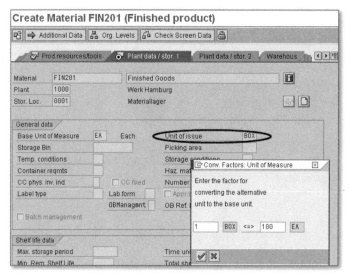

Figure 5.12   Unit of Issue in the Material Master

5.3   Inbound and Outbound Processes

Materials issue and receipt are the two major business processes in inventory management. As previously discussed, materials are received via goods receipts and issued via goods issues. The *inbound process* comprises all of the steps that must occur when goods are received into a storage location. The *outbound process* comprises all of the steps that must occur when goods are shipped out of a storage location.

In the following sections, we'll discuss the major aspects of inbound and outbound processes, including their definitions and configuration options.

5.3.1 Inbound/Outbound Process Definitions

In the SAP system, the inbound process pertains to all incoming goods. This can include receiving materials from a vendor against a PO or receiving return materials from a customer due to quality issues. Whenever goods arrive at the goods receiving area, the store keeper posts the goods receipt transaction in the system via Transaction MIGO (Figure 5.13). This creates a material document, which is proof of goods movement in a storage location. If required, the goods receipt slips can be printed. If incoming materials are subjected to quality inspection, materials will be received and kept as quality inspection stock.

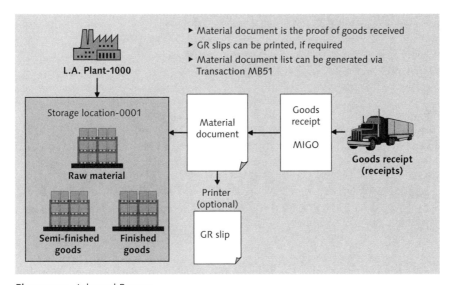

Figure 5.13 Inbound Process

The outbound process, on the other hand, pertains to all outgoing goods. This can include issuing goods to a customer against a sales order or returning materials to a vendor because of quality issues. Whenever goods are issued from storage locations, the store keeper posts the goods issue transaction in the system via Transaction

MIGO_GI (Figure 5.14). This creates a material document, which is proof of goods movement in a storage location.

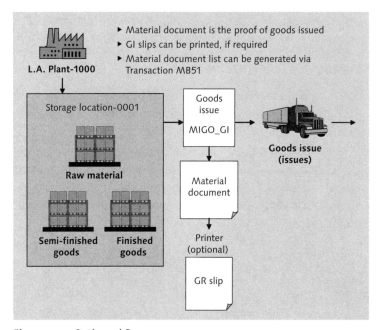

Figure 5.14 Outbound Process

In the outbound process, when post goods issue (PGI) is done, the system issues goods to the customer and posts a material document and an accounting document.

> **Note**
>
> You can set up outbound delivery for stock transport orders. For more information about this, see Chapter 4, Section 4.12.2.

5.3.2 Goods Movement (Transaction MIGO)

You can use Transaction MIGO to enter any type of goods movement (i.e. either issue or receipts). In the first list box (transaction) in Transaction MIGO, select the type of transaction such as GOODS RECEIPT, RETURN DELIVERY, or GOODS ISSUE as shown in Figure 5.15. By clicking the GOODS RECEIPT list item, you'll be able to choose from several different transaction options:

- ▶ GOODS RECEIPT

- ▶ TRANSFER POSTING

- ▶ GOODS ISSUE

- ▶ CANCELLATION

- ▶ DISPLAY

- ▶ PLACE IN STORAGE

- ▶ RELEASE GR BLOCKED STOCK

- ▶ REMOVE FROM STORAGE

- ▶ RETURN DELIVERY

- ▶ SUBSEQUENT ADJUSTMENT

- ▶ SUBSEQUENT DELIVERY

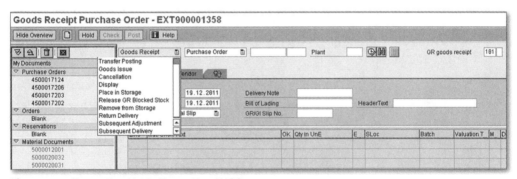

Figure 5.15 Transaction List in Transaction MIGO

After selecting the transaction, select a reference (you are creating the document with reference to which previous document) from the second dropdown menu. You can choose from the following references:

- ▶ INBOUND DELIVERY

- ▶ MATERIAL DOCUMENT

- ▶ ORDER

- ▶ OTHER (without reference)

- ▶ OUTBOUND DELIVERY

- ▶ PURCHASE ORDER

▶ RESERVATION

▶ DELIVERY NOTE

▶ TRANSPORT

▶ TRANSPORT ID CODE

The entries available for selection in the reference list box depend on the transaction selected.

5.3.3 Goods Movement with and without Reference

Goods receipts can contain a reference to another document such as a purchase order or production order. However, you may run into a situation where you may not have a preceding reference document. For such a scenario, you can post the transaction without reference to any other document. For example, when you implement SAP, you need to upload the initial stock balances from the legacy system to the SAP system. This requires you to post the goods receipt without reference to any purchase order or production order. Initial stock is posted via Transaction MIGO and movement type 561.

To post the goods receipt without reference, go to Transaction MIGO and select the transaction (i.e., GOODS RECEIPT, GOODS ISSUE, etc.). In the reference list, select OTHER to post any transaction without reference to any document as shown in Figure 5.16.

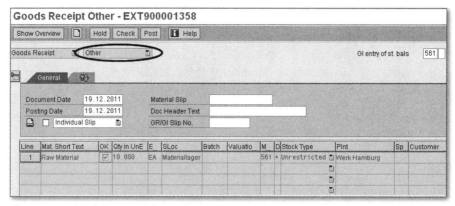

Figure 5.16 Goods Receipt Other in Transaction MIGO

Goods receipts without reference to any document belong to an unplanned goods movement because no information on material, quantity, and delivery date is stored in the system prior to the actual posting.

Other goods receipts are depicted using various movement types, as shown in Figure 5.17. As you can see, various goods receipt and goods issue transactions can be posted without reference to any document. Good examples of goods receipt without reference are receiving free of charge goods and initial stock upload.

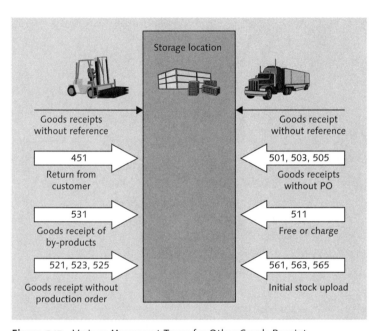

Figure 5.17 Various Movement Types for Other Goods Receipt

5.3.4 Inventory Management Configurations

In the following sections, we'll discuss the two ways you can configure inbound and outbound processes: by setting plant parameters and by defining number ranges for material documents. We'll also discuss the default parameters set in the system.

Setting Plant Parameters

In inventory management, you can define control parameters for each plant via menu path SAP IMG • MATERIALS MANAGEMENT • INVENTORY MANAGEMENT AND PHYSICAL INVENTORY • PLANT PARAMETERS. This allows you to define control parameters for categories such as GOODS MOVEMENTS, PHYSICAL INVENTORY, and NEGATIVE STOCKS (Figure 5.18).

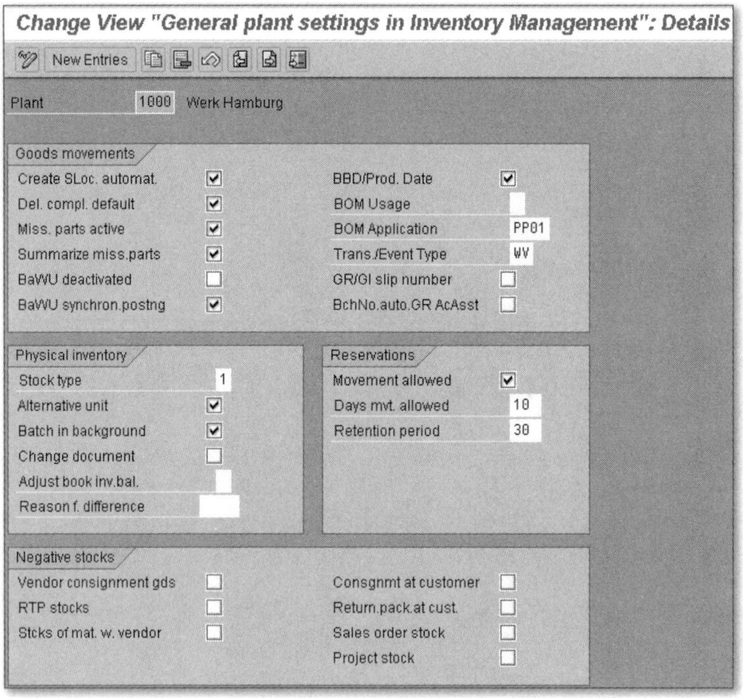

Figure 5.18 Plant Settings for Inventory Management

Negative stocks are necessary; for example, when goods issues are entered prior to the corresponding goods receipts, and the material is already physically located in the warehouse. After the goods receipts have been posted, the book inventory balance must again correspond to the physical stock; that is, the book inventory balance can no longer be negative.

For example, consider a scenario in which 1,000 pieces of material are physically available in a storage location. However, due to time limitations, the goods receipt document isn't posted in the system. In this case, the system stock will show up as zero:

▶ Physical stock: 1,000 pieces

▶ Book inventory stock: 0 pieces

Suddenly, 100 pieces of material must urgently be issued, and the goods issue is posted in the system. Because the book inventory balance was zero before, it will now be negative:

- Physical stock: 900 pieces
- Book inventory stock: (–)100 pieces

If you want to allow negative stock for a plant, go to menu path SAP IMG • MATE-RIALS MANAGEMENT • INVENTORY MANAGEMENT AND PHYSICAL INVENTORY • GOODS ISSUE/TRANSFER PROCESS • ALLOW NEGATIVE STOCK. In this step, you specify whether negative stocks are allowed for unrestricted-use stock in the valuation area, in the plant, and in the storage location (Figure 5.19).

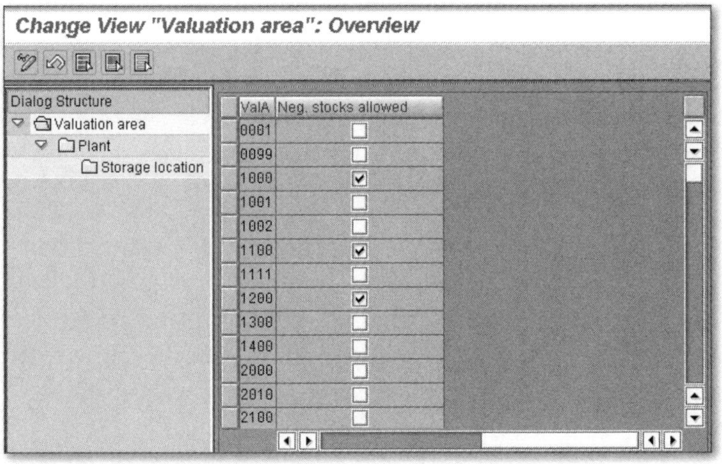

Figure 5.19 Allow Negative Stock for Valuation Area, Plant, and Storage Location

At a later time, the goods receipt is posted in the system, which updates the book inventory balance:

- Physical stock: 900 pieces
- Book inventory stock: 900 pieces

After the goods receipt is posted, the stock number in the system matches the actual physical stock. Now there is no more negative stock.

Defining Number Ranges for Material Documents

In the standard SAP system, the following document types are predefined for inventory management:

▶ WA: Goods issues, transfer postings, and other goods receipts

▶ WE: Goods receipts with reference to POs

▶ WF: Goods receipts with reference to production orders

▶ WI: Inventory differences

▶ WL: Goods issues with reference to deliveries (SD)

▶ WN: Net posting of goods receipts

▶ PR: Revaluation documents

Each document type is already assigned a number range. In company code 0001, number intervals are defined for each number range, both for the current and the previous fiscal year. Number range 49, with the year-related interval 4900000000 to 4999999999, is assigned to the document types for all goods movements, except goods movements with reference to purchase/production orders.

Document type WE is used for goods receipts with reference to POs and production orders. This document type is assigned number range 50, with the year-related interval 5000000000 to 5099999999. Note that net postings of goods receipts (document type WN) aren't active in the standard SAP system. If you want to post net goods receipts, you have to assign document type WN instead of WE to Transaction MB01.

Document type WI is used for posting inventory differences. This document type is assigned the number range 01, with the year-related interval 0100000000 to 019999999999.

If your company has different number ranges for different types of document based on some criteria to identity the document by its number only, you can define your own number range. To define your own number range, go to SAP IMG • MATERIALS MANAGEMENT • INVENTORY MANAGEMENT AND PHYSICAL INVENTORY • NUMBER ASSIGNMENT • DEFINE NUMBER ASSIGNMENT FOR MATERIAL AND PHYS. INV. DOC.

Number ranges for material documents are year-specific. Click on INSERT YEAR from the top menu, and enter the YEAR, FROM NUMBER, and TO NUMBER, as shown in Figure 5.20.

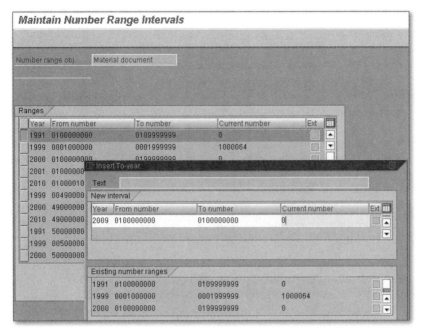

Figure 5.20 Define the Number Range for Material Documents

Default Settings

In the standard system, transaction/event types and number range intervals are preset as follows:

▶ **Physical inventory documents**

These have a number range interval from 0100000000 to 0199999999 and contain the following transaction/event types:

- ▶ IB: Physical inventory documents
- ▶ ID: Physical inventory documents for counts and difference without reference
- ▶ IN: Physical inventory documents for recounts
- ▶ IZ: Physical inventory documents for count without reference
- ▶ WV: Physical inventory documents for difference postings in the WM (Warehouse Management) system

▶ **Material documents for goods movements and inventory differences**

These have a number range interval from 4900000000 to 4999999999 and contain the following transaction/event types:

- ▶ WA: Goods issues, transfer postings, and other goods receipts

- ▶ WH: Goods movements for handling units (HU)

- ▶ WI: Material documents for inventory adjustment postings

- ▶ WL: Goods issues for delivery documents (SD)

- ▶ WQ: Goods movements for usage decisions (QM)

- ▶ WR: Goods movements for completion confirmations (PP)

- ▶ WS: Goods movements for running schedule headers (PP)

- ▶ WZ: Documents for batch status changes

- ▶ **Material documents for goods receipts**
  These have a number range interval from 5000000000 to 5999999999 and contain the following transaction/event types:

  - ▶ WE: Goods receipts for POs

  - ▶ WF: Goods receipts for production orders

  - ▶ WO: Subsequent adjustment of subcontract orders

  - ▶ WW: Subsequent adjustment of active ingredient materials

- ▶ **Inventory sampling numbers**
  These have number range intervals from 0200000000 to 0299999999 and contain transaction/event type SI.

> **Note**
>
> SAP recommends using default settings. In this case, no action is required on your part.

Now that we've covered the essential topics in inbound and outbound processes, let's move on to discuss the different stock types in inventory management.

5.4   Stock Types in Inventory Management

In inventory management, stock types vary depending on the business requirement. The stock type of a specific material specifies its usability, whether it's valuated or non-valuated, its availability for MRP, and more. The SAP system provides the following various types of stock:

- Standard stock (which includes unrestricted-use stock, quality-inspection stock, and blocked stock)
- Goods receipt blocked stock
- Special stock

We'll discuss each of these in more detail in the following subsections. Then we'll discuss how to change stock from one type to another.

5.4.1 Standard Stock Types

Three SAP-defined stock types are based on material usability:

- Unrestricted-use stock
- Quality-inspection stock
- Blocked stock

When you receive goods into a storage location via Transaction MIGO, you can select the stock type. The system will then update the stock quantity for that stock type (Figure 5.21). (Again, you can see stock overview reports via Transaction MMBE, which will display the stock available for each stock type.)

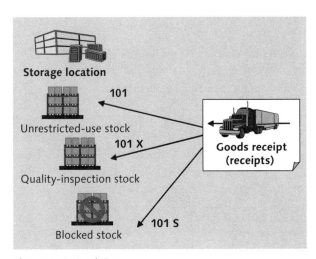

Figure 5.21 Stock Types

Let's go over the definition of each stock type.

Unrestricted-Use Stock

Unrestricted-use stock is company stock that's physically located in a storage location. It's valuated, and there's no restriction for usage. Unrestricted-use stock can be issued to production or customers.

You can receive the goods in unrestricted-use stock, when there are no quality issues with the material and no vendor disputes requiring the material to be returned to the vendor. Once you keep the stock in unrestricted-use stock, it can be issued.

Quality-Inspection Stock

Quality-inspection stock is company stock that's physically located in a storage location but is subjected to quality inspection. Quality-inspection stock is valuated and can't be issued to production or to a customer because it's under quality inspection. This means that the quality-management functionality has been implemented, and the materials are being inspected by a quality inspector. Based on the results of the inspection, usage decisions are made. Depending on this usage decision, quality-inspection stock can be changed to unrestricted-use stock or blocked stock.

In scenarios where the quality inspection is required for a material before it can be issued or used, you need to receive the materials in quality-inspection stock.

Blocked Stock

Blocked stock is company stock that can't be used because the status is blocked. The materials that are under dispute, of poor quality, or damaged are kept as blocked stock. If you want to issue these materials to production or to a customer, you need to transfer them to unrestricted-use stock.

As should be apparent from these three definitions, materials for production can be issued only from unrestricted-use stock. You can, however, withdraw a sample and scrap a quantity from blocked stock. Additionally, physical inventory can be carried out for all three types of stock, and differences can be posted.

You can change a material's stock type. This is called a *transfer posting* and is discussed in the next section.

In scenarios where you don't want to use the materials until the dispute with the vendor is resolved, you can keep such materials under block stock.

Transfer Postings

Although their names sound similar, a transfer posting is different from a stock transfer and is used for changing stock types of a material. For example, if you want to withdraw materials from blocked stock or quality-inspection stock, you have to first carry out a transfer posting into unrestricted-use stock via Transaction MIGO and transaction type Transfer posting, and then withdraw the material from unrestricted-use stock. Figure 5.22 illustrates the different movement types used for transfer postings.

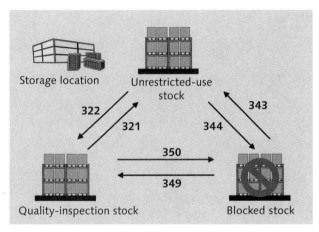

Figure 5.22 Transfer Posting Scenario

Transfer postings change stock types and batch numbers and may also involve physical stock transfers. Transfer postings always create a material document, and, if a change in valuation is involved, they also create an accounting document.

Material-to-Material Transfer

If the state of a material changes over time—for example, the properties of the original material defined in the material master record has changed over the period, and now these properties correspond to another material number—a material-to-material transfer becomes necessary. This is often the case in the chemical and pharmaceutical industries. One good example of this is wine; over a period of time, wine becomes the aged wine, and a material-to-material transfer posting is made. Ten-year-old wine is kept in the warehouse for the next 10 years to become

20-year-old wine that will be sold at a higher price. Movement type 309 is used for material-to-material transfers. You can perform material-to-material transfers via Transaction MIGO and movement type 309.

5.4.2 Goods Receipt Blocked Stock

When you post a goods receipt, the system updates the stock in a storage location. Alternatively, the stock is posted for direct consumption. However, there is another option in addition to these two: you can manage the stock as goods receipt blocked stock.

Business Scenario

Consider a car-manufacturing business that procures gear box assembly materials from a supplier. During the goods receipt, the company finds that some of the materials are damaged. They need to discuss the situation with the vendor and decide whether to use this material or send it back. Until this decision is made, this material needs to be kept in stock; however, the enterprise doesn't want to own it because it's under dispute.

The SAP system includes a goods receipt blocked stock functionality that allows the materials to be received but not valuated (Figure 5.23). The transaction is updated in the PO history.

If the material is sent back to the vendor, the system will create a material document and update the PO history. If it's transferred to the company's own stock, it becomes valuated and creates a material document and an accounting document. You can release goods receipt blocked stock to any other type of stock, such as unrestricted-use, quality-inspection, or blocked stock.

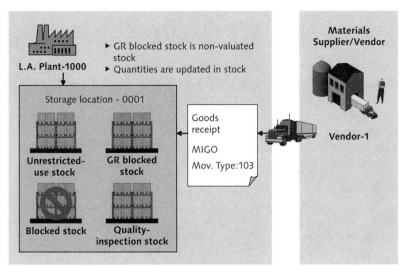

Figure 5.23 The Goods Receipt Blocked Stock Scenario

Process Steps

To configure the system to manage goods receipt blocked stock, follow these steps:

1. **Post the goods receipt.**
   Post the goods receipt with reference to a PO via Transaction MIGO and movement type 103. This will create a material document, and the stock quantity of goods receipt blocked stock will be updated in the plant stock.

2. **Release the goods receipt blocked stock, or return it.**
   To release goods receipt blocked stock to your own company, post a goods receipt with reference to a PO, using movement type 105. The system will release the goods receipt blocked stock to the company's own stock. A material document and an accounting document will be created.

To return goods receipt blocked stock to the vendor, post a goods return via Transaction MIGO with reference to the PO. Use movement type 124. The system will return the goods receipt blocked stock to the vendor.

In addition to the standard stock types and goods receipt blocked stock, special stock types also exist. We'll discuss these in the following section.

5.4.3 Special Stock Types

Special stocks are managed separately because they're either owned by a business partner (such as a vendor or customer), or stored in some other location (such as customer or vendor premises). These special stock types are split up into two groups: company-owned special stock and externally owned special stock. The list that follows shows which special stocks belong in each group (the letter in parentheses is the indicator in the SAP system):

► **Company-owned special stock**

  ► Subcontract stock (O)

  ► Customer consignment stock (W)

  ► Returnable transport packaging stock to customer (V)

► **Externally owned special stock**

  ► Vendor consignment stock (K)

  ► Returnable transport packaging stock to vendor (M)

  ► Sales order stock (E)

  ► Project stock (Q)

  ► Pipeline material (P)

Company-Owned Special Stock

Company-owned special stock is stock that's stored with the vendor or the customer. For example, material issued to a subcontractor is a company's stock that's stored on vendor premises.

The following are definitions of the company-owned special stocks available in the SAP system:

► **Subcontract stock**
  This is stock provided to the vendor for further processing.

► **Customer consignment stock**
  This is stock stored on customer premises. It's still owned by the company until it's consumed by the customer or transferred to the customer's own stock.

► **Returnable transport packaging stock to customer**
  This is packaging materials or means of transport (e.g., pallets or crates) that are supplied by your company to a customer and must be returned.

> **Note**
>
> Because these special stocks aren't located at your own company, they're managed at the plant level and not at the storage location level.
>
> Two stock types are possible: unrestricted-use stock and quality-inspection stock.

Externally Owned Special Stock

Externally owned special stock is stock that your customer or vendor stores at your company. The owner of the materials is still the customer or vendor, so it's not valuated in your stock valuation.

The following are definitions of the externally owned special stocks available in the SAP system:

- **Vendor consignment stock**
  This is stock provided by a vendor and kept at your company's storage location. The vendor remains the owner of the materials until they're consumed or transferred to the company's own stock.

- **Returnable transport packaging stock to vendor**
  This is packaging materials or means of transport (e.g., pallets or crates) that are supplied to your company by the vendor and must be returned.

- **Sales order stock**
  This is material that's procured directly for a sales order. Sales order stock can only be used to produce material ordered by the customer. Furthermore, the finished product can only be delivered to the customer via a sales order.

- **Project stock**
  This is material that's procured directly for a project. The project stock is allocated to a Work Breakdown Structure (WBS) element. Components can only be withdrawn for the WBS element.

> **Note**
>
> Because these special stocks are located at your company, they're managed at the storage location level.
>
> All three standard stock types are possible with this type of special stock.

5.5   Physical Inventory Management Processes

Physical inventory management is the process of physically verifying stock quantities in storage locations. If there are any differences in the system stock and physical stock, these differences are posted in the system. Many countries require by law that companies take a physical inventory of their material stocks. This physical inventory checks the material stocks for the current assets shown in the company's financial statement.

It's also important for internal reasons to establish the correct stock quantities on hand. Incorrect stock data leads to faulty availability figures. You can check the stock of material in the storage locations by counting the quantities in unrestricted-use stock, blocked stock, and quality-inspection stock. You can also carry out physical inventory for special stock and your own stock separately, using different physical inventory documents.

The physical inventory management process can be divided into three phases:

1. **Physical inventory preparation.**
   This phase includes creating physical inventory documents, blocking material for posting, and printing and distributing physical inventory documents.

2. **Physical inventory count.**
   This phase includes physically counting stock and entering the inventory count in the system.

3. **Physical inventory check.**
   In this phase, the physical count result is checked. If required, a recount can be initiated; otherwise, differences are accepted and posted. System stock is corrected after posting the differences.

Figure 5.24 illustrates the physical inventory process. The process starts with the creation of a physical inventory document. After physical counting, the inventory count and differences are posted in the system. Posting difference transactions will create a material document and an accounting document.

In the following sections, we'll discuss different types of physical inventory methods, as well as the process and configuration steps involved in physical inventory management.

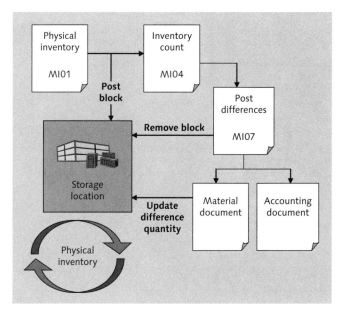

Figure 5.24 Physical Inventory Management Process

5.5.1   Process Steps

Follow these steps for the physical inventory process:

1. **Create a physical inventory document.**
   The first step is to create a physical inventory document via Transaction MI01. Enter the DOCUMENT DATE, PLANNED COUNT DATE, PLANT, and STORAGE LOCATION. You can block the posting by checking the POSTING BLOCK checkbox, as shown in Figure 5.25. If it's special stock, select the SPECIAL STOCK indicator. Press Enter. In the next screen, enter the material number for which you want to do a physical inventory, and then save. This will generate a physical inventory document, which can be printed via Transaction MI21.

> **Note**
>
> If you've selected the POSTING BLOCK indicator in a physical inventory document, you can't post any materials movement until you complete the inventory count.

2. **Enter the physical inventory count.**
   Enter the count result for the material via Transaction MI04, as shown in Figure 5.26.

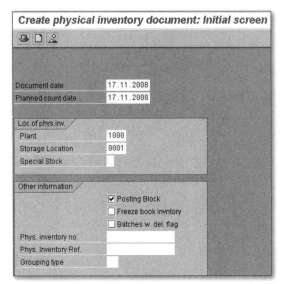

Figure 5.25   Creating a Physical Inventory Document

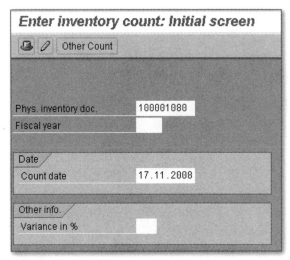

Figure 5.26   Entering the Inventory Count

3. **Post the difference.**

   You can post the difference with Transaction MI07, as shown in Figure 5.27. The system will create a material document for the difference quantity. It will also post an accounting document because discrepancies in stock quantity impact stock valuation.

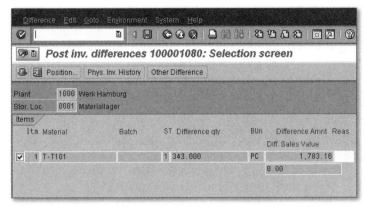

Figure 5.27 Posting Differences

With respect to account postings, if the physical inventory count is more than the system stock, the stock G/L account will be debited. If the physical inventory count is less than the system stock, the stock G/L account will be credited. For a gain in stock due to physical inventory, movement type 701 is used; for a loss in stock due to physical inventory, movement type 702 is used.

Now that you've learned the basics of the physical inventory process, let's discuss the different types of physical inventory methods.

5.5.2 Cycle Counting Method

There are a number of physical inventory methods that can be used. The following are provided by the SAP system:

▶ **Periodic inventory**
All company stocks are physically counted on the balance sheet key date. Every material has to be counted, and the entire storage location must be blocked for materials movement.

▶ **Continuous inventory**
Stocks are counted throughout the fiscal year. Every material is counted at least once during the fiscal year.

▶ **Cycle counting**
Materials are counted at regular intervals within a fiscal year. These intervals depend on the cycle counting indicator set for each material.

▶ **Inventory sampling**
Randomly selected company stocks are physically counted on the balance sheet key date. If the variances between the result of the count and the book inventory balances are small, it's presumed that the book inventory balances for other stocks are correct.

For our purposes, we'll focus on the cycle counting method because it's the most preferred method in the industry. With this method, all materials to be included in the inventory count are classified into different cycle categories such as A, B, C, and D (Figure 5.28). Each cycle category has a different time interval assigned to it. You can set these parameters via the CYCLE COUNTING indicator.

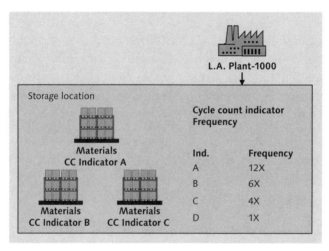

Figure 5.28   Cycle Counting Indicator

To customize the CYCLE COUNTING indicator and its frequency, go to SAP IMG • MATERIALS MANAGEMENT • INVENTORY MANAGEMENT AND PHYSICAL INVENTORY • PHYSICAL INVENTORY • CYCLE COUNTING. In this step, you configure the system settings for the physical inventory method of cycle counting by defining the individual cycle counting indicators for a given plant (Figure 5.29). The cycle counting indicators are used to group the materials together into individual categories.

For each plant, define the cycle counting physical inventory indicator (CC PHYS. INV. IND.). This indicates that a given material is subject to the cycle counting method of inventory. The indicator also defines at which time intervals a physical inventory should be carried out for the material.

Change View "Settings for Cycle Counting": Overview

New Entries

Plnt	CC phys. inv. ind	No.of phys.inv.	Interval	Float time	Percentage
0001	A	12	20	5	56
0001	B	6	41	10	28
0001	C	3	82	20	14
0001	D	1	247		2
1000	A	12	20	5	55
1000	B	6	41	10	28
1000	C	3	83	20	14
1000	D	1	249		2
1000	X	1	248	5	1
1001	A	12	20	5	56
1001	B	6	41	10	28
1001	C	3	82	20	14
1001	D	1	247		2
1002	A	12	20	5	56
1002	B	6	41	10	28
1002	C	3	82	20	14
1002	D	1	247		2

Figure 5.29 Defining the Cycle Counting Indicator

For materials that should be verified by the cycle counting method, you must assign the cycle count indicator in the material master record. This can be done either manually or automatically.

To set the physical inventory indicator manually, use Transaction MM02. Select the PLANT DATA/STOR. 1 view in the material master record, and select the CC PHYS. INV. IND. indicator (Figure 5.30).

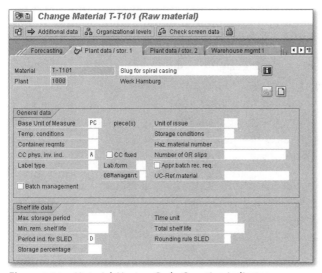

Figure 5.30 Material Master: Cycle Counting Indicator

To set the indicator automatically, execute Program RMCBIN00 via Transaction SE38, or use Transaction MIBC. This carries out ABC analysis (Figure 5.31). You can analyze based on requirements or consumption.

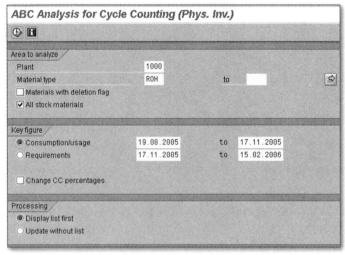

Figure 5.31 ABC Analysis for Cycle Counting

Performing an ABC analysis based on requirements means that you're analyzing the requirement values (planned independent requirements, sales orders, dependent requirements, and requirements from stock transport orders) for a specified period. Performing an ABC analysis based on consumption means you're analyzing consumption values for a specified period.

In either case, select the plant and material type, and then select the appropriate ABC analysis indicator. Under PROCESSING, select DISPLAY LIST FIRST, as shown in Figure 5.31. The system will display the material list with the new and old cycle counting indicator. If you want to update all of the material master records for the proposed cycle counting indicator and execute the report, select the UPDATE WITHOUT LIST checkbox in the PROCESSING section.

To create a physical inventory document automatically, use Program RM07ICN1 or Transaction MICN (Figure 5.32). This program automatically checks the due date for inventories for all cycle counting materials.

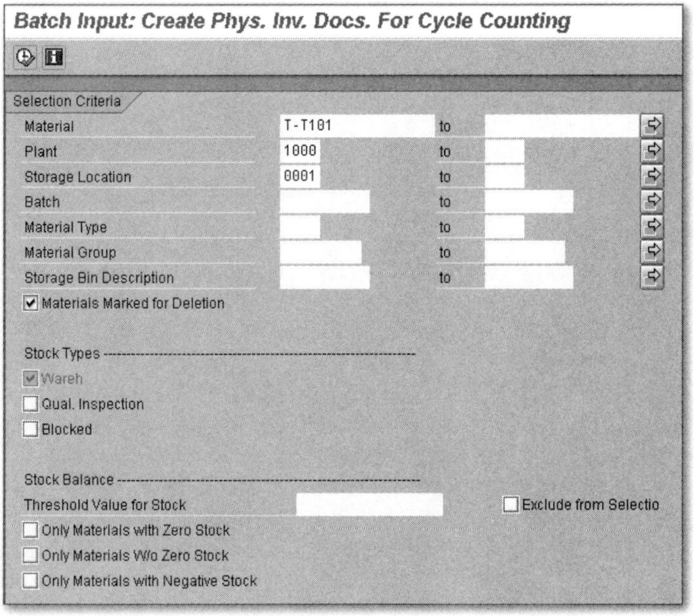

Figure 5.32 Creating a Physical Inventory Document Automatically

5.6 Vendor Return Process

There may be a scenario where you need to return materials to a vendor due to poor quality, damaged goods, or excess delivery. Vendor material can be returned through the following processes:

▶ Return without return PO

▶ Return with return PO

▶ Return with return PO and outbound delivery

We'll now discuss each of these scenarios in detail.

5.6.1 Return without Return Purchase Order

The return without return PO process is used when you don't want to process return POs. Materials are directly returned (i.e., issued) to the vendor with reference to the PO against which materials were received (Figure 5.33). In this case, material prices are picked up from the PO, and the returned quantity becomes the open quantity (the quantity to be delivered) in the PO.

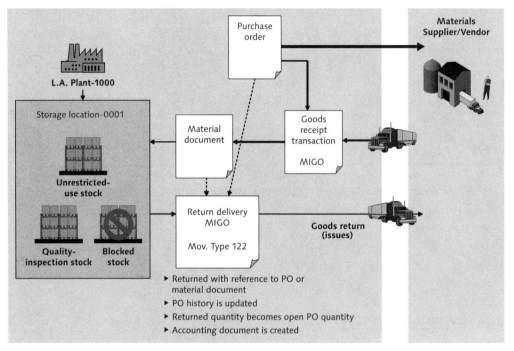

Figure 5.33 Vendor Return without Return PO

Materials can be returned to a vendor via Transaction MIGO. Select the goods receipt with reference to PO, enter the PO number (i.e., the PO number against which the material was received), and then enter "122" in the MOVEMENT TYPE field (Figure 5.34).

This transaction will issue the material to the vendor and update the PO history. The returned quantity will become the open quantity in the PO.

You can also return material via return delivery. Select the material document number (i.e., the material document number through which the material was received), and enter "122" in the MOVEMENT TYPE field. This transaction will be updated in the PO history.

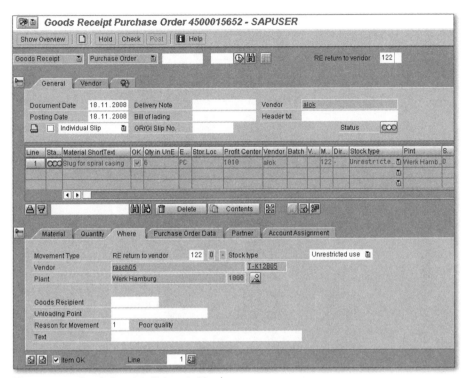

Figure 5.34 Goods Receipt: Return to Vendor

Regarding account postings, an accounting document will be created. The GR/IR (goods receipt/invoice receipt) account will be debited, and the stock G/L account will be credited.

> **Note**
>
> If you've accepted the goods conditionally and posted the goods receipt with movement type 103 in the non-valuated GR blocked stock, use movement type 124 for the return delivery. Because a non-valuated goods receipt is concerned in this case, the return delivery is also non-valuated.

What if you've already posted the invoice after the goods receipt is posted and now you want to return the material to the vendor? For such a scenario, you can make a setting for each movement type in Customizing for inventory management to specify whether a reversal of goods receipt or a return delivery is allowed in invoice verification based on goods receipts if you've already entered the relevant invoice.

These settings are in SAP IMG SAP IMG • MATERIALS MANAGEMENT • INVENTORY MANAGEMENT AND PHYSICAL INVENTORY • GOODS RECEIPT • FOR GR-BASED IV, REVERSAL OF GR DESPITE INVOICE (or you can use Transaction OMBZ).

Here you need to select the check box for the movement type for which you want to allow the reversal of GR despite invoice as shown in Figure 5.35.

Change View "For GR-Based IV, Reversal of GR Despite Invoice"

MvT	Movement Type Text	RevGR desp. IR
102	Reversal of GR	☑
106	Rev.GR from blocked	☐
122	RE return to vendor	☑
162	GR rtrns reversal	☑
802	RGR ad. Inv. + tax	☑
804	RGR AI ICMS/IPI	☑
806	RGR bl. AI w. tax	☐
812	RGR TP dely w tax	☑
816	RGR B TP dely w. tax	☐
822	RGR val. VS w. tax	☑
826	RGR B val. VS w. tax	☐
863	GI TF SD/MM return	☑
922	RE return to vendor	☑

Figure 5.35 Reversal or Return of GR Despite Invoice

5.6.2 Return with Return Purchase Order

The return with return PO scenario is used when you want to return materials via a return PO. This scenario is required when you don't have a record of the PO or goods receipt number against which the material was received. This may happen when you have multiple POs and goods receipts from the same vendor. In this case, a return PO is created, and materials are issued to the vendor via return delivery with reference to the return PO (Figure 5.36). A credit memo is issued to the vendor with reference to the return PO.

Follow these process steps for this type of return:

1. **Create a return PO.**
   Create a return PO via Transaction ME21N. Select the vendor, material, quantity, plant, and other identifying information. Then select the RETURNS ITEM checkbox, located in the PO item line (Figure 5.37). Use document type NB.

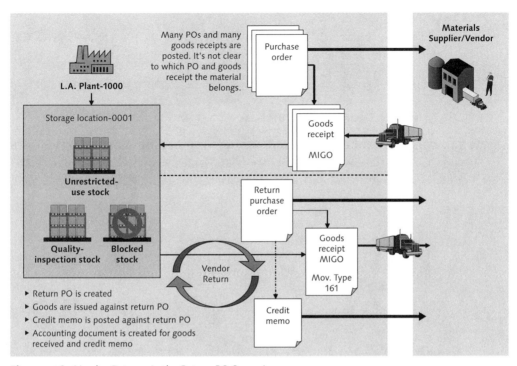

Figure 5.36 Vendor Return via the Return PO Scenario

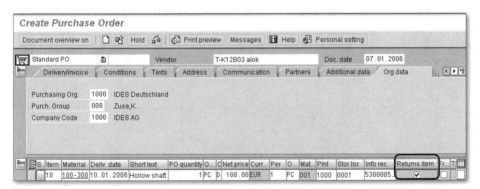

Figure 5.37 Purchase Order: Returns Item Indicator

2. **Post a goods issue.**

    Post a goods issue with reference to the return PO, via Transaction MIGO. Select movement type 161. A material document and an accounting document will be created in the system, the GR/IR account will be debited, and the stock G/L account will be credited.

3. **Post a credit memo.**

   Post a credit memo with reference to the return PO via Transaction MIRO. The system will create an accounting document, the GR/IR account will be credited, and the vendor account will be debited.

5.6.3 Return with Return Purchase Order and Outbound Delivery

The return with return PO and outbound delivery scenario is similar to the return with PO scenario except that the goods are issued via outbound delivery. The outbound delivery is created with reference to the return PO. Goods are issued, followed by the pick and pack process (Figure 5.38).

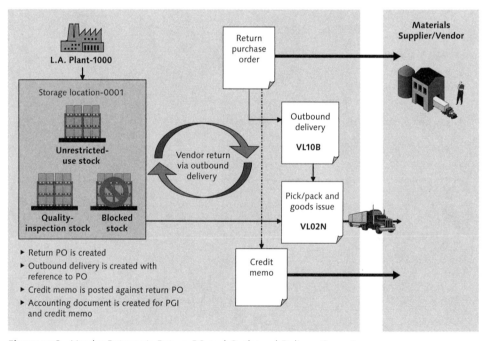

Figure 5.38 Vendor Return via Return PO and Outbound Delivery Scenario

Process Steps

Follow these process steps for a vendor return via return order and outbound delivery:

1. **Create a return PO.**
   Create a return PO via Transaction ME21N. Select the vendor, material, quantity, plant, and other identifying information. Then select the RETURNS ITEM checkbox, located in the PO item line. Use document type NB.
2. **Create an outbound delivery.**
   Create an outbound delivery with reference to the return PO via Transaction VL10B.
3. **Post a goods issue.**
   Perform the pick and pack activities and post the PGI via Transaction VL02N. Movement type 161 is used for a goods issue. The material document and accounting document are posted in the system.
4. **Post the credit memo.**
   Post the credit memo with reference to the return PO via Transaction MIRO. The system will create an accounting document, the GR/IR account will be credited, and the vendor account will be debited.

Configuration Steps

You can define the delivery type and supplying plant for a return PO. To do so, go to SAP IMG • MATERIALS MANAGEMENT • PURCHASING • PURCHASE ORDER • RETURNS ORDER • RETURNS TO VENDOR (Figure 5.39). In the standard system, return delivery type RL is used for vendor returns.

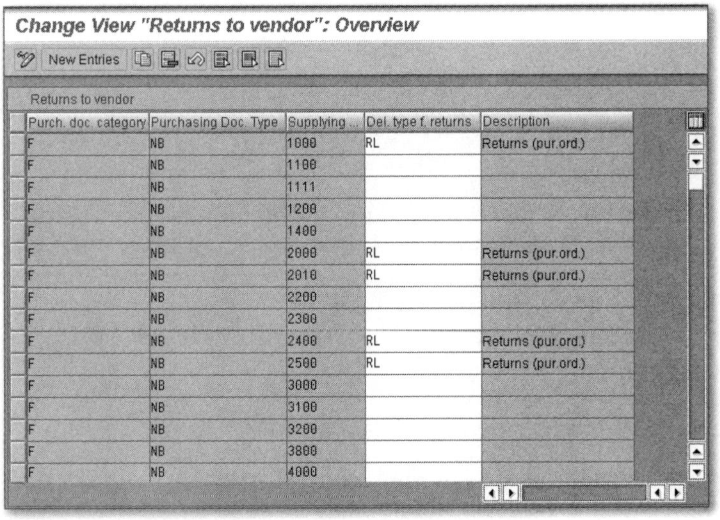
Change View "Returns to vendor": Overview

New Entries

Returns to vendor

Purch. doc. category	Purchasing Doc. Type	Supplying ...	Del. type f. returns	Description
F	NB	1000	RL	Returns (pur.ord.)
F	NB	1100		
F	NB	1111		
F	NB	1200		
F	NB	1400		
F	NB	2000	RL	Returns (pur.ord.)
F	NB	2010	RL	Returns (pur.ord.)
F	NB	2200		
F	NB	2300		
F	NB	2400	RL	Returns (pur.ord.)
F	NB	2500	RL	Returns (pur.ord.)
F	NB	3000		
F	NB	3100		
F	NB	3200		
F	NB	3800		
F	NB	4000		

Figure 5.39 Defining a Delivery Type for Vendor Returns

When processing returns in this manner, you must also edit the vendor master record. In the purchasing data screen under CONTROL DATA, select the RETURNS VENDOR checkbox (Figure 5.40). This indicator enables vendor returns to be carried out via the shipping process.

Figure 5.40 Vendor Master: Returns Vendor Setting

5.7   Cancellation of Material Document

If a materials document is posted by mistake or has an error, SAP provides an option to cancel the document.

You should always cancel the material document with reference to the original document because of the following advantages:

- You can copy the items to be reversed from the source document.
- The system automatically determines the reversal movement type.
- Reversal postings of goods issues, transfer postings, and goods receipts without reference are valuated with the value of the original document.
- Reversal postings of goods receipts with reference to purchase orders or production orders are valuated with the value determined from the purchase order or production order.
- You can use the list of cancelled material documents (Transaction MBSM) to analyze the cancelled material documents.

As a rule, the following is valid for the reversal movement type:

Reversal movement type = original movement type + 1

An example is given in Table 5.1.

Goods Movement	Movement Type	Reversal Movement Type
GR for PO	101	102
GR Blocked Stock	103	104
Return Delivery	122	123
Initial Stock Upload	561	562

Table 5.1 Movement and Reversal Movement Types

Process Steps

To cancel the document, go to Transaction MBST or Transaction MIGO and select the transaction CANCELLATION. Enter the material number you want to cancel and press Enter. You can see in Figure 5.41 that movement type 102—Reversal of GR—is automatically picked by the system.

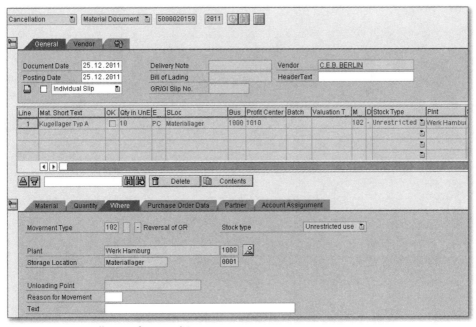

Figure 5.41 Cancellation of Material Document

If the original material document has an accounting document, the cancellation document will also create the accounting document, and the reversal entries in the G/L account will be posted.

5.8   Summary

In this chapter, we've discussed the processes involved in inventory management, including movement types, stock types, and types of returns. We've also covered some more technical topics, such as SAP system configuration for various processes. With the skills you've acquired in this chapter, you can now configure your customers' inventory management procedures so that they're perfectly tailored to the customers' requirements.

In the next chapter, we'll discuss another important process in MM: invoice verification.

This chapter explains the invoice verification process and how to customize your system to meet various business requirements involved in invoice verification such as invoice reduction, double invoice check, and subsequent debit/credit.

6 Invoice Verification

From a Materials Management (MM) perspective, the procurement process ends with invoice verification, which results in payments being issued to vendors by the finance and accounting department. An *invoice* is a legal document that vendors send as a record of goods supplied or services performed; it contains the item price, taxes, freight charges, discounts, and terms of payment. Purchasing departments verify the invoice using the purchase order (PO) and goods receipt, and then post it. Finally, the finance and accounting departments process the payment to the vendor.

Invoice verification creates an MM invoice document and a Financial Accounting (FI) invoice document (Figure 6.1). Invoice posting updates the PO history and, if materials are subjected to stock valuation, the valuation price in the material master record.

As shown in Figure 6.2, invoices can be posted in several different ways. With *manual entry*, invoices are received by mail or via a courier, and employees manually verify and enter the invoices into the system. In *EDI/XML*, invoices can be transmitted electronically in the form of intermediate documents (IDocs) via Electronic Data Interchange (EDI) or in XML format.

The system creates invoices using settlement programs that run at regular intervals for consignment, invoicing plans, and evaluated receipt settlement (ERS).

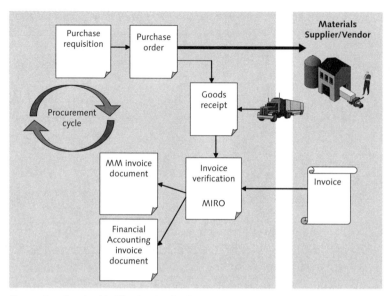

Figure 6.1 Invoice Verification in the Procurement Process

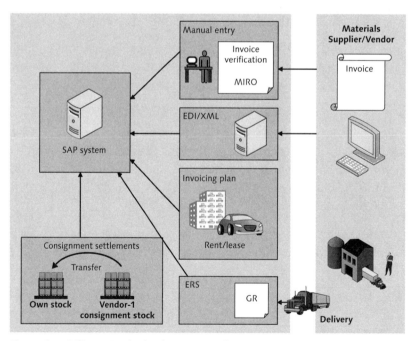

Figure 6.2 Different Methods of Invoice Verification

In this chapter, we'll discuss various scenarios in invoice verification including the following:

▶ PO-based invoice

▶ Goods receipt-based invoice

▶ Subsequent debit/credit

▶ Invoices for account-assigned POs (blanket PO)

▶ Evaluated receipt settlements

▶ Invoicing plans

▶ Credit memo and reversals

▶ Invoice verification in background

▶ Invoices with reduction

Before we proceed to discussing each of these scenarios, we'll cover the basic concepts of the invoice verification process in the SAP system.

6.1   Basics of Invoice Verification

In general, an invoice from a vendor contains a number of fields, as illustrated in Figure 6.3. Important fields are the invoice number, item description, item quantity, item amount, and taxes.

ABC Materials Inc.	12/1, Sea Rock Road, CA VAT - 99119900

Invoice Number: 100-1201	Date: 02/09/2009
Reference PO 4500000045	

Item	Qty	Amount
Valve	2 pcs	50
Seal	2 pcs	20
Basic Cost		70
Discount		10
		60
Tax @ 10%		06
Fright		05
Total		71

Terms & Conditions:
Payment is due within 30 days.

Figure 6.3   Sample Invoice

As shown in Figure 6.4, invoice verification in the SAP system is carried out via Transaction MIRO. This transaction allows you to post invoices pertaining to different scenarios by simply selecting the required option from a dropdown list. In addition, incoming invoices can be directly posted with reference to a material or a G/L account. Transaction MIRO also provides various layouts that ease the invoice verification process.

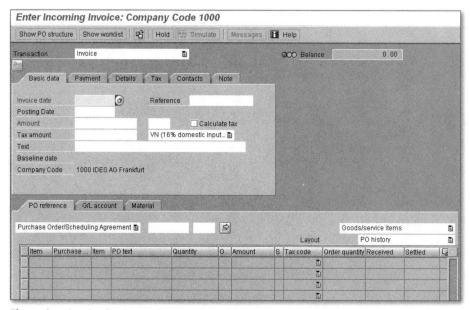

Figure 6.4 Invoice Posting via Transaction MIRO

Figure 6.4 shows a typical screen layout in Transaction MIRO. The following list is an explanation of the most important fields in this transaction:

▶ HOLD
You click on this button when you have insufficient information to post the invoice but want to save the partially entered data. Held invoices can be posted later when entering the missing information.

▶ SIMULATE
Before posting an invoice, it's possible to check the different G/L account postings using the SIMULATE button.

▶ MESSAGES
You click on this button to see the messages issued by the system.

- TRANSACTION
  In this field, you can select any one of the four options available from the drop-down list: INVOICE, CREDIT MEMO, SUBSEQUENT DEBIT, and SUBSEQUENT CREDIT. Based on the selected option, the screen layout will change.

- BALANCE
  This shows the balance between the PO value and the invoice value. It's for display only.

- BASIC DATA
  This tab contains several fields such as INVOICE DATE, POSTING DATE, and AMOUNT. INVOICE DATE is the date printed on the invoice, POSTING DATE is the date on which you want to post the invoice, and AMOUNT is the amount mentioned in the vendor invoice (this is a mandatory field). You can also enter references and tax amount in their respective fields. If you select the CALCULATE TAX checkbox, the system calculates tax based on the selected tax code.

- PO REFERENCE
  On this tab, from the leftmost dropdown list, you can select any option with reference to which you want to post an incoming invoice. The options include PURCHASE ORDER/SCHEDULING AGREEMENT, DELIVERY NOTE, BILL OF LADING, and SERVICE ENTRY SHEET.

- LAYOUT
  Also located on the PO REFERENCE tab, you can select a layout from the LAYOUT dropdown list. The layout plays a vital role for invoice reduction because the system will display the fields based on the layout.

After all of the required information has been supplied, an invoice can be posted. Invoice posting has the following effects:

- MM and FI invoice documents are generated.

- Various G/L accounts are debited or credited.

- The PO history is updated to reflect the invoice posting.

- Payment can be processed to the vendor.

Now that you've learned about the basic concepts involved in invoice verification, let's move on to discuss the different types of invoice verification, starting with PO-based verification.

6.2 PO-Based Invoice Verification

In PO-based invoice verification, the system allows invoice posting with reference to a PO, even though goods haven't yet been delivered. The line items of the PO are copied into the invoice posting screen at the time of invoice verification. As shown in Figure 6.5, the invoice can be posted both before and after the delivery of goods.

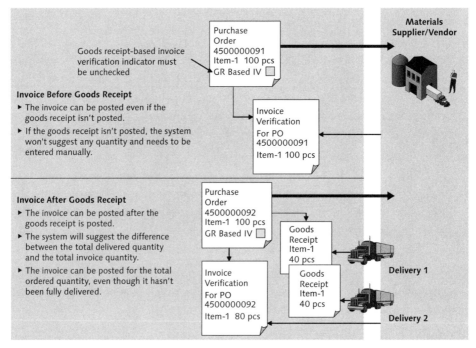

Figure 6.5 PO-Based Invoice Verification

> **Note**
>
> The PO line item details are shown on the INVOICE tab. This includes the GR-BASED INVOICE VERIFICATION indicator, which should be unchecked for PO-based invoice verification.

6.3 GR-Based Invoice Verification

In this scenario, the SAP system allows you to post invoices only after the goods receipt has been posted in the system (Figure 6.6) and invoices are matched with the received quantity of a PO. For multiple deliveries, the system supplies each delivery on a separate line.

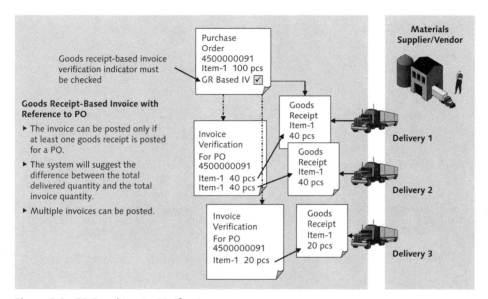

Figure 6.6 GR-Based Invoice Verification

6.4   Invoices for Account-Assigned Purchase Orders

As you learned in Chapter 4, POs for materials procured for consumption are account-assigned POs. We'll now explain how to post an invoice for an account-assigned PO.

The account assignment category is used to define account assignment and can be configured via SAP IMG • MATERIALS MANAGEMENT • PURCHASING • ACCOUNT

ASSIGNMENT • MAINTAIN ACCOUNT ASSIGNMENT CATEGORIES. As shown in Figure 6.7, the account assignment category controls the following:

▶ Goods receipt posting is allowed (GOODS RECEIPT)

▶ Invoice receipt posting is allowed (INVOICE RECEIPT)

▶ Account assignment is changeable at the time of invoice receipt (AA CHANGEABLE AT IR)

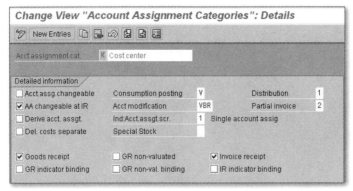

Figure 6.7 Account Assignment Category Configuration

If the AA CHANGEABLE AT IR checkbox is selected, and a valuated goods receipt isn't allowed, the account assignment category defined in the PO can be changed at the time of invoice posting.

In the following sections, we'll discuss account postings and the process steps for posting an invoice for an account-assigned PO.

6.4.1 Account Postings

As shown in Figure 6.8, if a valuated goods receipt is defined for a PO with account assignment, the consumption G/L account is debited during goods receipt. The offsetting entry is posted into the GR/IR account. Furthermore, during the invoice posting, the GR/IR account is debited, and the vendor account is credited. If a price variance exists in the invoice, the difference is posted to the consumption account.

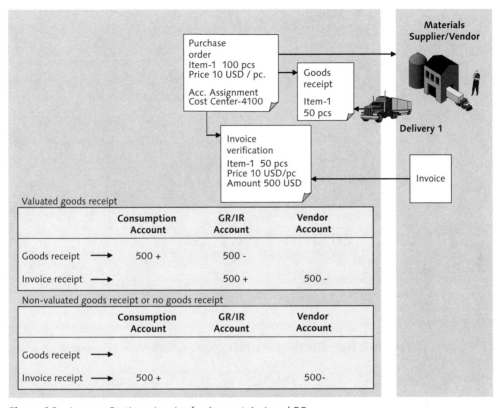

Figure 6.8 Account Postings: Invoice for Account-Assigned PO

For a non-valuated goods receipt, there isn't an account posting. The invoice posting debits the consumption account and credits the vendor account.

6.4.2 Process Steps

You can post invoices via Transaction MIRO. Enter the PO number and press Enter. As shown in Figure 6.9, two line items are supplied from the PO. The first line item is defined as a valuated goods receipt in the PO; therefore, the account assignment is in display mode only and can't be changed. The second line item is defined as a non-valuated goods receipt in the PO and has account assignment category K (cost center, changeable). This means that the account assignment can be changed and that multiple account assignments are possible.

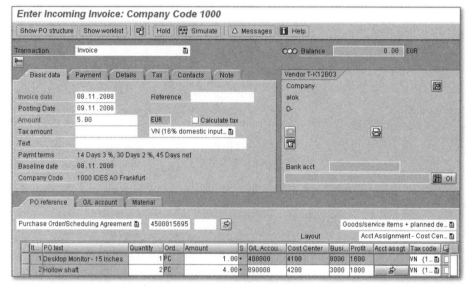

Figure 6.9 Invoice Posting for Account-Assigned PO

6.5 Invoices for Blanket Purchase Orders

Blanket POs are used to procure consumable materials or services when you don't want to create a PO each time. Blanket POs are valid for a longer period, and invoices can be directly posted for the materials and services procured. When posting an invoice for a blanket PO, the system checks for the validity date and limits that are defined in the PO. Tolerances for value limits and validity periods can also be configured in the system; if the invoice exceeds these tolerance limits, it's blocked.

To configure the tolerance limits for a blanket PO, go to SAP IMG • MATERIALS MANAGEMENT • LOGISTICS INVOICE VERIFICATION • INVOICE BLOCK • SET TOLERANCE LIMITS. In the standard system, tolerance key LA is defined for blanket PO value limits, and tolerance key LD is defined for blanket PO time limits (Figure 6.10).

Change View "Tolerance Limits": Overview

Co...	Company Name	TIKy	Description
1001	IDES AG	LA	Amount of blanket purchase order
1001	IDES AG	LD	Blanket PO time limit exceeded

Figure 6.10 Tolerance Limits

Figure 6.11 shows an example of how you might define tolerance limits.

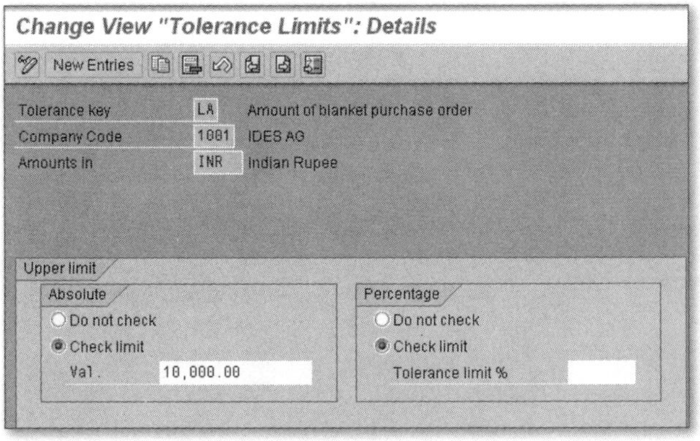

Figure 6.11 Tolerance Limits: Details

6.6   Evaluated Receipt Settlements

With the evaluated receipt settlements (ERS) scenario, the system automatically posts invoices after the goods receipt is posted in the system. This effectively reduces paperwork and data entry errors.

6.6.1   Business Scenario

Consider a car manufacturer with a vendor that delivers goods based on PO quantities and delivery schedules. The company posts the invoices based on the goods receipts, and subsequently, the vendor is paid. In this scenario, the vendor doesn't send invoices (see Figure 6.12). The system uses the prices and discount conditions from the PO, and settlement information is sent to the vendor via messages generated at the time of settlement.

In the following sections, we'll discuss the prerequisites in the master data and process steps as they relate to ERS.

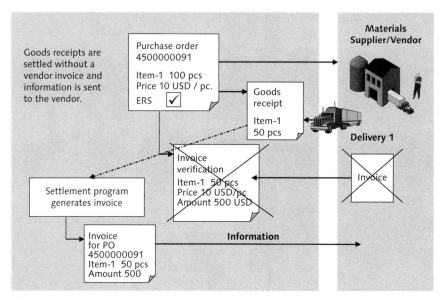

Figure 6.12   ERS Scenario

6.6.2   Prerequisites in Master Data

For the ERS functionality, you must configure certain settings in the vendor master data and in the info record. In the vendor master data, activate the ERS indicator and the GR-BASED INVOICE VERIFICATION indicator. If the vendor is already defined, use Transaction XK02 (Change Vendor). If you're creating a new vendor, use Transaction XK01 (Create Vendor). Under CONTROL DATA in the PURCHASING view, select the checkbox for GR-BASED INV. VERIF. and AUTOEVALGRSETMT DEL., as shown in Figure 6.13.

In the info record, set the ERS indicator for a material and vendor combination, and define the tax code so that it's copied at the time of PO creation. Use Transaction ME11 (Create Info Record), and enter the material, vendor, and purchase organization. Then go to the PURCHASE ORGANIZATION DATA view, and select the GR-BASED IV indicator. Don't select the NO ERS checkbox. Enter the tax code as well (Figure 6.14).

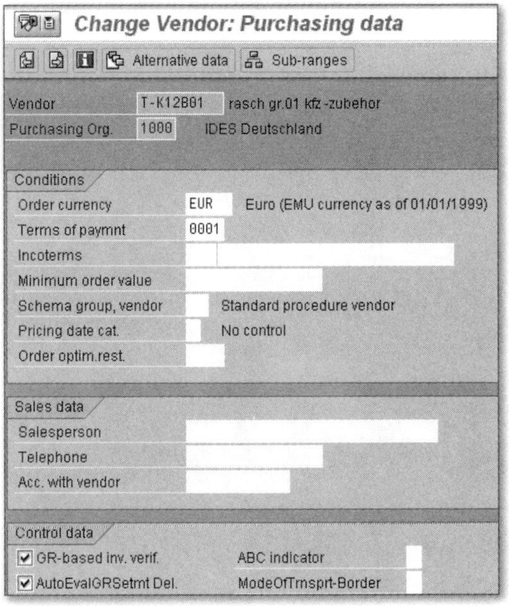

Figure 6.13 Vendor Master Data: ERS Indicator

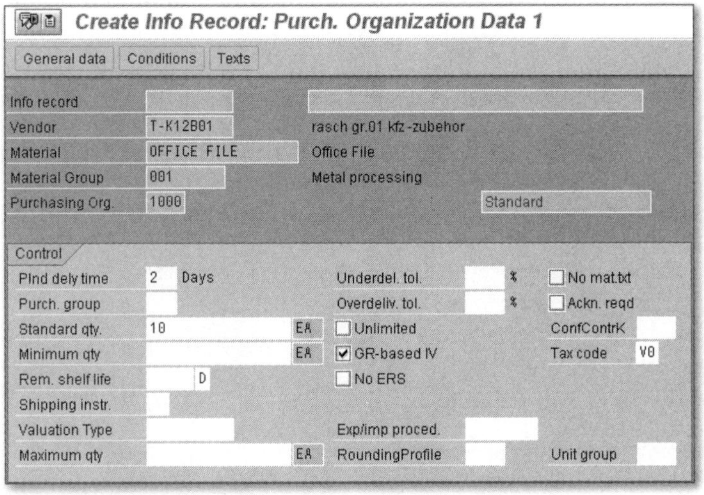

Figure 6.14 Purchasing Info Record: ERS Indicator

6.6.3 Process Steps

For an ERS scenario, follow these process steps:

1. **Create the PO.**
   Go to Transaction ME21N and enter the vendor, company code, purchasing organization, purchase group, material, quantity, and delivery date. Check the GR-BASED IV and ERS indicators on the INVOICE tab of the item details, as shown in Figure 6.15.

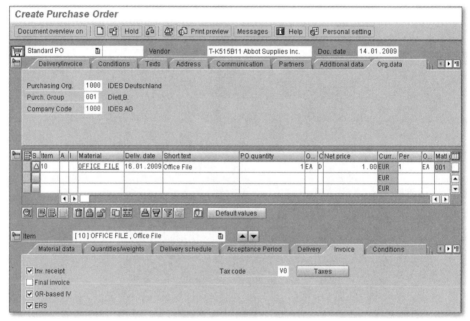

Figure 6.15 PO Creation: ERS Indicator

2. **Post the goods receipt.**
   Go to Transaction MIGO and post the goods receipt for the PO.

3. **Execute the settlement program for ERS.**
   Go to Transaction MRRL and enter the company code, plant, and vendor (Figure 6.16). Select DOC. SELECTION in the PROCESSING OPTIONS section and execute. The system will create the invoice document.

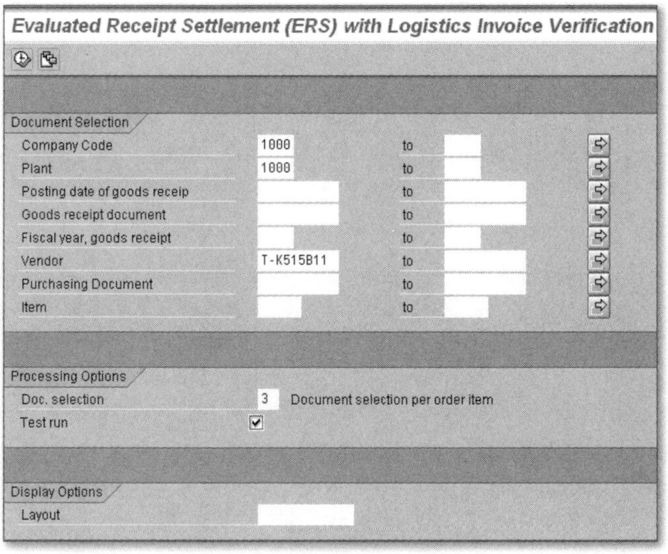

Figure 6.16 ERS Execution via Transaction MRRL

Invoices can be generated with the following options:

▶ One invoice document per vendor

▶ One invoice document per PO

▶ One invoice document per PO item

▶ One invoice document per delivery document/service entry sheet

Choose any of these options while processing the ERS via Transaction MRRL. You can see these options in the Doc. Selection field.

Note

To create invoices automatically, you can define ERS as a batch job. Schedule the batch job with Program RMMR1MRS and the required variant. The system will automatically pick up the deliveries due to ERS and post the invoices.

6.7 Invoicing Plans

An *invoicing plan* consists of a series of invoicing dates and values and involves invoices that are automatically posted by the system. For example, an enterprise that wants to automatically generate invoices for the monthly office rent might use an invoicing plan.

6.7.1 Business Scenario

A leading FMCG (fast-moving consumer goods) company with operations across the world rents warehouses in various cities and that are paid on a monthly basis. The company also has various sales offices on a monthly rental basis. These rents are supposed to be paid on a specific date of each month. The company wanted a system to create the invoices automatically based on the rent due date and process the payments to vendors. ERS functionality accomplished this and helped reduce manual efforts and lessen the chance that someone would forget to raise the invoice on the due dates.

An invoicing plan is defined in the PO for repetitive procurement transactions such as rental, leasing, or service agreements. There are two types of invoicing plans:

▶ Periodic invoicing plan: This is used when invoicing is generated on regular intervals (monthly, yearly and so on).

▶ Partial invoicing plan: This is used when invoicing is generated based on a milestone and for a partial amount. Invoices are generated based on the progress of work.

We'll discuss both invoicing plans in detail in the following sections.

6.7.2 Periodic Invoicing Plan

Periodic invoicing plans are used for repetitive procurement transactions such as building rent, car rentals, leased machines, and so on (see Figure 6.17). As you can see in Figure 6.17, the PO is created for the office space procurement on a rental basis (1000 USD per month), and this PO is marked for ERS. The vendor doesn't need to send the invoice each month because the system will generate the invoice each month based on the invoicing plan and due dates. In these plans, the total value of the PO is invoiced on each due date.

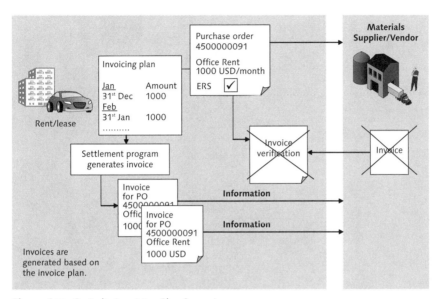

Figure 6.17 Periodic Invoicing Plan Scenario

6.7.3 Partial Invoicing Plan

Partial invoicing plans are used for transactions involving invoicing in stages. For example, construction projects use partial invoicing plans, where the total value of the project is invoiced and paid in partial increments throughout the life of the project. If a model invoicing plan is defined in the system, invoice due dates are automatically supplied. Otherwise, the due dates have to be defined manually in the PO.

The total value of a PO can be split among due dates on either a percentage or absolute value basis. Figure 6.18 shows the construction project example. In the PO, the partial invoicing plan is defined based on the completion of each stage of the project.

In the following sections, we'll discuss the customization options available and the process steps involved in invoicing plans.

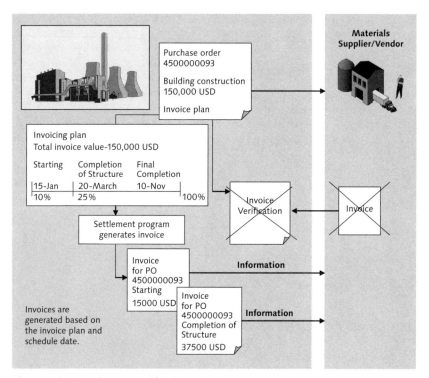

Figure 6.18 Partial Invoicing Plan Scenario

6.7.4 Customization

Previously, we discussed the invoicing plan types and also how they can be customized. Now let's explore some more customizing parameters.

Maintain Periodic Invoicing Plan Types

To maintain partial invoicing plan types, go to SAP IMG • MATERIALS MANAGEMENT • PURCHASING • PURCHASE ORDER • INVOICING PLAN • INVOICING PLAN TYPES • MAINTAIN PERIODIC INVOICING PLAN TYPES. In this step, you define the periodic invoicing plan types by specifying the relevant control data (Figure 6.19). Enter the STARTING DATE, END DATE, and HORIZON in the ORIGIN OF GENERAL DATA section. In the INVOICE DATA: SUGGESTION FOR DATES section, select the periodic invoice date to determine the next billing date.

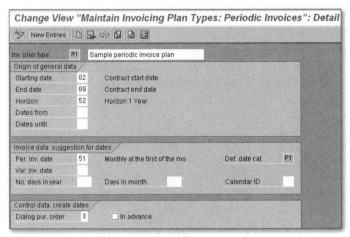

Figure 6.19 Maintain Invoicing Plan Types: Periodic Invoicing

Maintain Partial Invoicing Plan Types

To maintain partial invoicing plan types, go to SAP IMG • MATERIALS MANAGEMENT • PURCHASING • PURCHASE ORDER • INVOICING PLAN • INVOICING PLAN TYPES • MAINTAIN PARTIAL INVOICING PLAN TYPES. In this step, you define the partial invoicing plan types by specifying the relevant control data (Figure 6.20).

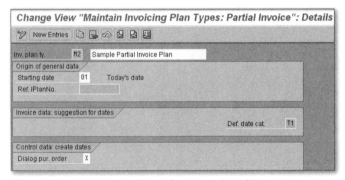

Figure 6.20 Maintain Invoicing Plan Types: Partial Invoices

Maintain Date IDs

Date IDs are texts briefly describing the relevant dates in the invoicing plan. The descriptions are merely to differentiate between the invoicing dates and have no control character.

To define date IDs, go to SAP IMG • MATERIALS MANAGEMENT • PURCHASING • PUR-CHASE ORDER • INVOICING PLAN • MAINTAIN DATE IDs. In this step, you can define the DATE DESCRIPTION as shown in Figure 6.21.

Enter an alphanumeric key of maximum four characters in length, plus a language key and a descriptive text for each date.

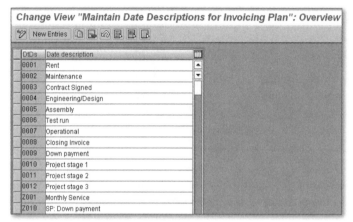

Figure 6.21 Maintain Date IDs

Maintain the Date Category for Invoicing Plan Types

In this step, you can make relevant settings for the date category. The date category has control functions for the invoicing plan. For example, it determines whether invoicing dates can be blocked (and if so, how), and it specifies the calculation rule for apportioning the values among the invoicing dates.

To define a date category, go to SAP IMG • MATERIALS MANAGEMENT • PURCHASING • PURCHASE ORDER • INVOICING PLAN • DATE CATEGORIES • MAINTAIN DATE CATEGORY FOR INVOICING PLAN TYPE. In this step, you can assign one or more date categories to each invoicing plan type (Figure 6.22). Enter the DATE CATEGORY, and select the DATE DESCRIPT. and CALC. RULE, which defines how the billed value is determined.

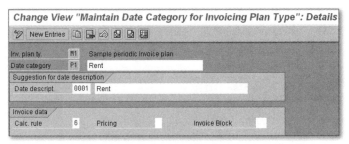

Figure 6.22 Maintain a Date Category for the Invoicing Plan Type

Define the Default Date Category for the Invoicing Plan Type

We have seen in an earlier step that several date categories can be assigned to an invoicing plan. In this step, you can define the default value for invoicing plant types. To define a default date category, go to SAP IMG • MATERIALS MANAGEMENT • PURCHASING • PURCHASE ORDER • INVOICING PLAN • DATE CATEGORIES • DEFINE DEFAULT DATE CATEGORY FOR INVOICING PLAN TYPE. In this step, you can define a DATE CATEGORY as the default value for each INVOICING PLAN TYPE (Figure 6.23).

Change View "Assign Date Proposal Category to Invoicing Plan": Overvie

Inv. pl. ty.	Invoicing plan type	DD	Date category	
M1	Sample periodic invoice plan	P1	Rent	
M2	Sample Partial Invoice Plan	T1	Percentage partial invoice	
MM		P1	Rent	
PR		P1	Rent	
TR		T1	Percentage partial invoice	

Figure 6.23 Assign a Date Proposal Category to the Invoicing Plan

Maintain the Date Proposal for Partial Invoicing Plans

In this step, you can maintain a date sequence proposal for partial invoicing plans. A date sequence proposal defines a series of dates that can be referenced for the purposes of date determination during PO processing.

> **Note**
>
> The date sequence proposal is relevant to partial invoicing plans only—not to periodic invoicing plans.

When a partial invoicing plan is created for a PO, the invoicing dates are taken from the reference object that has been defined in Customizing for the relevant invoicing plan type.

To maintain date proposals for partial invoicing plans, go to SAP IMG • MATERIALS MANAGEMENT • PURCHASING • PURCHASE ORDER • INVOICING PLAN • MAINTAIN DATE PROPOSAL FOR PARTIAL INVOICING PLANS (Figure 6.24).

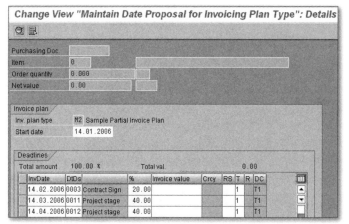

Figure 6.24 Maintain Date Proposals for the Invoicing Plan Type

6.7.5 Process Steps

Follow these process steps to use invoicing plans:

1. **Create a PO.**

   Create a PO via Transaction ME21N. Document type FO (framework order) is used for POs with invoicing plans. Select the account assignment category and the cost object (such as cost center) for account assignment category K (Figure 6.25). If you want to select the GR indicator in the PO, you must select the non-valuated goods receipt indicator as well.

> **Note**
>
> Invoicing plan functionality doesn't work with valuated goods receipts.

   Click on the INVOICING PLAN button located on the INVOICE tab of the item details, and select the invoicing plan type. The system will propose the invoice schedules from the template created in Customizing.

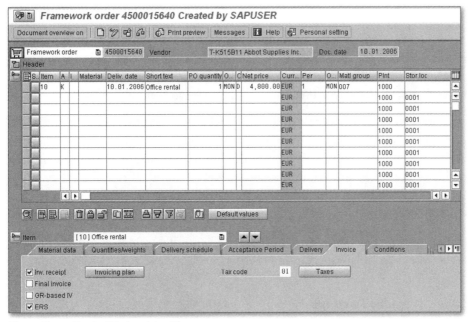

Figure 6.25 Create PO: Invoicing Plan

2. **Execute the invoicing plan settlement.**

Go to Transaction MRIS (Invoicing Plan Settlement); enter the COMPANY CODE, PLANT, and VENDOR; and click on EXECUTE. The system will generate the invoices. You can check the invoice status on the INVOICING PLAN tab of the PO. Billing status C stands for completely processed.

> **Note**
>
> To create invoices automatically, you can define invoicing plan settlement via a batch job. Schedule the batch job with Program RMMR1MIS and the required variant. The system will automatically pick up the items due for billing from the PO invoicing plan.

6.8   Subsequent Debit/Credit

Subsequent debit or credit happens when an invoice or credit memo is received from a vendor after the invoice for a particular PO has already been posted.

6.8.1 Business Scenario

Let's say that a business receives invoices or credit memos for a PO that has already been invoiced. Additional invoices are sent by a vendor because the original invoices contained prices that were too low. Similarly, credit memos may be sent by a vendor if the original invoice contained prices that were too high.

The SAP system provides the subsequent debit or credit functionality to handle situations where invoices or credit memos are received from a vendor after posting an invoice for a particular PO. Subsequent debits and credits are posted with reference to a PO, which changes the PO value but doesn't affect the total quantity. Subsequent debit or credit may be posted for a PO item only if the invoice has already been posted, and the PO history is updated.

In the following sections, we'll discuss the account postings and process steps involved in invoice verification for subsequent debit/credit.

6.8.2 Account Postings

Subsequent debit and credit transactions update the G/L account based on different scenarios.

For stock materials with price control V (moving average price), the subsequent debit/credit amount is posted to the vendor and GR/IR account. Figure 6.26 shows an example of an account posting for a subsequent debit transaction. A PO is issued for 10 pieces of material Mat-1 with a price of $10 per piece. After the goods receipt and invoice receipt are posted for a total quantity of 10 pieces with an amount of $100, the vendor realizes that the amount charged is less by $20 and sends another invoice for $20. A subsequent debit is posted for an amount of $20 for 10 pieces of material. Different transactions involved in the entire process will update the G/L accounts as follows:

- **Goods receipt:** stock account (+) 100, GR/IR account (–) 100
- **Invoice receipt:** GR/IR account (+) 100, vendor account (–) 100
- **Subsequent debit:** stock account (+) 20, vendor account (–) 20

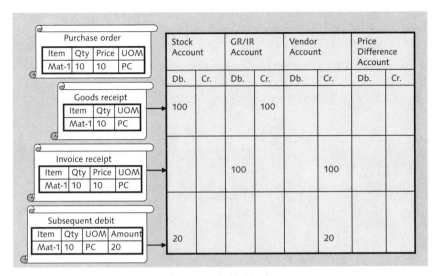

Figure 6.26 Account Posting: Subsequent Debit/Credit

In the following scenarios, the account posting may differ:

▶ **Stock material with price control "S" (standard price)**
For stock material with price control S (standard price), the subsequent debit/credit amount is posted to the vendor account and the price difference account.

▶ **Consumable materials (account-assigned POs)**
For account-assigned POs (which are used for consumable materials), subsequent debit/credit transactions update the vendor account and post the offsetting entry to the cost account.

▶ **Subsequent debit/credit before the goods are delivered**
For situations where there is a subsequent debit/credit transaction before the goods are delivered (i.e., before the goods receipt transaction), the vendor and GR/IR accounts are posted. At the time of the goods receipt, the stock account or price difference account will be posted, depending on the price control of the material master data.

Now that we've gone through the subsequent debit/credit business scenario and various account postings, let's go through the process steps.

6.8.3   Process Steps

Subsequent debit/credit is posted via Transaction MIRO. Select SUBSEQUENT DEBIT or SUBSEQUENT CREDIT in the TRANSACTION field, as shown in Figure 6.27. After you enter the PO number, the system will supply the material and quantity. Enter the amount and save. The PO history will be updated.

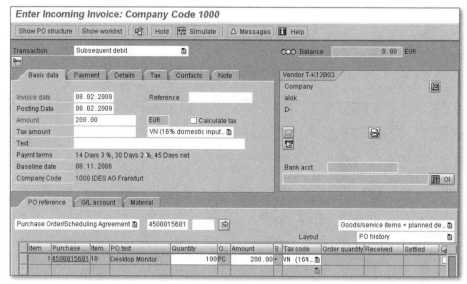

Figure 6.27   Subsequent Debit Posting via Transaction MIRO

6.9   Credit Memos and Reversals

Credit memos are used to adjust amounts owed to a vendor. Credit memos are different from subsequent debits/credits, which don't change the invoiced quantity but only post the amounts. Your business will use credit memos when the invoice is posted for more than the received quantity. With a credit memo, the invoiced quantity is updated.

6.9.1   Business Scenario

Imagine that a vendor has sent your company an invoice for a larger quantity of material than was delivered, and this invoice is posted to the system.

In this scenario, a vendor credit memo is posted with reference to the PO for the excess quantity (Figure 6.28). The credit memo updates the G/L accounts and PO history.

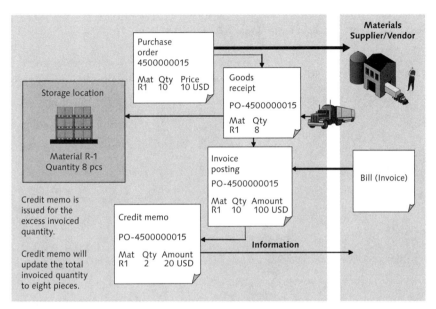

Figure 6.28 Credit Memo Scenario

Credit memos are also used in cases of reversal (cancellation) of an invoice. In the SAP system, canceling an invoice isn't possible, but it can be reversed by posting a credit memo. Credit memos will update the same G/L accounts (with opposite debit/credit entries) that were posted with the invoice.

Let's move on to learning how to post a credit memo in the system.

6.9.2 Process Steps

Credit memos are posted via Transaction MIRO. Access the transaction, select CREDIT MEMO in the TRANSACTION field, and enter the PO number and POSTING DATE (Figure 6.29). The system will propose the total invoiced quantity and amount from the PO. With partial reversals, you can change the quantity and amount.

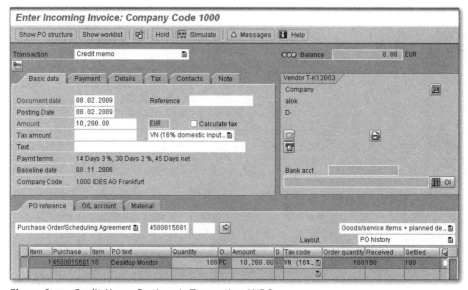

Figure 6.29 Credit Memo Posting via Transaction MIRO

Note

An invoice and a credit memo are also used to cancel each other. For example, if you've posted an incorrect credit memo and you want to reverse (cancel) it, you need to post an invoice document by Transaction MIRO with reference to the PO.

6.10 Invoice Verification in Background Processing

When you post an invoice, the system compares the invoice amount with the PO value. For large invoices with hundreds of line items, this process can take a long time. Thus, to save time, large invoices can be processed via *background processing*.

6.10.1 Business Scenario

Consider an example of a business involved in car manufacturing. The business receives an invoice from a vendor and posts it online via Transaction MIRO. However, sometimes the business receives large invoices that contain several line items, and due to time limitations and large workloads, it becomes difficult to post the invoices online via Transaction MIRO. These invoices can be posted via invoice verification in the background.

For invoice verification in background processing, enter the general invoice data such as invoice amount, tax information, dates, PO number, and so on. This data is saved in the invoice document. Item data isn't entered manually but is instead created by the settlement program. The system checks the total quantity and amount that should be invoiced from the PO, with the amount and tax data entered.

If the total balance amount is zero or within tolerance limits, the SAP system posts the invoice document in the background. If the balance exceeds the tolerance limits, the invoice document and the items created are saved and must be processed later. Settlement Program RMBABG00 is used for background processing. This program can be scheduled in the batch job.

Next, you'll learn how to post invoices through the invoice verification in background functionality.

6.10.2 Process Steps

Follow these steps to post invoices with invoice verification in the background:

1. **Enter the invoice via Transaction MIRA.**
   Enter the invoice via Transaction MIRA, as shown in Figure 6.30. Enter the INVOICE DATE, POSTING DATE, AMOUNT, TAX AMOUNT, and PO number. Upon saving, the system will generate an invoice document number.

2. **Execute the settlement program to post the invoice in the background.**
   Execute Program RMBABG00 via Transaction SA38. Enter the COMPANY CODE, as shown in Figure 6.31, and execute the transaction.

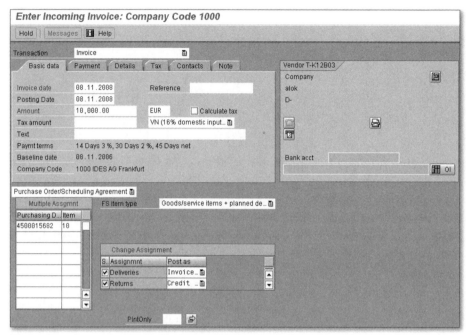

Figure 6.30 Process Invoice for Background Processing via Transaction MIRA

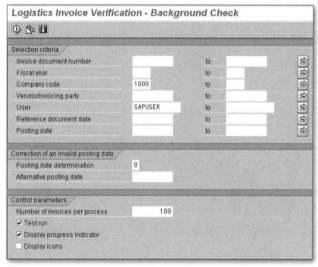

Figure 6.31 Invoice Verification in Background Processing

You'll receive a report of results, as shown in Figure 6.32.

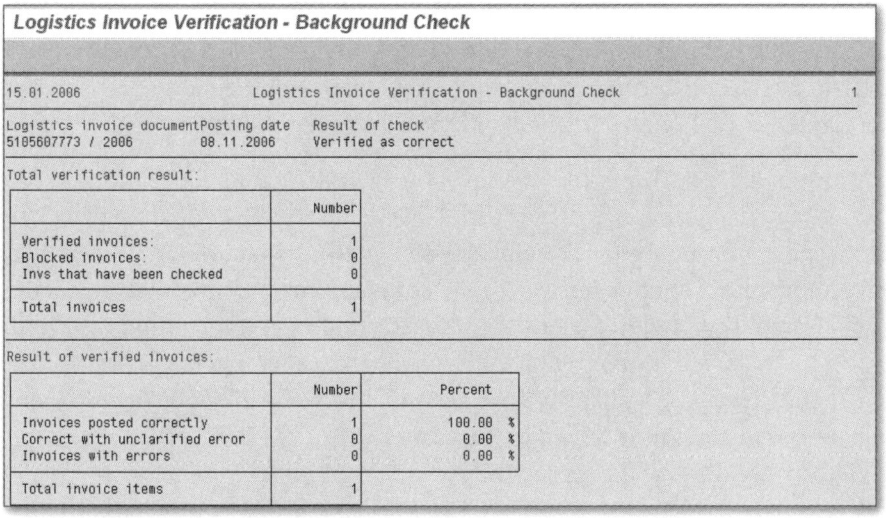

Figure 6.32 shows a report titled "Logistics Invoice Verification - Background Check" containing the following information:

```
Logistics Invoice Verification - Background Check

15.01.2006                    Logistics Invoice Verification - Background Check                    1

Logistics invoice documentPosting date    Result of check
5185607773 / 2006       08.11.2006        Verified as correct

Total verification result:

                                    | Number
    Verified invoices:              |      1
    Blocked invoices:               |      0
    Invs that have been checked     |      0

    Total invoices                  |      1

Result of verified invoices:

                                    | Number |    Percent
    Invoices posted correctly       |      1 | 100.00  %
    Correct with unclarified error  |      0 |   0.00  %
    Invoices with errors            |      0 |   0.00  %

    Total invoice items             |      1
```

Figure 6.32 Results of Invoice Verification in Background Processing

The results report for background processing will also show the error log for an invoice document that contained errors. Invoices with error statuses need to be changed manually. They can then be posted manually, or they can be marked for another background processing job.

6.11 Invoice Reductions

In cases where the invoice amount sent by the vendor is too high, and you want to post an invoice with the correct amount (which is a reduced amount), you can use the invoices with reduction functionality. The system handles this by generating a credit memo.

6.11.1 Business Scenario

A manufacturing enterprise has a procedure to post invoices for delivered materials and their quantities. Sometimes, however, the enterprise receives invoices for both delivered quantities and pending delivery quantities due to a vendor error. During the invoice posting, the manufacturing company wants to reduce the invoice amount so that it doesn't include the undelivered quantity.

The SAP system functionality for invoice posting with reduction allows you to post invoices that contain a greater quantity/value due to a vendor error. While posting the invoice, you can reduce the quantity or value. In this case, the system creates two accounting documents: the first document contains the actual quantities and value, and the second document contains a credit memo for the difference between the actual invoiced quantities/values and the system-suggested quantities/values.

Take a look at Figure 6.33. In this example, the PO is issued to the vendor for 100 pieces of material Mat-1 at $10 per piece. The vendor delivers only part of the order, 60 pieces, and the goods receipt is posted in the system. However, you then receive an invoice from the vendor for the entire 100 pieces instead of the delivered 60. Naturally, you don't want to pay for the undelivered quantity; therefore, you post an invoice with the reduction functionality. When posting the invoice, the system will propose a quantity of 60 pieces and a value of $600. You can enter the quantity and amount specified in the vendor invoice in the VENDOR QUANTITY and VENDOR AMOUNT fields, respectively.

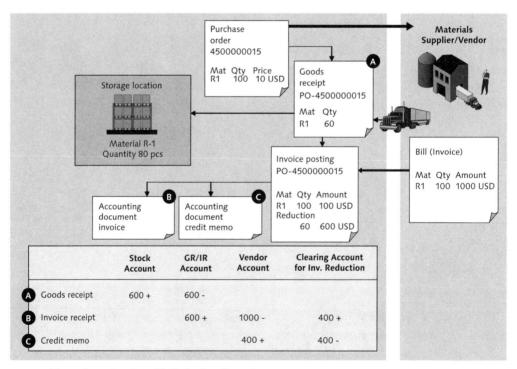

Figure 6.33 Invoice with Reduction Scenario

> **Note**
>
> With the invoice reduction functionality, you don't actually reduce the invoice. Instead, you post an invoice for the actual quantities and values specified in the vendor invoice, and the system posts a credit memo for the amount that needs to be reduced.

The following sections discuss the account postings and process steps involved in invoice reductions.

6.11.2 Account Posting

In an invoice reduction, the system creates an invoice and credit memo, which means that two accounting documents will be created. An example of an account posting was shown in Figure 6.32 in the previous section.

6.11.3 Process Steps

Follow these process steps when handling an invoice reduction:

1. **Create a PO.**
   Create a PO for the vendor via Transaction ME21N. In our example, you would create a PO for 100 pieces at $10 apiece.

2. **Post the goods receipt.**
   Suppose that the vendor has delivered a partial quantity. Post the goods receipt for the partial quantity via Transaction MIGO. In our example, you would post a goods receipt for 60 pieces.

3. **Post the invoice with reduction.**
   For our example, say you've received an invoice for 100 pieces for a total amount of $1,000, instead of for 60 pieces and an amount of $600. Post an invoice with reduction via Transaction MIRO. Then enter the PO number and select INVOICE REDUCTION in the LAYOUT field. The system will propose the quantity and amount due, as shown in Figure 6.34. In the INVOICE POSTING screen, you also see two fields called INVOICE QTY ACC. TO VENDOR and INVOICE AMOUNT ACC. TO VENDOR. These fields are there to enter the quantity and amount, respectively, as specified in the vendor invoice.

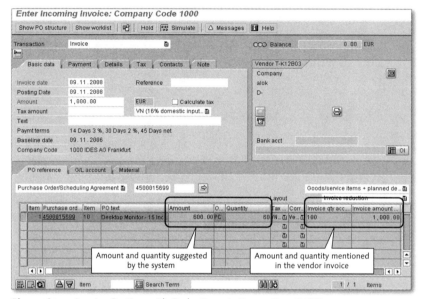

Figure 6.34 Invoice Posting with Reduction via Transaction MIRO

You can view the accounting documents from the DISPLAY INVOICE DOCUMENT screen by clicking the FOLLOW-ON DOCUMENTS button. The system has created two accounting documents (as shown in Figure 6.35): one for the invoice and one for the credit memo.

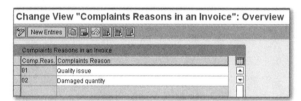

Figure 6.35 Display Invoice: Accounting Documents

6.11.4 Customization Steps for Invoices with Reduction

You can use the MM business function LOG_MM_CI_1 to record the reason for an invoice reduction. You can turn on this business function via Transaction SFW5. This function is available in SAP ERP 6.0, since EHP2.

After you turn on the business function, you'll get the new customizing Transaction SPRO. To access this, go to SAP IMG • MATERIALS MANAGEMENT • LOGISTICS INVOICE VERIFICATION • INCOMING INVOICE • MAINTAIN REASONS FOR INVOICE REDUCTION.

To define the reasons for invoice reduction, enter the reason code and description (see Figure 6.36).

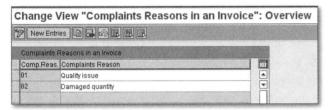

Figure 6.36 Complaints Reasons for Invoice Reductions

After you've defined your reasons, you're ready to use this feature. Go to Transaction MIRO, enter the PO number for the invoice that is due, and select the layout as INVOICE REDUCTION. You'll see a new field COMPLAINTS REASONS; here you can select the reason for reduction as shown in Figure 6.37. You'll get the list of options that you've created in Customizing.

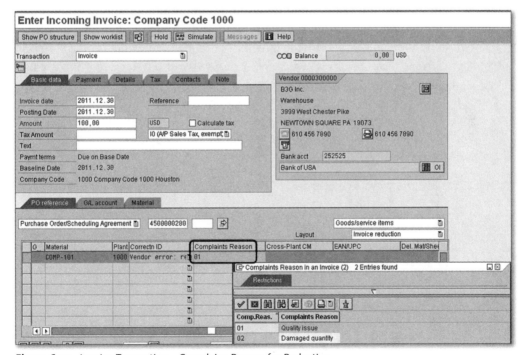

Figure 6.37 Invoice Transaction—Complains Reason for Reduction

You can specify the reason for invoice reduction for each item in an invoice.

6.12   Invoices with Variances

For a particular purchase, the total amount of money on the vendor invoice and the total amount suggested in the system may have a variance, meaning that their values are different from one another. This may happen due to a price difference in any one or more line items. For invoices with more than 100 line items, it becomes very tedious to find those that are causing the difference. Let's discuss the business scenario where this situation can occur and how the SAP system deals with such scenarios.

6.12.1   Business Scenario

A vendor is responsible for supplying several components required in a leading car manufacturing company. Most of the time, the POs contain as many as 200 line items, and sometimes the vendor invoice total amount and the system-suggested total amount don't match. In such a scenario, it becomes cumbersome and time-consuming to quickly identify the line item or items responsible for the variance. Therefore, you can posts an invoice reduction without reference to a specific line item. This scenario is called *total-based invoice reduction*. The business also has another requirement that can be customized in the system, where in the event of a small difference in total amount, the system should accept the vendor invoice and post the difference into a small differences G/L account. The small difference G/L account is a P&L (profit & loss) account type.

There are two ways to do this:

▶ Total-based invoice reduction

▶ Total-based invoice acceptance

We'll now look at the account postings in both scenarios.

6.12.2   Account Posting

The G/L account posting will vary for these scenarios; thus, we'll discuss how the G/L account postings will be carried out in each scenario.

Account Posting in the Total-Based Invoice Reduction Scenario

In total-based invoice reduction, the system creates two accounting documents; the first contains the invoice posting, and the second contains a credit memo for the difference amount. Figure 6.36 shows an example of this. In this figure, you can see that the vendor invoice contains 100 line items and has a total amount of $100,480. However, while posting this invoice, the system supplies a total amount of $100,470. This is a variance of $10. Because there are 100 line items on the invoice, it's time-consuming to identify the line item responsible for the difference; therefore, the invoice should be posted using the total-based reduction functionality. Figure 6.38 also shows the account postings for total-based reductions.

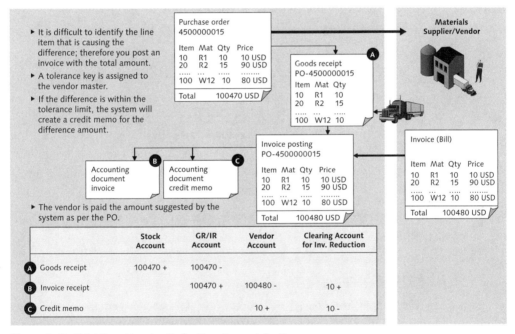

Figure 6.38 Total Based Invoice Reduction: Account Posting

Account Posting in Total-Based Invoice Acceptance Scenario

In total-based invoice acceptance, the system posts the difference amount into a non-operating expense or revenue account, as shown in Figure 6.39.

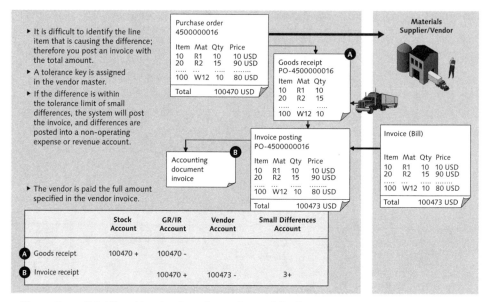

Figure 6.39 Total-Based Invoice Acceptance: Account Posting

In total-based invoice reduction, the system posts the difference to a clearing account and generates a credit memo in a second document to clear this difference. In acceptance-based invoice reduction, the system automatically generates a difference line in an income or expense account.

Let's now take a look at how to post invoices with total-based reduction and total-based acceptance.

6.12.3 Process Steps

The process steps in total-based reduction and total-based acceptance are similar to the standard invoice verification process. You post an invoice via Transaction MIRO, and enter the invoice amount and PO number. The system will show the difference in the BALANCE field, and if this difference is within the tolerance limits, the status will be green.

The system decides whether to proceed with total-based reduction or total-based acceptance by checking the relative tolerance differences. If an invoice difference is within acceptable limits (per the tolerance limit defined in the system), the invoice is posted using the total-based acceptance scenario. If the invoice difference is outside of these limits, the system checks the difference limits for total-based reductions. If the difference is within these limits, the system posts the invoice with total-based reduction. If, however, the difference exceeds these limits, the invoice can't be posted with the difference amount. We'll discuss the setting of tolerance limits in the next section.

6.12.4 Configuration Steps

Follow these configuration steps for total- and acceptance-based invoice reductions:

1. **Define vendor-specific tolerances.**
   During configuration, you can create tolerance groups for each company code, which are then assigned to each vendor in the vendor master record. You define tolerances for both total-based acceptance and total-based invoice reduction. To do this, go to SAP IMG • MATERIALS MANAGEMENT • LOGISTICS INVOICE VERIFICATION • INCOMING INVOICE • CONFIGURE VENDOR-SPECIFIC TOLERANCES.

Figure 6.40 Define Vendor-Specific Tolerances

Enter the small difference limits for positive differences and negative differences, as shown in Figure 6.40. You can enter both absolute value limits and percentage limits. These limits are for total-based invoice acceptance. The last section in the screen is for automatic invoice reduction (total-based invoice reduction) limit values.

2. **Assign tolerance groups in the vendor master record.**
   Assign tolerance groups in the vendor master record via Transaction XK02. Go to the Payment Transaction view, and in the INVOICE VERIFICATION section, enter the TOLERANCE GROUP, as shown in Figure 6.41.

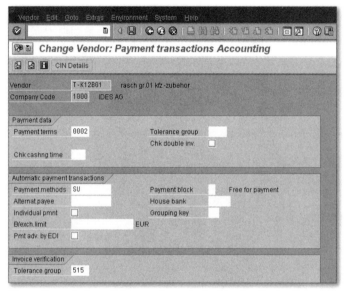

Figure 6.41 Assign a Tolerance Group in the Vendor Master Record

6.13   Taxes in Invoice Verification

Most invoices are taxable. This means that you need to verify that taxes can be entered for value-added tax (VAT) amounts, and according to various tax procedures. During the purchase and sale of goods, taxes are calculated and paid to the vendor or charged to customers, respectively, as shown in Figure 6.42. For VAT, the tax is calculated on the difference between the purchase and sales price. The tax amounts collected from customers are paid to tax authorities.

In the following sections, we'll discuss the information you need to correctly handle taxes during invoice verification.

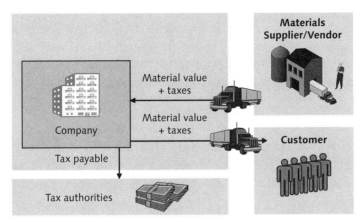

Figure 6.42 Tax Scenario

6.13.1 Entering Tax Data in an Invoice

When posting an invoice in the system, you can select the tax code and enter the tax amount. Alternatively, if you want the system to calculate the tax amount, you can select the Calculate tax checkbox in the invoice transaction screen, as shown in Figure 6.43. The system calculates the tax based on the tax code defined for each line item. Tax codes are configured in the system for various types of taxes.

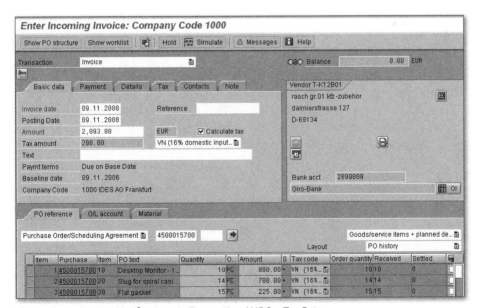

Figure 6.43 Invoice Verification via Transaction MIRO—Tax Entry

6.13.2 Configuration Steps

Tax codes and tax procedures are configured by the person responsible for financial accounting. The SAP system also provides an option to link to an external tax calculation system, such as Taxware, which many customers find helpful.

MM allows you to maintain default values for tax codes. To do so, go to SAP IMG • MATERIALS MANAGEMENT • LOGISTICS INVOICE VERIFICATION • INCOMING INVOICE • MAINTAIN DEFAULT VALUES FOR TAX CODES. In this step, you can define the default tax codes for each company code. Click on the NEW ENTRIES button and enter the company code, the default tax code, and the default tax code for unplanned delivery costs (Figure 6.44).

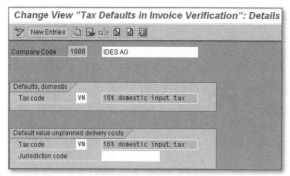

Figure 6.44 Maintain Default Tax Codes

6.14 Discounts in Invoice Verification

You may have a scenario where a vendor offers you discounts based on payment settlement dates. For example, the vendor may tell you that if you make payment within 10 days from the date of invoice, you get a discount of 5%; if you make payment within 15 days, you get a discount of 2%; and after 15 days, you don't get a discount. Such scenarios can be managed via the PAYMENT tab in the SAP system. You can define the payment terms in configuration, and these payment terms can be selected in the PO. When posting an invoice, the system copies the payment terms from the PO.

During invoice verification, you can enter the payment terms of fixed cash discount amounts, as shown in Figure 6.45. The PAYMENT tab displays the payment terms that are supplied from the PO, which can be changed here.

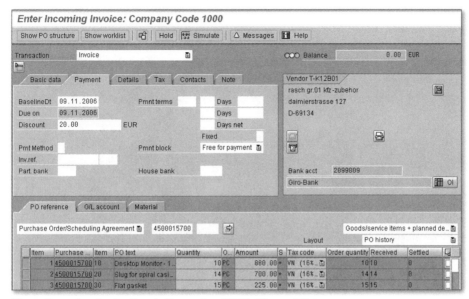

Figure 6.45 Invoice Posting via Transaction MIRO: Discount Entry

6.14.1 Account Postings

Cash discounts can be posted via either gross posting or net posting. We'll discuss both ways of posting in detail.

Gross Posting

In gross posting, the system ignores the cash discount amount at the time of the invoice posting and posts the cash discount amount into the cash discount G/L account at the time of payment. In this scenario, the cash discount amount isn't credited into stock accounts or cost accounts. Figure 6.46 shows an illustration of the gross-posting scenario.

Net Posting

In net posting, the system posts the cash discount amount to the cash discount clearing account at the time of the invoice posting, and the cash discount clearing G/L account is cleared at the time of payment. Figure 6.47 shows an illustration of the net-posting scenario.

You can define whether postings should be gross or net for each document type in Customizing.

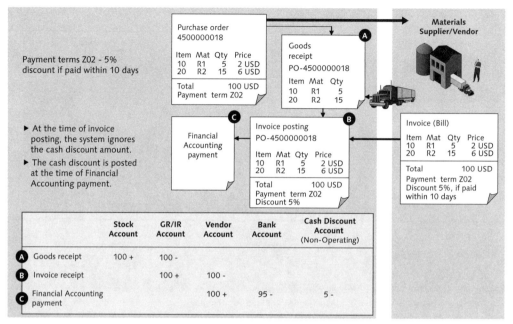

Figure 6.46 Account Posting: Cash Discounts Gross Posting

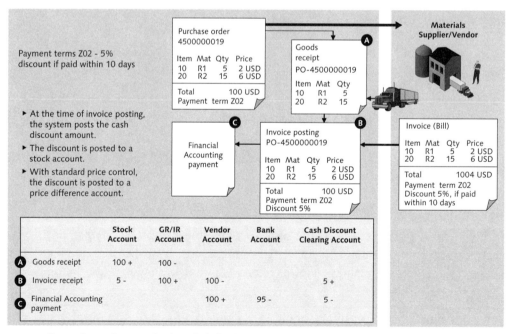

Figure 6.47 Account Posting: Cash Discounts Net Posting

6.14.2 Configuration of Gross/Net Posting

To configure gross or net posting for a document type, go to SAP IMG • Financial Accounting • Accounts Receivable and Accounts Payable • Business Transactions • Incoming Invoices/Credit Memos • Carry Out and Check Document Settings • Define Document Types. You'll see a list of document types. Select the document type for invoice verification, and click on the Details button. If you want net posting, select the Net document type checkbox in the Control data section. If you want gross posting, leave this checkbox blank (Figure 6.48).

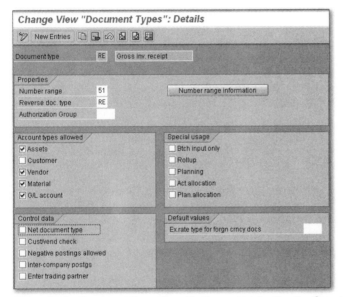

Figure 6.48 Document Type: Gross Posting or Net Posting Configuration

6.14.3 Configuration of Payment Terms

To configure payment terms, go to SAP IMG • Financial Accounting • Accounts Receivable and Accounts Payable • Business Transactions • Incoming Invoices/Credit Memos • Maintain Terms of Payment. You'll see a list of payment terms defined by SAP (Figure 6.49). Here, you can change existing payment terms or define new payment terms.

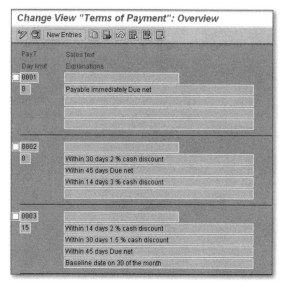

Figure 6.49 Defining Payment Terms

6.15   Invoice Blocking

After vendor invoices are verified and posted into the system, the finance department makes the payment to the vendor. However, there may be a scenario where you want to block the invoice for payment processing for a specific reason, such as quantity or price variance.

6.15.1   Business Scenario

Imagine a situation where an enterprise receives invoices for a higher amount than expected. As a result, the company wants to block the invoices for payment processing until the differences are resolved with the vendor. Invoices can be blocked manually or automatically due to a variety of different variance types, as follows:

- ▶ Blocking due to a quantity variance
- ▶ Blocking due to a price variance
- ▶ Blocking due to a quality inspection
- ▶ Blocking due to an amount
- ▶ Stochastic blocking

The SAP system allows you to define tolerance limits for each variance type. When posting an invoice, the system checks for different variances, and if the variance is more than the tolerance limit, the system will automatically block the invoice for payment. Figure 6.50 shows an example of invoice blocking due to a price variance. The blocking reason is filled in the vendor line item in the FI document. You can also select the blocking reason manually.

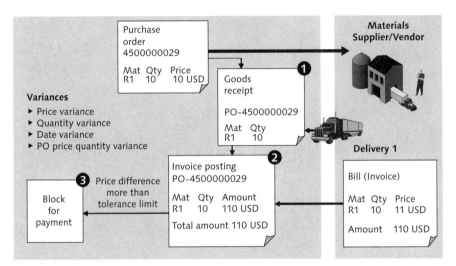

Figure 6.50 Invoice Blocking Scenario

Payment won't be released when invoices are blocked for payment. When the variances are resolved, you must indicate this by releasing the invoice for payment processing (discussed later in this section).

In the following sections, we'll discuss the most important variance types.

6.15.2 Quantity Variance

A quantity variance occurs if the invoice quantity is more than the goods receipt quantity. Invoices that are blocked because of a quantity variance can be released when you receive the balance quantity of the goods. Figure 6.50 shows a quantity variance example. A PO for 10 pieces of material R1 at $10/piece is issued to the vendor. However, the vendor delivers only 8 pieces of material R1. After the goods receipt, you receive an invoice for 10 pieces, and the invoiced quantity is more than the goods receipt quantity. This invoice can be blocked due to quantity variance.

After some time, you receive the balance quantity and post another goods receipt. Now the variance no longer exists, and the invoice can be released for payment. All three documents (the goods receipt for 8 pieces, the invoice receipt for 10 pieces, and the goods receipt for 2 pieces) create accounting documents and post to different G/L accounts. Figure 6.51 shows the account postings for a quantity variance.

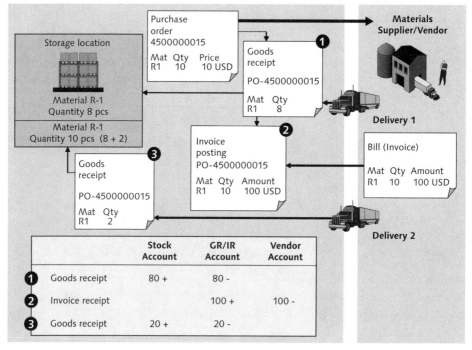

		Stock Account	GR/IR Account	Vendor Account
①	Goods receipt	80 +	80 -	
②	Invoice receipt		100 +	100 -
③	Goods receipt	20 +	20 -	

Figure 6.51 Quantity Variance Scenario and Account Posting

6.15.3 Price Variance

A price variance occurs if the invoice price is more than the PO price of an item. Figure 6.52, in the next subsection, shows a price variance example. A PO for 10 pieces of material R1 at $10/piece is issued to the vendor. Goods are received against the PO, but the invoice received from the vendor has a price of $11/piece. In this case, the invoice should be blocked until the price variance is resolved.

The account postings for a price variance depend on the price control defined in the material master record and can be either posted with a standard price, or posted with a moving average price.

Account Posting

Figure 6.52 shows the account postings for standard price valuation. The price difference amount is posted to the price difference G/L account. In this case, the standard price, as defined in the material master, can't be changed.

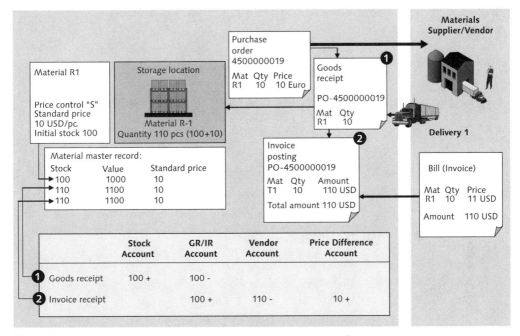

Figure 6.52 Price Variance: Account Posting for Standard Price Control

Account Posting with Moving Average Price

Figure 6.53 shows the account postings for a moving average price. In this case, the price difference amounts are posted into stock accounts, and the moving average price is changed. If there's insufficient stock quantity of the material, the system will post the price difference amount to the price difference G/L account.

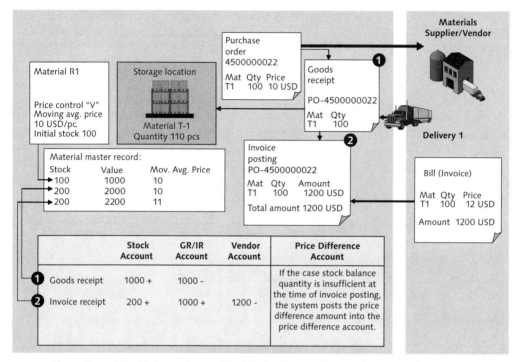

Figure 6.53 Price Variance: Account Posting for Moving Average Price Control

6.15.4 Stochastic Blocking

Stochastic blocking allows for the system to randomly check invoices and then block invoices based on threshold values defined in the configuration. This blocking process is used to check that users are verifying and posting invoices accurately.

Stochastic blocking is configured in two steps:

1. **Activate stochastic blocking.**
   To activate stochastic blocking for a company, go to SAP IMG • MATERIALS MANAGEMENT • LOGISTICS INVOICE VERIFICATION • INVOICE BLOCK • STOCHASTIC BLOCK • ACTIVATE STOCHASTIC BLOCK. Then select the checkbox next to the appropriate company code (Figure 6.54).

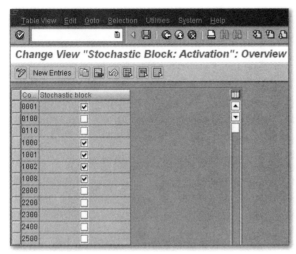

Figure 6.54 Activating Stochastic Block

2. **Set the stochastic block.**

In this step, you define the degree of probability that an invoice will be stochastically blocked. The degree of probability depends on the invoice value. For example, if the threshold value is $2,000 for a particular company code and the probability is 50%, an invoice with a value of $2,000 would have a 50% probability of being blocked. An invoice with a value of $1,000 would have a 25% probability of being blocked.

> **Note**
>
> Probability percentages increase or decrease based on the threshold value and the value of the invoice.

To define threshold values and percentage probabilities for each company code, go to SAP IMG • MATERIALS MANAGEMENT • LOGISTICS INVOICE VERIFICATION • INVOICE BLOCK • STOCHASTIC BLOCK • SET STOCHASTIC BLOCK. Enter the threshold value and percentage probability for the company code, as shown in Figure 6.55.

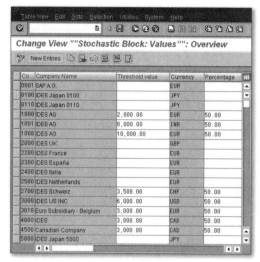

Figure 6.55 Define Stochastic Block Values

6.15.5 Manual Blocking

Users can manually block invoices at the time of the invoice posting via Transaction MIRO. This can be done at the header level, without reference to a particular line item. To do so, go to the PAYMENT tab and select BLOCKED FOR PAYMENT in the PMNT BLOCK dropdown list (Figure 6.56).

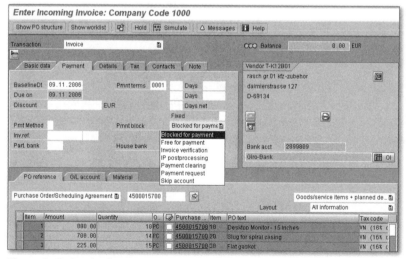

Figure 6.56 Invoice Posting via Transaction MIRO: Manually Blocking an Invoice

You can also block a particular line item during invoice posting. To do so, select the MANUAL BLOCK checkbox, as shown in Figure 6.57 for the first line item.

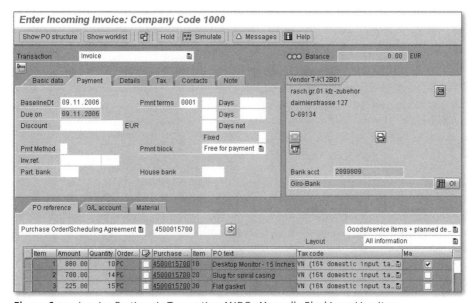

Figure 6.57 Invoice Posting via Transaction MIRO: Manually Blocking a Line Item

We've now discussed the various blocking reasons and ways of blocking invoices such as automatic blocking and manual blocking. Furthermore, you must define tolerance limits to automatically block invoices. We'll now explain how these tolerances can be configured in the system.

6.15.6 Tolerances

Tolerance limits can be defined for different variances, and they can be absolute values or percentage limits. Reasons for blocking are defined as tolerance keys. The SAP-defined tolerance keys are as follows:

▸ **AN:** Amount for item without order reference

▸ **AP:** Amount for item with order reference

▸ **BD:** Form small differences automatically

- ▶ **BR:** Percentage order price quantity unit variance (invoice receipt before goods receipt)
- ▶ **BW:** Percentage order price quantity unit variance (goods receipt before invoice receipt)
- ▶ **DQ:** Exceeded amount—quantity variance
- ▶ **DW:** Quantity variance—goods receipt quantity equals zero
- ▶ **KW:** Variance from condition value
- ▶ **LA:** Amount of blanket PO
- ▶ **LD:** Blanket PO time limit exceeded
- ▶ **PP:** Price variance
- ▶ **PS:** Price variance of the estimated price
- ▶ **ST:** Date variance (value × days)
- ▶ **VP:** Moving average price variance

To configure tolerance limits, go to SAP IMG • Materials Management • Logistics Invoice Verification • Invoice Block • Set Tolerance Limits. You'll see a list of tolerance keys for each company code (Figure 6.58). To define the limit, select the tolerance key and company code combination, and click on the Details button.

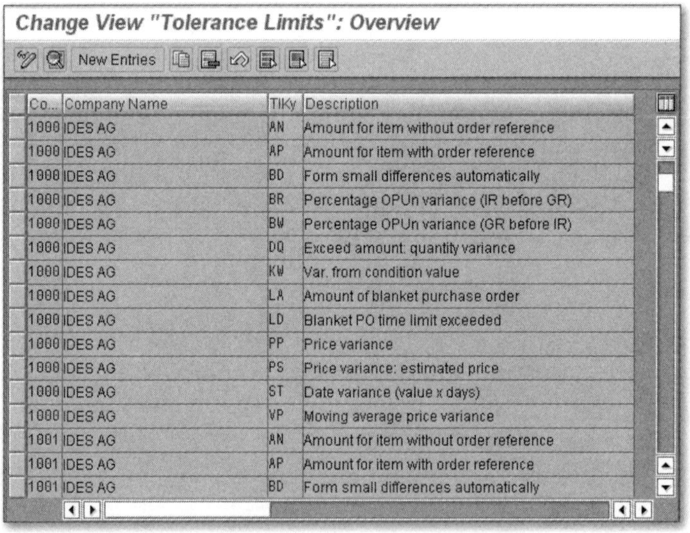

Figure 6.58 Defining Tolerance Limits

You can define the lower and upper limits for the tolerance key, as shown in Figure 6.59. If you select the DO NOT CHECK radio button, the system won't check the tolerance limit. You can also define absolute values and/or percentage values; if you define both, the system will check the lower value.

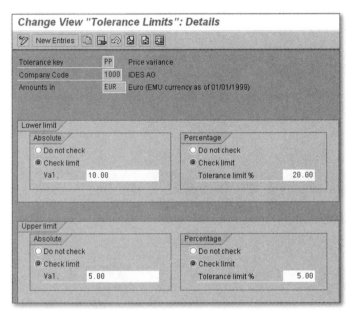

Figure 6.59 Defining Tolerance Limits: Details

Now that you understand how and why invoices are blocked, let's discuss how they can be released for payment processing.

6.15.7 Releasing Blocked Invoices

When the variance issue is resolved, you can release the invoice for payment processing either automatically or manually. To release invoices, use Transaction MRBR and enter the selection criteria (Figure 6.60).

Next, select the PROCESSING option as RELEASE MANUALLY or RELEASE AUTOMATI-CALLY. With manual release, the system displays the list of blocked invoices and allows you to select which ones you want to release (Figure 6.61).

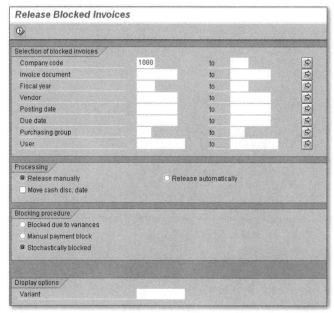

Figure 6.60 Release Blocked Invoice: Transaction MRBR

Release Blocked Invoices

Doc. no.	Year	Crcy	TransIDate	Exch.r...	T...	Posting Date	CoCd	Invoicing pty.	Name	User name	Bline date	...Dy...	Disc.1
5105607403	2006	EUR	20.02.2006	1.000...	RE	20.02.2006	1000	T-K12C01	C.E.B Berlin Gr.01	SAPUSER	22.02.2006	0	0.000
5105607403	2006	EUR	20.02.2006	1.000...	RE	20.02.2006	1000	T-K12C01	C.E.B Berlin Gr.01	SAPUSER	22.02.2006	0	0.000
5105607433	2006	EUR	21.03.2006	1.000...	RE	21.03.2006	1000	T-K12D01	Burohandel Leifritz Gr.01	SAPUSER	21.02.2006	0	0.000
5105607434	2006	EUR	21.03.2006	1.000...	RE	21.03.2006	1000	T-K12D01	Burohandel Leifritz Gr.01	SAPUSER	21.02.2006	0	0.000
5105607435	2006	EUR	21.03.2006	1.000...	RE	21.03.2006	1000	T-K12D01	Burohandel Leifritz Gr.01	SAPUSER	21.02.2006	0	0.000
5105607482	2006	EUR	10.05.2006	1.000...	RE	10.05.2006	1000	T-K515A01	Sapsota Company Limited	SAPUSER	10.05.2006	10	2.000
5105607522	2006	EUR	28.07.2006	1.000...	RE	28.07.2006	1000	T-L20C03	KAKE	SAPUSER	28.08.2006	0	0.000
5105607562	2006	EUR	02.09.2006	1.000...	RE	02.09.2006	1000	T-K10B01	kavita	SAPUSER	30.09.2006	0	0.000
5105607562	2006	EUR	02.09.2006	1.000...	RE	02.09.2006	1000	T-K10B01	kavita	SAPUSER	30.09.2006	0	0.000
5105607582	2006	EUR	06.09.2006	1.000...	RE	06.09.2006	1000	T-K12C01	C.E.B Berlin Gr.01	SAPUSER	06.09.2006	0	0.000
5105607602	2006	EUR	19.09.2006	1.000...	RE	19.09.2006	1000	T-K12B01	rasch gr.01 kfz -zubehor	SAPUSER	19.09.2006	0	0.000
5105607602	2006	EUR	19.09.2006	1.000...	RE	19.09.2006	1000	T-K12B01	rasch gr.01 kfz -zubehor	SAPUSER	19.09.2006	0	0.000
5105607622	2006	EUR	03.10.2006	1.000...	RE	03.10.2006	1000	T-K12C01	C.E.B Berlin Gr.01	SAPUSER	31.10.2006	0	0.000
5105607652	2006	EUR	17.10.2006	1.000...	RE	17.10.2006	1000	T-L15A01	T-L15A01	SAPUSER	18.10.2006	0	0.000
5105607652	2006	EUR	17.10.2006	1.000...	RE	17.10.2006	1000	T-L15A01	T-L15A01	SAPUSER	18.10.2006	0	0.000

Figure 6.61 Release Blocked Invoice Manually: Transaction MRBR

Note

You can also define a batch job via Transaction SM36 to execute the automatic release of blocked invoices by using Program RM08RELEASE.

6.16 GR/IR Account Maintenance

A goods receipt/invoice receipt (GR/IR) account is an intermediate account used for clearing goods receipts and invoices. A GR/IR clearing account is cleared for a PO item when the delivered quantity and the invoiced quantity are the same. The quantity differences between the goods receipt and invoice receipt for a PO result in a balance on the GR/IR account.

If an invoice quantity is more than the quantity delivered, this results in a balance amount on the GR/IR account, and the system expects additional goods receipts.

If the goods receipt quantity is more than the invoiced quantity, this results in a balance amount on the GR/IR account, and the system expects additional invoice postings.

If no additional goods invoice receipts are expected in the preceding scenario, you must manually clear the GR/IR account. Figure 6.62 shows an example of GR/IR account maintenance. One hundred pieces of a material are delivered, as requested in the PO. However, an invoice is posted for only 80 pieces, and no additional invoices are expected from the vendor. The quantity difference of 20 pieces results in a balance of $200 in the GR/IR account. When you clear the GR/IR account with the GR/IR account maintenance transaction, the system will create an accounting document and clear the GR/IR difference of $200.

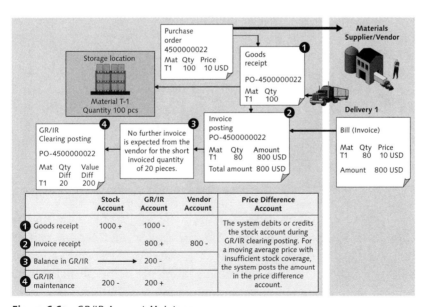

Figure 6.62 GR/IR Account Maintenance

6.16.1 Account Posting

The GR/IR account clearing transaction posting will post an accounting document. Refer to Figure 6.63 for an example of a G/L account posting.

We'll now look at the process steps used to clear a GR/IR account.

6.16.2 Process Steps

You can clear the GR/IR account via Transaction MR11, as shown in Figure 6.62. Enter the different selection criteria and execute the transaction.

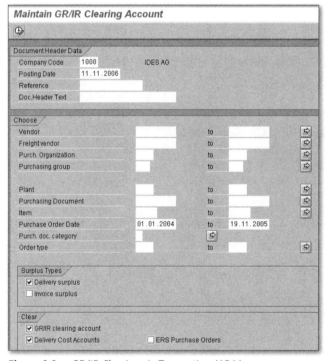

Figure 6.63 GR/IR Clearing via Transaction MR11

If the PREPARE LIST processing option is selected, you'll see a list of POs causing the balance in the GR/IR account (Figure 6.64). This list displays the PO number, line item number, quantity difference, value difference, and so on. Select the appropriate line, and click on the POST button to clear the difference in the GR/IR account.

Maintain GR/IR Clearing Account

| Purch.Doc. | Item | PO date | Name 1 | | | Material | | Plnt | Short text | | |
Purch.Doc.	Item	Account key name		FYrRef	Ref. doc.	Received quantity	Quantity invoiced			Difference qty	Difference value
4500015473	10	28.04.2006	C.E.B Berlin Gr.01			T-B111		1000	Casing		
4500015473	10	GR/IR clearing				100	110			10-	750.00-
4500015420	10	05.03.2006	Eletroblitz GmbH Gr.01					1000	paintingeee		
4500015420	10	GR/IR clearing		2006	100000131					1	225.00
4500015496	10	28.08.2006	KAKE					1000	Painting		
4500015496	10	GR/IR clearing		2006	100000132					1	500.00

Company code 1000 IDES AG
Currency EUR

Figure 6.64 GR/IR Clearing: Process Manually from Purchase Order List

The GR/IR clearing document is updated in the PO history.

If GR/IR account maintenance has been executed for a PO item, the account maintenance document is displayed in a separate transaction in the PO history. If there is an unexpected goods receipt or invoice receipt for the PO item after account maintenance, you can cancel the account maintenance document. To do so, choose LOGISTICS • MATERIALS MANAGEMENT • LOGISTICS INVOICE VERIFICATION • GR/IR ACCOUNT MAINTENANCE • DISPLAY/CANCEL ACCOUNT MAINTENANCE DOCUMENT (Transaction MR11SHOW), and enter the document number. Press Enter, and in next screen click the REVERSE button and save it. This will create a reverse accounting document that will also be updated in the PO history. You can now post the GR or IR against the PO.

6.17   Duplicate Invoice Check

Imagine a scenario where a vendor mistakenly sends you an invoice twice, resulting in duplicate invoices being posted in your system. For this scenario, the SAP system provides the *duplicate invoice check* functionality that prevents incoming invoices from being accidentally entered and paid more than once. To set up this functionality, go to SAP IMG • MATERIALS MANAGEMENT • LOGISTICS INVOICE VERIFICATION • INCOMING INVOICE • SET CHECK FOR DUPLICATE INVOICES. FOR EACH COMPANY CODE, and then select whether to activate or deactivate the check criteria for the company code, reference document number, and invoice date (Figure 6.65). The system will check for duplicate invoices only for the selected criteria. For example, if you've selected CHECK REFERENCE for a company code, then posting two invoices in the same company code with the same reference number will result in a "Duplicate Invoices Found" message.

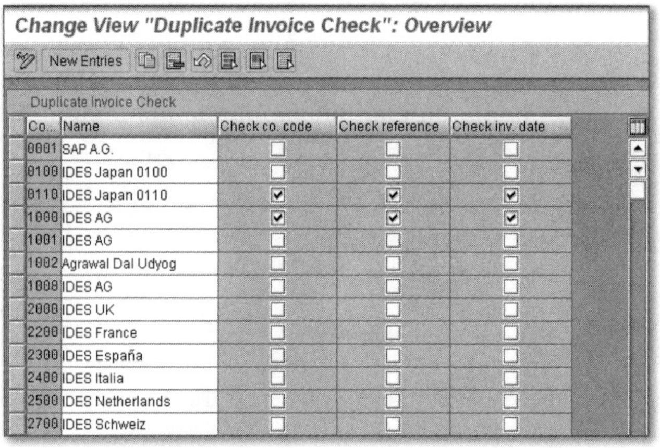

Co...	Name	Check co. code	Check reference	Check inv. date
0001	SAP A.G.	☐	☐	☐
0100	IDES Japan 0100	☐	☐	☐
0110	IDES Japan 0110	☑	☑	☑
1000	IDES AG	☑	☑	☑
1001	IDES AG	☐	☐	☐
1002	Agrawal Dal Udyog	☐	☐	☐
1008	IDES AG	☐	☐	☐
2000	IDES UK	☐	☐	☐
2200	IDES France	☐	☐	☐
2300	IDES España	☐	☐	☐
2400	IDES Italia	☐	☐	☐
2500	IDES Netherlands	☐	☐	☐
2700	IDES Schweiz	☐	☐	☐

Figure 6.65 Settings for Duplicate Invoice Checking

6.18 Invoices for POs with Down Payments

A down payment is a type of payment made in advance during the onset of the purchase of goods and services. The payment typically represents only a percentage of the full purchase price; in some cases, it isn't refundable if the deal falls through. Financing arrangements are made by the purchaser to cover the remaining amount owed to the seller. Making a down payment and then paying the rest of the price through installments is a method that makes expensive assets more affordable for the typical person. Down payment functionality in Purchasing is available from SAP ERP 6.0, EHP4. Let's discuss the down payment business scenario, process steps, and configuration steps.

6.18.1 Business Scenario

A leading heavy-engineering company in Asia is involved in manufacturing boilers, heat exchangers, and so on. Whenever your company wants to buy any specific machinery or plant equipment from this manufacturer, your company needs to make the advance payment (down payment), and then the company manufactures and delivers the material. The remaining balance of the total payment is paid upon the delivery of the goods.

You can define the down payment amount in a PO, and the down payment can be processed to the vendor with reference to the PO. Let's discuss how to set this up in a step-by-step process.

6.18.2 Process Steps

Follow these steps to run through the complete down payment scenario:

1. **Create a PO with the down payment amount.**
   Go to Transaction ME21N; enter the vendor, material, quantity, and so on; and then click on the PAYMENT PROCESSING tab in the PO header. Select the down payment category in DP CATEGORY. Enter the down payment amount in DOWN PAYMENT AMT or enter an amount in DOWN PAYMENT %, and then enter the due date in DP DATE as shown in Figure 6.66. After entering all of the details, save the PO.

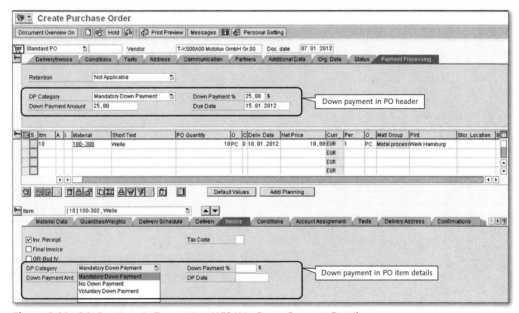

Figure 6.66 PO Creation via Transaction ME21N—Down Payment Details

The standard SAP system contains the following categories of predefined down payments:

- ▸ **M:** The down payment request/down payment is mandatory.
- ▸ **V:** The down payment request/down payment is voluntary.
- ▸ **N:** No down payment request/down payment is necessary.
- ▸ **(blank):** The down payment request/down payment isn't active (field is blank).

You can enter the down payment either on a header level or an item level. If you enter in the header level, the down payment is applicable for all of the items and is calculated on the total value of the PO. If you have multiple lines items, and only a few items are under the down payment condition, you can enter at the item level instead of header level.

2. **Process the down payment.**

   For making the down payments for the PO, there is a transaction called Down-Payment Monitoring for PO. Access Transaction ME2DP, go to SAP MENU • LOGISTICS • MATERIALS MANAGEMENT • PURCHASING • PURCHASE ORDER • REPORTING • DOWN-PAYMENT MONITORING FOR PO, or use Report RM06DPMONITOR.

   In the first selection screen, you can enter the various search criteria such as vendor, purchasing document number, and so on, and then execute the report. After execution, you'll get a list of POs due for down payment as shown in Figure 6.67.

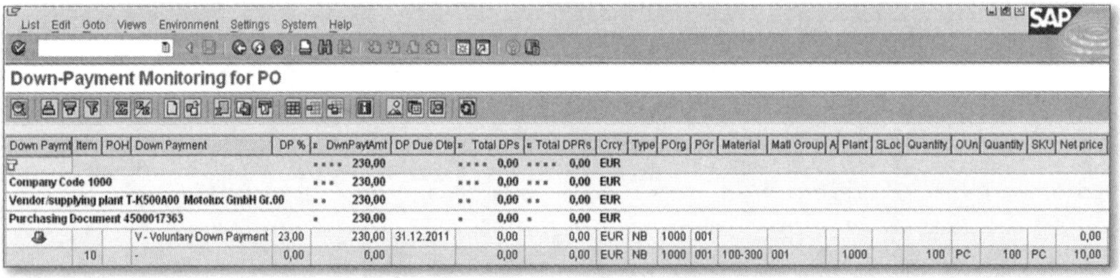

Figure 6.67 Down Payment Monitoring

You can create the down payment request or down payment from this screen by selecting the PO and clicking on the CREATE button or by pressing [Shift] +

F8 . You'll see a screen as shown in Figure 6.68 showing the PO number and providing an option to select either DOWN PAYMENT REQUEST or DOWN PMNT.

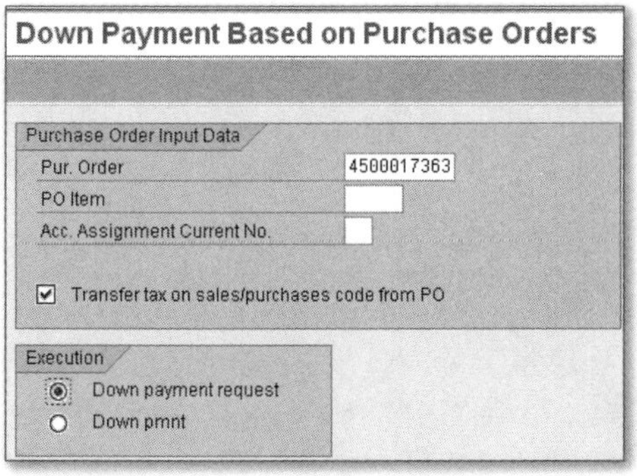

Figure 6.68 Down Payment Creation

After selecting the appropriate option, press Enter , and the screen shown in Figure 6.69 appears. Enter the down payment amount and press Enter .

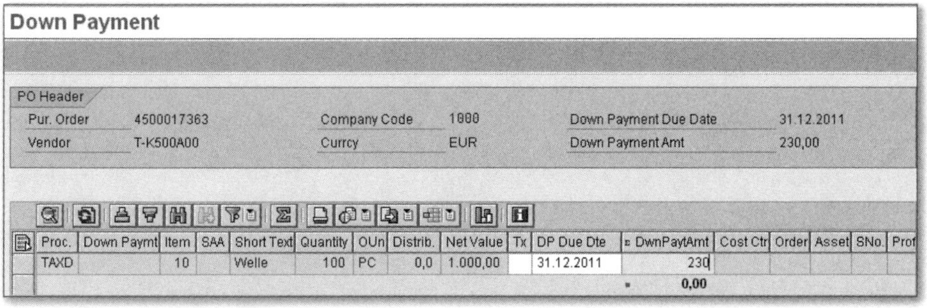

Figure 6.69 Down Payment Entry Screen

Next, you'll see a down payment processing screen as shown in Figure 6.70. This is the down payment transaction used in FI (Transaction F-47 for Down Payment Request and F-48 for Down Payment). Enter the bank account number you want to use to make the down payment, select the SPECIAL G/L IND, and save.

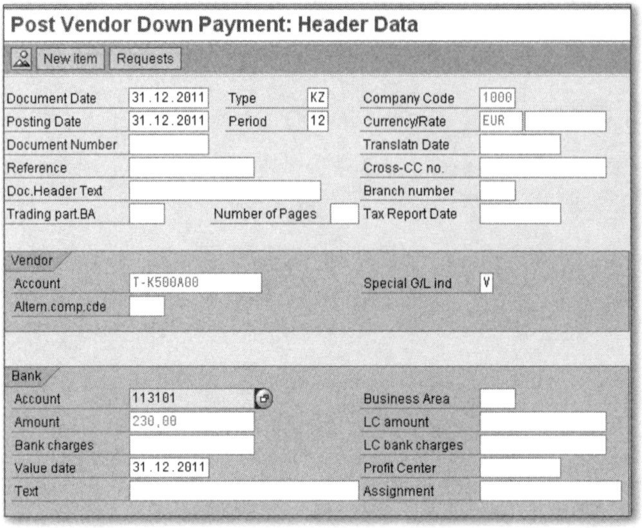

Post Vendor Down Payment: Header Data

New item | Requests

Document Date	31.12.2011	Type	KZ	Company Code	1000
Posting Date	31.12.2011	Period	12	Currency/Rate	EUR
Document Number				Translatn Date	
Reference				Cross-CC no.	
Doc.Header Text				Branch number	
Trading part.BA		Number of Pages		Tax Report Date	

Vendor
Account	T-K500A00	Special G/L ind	V
Altern.comp.cde			

Bank
Account	113101	Business Area	
Amount	230,00	LC amount	
Bank charges		LC bank charges	
Value date	31.12.2011	Profit Center	
Text		Assignment	

Figure 6.70 Down Payment Posting Screen

After posting the down payment, you can check the PO status by accessing Transaction ME2DP as shown in Figure 6.71.

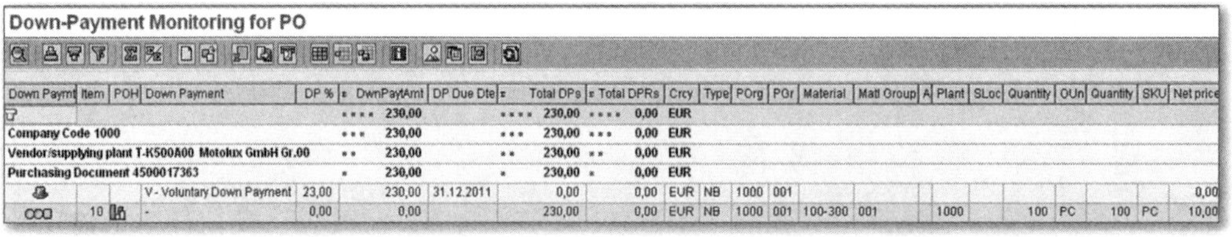

Down-Payment Monitoring for PO

Down Paym	Item	POH	Down Payment	DP %	DwnPayAmt	DP Due Dte	Total DPs	Total DPRs	Crcy	Type	POrg	POr	Material	Matl Group	A	Plant	SLoc	Quantity	OUn	Quantity	SKU	Net price
					230,00		230,00	0,00	EUR													
Company Code 1000					230,00		230,00	0,00	EUR													
Vendor/supplying plant T-K500A00 Motolux GmbH Gr.00					230,00		230,00	0,00	EUR													
Purchasing Document 4500017363					230,00		230,00	0,00	EUR													
			V - Voluntary Down Payment	23,00	230,00	31.12.2011	0,00	0,00	EUR	NB	1000	001									0,00
	10		-		0,00		230,00	0,00	EUR	NB	1000	001	100-300	001		1000		100	PC	100	PC	10,00

Figure 6.71 Down Payment Monitoring

The green traffic signal light means the down payment has been posted. You can also click on the PO history symbol to see the down payment transaction listed in the PO history.

3. **Post the goods receipt.**
Post the GR with reference to the PO by using Transaction MIGO.

4. **Post the invoice.**
To post the invoice, go to Transaction MIRO, enter the date and PO numbers, and press Enter. An information message will pop up as shown in Figure 6.72 stating that down payments for POs exist.

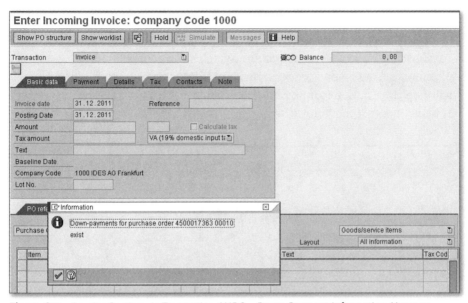

Figure 6.72 Invoice Posting via Transaction MIRO—Down Payment Information Message

Enter the amount and other required details in the invoice and press ⌷Enter⌷. The pop-up message shown in Figure 6.73 appears.

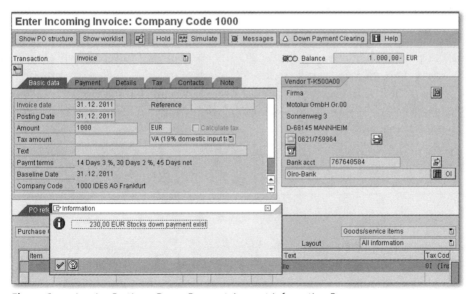

Figure 6.73 Invoice Posting—Down Payment Amount Information Popup

This message alerts the user that his down payment exists and can be settled during posting.

To adjust the down payment amount (which you've already posted as a down payment) during invoice, click on the DOWN PAYMENT CLEARING button, which will pop up a new screen as shown in Figure 6.74. Enter the down payment amount and post the invoice.

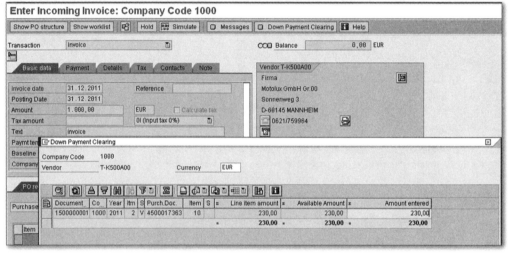

Figure 6.74 Invoice Posting—Down Payment Clearing Screen

After posting the invoice, go to the PO HISTORY tab via Transaction ME23N. As shown in Figure 6.75, you'll see the GR, invoice, and two down payment transactions. The first is when you made the down payment, and the second is posted automatically during invoice verification; the down payment amount is adjusted with the invoice amount.

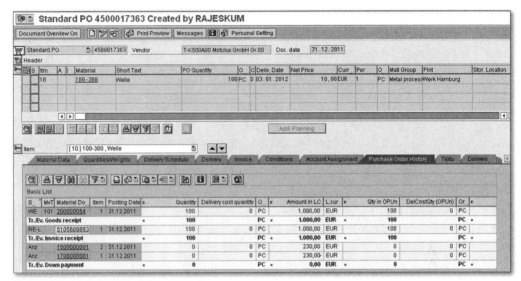

Figure 6.75 Display PO—History Details

You can also check the vendor line item display in FI via Transaction FBL1N as shown in Figure 6.76.

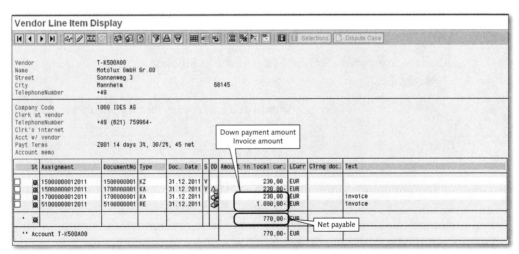

Figure 6.76 Vendor Account Line Item List—Transaction FBL1N

You can see the net open payable to vendor is different from the invoice amount and down payment amount, which was already paid. You can see that 230 Euro was paid to the vendor as down payment, and the invoice is posted with 1000 Euro. The net open payable to the vendor is 770 Euro.

6.18.3 Activate Down Payment in Purchasing

To use the down payment in the Purchasing functionality you need to activate the business function LOG_MMFI_P2P in Transaction SFW5 (Figure 6.77).

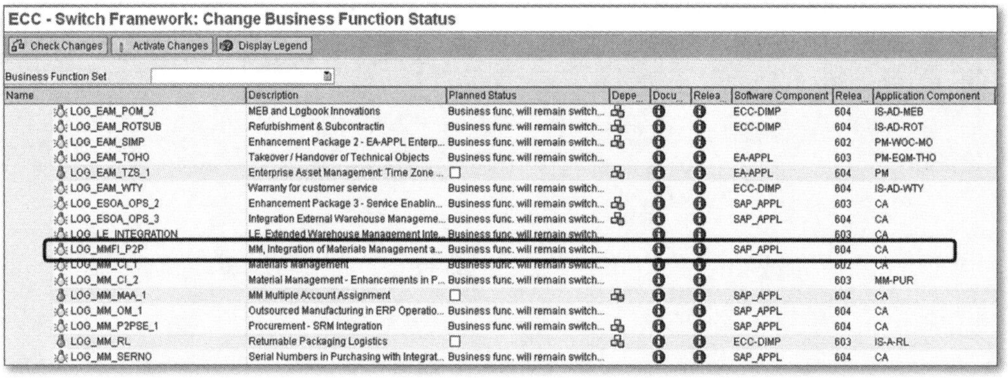

Figure 6.77 Switch Framework—Activation of Business Function

Additional enhancements in the down payment process can be done through the following BAdIs:

▶ ME_PROCESS_PO_CUST (Enhancement for Processing the Enjoy Purchase Order [Customer])
Define the conditions when down payments are mandatory, in the methods CHECK, PROCESS_HEADER, and PROCESS_ITEM. For example, you can define that down payments are required for PO values as of a specific value.

▶ BADI_CALC_DP_VALUES (Default Values for Vendor Down Payment Clearing)
Define default values for down payment clearing in logistics invoice verification. BAdI method CALC_PROPOSED_VALUES contains two new import parameters to help you do this.

▶ MRM_DOWNPAYMENT (Down Payments)
Control whether down payment clearing is possible directly in logistics invoice verification. If you specify that the system does not output the message "Down payments exist for this purchase order" (Message code M8 318), the DOWN PAYMENT CLEARING pushbutton isn't displayed, and the DOWN PAYMENT CLEARING option isn't available.

6.19   Invoices for POs with Retention Money

Retention money is part of an invoice amount that is retained until a defined due date (e.g., the end of the warranty period) to ensure that the delivery of materials or the performance of services is as defined in the contract.

As of SAP ERP 6.0 EHP4 (SAP_APPL 604), Business Function MM, Integration of Materials Management and Financial Accounting (LOG_MMFI_P2P), you can retain parts of the invoice amount until a defined due date to ensure the fulfillment of the contract when materials are delivered or services performed.

6.19.1   Business Scenario

A utility company in Mauritius is involved in power generation, transmission, and distribution, and they procure various materials and services via tender process. (*Tender* means they issue the request for a quotation on their website, and submit their quotation on or before the final submission date based on the information seen in leading newspapers regarding other interested vendors.) The company selects the most competitive vendor with the terms and condition that 20% of the total purchase value will be retained as a warranty of material/services provided. This 20% amount will be paid to the vendor after one year from the date of materials/ services receipt.

The 20% of amount is a type of security. If the product is faulty or the services are unsatisfactory, the company can deduct the amount from this retained money.

Let's consider the scenario in SAP. If you look at Figure 6.78, you can see that the PO has been sent to the vendor with retention money of 10% and a total PO value of 100 Euro.

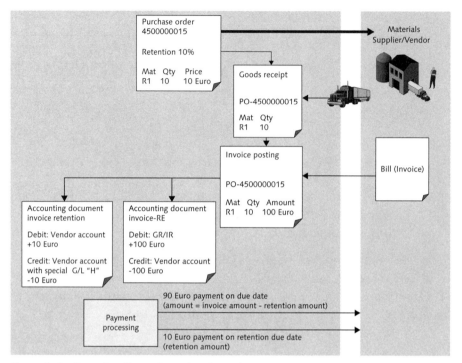

Figure 6.78 Retention Money Scenario—Example

After the goods receipt, when the invoice is posted, the system creates two accounting documents:

▶ **Accounting Document—Retention Document**
In this document, the system will debit the vendor account by 10 Euro and credit the vendor account with the special G/L indicator "H" by 10 Euro.

▶ **Accounting Document—Invoice Document (RE)**
This is the usual accounting document, which is created during invoice posting, where the vendor account is credited by 100 Euro, and the GR/IR account is debited by 100 Euro.

When payment processing is done, the system will propose only 90 Euro on the payment due date, and the remaining 10 Euro is retained until the retention date and paid after the retention period is over.

Let's discuss the process steps and the configuration steps required for the retention money scenario.

6.19.2 Process Steps

Follow these process steps for the retention money scenario:

1. **Create the PO.**
   Create a PO via Transaction ME21N; enter all of the required details such as vendor, material, quantity, and so on. Click on the PAYMENT PROCESSING tab on the PO header as shown in Figure 6.79.

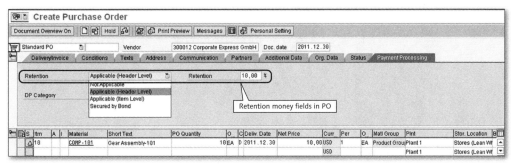

Figure 6.79 PO Creation—Retention Money Entry

In the RETENTION category, you'll see the following five options in the standard system:

▸ **Not Applicable:** Retention money is not applicable.

▸ **Applicable (Header Level) H:** Retention has been defined at the header level. In this case, the RETENTION % field must be populated. It isn't possible to process the value at the item level.

▸ **Applicable (Item Level) I:** Retention has been defined at the item level. In this case, the RETENTION % field can be populated at the item level in the invoice view.

▸ **Secured by Bond B:** The retention has been secured by a bond. It isn't possible to define the RETENTION % field (either at the header level or at the item level).

▸ **(blank):** No retention has been defined. The RETENTION % field can't be populated.

Select the retention at header level or at item level, enter the percentage in the RETENTION % field, and save the PO.

2. **Post the goods receipt.**

Via Transaction MIGO, post the goods receipt for the PO created in the previous step.

3. **Post the invoice.**

Post the invoice via Transaction MIRO, enter the PO number and dates, and press Enter. After you press Enter, if the PO is subjected to retention money it will give a pop-up message as shown in Figure 6.80.

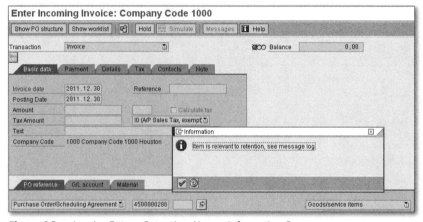

Figure 6.80 Invoice Entry—Retention Money Information Popup

Enter the RETENTION DUE date as shown in Figure 6.81, and post the invoice.

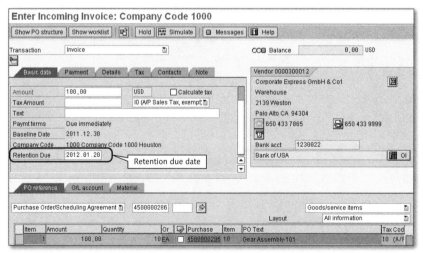

Figure 6.81 Invoice Posting—Retention Money Due Date Entry

After you post the invoice, the system will create two accounting documents, one for the total invoice amount as a credit to the vendor and a debit to the GR/ IR account, and a second document for the retention amount with the vendor account debit and the vendor account credit with the special G/L indicator.

Note

Special G/L indicator "H" is defined in the standard system for retention money.

6.19.3 Customizing Steps

To use the retention money in Purchasing functionality, you need to activate the business function LOG_MMFI_P2P in Transaction SFW5 as discussed in the previous section:

1. **Define the default due date for retention.**
   To define the default due date for retention, go to SAP IMG • MATERIALS MAN-AGEMENT • LOGISTICS INVOICE VERIFICATION • INCOMING INVOICE • RETENTION • DEFINE DEFAULT DUE DATE FOR RETENTION.

   You can define the retention period for each material group as shown in Figure 6.82. You can use the DATE CATEGORY and WARRANTYT DURATION fields to control the validity period. The system calculates the due date for retention as follows:

   Due date of retention = due date for net payment of incoming invoice + user-defined validity period

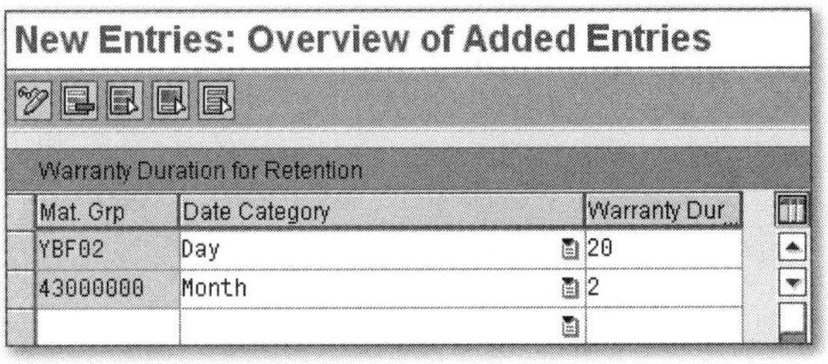

Figure 6.82 Default Retention Duration for Material Group

2. **Define tax handling for retention.**
   You can define country-specific parameters for tax calculation in the retention document. Depending on the tax code, you define whether the system calculates

retention amounts as gross or net. If a tax jurisdiction is required for the tax calculation schema assigned to the specified country, you must assign a tax jurisdiction. In this case, the Tax Jurisdiction field is ready for input. The system uses the tax code and tax jurisdiction (if entered) to determine whether retention amounts are posted as gross or net. The Tax Reduction for Retention indicator is copied to the invoice item as a default value and can be changed there.

> **Note**
>
> Tax settings are based on the country, and in the invoice document system, these settings determine the country from the plant.

3. **Define the control parameters for retention.**
   In this step, you can define the various parameters for retention for each company code as shown in Figure 6.83.

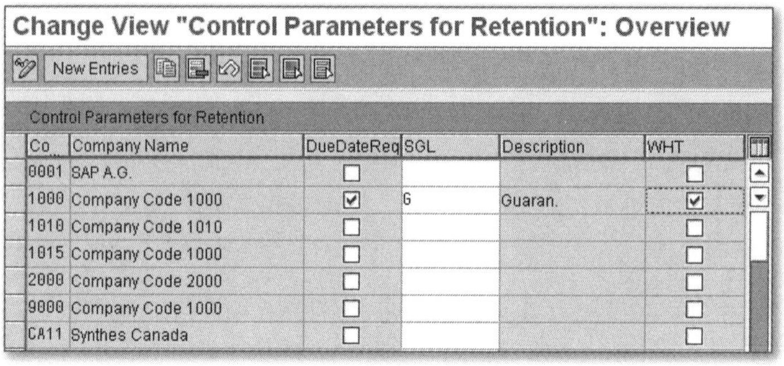

Co...	Company Name	DueDateReq	SGL	Description	WHT
0001	SAP A.G.	☐			☐
1000	Company Code 1000	☑	G	Guaran.	☑
1010	Company Code 1010	☐			☐
1015	Company Code 1000	☐			☐
2000	Company Code 2000	☐			☐
9000	Company Code 1000	☐			☐
CA11	Synthes Canada	☐			☐

Figure 6.83 Retention Money Control Parameter Configuration

The significance of each parameter is described in the following list:

- DueDateReq
  If you set this indicator, the Due Date for Retention field in the incoming invoice becomes a required field. You can use the BAdI Default Values and Input Parameters for Retention to override this Customizing setting.
- SGL
  Enter the special G/L indicator that you want to use to post retention amounts from Logistics Invoice Verification. If you don't specify a special G/L indicator, the system uses the H special G/L indicator for retention.

▶ WHT

This field is only relevant if withholding tax is posted in the incoming invoice. If you set this indicator, the system posts withholding tax in the retention document.

4. **Define the document type for retention.**

You need to define the document type, assign the number range, and assign this document type as the default value in the invoice document. Go to SAP IMG • MATERIALS MANAGEMENT • LOGISTICS INVOICE VERIFICATION • INCOMING INVOICE • NUMBER ASSIGNMENT • MAINTAIN NUMBER ASSIGNMENTS FOR ACCOUNTING DOCUMENTS.

After creating the document type, assign the number range and then assign this as the default document type for retention for Transaction MIRO as shown in Figure 6.84.

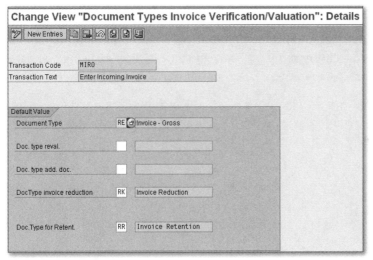

Figure 6.84 Define the Document Type for Retention for Transaction MIRO

Keep these important points in mind if you are using the retention money functionality:

▶ You can't use retention together with prepayment of an invoice.

▶ An amount split isn't possible for retention.

▶ If you've activated valuation areas for the material ledger, you can't define retentions for PO items with these valuation areas.

- You can't use retention together with installment payments.

- If you have multiple account assignments, no different tax codes are possible.

- Delivery costs aren't included when retentions are calculated.

Note

The BAPIs `BAPI_CONTRACT_CREATE` and `BAPI_CONTRACT_CHANGE` are available for creating and changing retentions for contracts. You can only display the retention data you entered with the `BAPI BAPI_CONTRACT_GETDETAIL`, not in the contract itself.

6.20 Summary

This chapter explained the various invoice verification processes. You also learned how invoices are blocked for payment for variance in price or quantity and that subsequent debit/credit and invoice with reduction are very important processes in invoice verification. In this chapter, we also discussed the account postings in most of the scenarios. Furthermore, we showed that ERS and invoicing plans are very important processes that save a lot of time and reduce data entry errors.

The next chapter describes inventory valuation, which is very important for the financial book of accounts. Let's move on to learn about the various valuation methods and their impact in accounting.

In addition to quantity, inventory maintained in an organization has value attached to it. This inventory value is maintained in the company's book of accounts and, unlike quantity, may fluctuate depending on the market price.

7   Inventory Valuation

Whenever any valuated material is received into stock or issued from stock, the value of the total stock is changed and recorded in the financial accounts. This process is called *inventory valuation*. Inventory valuation in the SAP system is carried out based on the standard price or moving average price. In this chapter, you'll see how you can customize the various valuation methods based on your business scenarios. Before we get into the details of each of the valuation methods and its customization, however, you need to understand the term *valuation area*.

First we'll go over the financial terms and key elements of Financials and Controlling in SAP. This will also help you understand the integration between Materials Management (MM) and Financial Accounting/Controlling (FI/CO).

7.1   Financial Accounting and Controlling Overview

You need to understand how the financials and controlling functions in SAP work, as well as the basic terminology used in finance before we get into details of inventory valuation.

Accounting must fulfill many different tasks. Fulfilling external requirements, which include legal restrictions such as the creation of balance sheet and profit and loss (P&L) statements, is just as important as fulfilling internal requirements; for example, the analysis of overheads, calculation of products, and the results analysis at the company level.

7.1.1   Financial Accounting

The General Ledger (G/L), Accounts Receivables (AR), Accounts Payable (AP), and Asset Accounting (AA) are the key areas in Financial Accounting (FI). All records of accounting-level business transaction are stored in the G/L. The G/L is stored in the chart of accounts, which contains all of the definitions of G/L accounts in a structured manner, including categorization of the G/L account as an income statement or balance sheet account and the account number. Often, however, only collective postings are maintained in the G/L for clarity. And in such times, the posting data is represented by subledgers. Subledgers pass their compressed data to the G/L. The subledgers are linked to the G/Ls in real time by reconciliation accounts. When a posting is made to a subledger account, the same is updated in the respective reconciliation account of the G/L. In MM, each vendor account equals a subledger account, and a group of vendors is assigned to one reconciliation account, which is a G/L account.

The G/L manages data at the company code level. The P&L statement and the balance sheets required by legislation are also compiled. The company assets, segregated further into assets (application of funds) and liabilities (source of funds), are listed in the balance sheet. To talk about integration, the business transactions entered in the subledgers and MM are flown in real time into the balance sheet. Figure 7.1 shows the following key elements of FI:

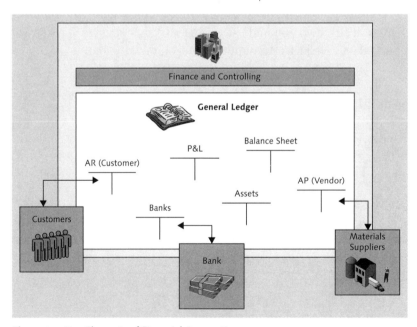

Figure 7.1 Key Elements of Financial Accounting

- Balance sheet
- P&L statement
- Accounts Payable (AP)
- Accounts Receivable (AR)
- Asset Accounting (AA)
- Bank accounting

The aim of recording business transactions is to create a balance sheet and P&L statement in the form of a report. These reports must be adapted to the specific legal requirements.

7.1.2 Management Accounting

MM has strong integration with FI and management accounting (Controlling, CO), as most of the time a materials movement will have a financial impact. To understand the integration, you need to understand the basics of management accounting. Management accounting is assigned the task of recording all business-related expenses and revenues, in detail, to provide more exact information about the utilization of costs and assets within the company.

The SAP ERP application component FI is a primary data source for management accounting. Most expense postings that relate to the G/L results in a costs posting in CO. The two key elements of CO are the profit center and cost center, which we'll discuss in the following subsections.

Profit Centers

You can use Profit Center Accounting (PCA) to analyze internal profit and loss for profit centers. This enables you to valuate different areas or units in your enterprise. A profit center can represent many things:

- An organizational unit within the company (such as a plant)
- A line of business
- A geographical location

> **Note**
>
> In earlier releases of SAP, the profit center was part of only CO, but in New G/L account-ing, profit centers are part of FI. Profit centers function as a dimension for reporting, similar to a company code.

Cost Centers

Cost Center Accounting (CCA) is used to determine where costs are incurred in your organization. When costs are incurred, you assign or post them to the correspond-ing cost center. These costs can include personnel costs, rental costs, or any other costs that can be assigned to an existing cost center.

Because material valuation is also an important part of FI, before we get into the various types of valuation, we'll first discuss the valuation area.

7.2 Valuation Area

A *valuation area* is the organizational level at which materials are valuated such as at the plant or company code level, as illustrated in Figure 7.2.

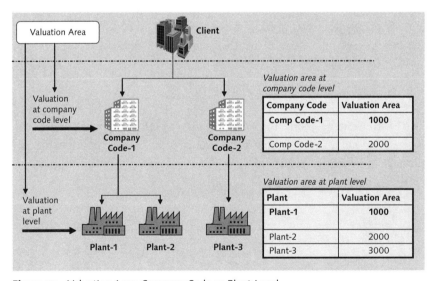

Figure 7.2 Valuation Area: Company Code or Plant Level

When the valuation area is at the plant level, you can valuate a material in different plants at different prices. When the valuation area is at the company code level, the valuation price of a material is the same in all of the plants of the company code.

> **Note**
>
> SAP recommends that you valuate materials at the plant level. Material valuation at the plant level is mandatory if your system is a retail system, or if you want to use either the Production Planning (PP) or Product Cost Accounting components.

To define the valuation area at the company code or plant level, go to SAP IMG • ENTERPRISE STRUCTURE • DEFINITION • LOGISTICS GENERAL • DEFINE VALUATION LEVEL.

Select the valuation area level either at the plant or company code level as per your requirement, as shown in Figure 7.3.

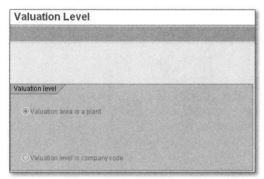

Figure 7.3 Define the Valuation Area Level

> **Note**
>
> The valuation level is a fundamental setting and is very difficult to reverse after it's been selected.

In the following sections, we'll discuss the major concepts involved in inventory valuation including valuation procedures, material price changes, and split valuation.

7.3 Valuation Methods: Moving Average Price and Standard Price

Material valuation is carried out according to the price controls set in the SAP system. In this section, we'll discuss the following valuation methods: moving average price (price control V) or standard price (price control S). We'll also see how material valuation can be used depending on the business scenarios and go through the customization steps (see Figure 7.4).

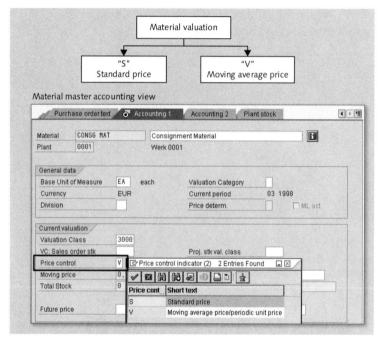

Figure 7.4 Valuation Methods

In the standard price procedure, the valuation price is defined and fixed in the material master record. If a PO price is different (either more or less) from the standard price, the difference amounts are posted into a price difference account.

Moving average price, on the other hand, is a weighted average price. The movements of materials such as goods issue or goods receipts may impact moving average prices.

The valuation method is defined in the accounting view screen of the material master as shown in Figure 7.4.

We'll discuss both valuation methods in detail in the following subsections.

7.3.1 Moving Average Price "V"

The moving average price is the weighted average price of a material and will change regularly if the PO prices of a material are changed regularly. This price is calculated based on total stock and total value using the following equation:

Moving average price = total stock value / total stock quantity

Consider, for example, a case where you have an initial stock of 100 pieces of material (called Mat-1) at a price of $8/piece (see Figure 7.5). In the meantime, you've created a PO for 100 pieces of material Mat-1 at $10/piece. (Keep in mind that at the time of the PO, an accounting document doesn't yet exist.) After you receive the 100 pieces from the vendor, you enter the goods receipt with reference to the PO.

When you post the goods receipt, an accounting document is created. The stock account is debited $1,000 (100 × 10), and the GR/IR account is credited $1,000, both according to the PO price. The total stock quantity becomes 200 pieces (100 + 100), and the total stock value becomes $1,800 ($800 + $1000). Plugging these numbers into the moving average price equation yields the following result:

Moving average price = total stock value / total stock quantity

= 1,800 / 200

= 9

As you can see, the moving average price for the stock is now $9.

If you post the invoice with the same price as in the PO, the GR/IR account will be debited with $1,000, and the vendor account will be credited with $1,000.

After the invoice posting, the moving average price will remain $9 each because there's no price difference between the PO and the invoice.

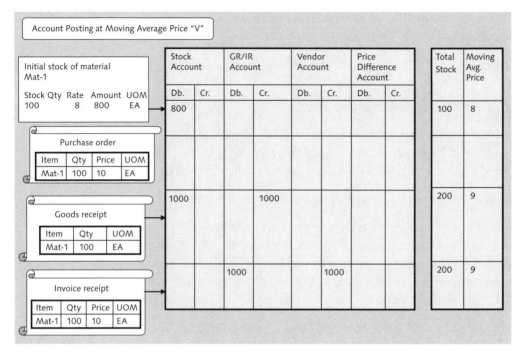

Figure 7.5 Moving Average Price Scenario

The material master record will always be updated with the current moving average price. You can check the price in the material master in the accounting view using Transaction MM03.

7.3.2 Standard Price "S"

A standard price is a fixed price defined in the material master record. In general, you use the standard price for finished goods. Consider a case where you have an initial stock of 100 pieces of material Mat-1. The standard price in the material master record is $8/piece (Figure 7.6). In the meantime, you've created a PO for material Mat-1 at a price of $10/piece. (Keep in mind that at the time of the PO, the accounting document has not yet been created.)

After you receive the 100 pieces of material Mat-1, you enter the goods receipt for the PO. When you post the goods receipt, an accounting document is created. In this case, the stock account is debited by $800 (100 × 8)—even though the PO lists a price of $10/piece. This is because the material uses a standard price valuation, which is $8. The GR/IR account, however, will be credited with *$1000* because the GR/IR account is based on the PO and goods receipt, not the standard price. Because of the difference in costs, the price difference account is debited $200.

The bottom line is that the standard price is always fixed, and any difference between the standard price and the PO price is posted in the price difference account.

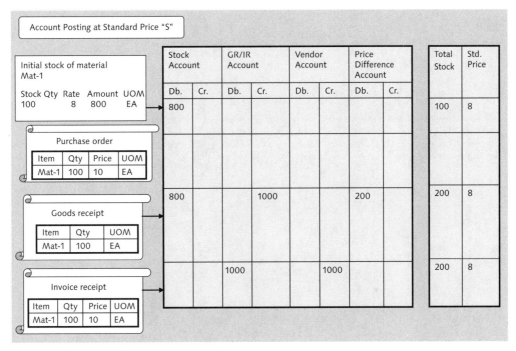

Account Posting at Standard Price "S"

	Stock Account Db.	Stock Account Cr.	GR/IR Account Db.	GR/IR Account Cr.	Vendor Account Db.	Vendor Account Cr.	Price Difference Account Db.	Price Difference Account Cr.	Total Stock	Std. Price
Initial stock of material Mat-1 — Stock Qty 100, Rate 8, Amount 800, UOM EA	800								100	8
Purchase order — Item Mat-1, Qty 100, Price 10, UOM EA										
Goods receipt — Item Mat-1, Qty 100, UOM EA	800			1000			200		200	8
Invoice receipt — Item Mat-1, Qty 100, Price 10, UOM EA			1000			1000			200	8

Figure 7.6 Standard Price Scenario

We'll discuss the configuration and process steps for standard prices and moving average prices in the following sections.

7.3.3 Configuration Steps

Price control S (standard price) and price control V (moving average price) are both predefined in the SAP system. While creating the material master record, you must assign the valuation method in the accounting view. However, you can assign the price control to material types so that each time you create an accounting view of the material master, the price control is assigned automatically by the system. To do so, go to SAP IMG • Logistics-General • Material Master • Basic Settings • Material Types • Define Attributes of Material Types.

The valuation method can be selected on the Valuation section, as shown in Figure 7.7. It's then used as a default (proposed by the system) in the creation of the material master record but can be changed at the time of material master creation. You can make a particular valuation method mandatory by selecting the Price Ctrl mandatory checkbox in the Valuation section of material type, as shown in Figure 7.7. If the valuation method is made mandatory, the default valuation method can't be changed in the material master record.

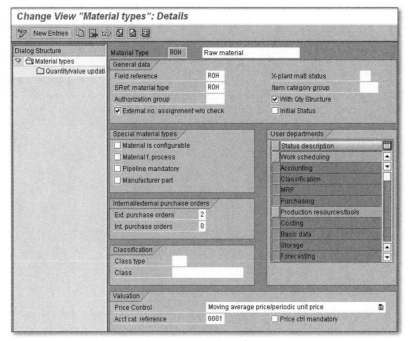

Figure 7.7 Material Type: Valuation Method Configuration

7.3.4 Process Steps

During materials movement such as goods receipt, goods issue, and invoice posting, the system automatically posts the entries in the stock G/L account, and the valuation amount is calculated based on the valuation method defined in the material master.

You can view the total stock quantity, total value, and valuation method of a material in the material master ACCOUNTING view. To do so, use Transaction MM03, as shown in Figure 7.8.

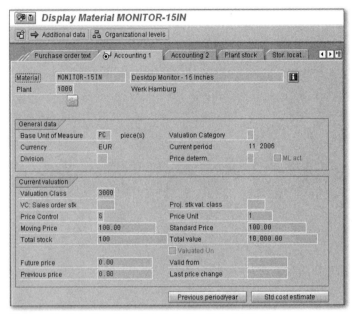

Figure 7.8 Valuation Price Details in the Material Master

Valuation methods are directly related to the idea that materials experience price changes. In the following section, we'll discuss the concept of price changes in more detail.

7.4   Material Price Changes

Material prices can change over a period of time due to changes in the market price. The SAP system includes functionality to accommodate these changes, and stock valuation is revaluated as per the current market price.

7.4.1   Business Scenario

A computer hardware manufacturer wants to change the valuation price of a material (desktop monitor) due to a change in the market price.

The company has 100 pieces in stock with a stock value of $10,000. The material is maintained with the valuation method standard price, and the price is $100/piece. The market price of desktop monitors has since been reduced to $60/piece, and the company would like to update its stock valuation per the current market price.

Valuation prices can be changed based on business requirements for three scenarios:

▸ A price change during the current posting period

▸ A price change during the previous posting period and changes not carried over to the current period

▸ A price change during the previous posting period or year and changes carried over to the current period

> **Note**
>
> Keep in mind that changing the material price doesn't involve changing the material master record; it's an accounting transaction in which the total stock for a valuation area is revaluated.

Let's discuss these three different types of price changes.

Price Change in the Current Posting Period

A material price change in the current posting period changes the material price and creates an accounting document. Figure 7.9 shows an example of a price change in the current period. Material Mat-1 has a stock balance of 100 pieces, a price of $12/piece, and a total stock value of $1,200.

Now the market price is changed from $12/piece to $20/piece, and to revaluate your stock valuation as per the current market price, you need to post a price change document. After you've posted the price change document in the system, an accounting document is created, the stock G/L account is debited $800 (the difference between the original value of $1,200 and the new value of $2,000), and the expense/revenue from the revaluation G/L account is credited $800. The material price change is now complete, and the price stands at $20/piece.

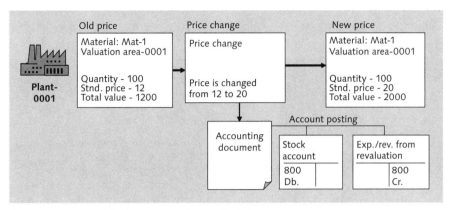

Figure 7.9 Material Price Change in Current Period

Price Change in the Previous Period/Year, with the Change Effective Only in that Period/Year

A material price change in the previous period or year changes the material price only in the previous period; that is, the current price and valuation remain the same. In this scenario, the price change transaction creates two accounting documents: one for the previous year, and one for the current year.

Figure 7.10 shows an example of this process. When you change the price from $12 to $20 in the previous period or year, the previous period's stock account is debited $800, and revenue from the revaluation account is credited $800. To keep the price in the current valuation period the same, the system then posts one more accounting documents for the current period, the stock account is credited, and the expense from revaluation account is debited.

Price Change in the Previous Period/Year, with the Change Also Effective for the Current Period

In this scenario, the price change in the previous period or year is carried forward to the current period. Figure 7.11 shows an example where the material price is changed to $20. In the previous period, the material price was $12 and total stock was 100 pieces. In the current period, the material price is $15 and the total stock is 120 pieces.

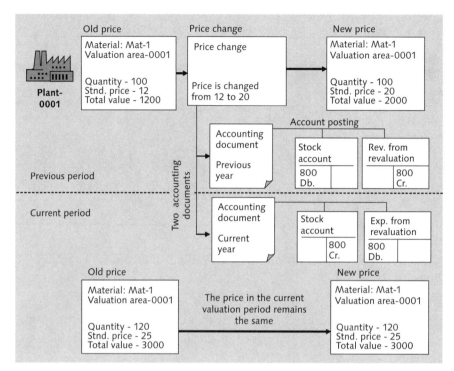

Figure 7.10 Material Price Change in Previous Posting Period/Year (Not Carried Over to Current Period)

As with the previous scenario, this transaction will create two accounting documents; the first accounting document is posted for the previous period and the second accounting document is posted for the current posting period. The following list details both of these documents:

1. **First accounting document (posted for previous period)**
   The material price is increased by $8 (the new price is $20, the old price was $12); therefore, the stock value will be increased in the previous period by $800 (increased price of $8 × stock quantity of 100 for the previous period). $800 Euro ($8 × 100) is debited to the stock G/L account, and $800 is credited to the revenue from the revaluation G/L account.

2. **Second accounting document (posted for current period)**
   For the current posting period, the stock quantity is 120 pieces and the price is $15. Therefore, the calculation for the accounting posting will be as follows:

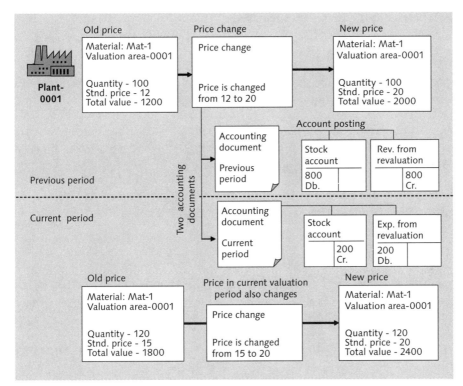

Figure 7.11 Material Price Change in Previous Posting Period/Year (Carried Over to Current Period)

- **Reversal of price change in the current period**
  Reversal of the amount posted in the last posting period via the first accounting document:
  - Stock G/L account: $800 credit
  - Expense from revaluation account: $800 debit

- **Carry over price change into the current period**
  Because the new price needs to be carried over to the current period, the price difference amount results from the change in price from $15 per piece to $20 per piece in the current period:
  - Stock G/L account: $600 debit (120 pieces × $5 is the price difference)
  - Revenue from revaluation account: $600 credit

▶ **Net effect of the previous calculation**
The net value is calculated from the previous two calculations and posted via the second accounting document:

– Stock G/L account: $200 credit

– Expense from revaluation account: $200 debit

As shown in Figure 7.11, the accounting document posted in the current posting period has credited $200 to the stock G/L account and debited $200 to the expense account from the revaluation account.

Now that we've discussed the three possible price-change scenarios, let's look at the process and configuration steps involved in prices changes.

7.4.2 Process Steps

You can change prices via Transaction MR21, as shown in Figure 7.12. Then check the new valuation price and value of the stock in the material master accounting view via Transaction MM03. You can post a material debit/credit via Transaction MR22.

This scenario is required primarily when materials are valuated with standard price control.

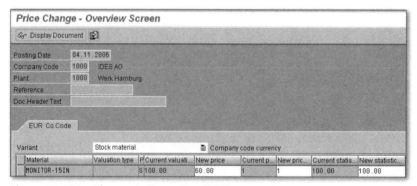

Figure 7.12 Price Change via Transaction MR21

7.4.3 Configuration Steps for Price Changes in the Previous Period/ Year

For a price change in the previous period or year, you must define whether the change also applies to the current period. To do so, go to SAP IMG • MATERIAL

Management • Valuation and Account Assignment • Configure Price Change in Previous Period/Previous Year and select the Price Carr.over checkbox to activate the price change carryover (Figure 7.13).

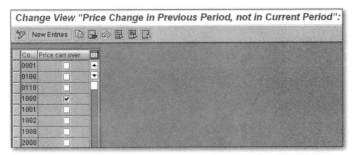

Figure 7.13 Previous Period Price Change Carryover Configuration

Now that we've covered two of the main topics in inventory valuation—valuation methods and material price changes—let's look at a specific type of inventory valuation called split valuation.

7.5 Split Valuation

Split valuation enables you to valuate sub-stocks (sub-stock means part of the total stock) of a material in different ways. There are a number of reasons you might want to valuate sub-stocks separately, such as:

▶ The material has different origins (i.e., comes from different countries)

▶ The material is acquired via different types of procurement (i.e., external procurement vs. internal procurement)

▶ The material has different categories of quality (i.e., damaged, poor quality, or good quality)

7.5.1 Business Scenario

Imagine a car manufacturing company that procures engine valves from both a domestic vendor and an overseas vendor. Naturally, the vendor prices for the material are different; therefore, the company wants to valuate the stock separately. Figure 7.14 shows an illustration of this concept.

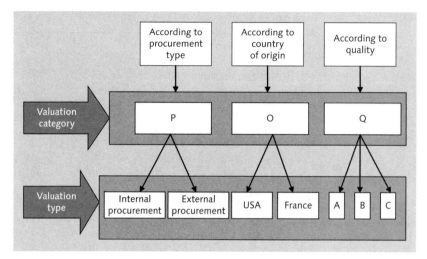

Figure 7.14 Split Valuation Types

> **Note**
>
> Split valuation is used only with the moving average price control, and materials subjected to split valuation can be valuated only via the moving average price method.

Look closely at the example illustrated in Figure 7.15. Material Mat-1 is procured for Plant 0001 from Vendor-1 and Vendor-2, located in the US and France, respectively. The material is designated for split valuation based on the origin of material. From Vendor-1, Plant 0001 has procured 60 pieces of the material at a price of $10/piece. From Vendor-2, Plant 0001 has procured 40 pieces of the material at a price of $15/piece. While posting the goods receipt, the appropriate valuation type (either USA or France) needs to be selected for each vendor.

After this is done, you can see the total stock quantity and stock value at Plant 0001, and you can also see the material valuation based on the origin of the material. The stock value of the material procured from the US is $600, and the valuation price is $10/piece. The stock value of the material procured from France is $600, and the valuation price is $15/piece. The stock quantities and stock values of split-value materials are cumulated at the valuation area level.

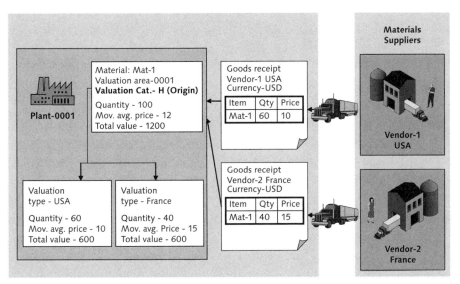

Figure 7.15 Split Valuation Example

This example introduces two essential concepts in split valuation: *valuation category* and *valuation type*. The valuation category indicates whether a material's stock should be valuated as one unit or in parts. It's also a key that indicates the criteria for defining partial stock, and determines which valuation type is allowed.

The *valuation type* is a key that identifies split-valuated stocks of a material and indicates the characteristic of a partial stock. The valuation category is assigned in the material master record, and selected during material transactions such as goods issues and goods receipts.

7.5.2 Configuration Steps

To configure split valuation, follow these steps:

1. **Activate split valuation.**
   To activate split valuation, go to SAP IMG Customizing Implementation Guide • Material Management • Valuation and Account Assignment • Split Valuation • Activate Split Valuation (Figure 7.16). If you allow split valuation, this doesn't mean that you must only valuate material on a split valuation basis. Split valuation is used only when the valuation category is assigned in a material master record.

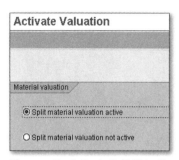

Figure 7.16 Activate Split Valuation

2. **Configure split valuation.**

To configure split valuation, go to SAP IMG • MATERIAL MANAGEMENT • VALU-
ATION AND ACCOUNT ASSIGNMENT • SPLIT VALUATION • CONFIGURE SPLIT VALUA-
TION. You now have to define the global types and global categories.

First, click on the GLOBAL TYPES button. In this step, you create valuation types
and define their attributes (Figure 7.17). To create a new valuation type, click
on the NEW button and enter the valuation type. Define the following attributes:

Global Valuation Types

Create	Change	Delete

Valuation Type	Ext. POs	Int. POs	ARef	Description
009	0	1	0001	Reference for raw materials
01	0	2	0001	Reference for raw materials
02	2	0	0001	Reference for raw materials
C1	2	2	0003	Reference for spare parts
C2	2	2	0003	Reference for spare parts
C3	2	2	0003	Reference for spare parts
EIGEN	0	2	0001	Reference for raw materials
FREMD	2	0	0001	Reference for raw materials
LAND 1	2	0	0001	Reference for raw materials
LAND 2	2	0	0001	Reference for raw materials
RAKTION	2	2	0005	Reference for trading goods
RNORMAL	2	2	0005	Reference for trading goods

Figure 7.17 Define Global Types: Valuation Types

▶ EXT. POs
This indicates whether external POs are allowed.

▶ INT. POs
This indicates whether internal POs (i.e., production orders) are allowed.

▶ AREF (account category reference)
This is used to group valuation classes. Specify for which account category reference this valuation type is allowed.

3. **Create global categories.**
Now, click on the GLOBAL CATEGORY button. In this step, you create global categories, as shown in Figure 7.18. To define a valuation category, click on the CREATE button. Enter the category code and description.

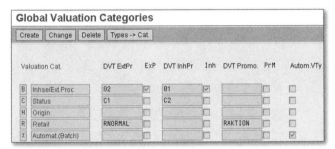

Figure 7.18 Define Global Category

You can define the following attributes for a valuation category (Figure 7.19):

▶ DEFAULT: VAL.TYPE EXT. PROCURE
The valuation type selected in this field is proposed at the time of PO creation.

▶ DEFAULT: VAL.TYPE EXT.PROC. MAND.
If you select this checkbox, the default valuation type is mandatory and can't be changed in the PO.

▶ DEFAULT: VAL.TYPE IN-HOUSE PROD
The valuation type selected in this field is proposed at the time of production order creation.

▶ DEFAULT: VAL.TYPE IN-HOUSE MAND.
If you select this checkbox, the default valuation type is mandatory and can't be changed in the production order.

▶ DETERMINE VAL. TYPE AUTOMAT.
If this checkbox is selected, the system will automatically determine the valuation type at the time of the goods receipt. This indicator is only useful for materials that are managed in batches. A valuation record is automatically created for each batch.

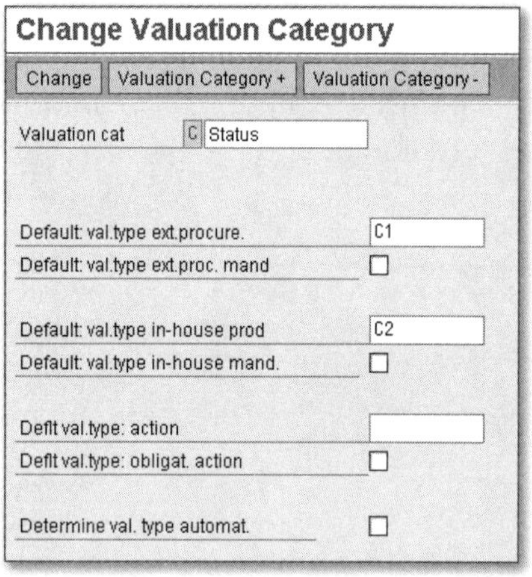

Figure 7.19 Valuation Category Details

You must activate valuation types for the valuation category by clicking on TYPES • CAT or by pressing F7. As shown in Figure 7.20, valuation types LAND 1 and LAND 2 are active for valuation category H (Origin).

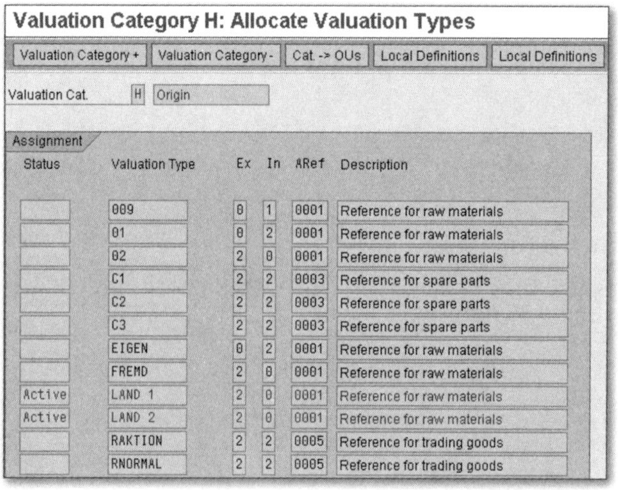

Figure 7.20 Activate Valuation Types for Valuation Category

7.5.3   Process Steps

To understand how the process of split valuation is carried out in the SAP system, follow these split valuation process steps:

1. **Assign a valuation category in the material master record.**
   After your configuration is complete, you must assign a valuation category to the material master record in the ACCOUNTING view. You can choose the relevant valuation category from the drop down list. For example valuation category H is assigned for the material shown in Figure 7.21. Valuation category H represents the origins of a material and is provided by SAP.

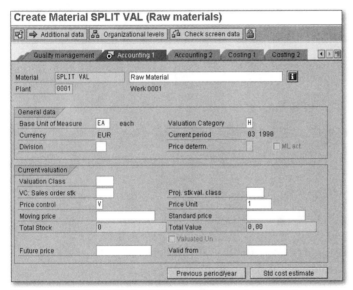

Figure 7.21   Material Master: Valuation Category Assignment

2. **Create a PO.**
   Create a PO via Transaction ME21N and enter the material, quantity, plant, vendor, and all other required data. As shown in Figure 7.22, the default valuation type is copied on the DELIVERY tab of the PO. You can change the default value and select the required valuation type.

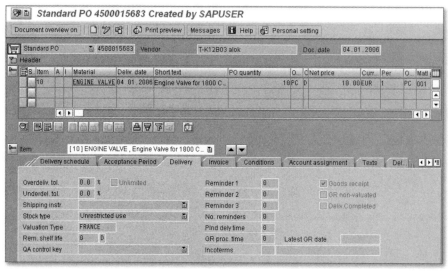

Figure 7.22 PO: Valuation Type in the Delivery Tab

3. **Post the goods receipt.**

   Post the goods receipt via Transaction MIGO. You can see the valuation type entry on the MATERIAL tab (Figure 7.23).

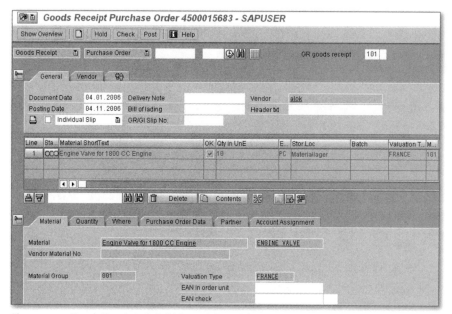

Figure 7.23 Goods Receipt: Split Valuated Material

4. **Display the valuation price in the material master record.**
   You can view the valuation price in the material master ACCOUNTING view via Transaction MM03. This will show you the valuation price at the plant level. If you select a valuation type at the organizational level, the system will display the stock valuation for the selected valuation type.

   For example, for the material Engine Valve, the value is assigned for split valuation based on origin. Valuation Types France and USA are configured. In the material master record, the stock valuation for a plant will be the total valuation that's procured from both France and the US (Figure 7.24). You can also display the valuation price for each valuation type.

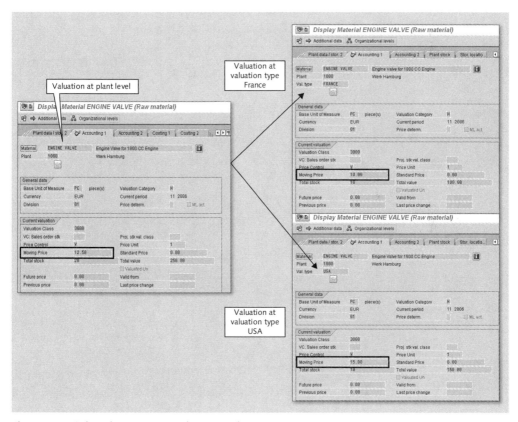

Figure 7.24 Split Valuation Price in the Material Master

337

7.6   Summary

In this chapter, you've learned about valuation methods, material price changes, and how to configure split valuations. Now that you understand these concepts, you should be able to better meet the business requirements of your customers.

In the next chapter, we'll discuss some of the key configurations involved in MM.

Many SAP system configurations are common across business processes. This chapter explains these key configurations.

8 Key Configurations in Materials Management in SAP

This chapter discusses the following most common configurations required across business processes:

- Release strategy
- Pricing procedure
- Automatic account determination
- Document type
- Version management
- Message determination
- Serial numbers in purchasing
- Templates in POs and purchase requisitions
- Blocking and unblocking POs with reasons

While implementing Materials Management (MM), you need to configure the pricing procedure and automatic account determination, which are required for all of the business processes.

The release strategy and version management may be implemented based on your customer's requirements.

SAP has introduced the serial number functionality in Purchasing since the release of EHP4. This allows you to track each quantity of a material with serial numbers.

We'll first discuss the topic of release strategy, including a business scenario where it can be implemented, as well as the step-by-step configurations and possible customizations.

8.1 Release Strategy

Release procedures are approval procedures for purchasing documents such as purchase requisitions and purchase orders (POs). The manner in which you configure these procedures is called a *release strategy*. A release strategy involves a process whereby an approver verifies document data (such as material, quantity, and value) and then gives the authorization to purchase. The process takes place online, which saves time and is more efficient than a manual approval process.

8.1.1 Business Scenario

Say a manufacturing organization wants all external documents (such as POs, contracts, and scheduling agreements) to be approved by a manager and vice president based on their value, with low amounts requiring no approval, medium amounts requiring manager approval, and high amounts requiring both manager and vice president approval. To accomplish this, you can configure release strategies for both internal and external purchasing documents.

You can set up a scenario where purchase requisitions and POs need to be approved by certain people either by value limit or some other criteria such as document type, purchasing group, and so on.

For example, you may have a scenario where a purchase requisition needs to be approved by different levels of responsible people based on value limits such as the following:

▶ $0 – $1000: No approval required

▶ $1000 – $5000: Manager needs to approve

▶ More than $5000: Manager and vice president need to approve

Figure 8.1 shows the approval process flow for purchase requisitions and POs. When a release strategy is used, purchase requisitions must be approved before you can create any related documents (such as RFQs or POs). The system also prohibits circulation of the document via printouts, faxes, or email.

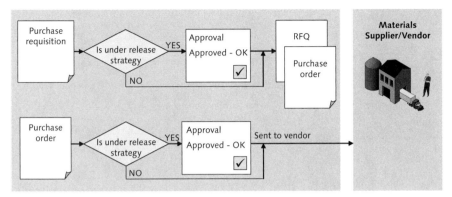

Figure 8.1 Release Procedure: Process Flow

In the following sections, we'll provide an introduction to the concept of release strategy and then explain the configuration and process steps involved.

8.1.2 Basic Concepts of Release Strategy

The SAP system provides two different types of release procedures:

▶ **Release procedure without classification**
The release procedure without classification can be configured only for item-level release. Therefore, it can only be used for internal documents (such as purchase requisitions). This is because external documents (such as POs) must be sent to vendors and therefore can't be partially approved. In the procedure without classification, you can set the release based on the following four criteria:

- ▶ Plant
- ▶ Value
- ▶ Material group
- ▶ Account assignment category

▶ **Release procedure with classification**
The procedure with classification offers many more criteria to define the release strategy.

You can use either of these procedures for purchase requisitions. For POs and RFQs, you must use the release procedure with classification (Figure 8.2).

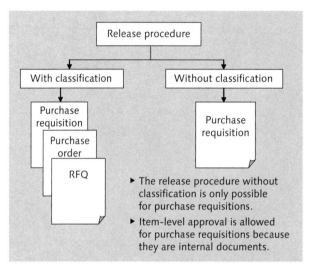

Figure 8.2 Release Procedure Types: With Classification and Without Classification

Before we get into the release procedure configuration steps, we'll define the key terms used in release procedures, as follows:

▶ **Release strategy**
Defines the entire approval process and consists of release conditions, release codes, and release prerequisites.

▶ **Release conditions/criteria**
Determines which release strategy applies for a particular purchasing document. For example, if the value of a requisition item is $1000, it may require a certain strategy; if the value of the item is $100,000, it may require a different strategy. If purchasing documents fulfill release conditions, they must be approved before they can be processed further.

▶ **Release code/point**
Two-character key that represents an individual or department that must give approval. Each person involved in the release procedure signifies approval in a release transaction using his release code.

▶ **Release prerequisite**
Sets the order in which approval must take place. For example, a manager must approve a document before the vice president approves it.

▶ **Release status/indicator**

Represents the current status of the item or document such as blocked and released. For example, if the document isn't fully approved, it may have a blocked status.

Now that you have an understanding of the basic concepts of a release strategy, let's move on to the configuration steps involved. We'll discuss two types of configuration: without classification and with classification.

8.1.3 Configuration Steps for Release Procedure without Classification

Follow the menu path SAP IMG • MATERIALS MANAGEMENT • PURCHASING • PURCHASE REQUISITION • RELEASE PROCEDURE • SET UP PROCEDURE WITHOUT CLASSIFICATION. This will display five activities, as shown in Figure 8.3.

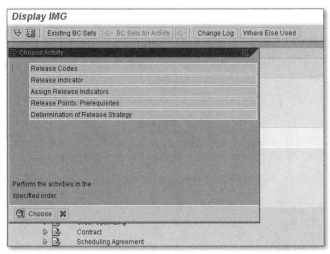

Figure 8.3 Release Procedure Configuration: Activities

You need to select each activity, one by one, as follows:

1. **Select release codes.**

   The release code is used to approve the document. Click on NEW ENTRIES and enter the two-digit RELEASE CODE key and DESCRIPTION, as shown in Figure 8.4. The release code can be your decision of either numeric or alphanumeric entries.

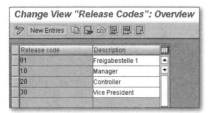

Figure 8.4 Release Procedure Configuration: Release Codes

2. **Select the release indicator.**

   This specifies the release status of the purchase requisition. You can define the release indicator as shown in Figure 8.5. Click on NEW ENTRIES and enter the one-digit release indicator and description.

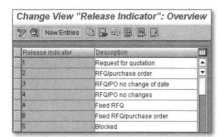

Figure 8.5 Define Release Indicator

You also need to define controlling indicators and a field selection key for the release indicator, as shown in Figure 8.6. Let's discuss the impact of each indicator and selection key:

Figure 8.6 Release Indicator Details

▶ FIXED FOR MRP
If you select this checkbox, the purchase requisition can't be changed by material requirements planning (MRP).

▶ RELEASED FOR QUOT.
This indicator specifies that quotations and RFQs may be processed with reference to purchase requisitions. If you select this checkbox, it means that the purchase requisition is available for RFQ and quotation processing.

▶ REL. FOR ORDERING
This indicator specifies whether POs can be generated with reference to purchase requisitions.

▶ FIELD SELECTION KEY
When setting up a release strategy and release indicators, you can use the field selection key to determine whether certain fields in a purchase requisition may or may not be changed on approval. For example, you may have a requirement to configure the system in such a way that the requested quantity in the purchase requisition can't be changed after this release indicator is set in the purchase requisition. For this requirement, you can configure the order quantity field as "display only" in the field selection key.

▶ CHANGEABIL.
This defines how the system reacts if a purchasing document is changed after the start of the release procedure, as shown in Figure 8.7.

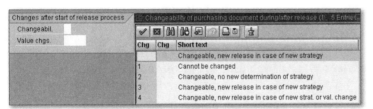

Figure 8.7 Changeable Option Selection

▶ VALUE CHGS.
Specifies the percentage by which the value of the purchase requisition can be changed after the release procedure has started. If the requisition is changed more than the specified limit entered here, it's subjected again to the release procedure.

3. **Assign the release indicators.**

In this step, you assign the release indicators to a release strategy as shown in Figure 8.8. Click the NEW ENTRIES button, enter the release strategy code, select the release indicator, and save.

Rel.strat.	C1	C2	C3	C.	C.	C.	C.	C.	ReleaseInd	Description
R1	X								1	Request for quotation
R1	X	X							2	RFQ/purchase order
S1	X								2	RFQ/purchase order

Figure 8.8 Assign Release Indicators to a Release Strategy

This indicator specifies the release sequence; that is, which release point(s) must have a released requisition before the current individual or department is allowed to release that requisition. Look at Figure 8.8 for an example. For release strategy R1, release indicators 1 and 2 have been defined. If release indicator 1 is set, the RFQ can be created from the purchase requisition. Release indicator 2 can be set only after release indicator 1 is set, and release indicator 2 means that RFQs or POs can be created.

4. **Select release points as prerequisites.**

In this step, you configure the sequence of release codes and the prerequisites they must fill before they can be released. Look at Figure 8.9 for an example. For release strategy R1, there are two release codes: 10 and 20. Release code 10 has no prerequisite, which means it can approve the purchase requisition. Release code 20, however, does have a prerequisite, which means that it must be approved by release code 10 before it can be approved by release code 20. (Remember, release codes are references to specific people.)

Rel. strategy	Release code	Description	C.	C.	C.	C.	C.	C.	C.	C.
R1	10	Manager	X							
R1	20	Controller	+	X						
S1	01	Freigabestelle 1	X							

Figure 8.9 Select Release Points

Test your sequence and prerequisites by clicking on the SIMULATE RELEASE button, as shown in Figure 8.9. After clicking on this button, you see a popup window where you can test your release strategy (Figure 8.10).

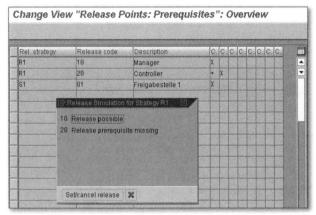

Figure 8.10 Release Strategy Simulation

Release strategy R1 has two release indicators, which we assigned in step 2. When release code 10 releases the purchase requisition, release indicator 1 is set. This means that you can create an RFQ even though the purchasing document hasn't yet been released by release code 20. When the document is released by release code 20, release indicator 2 is set. This allows the creation of POs.

5. **Determine when to apply a specific release strategy.**
   In this step you define when the purchase requisition is considered for a release procedure and which release strategy is applicable. The without classification release strategy can be configured with only four criteria: account assignment category, material group, plant, and value. In Figure 8.11, you can see that for account assignment category F, material group 011, plant 3000, and value 2,000.00 USD, release strategy R1 is applicable. When a purchase requisition is created with these attributes, the system will automatically assign release strategy R1 and will follow the approval process configured in this strategy.

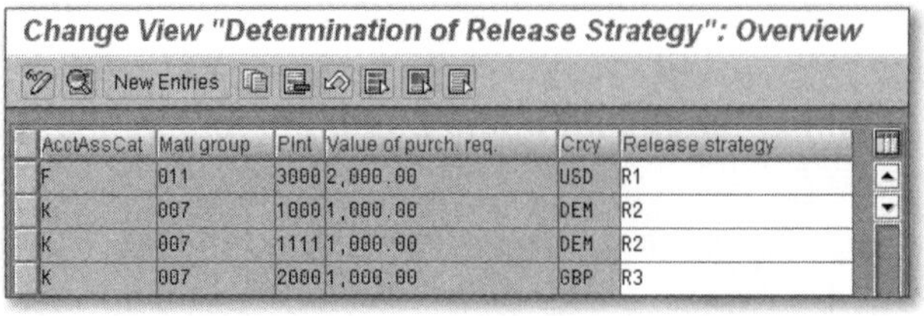

Figure 8.11 Release Strategy Determination

8.1.4 Configuration Steps for the Release Procedure with Classification

A release procedure with classification can be defined for internal documents (purchase requisitions) and external documents (POs, RFQs, contracts, and scheduling agreements). You must define both characteristics and classes for a release procedure with classification. We'll now discuss the steps involved in this process. Because some of these steps are fairly complex, we'll give each its own section.

Step 1: Edit Release Characteristics

In this step you create classification characteristics for a release procedure. These characteristics are the criteria for a release condition; if the characteristics are satisfied, the associated release strategy is assigned to the purchasing document. For example, the release condition for release strategy S1 has the characteristic as defined in Table 8.1.

Characteristic	Characteristic Value
Total net value of PO	Over $1,000

Table 8.1 Characteristics of a Release Condition

This means that if the total value of a PO exceeds $1000, release strategy S1 is assigned to the PO.

The SAP system provides the communication structures CEBAN for mapping characteristics for purchase requisitions, and CEKKO for mapping characteristics for POs. In communication structure CEKKO, you'll find all of the fields that can be used as characteristics for a release condition. For example, BSART is used for the order type, and GNETW is used for the total order value.

To define a characteristic, go to SAP IMG • Materials Management • Purchasing •
Purchase Order • Release Procedure for Purchase Order • Edit Characteristic.
(The menu paths will be slightly different for each purchasing document; select
the appropriate document from the Purchasing menu.) Click on New, and enter
the characteristic name and validity start date. On the Basic data tab, enter the
description and set the status, as shown in Figure 8.12.

In the Value assignment section, select Single-value or Multiple Values. In the
Format section, fill in the Data Type and the Number of Chars fields. (The data
type will depend on the field you're selecting from the CEKKO table.)

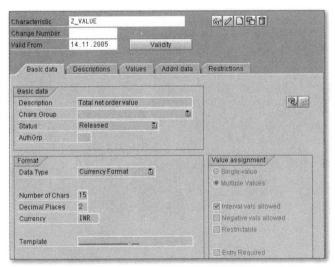

Figure 8.12 Define Characteristic

On the Addnl data tab, enter table name "CEKKO" (if configuring for POs) or
"CEBAN" (if configuring for purchase requisitions). Enter the field name from the
purchasing document (e.g., GNETW means total value in POs).

On the VALUES tab, you can define a list of different values for the characteristic. Alternatively, you can leave this blank; in this case, values can be defined in the release strategy.

Step 2: Edit Classes

In this step you create classes for a release procedure. Classes are used to group together characteristics that constitute a release condition for a release strategy. For example, if you want to have release strategy based on a purchasing organization, purchasing group, total amount, and plant combination, you need to define all of these elements as characteristics and assign them to one class. To define a class, go to SAP IMG • MATERIALS MANAGEMENT • PURCHASING • PURCHASE ORDER • RELEASE PROCEDURE FOR PURCHASE ORDER • EDIT CLASS. Click on CREATE, and enter the class name and class type, which is always "032" (this is the class type used for release procedures). On the BASIC DATA tab, enter the DESCRIPTION, STATUS, and VALIDITY. On the CHAR. tab, select the different characteristics that should be grouped in this class, as shown in Figure 8.13.

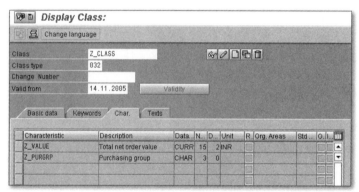

Figure 8.13 Define Class

Note

Classes and characteristics are treated as master data in the SAP system. This means that you can't transport them from development to quality and production clients through transport requests. Instead, you must manually create them in each client, or automatically upload them via SAP-provided Application Linking and Enabling (ALE). Transactions BD91, BD92, and BD93 can be used to transfer classes and characteristics via ALE. You can manually assign classes and characteristics to release strategies in each client by using Transaction CL24N.

Step 3: Define the Release Procedure for Purchase Orders

In this last step you define the release procedure for POs. To do so, go to SAP IMG • MATERIALS MANAGEMENT • PURCHASING • PURCHASE ORDER • RELEASE PROCEDURE FOR PURCHASE ORDER • DEFINE RELEASE PROCEDURE FOR PURCHASE ORDERS. You'll see a list of five activities; select each activity, one by one, as follows:

1. **Select the release groups.**
   A release group contains one or more release strategies. You can define different release strategies with the same key for different release groups. For example, release group 01 is defined for purchase requisitions, and release group 02 is defined for POs. You can define a release strategy for both release groups 01 and 02 with the same key: in our example, S3 is used. Click on NEW ENTRIES, and enter the REL. GROUP code and REL. OBJECT (1 for purchase requisitions, and 2 for POs). Enter the CLASS name and DESCRIPTION, as shown in Figure 8.14.

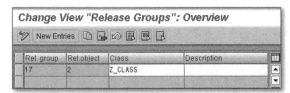

Figure 8.14 Define Release Groups

2. **Select the release codes.**
   In this step, you define different release codes. These can be defined however you choose. In the example in Figure 8.15, three release codes have been defined: AA, AB, and AC.

Figure 8.15 Define Release Codes

3. **Select the release indicator.**
   The release indicator specifies whether the purchasing document can be processed or is blocked. Based on the requirement and approval matrix, you would know when the documents should be under released status and when it should be under blocked status.

> **Example**
>
> Let's say you have a requirement where you have two approvers: a department head and a vice president. The first approver is the department head, but after his approval, the document should still be in blocked status. After the vice president approves, then the document should be released. In this scenario, the release code for the vice president will have the release indicator set to RELEASED.

4. Click on NEW ENTRIES, enter the RELEASE IND., check the RELEASED checkbox (which indicates whether the document is released or not), and fill in the CHGABLE, VALUE CHANGE %, and DESCRIPTION fields (Figure 8.16).

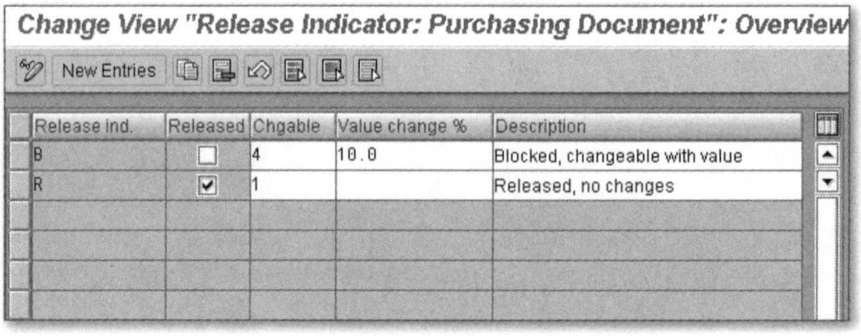

Release ind.	Released	Chgable	Value change %	Description
B	☐	4	10.0	Blocked, changeable with value
R	☑	1		Released, no changes

Figure 8.16 Define the Release Indicator

5. **Select the release strategies.**
   In this step you configure the different release strategies. Click on NEW ENTRIES and select the RELEASE GROUP (which you created in step 1). Enter the REL. STRATEGY key and description, and select the release codes applicable for the release strategy. There are four options in the bottom of the screen as shown in Figure 8.17: RELEASE PREREQUISITES, RELEASE STATUSES, CLASSIFICATION, and RELEASE SIMULATION.

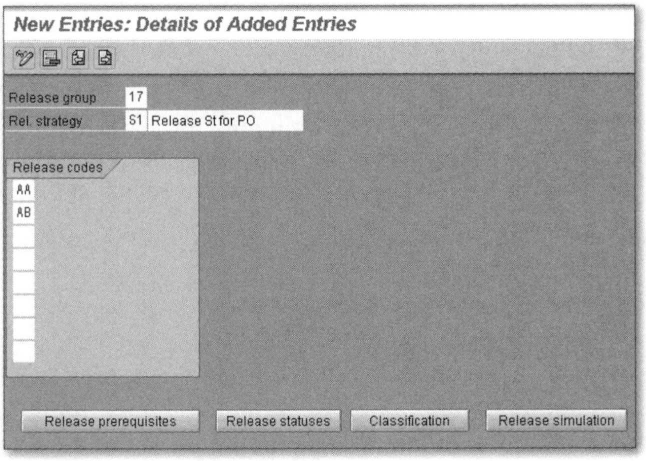

Figure 8.17 Define the Release Strategy

First, click on RELEASE PREREQUISITES. If you have multiple release codes, you need to define the release prerequisite for each code. For example, release code AB can approve only if release code AA has approved.

Next, click on RELEASE STATUSES. Here, you define the different release indicators at different statuses of the release procedure. For example, Figure 8.18 shows that release indicator B is set until it's been approved by both release codes, whereas release indicator R is set only when it has been approved by both release codes.

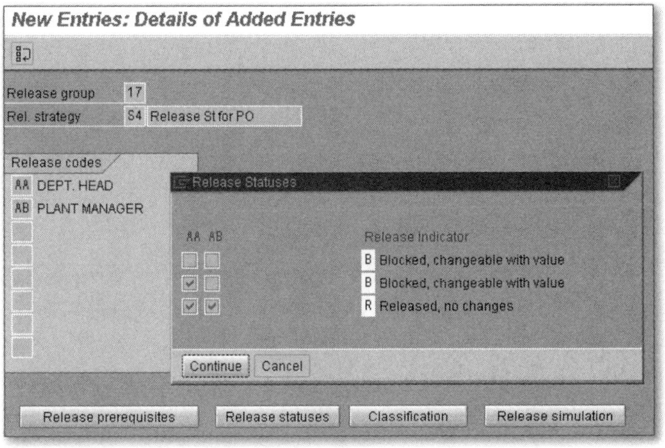

Figure 8.18 Define the Release Status

Next, click on CLASSIFICATION and enter the characteristic's values. Based on these values, this release strategy will be picked up in the appropriate purchasing documents. For example, two characteristics are selected in Figure 8.19. The first characteristic, TOTAL NET ORDER VALUE, has a value of greater than 2,000 USD, and the second characteristic, PURCHASING GROUP, has two values, purchase group 1 and purchase group 2. Therefore, if a PO is created with a value of more than $2000 and purchase group 1 or purchase group 2, release strategy S1 will be assigned to the PO.

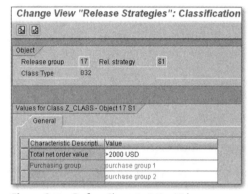

Figure 8.19 Define Characteristics Values

Finally, click on the RELEASE SIMULATION button (refer back to Figure 8.18) to test whether your release strategy is working in the correct sequence. This will display a screen with the release codes and status.

6. **Select the workflow.**

   You can also define a workflow for release procedures. Employees involved in the approval process are defined as agents. Define the agent for each release code, and this agent will be configured in the workflow. This step is optional. You would need technical consultants to help who have expertise in SAP Business Workflow to write the various workflows based on the requirements.

This completes the configuration steps for release procedures with classification. Before we move on to the process steps, however, there's one last topic we must cover: item-level release procedures.

Item-Level Release for Purchase Requisition

Releasing each line item separately is called *item-level release*. A purchase requisition may contain one or more line items. With item-level release, a particular line item can be released while other line items may be pending for approval or rejection. It isn't possible to perform item-level release procedures using a release procedure with classification for external documents because external documents are always released or blocked as a whole document. However, for internal documents, you can configure line-item level approval or complete document approval using the release procedure with classification.

To configure item-level release for a purchase requisition, go to SAP IMG • MATERIALS MANAGEMENT • PURCHASING • PURCHASE REQUISITION • DEFINE DOCUMENT TYPES. Select the OVERREQREL checkbox to enable overall release of a purchase requisition. If you want item-level approval, don't select this checkbox. In Figure 8.20, document type NB has OVERREQREL selected; therefore, any purchase requisition created with document type NB will be released as a whole document.

	Type	Doc. type descript.	Item...	NR int.as.	No.rng.ext	Field sel.	Cont...	OverReqRel	Variant	
	EC	Purch.requis. EBP	10	01		RQ	NBB		☐		
	FO	Framework requisn.	10	01	02	FOF			☐	SRV	
	IN	Purch.requis. I-Comm	10	01	02	NBB			☐		
	MV	Model specification	10	01	02	RVB	R		☐		
	NB	Purch.requis. Stand.	10	01	02	NBB			☑		
	RV	Outl. agmt. requisn.	10	01	02	RVB	R		☐		

Figure 8.20 Item-Level Release Configuration

8.1.5 Process Steps

When you create a purchasing document, the system will automatically assign the relevant release procedure. Figure 8.21 shows a PO that has been assigned to release strategy S4. This PO can't be sent to the vendor because it's in a blocked state (release indicator B means blocked). This PO requires two levels of approval: from the plant manager (release code AB) and the department head (release code AA).

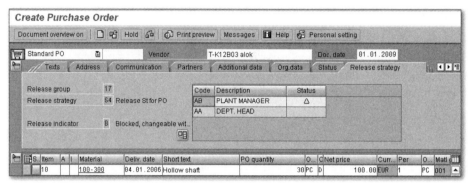

Figure 8.21 PO Release Strategy Assignment

You can release purchasing documents individually or collectively. In individual release, one document is released at a time. Go to Transaction ME29N for the individual release of POs, and go to Transaction ME54N for the individual release of purchase requisitions. Click on the RELEASE button, which you'll find on the RELEASE STRATEGY tab (Figure 8.22). After a PO is approved by all of the approvers, it can be sent to the vendor.

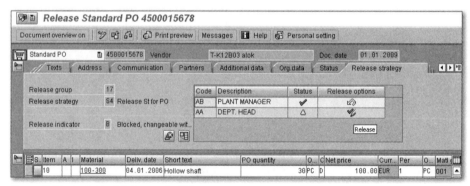

Figure 8.22 Individual Release of a PO

You can also release purchasing documents collectively, which means that documents are released as a group instead of individually. The following transaction codes are used for collective release:

▶ Transaction ME28: PO release

▶ Transaction ME55: Purchase requisition release

- ▸ Transaction ME35K: Contract release

- ▸ Transaction ME35L: Scheduling agreement release

8.2 Pricing Procedure

A *pricing procedure* is used to determine the price of a material in a PO. The net price of a material depends on discounts, surcharges, taxes, freight, and so on.

8.2.1 Business Scenario

A purchasing department in an enterprise calculates the net price of the materials based on the gross price, discounts, taxes, freight charges, and so on. These values are referred to while creating a PO and contracts.

In the SAP system, the price, discounts, surcharges, freight costs, and so on are represented in the form of *condition types*. Condition types are used in the determination of net and effective prices in POs. Each condition type has condition records (i.e., values), and these records are defined in condition tables. The sequence in which condition records are referred is defined in the access sequence, and this sequence is assigned to condition types.

Various condition types are grouped in a sequence in a *calculation schema*. A calculation schema is assigned for a combination of vendor schema groups and purchasing organization schema groups.

> **Note**
>
> Conditions can be time-dependent or time-independent. Time-dependent conditions are defined for a certain validity period; time-independent conditions don't have a validity period. Conditions in info records and contracts are always time-dependent conditions. Conditions in POs are always time-independent.

In the following sections, we'll discuss the process and configuration steps for the pricing procedure.

8.2.2 Process Steps

As shown in Figure 8.23, the pricing procedure begins with Step 1 and ends with Step 9. Using this figure, we'll go through each of the steps for the SAP Business Workflow as determined by the system, and explain how the price for Material Mat-1 was determined in the PO created with Vendor ABC and Purchasing Organization 1000.

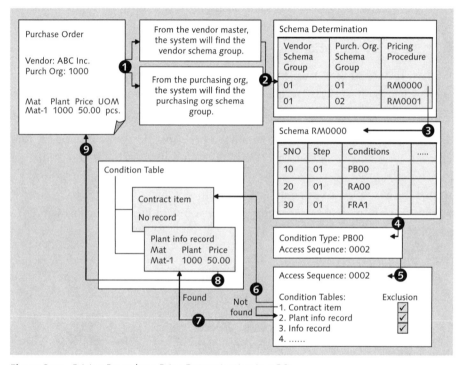

Figure 8.23 Pricing Procedure: Price Determination in a PO

❶ **Determine the vendor schema group and the purchasing organization schema group.**

The system determines this information from the vendor master record and the purchasing organization. In this example, it's Vendor Schema Group 01 and Purchasing Organization Schema Group 01.

❷ **Determine the calculation schema.**

The system determines the relevant calculation schema. This is based on a combination of the vendor schema group and the purchasing organization schema group. In this example, the calculation schema is RM0000.

❸ **Determine the condition type.**
The calculation schema consists of various condition types listed in a sequence. Here, Condition Type PB00 is defined for the material price.

❹ **Determine the access sequence.**
The system uses the calculation schema to determine the access sequence (in this example, 0002) assigned to the condition type (in this example, PB00).

❺ **Determine the condition tables.**
The system determines the condition tables assigned to the access sequence (in this example, 0002).

❻ **Determine the condition record (Part I).**
The condition table of access sequence 0002 consists of many condition records of which contract item has the highest priority. A system search yields no value for this condition record.

❼ **Determine the condition record (Part II).**
In the previous step, the system search yielded no result for the highest priority condition record, which is contract item. Therefore, the system moves to the next condition record, which is plant info record.

❽ **Determine the material price.**
The system search yields a value of $50.00 for plant info record. This value for Condition Type PB00 is assigned to the material as the price in the PO.

❾ **Material price is copied in the PO.**
Once the system finds the value for the condition type, it assigns the value in the PO.

> **Note**
>
> Material-specific discounts and surcharges are supplementary conditions linked to the gross price (condition type PB00). No access sequence is assigned to supplementary conditions, and no separate price determination is carried out for them. They're found using the condition records for the gross price.

Settings made in Customizing determine the details of these pricing elements and how the price is computed.

8.2.3 Configuration Steps

Follow these steps for pricing procedure configuration:

1. **Define condition types.**

   The condition types are used to represent pricing elements such as prices, discounts, surcharges, taxes, or delivery costs in the SAP system. For example, the condition type is PB00 for gross price. These are stored in the system in the form of condition records. Condition types have control parameters and are differentiated by condition class. For condition types for which you want to maintain records with their own validity period, you must specify an access sequence. The access sequence is used to search valid condition records.

   To configure condition types, go to SAP IMG • MATERIALS MANAGEMENT • PURCHASING • CONDITIONS • DEFINE PRICE DETERMINATION PROCESS • DEFINE CONDITION TYPES. Here, you'll see a list of condition types provided by the SAP system (Figure 8.24). You can create new condition types by clicking on NEW ENTRIES or by copying from existing SAP-provided condition types.

Change View "Conditions: Condition Types": Overview

New Entries

CTyp	Condition Type	Condition class	Calculation type
A001	Rebate	Expense reimbursement	Percentage
A002	Material Rebate	Expense reimbursement	Quantity
A003	Hierarchy Rebate	Expense reimbursement	Percentage
A004	Hierarchy rebate/mat	Expense reimbursement	Quantity
AK01	Customer Rebate	Expense reimbursement	Percentage
AMO1	Internal Amort. %	Discount or surcharge	Percentage
AMO2	Internal Amort./Qty	Discount or surcharge	Quantity
CU00	Gross price cust.sim	Prices	Quantity
CUAC	Antidumping cus.qty	Discount or surcharge	Quantity
CUAD	Anti-dumping cust %	Taxes	Percentage
CUAE	Antidumping cust.wt	Discount or surcharge	Net weight
CUAS	Customs exemption %	Taxes	Percentage
CUDC	3rd country cust qty	Discount or surcharge	Quantity
CUDE	3rd country weight	Discount or surcharge	Net weight
CUDL	3rd country cust %	Taxes	Percentage
CUFR	Freight qty customs	Discount or surcharge	Quantity
CUIN	Insurance customs	Discount or surcharge	Quantity
CUP1	Preference qty cust	Discount or surcharge	Quantity
CUP2	Preference wt cust.	Discount or surcharge	Net weight

Figure 8.24 Define Condition Types

> **Note**
>
> If you define your own condition types, the key should begin with the letter "Z" because SAP keeps these name slots free in the standard system. You shouldn't change the condition types that are included in the standard SAP system.

Figure 8.25 shows the details of the condition types. In the CONTROL DATA 1 section, you can see the COND. CLASS, CALCULAT.TYPE, COND. CATEGORY, ROUNDING RULE, and PLUS/MINUS fields.

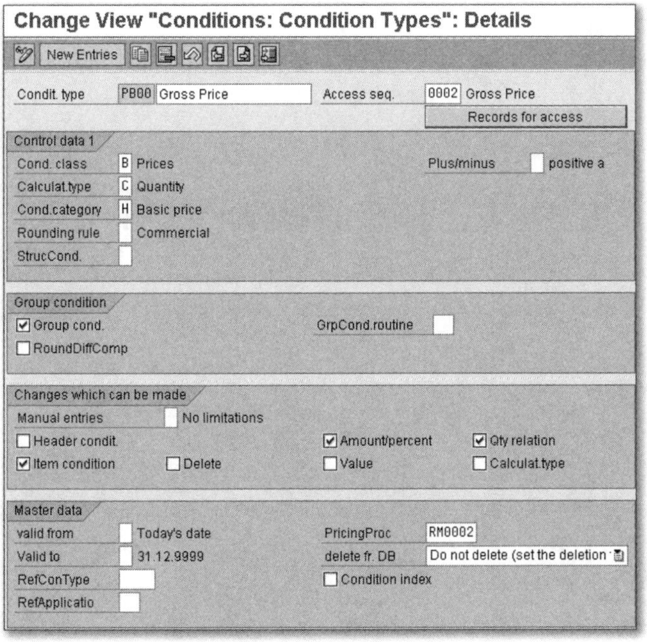

Figure 8.25 Define Condition Types: Details

The *condition class* is used for grouping similar condition types; for example, condition class A is used for discounts and surcharges, and condition class B is used for prices. The *calculation type* determines how the condition value should be calculated, that is, whether it's based on quantity, weight, or volume. *Plus/ minus* controls whether the condition results in an amount that's negative (a discount), positive (a surcharge), or whether both positive and negative amounts are possible.

Based on your requirements, you need to define all of the control data for the condition type you want to create.

2. **Define an access sequence.**

An access sequence is a search strategy the SAP system uses to search for valid condition records of a certain condition type. For example, when supplying a price, you can stipulate that the SAP system first searches for the price for a specific plant and then for a generally applicable price. For condition types for which you want to maintain records with their own validity period, you must assign an access sequence. With this, you define which fields the SAP system checks when searching for a valid condition record.

To define an access sequence, go to SAP IMG • MATERIALS MANAGEMENT • PURCHASING • CONDITIONS • DEFINE PRICE DETERMINATION PROCESS • DEFINE ACCESS SEQUENCE. The system will list the SAP-provided access sequences, as shown in Figure 8.26.

Note

Access sequence is a cross-client setting; that is, each change you make will have an effect on all other clients in the system.

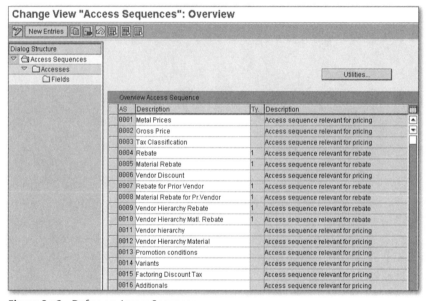

Figure 8.26 Define an Access Sequence

Note

If you define your own access sequence, the key should begin with the letter "Z" because SAP keeps these name slots free in the standard system. You shouldn't change the access sequences that are included in the standard SAP system.

Select the access sequence, and then select ACCESSES, located in the left tree menu. This will open the sequence of condition tables for an access sequence, as shown in Figure 8.27.

Change View "Accesses": Overview

New Entries

Dialog Structure
▽ ☐ Access Sequences
　▽ ☐ Accesses
　　☐ Fields

Access sequence `0002` Gross Price

Overview Accesses

No.	Tab	Description	Requiremnt	Exclusive
5	118	"Empties" Prices (Material-Dependent)	43	☑
10	68	Outline Agreement Item: Plant-Dependent		☑
13	16	Contract Item		☑
15	16	Contract Item		☑
20	67	Plant Info Record per Order Unit	36	☑
25	17	Material Info Record (Plant-Specific)	35	☑
30	66	Info record per order unit	34	☑
35	18	Material Info Record		☑
40	25	Info Record for Non-Stock Item (Plant-Specific)	38	☑
45	28	Info Record for Non-Stock Item	11	☑
60	67	Plant Info Record per Order Unit	37	☑
65	17	Material Info Record (Plant-Specific)	37	☑
70	66	Info record per order unit	37	☑
75	18	Material Info Record	37	☑

Figure 8.27 Define Access Sequence: Condition Tables

For example, if you've defined access sequence 0002 for the gross price condition PB00, the system will search the valid condition record in this sequence. The system will pick the lowest number table first and search for the condition record. If it isn't found, the system will search in the next table and so on.

The EXCLUSIVE checkbox controls whether the system stops searching for a record after a successful result has been obtained.

3. **Define the calculation schema or pricing procedure.**

In a *calculation schema*, you define the complete structure of different price components (i.e., conditions) with a sequence and control parameters. While creating a PO, the system finds the calculation schema and, based on the schema system, finds the value of each condition defined in that schema. For example, you might have a scenario where you have the gross price of a material and additional freight charges and handling charges. You also may have discounts. You need to define all of these conditions in the schema.

To define a calculation schema, go to SAP IMG • MATERIALS MANAGEMENT • PURCHASING • CONDITIONS • DEFINE PRICE DETERMINATION PROCESS • DEFINE CALCULATION SCHEMA. SAP-provided calculation schemas can be used, or you can create your own. To create your own, click on NEW ENTRIES or copy an existing calculation schema (Figure 8.28).

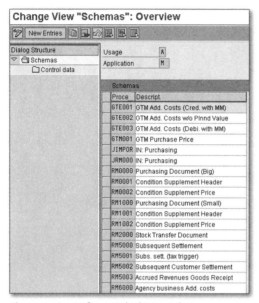

Figure 8.28 Define a Calculation Schema

Select the calculation schema, and then select CONTROL DATA in the left tree menu. The system will display the screen shown in Figure 8.29.

Change View "Control data": Overview

New Entries

Dialog Structure	Procedure				RM0000	Purchasing Document (Big)										
▽ ☐ Schemas	Control data															
☐ Control data	Reference Step Overview															

Step	Co	CTyp	Description	Fro	To	Ma	R	Stat	P	SuTot	Reqt	CalTy	BasTy	AccK	Accru
1	1	PB00	Gross Price			☐	☐	☐	X	9					
1	2	PBXX	Gross Price			☐	☐	☐	X	9	5				
2	0	VA00	Variants/Quantity			☐	☐	☐	X						
3	0	VA01	Variants %			☐	☐	☐	X						
4	0	GAU1	Orignl Price of Gold			☑	☐	☐	X			31			
5	0	GAU2	Actual Price of Gold			☐	☐	☐	X		31	32	32		
10	1	RB00	Absolute discount			☑	☐	☐	X						
10	2	RC00	Discount/Quantity			☑	☐	☐	X						
10	3	RA00	Discount % on Net			☑	☐	☐	X						
10	4	RA01	Discount % on Gross	1		☐	☐	☐	X						
10	5	HB00	Header Surch.(Value)			☑	☐	☐	X						
10	6	ZB00	Surcharge (Value)			☑	☐	☐	X						
10	7	ZC00	Surcharge/Quantity			☑	☐	☐	X						

Figure 8.29 Calculation Schema Control Data

The following list provides an explanation of the different controlling fields in calculation schemas:

- STEP
  Determines the sequence of the condition types.

- COUNTER
  The access number of the conditions within a step in the pricing procedure.

- CTYPE
  Defines the condition type you want to include in the pricing procedure.

- FROM/TO
  Calculates the number of condition types based on which the amount needs to be calculated for that condition. For example, to calculate the surcharge on the gross price, you need to define the sequence number of the gross price in the FROM field. The system will then calculate the surcharge based on the gross price.

- MANUALLY
  Defines manually entered conditions.

- REQUIRED
  Defines mandatory conditions.

- STATISTICAL
  Set for the conditions that are required for some other calculation. The value of this condition isn't directly included in the pricing.

4. **Define the schema group.**
   A company may have multiple calculation schemas that are used based on the purchasing organization or vendor. Defining a *schema group* helps you keep track of this by grouping together the purchasing organizations or vendors that use the same calculation schemas. For example, if you have a set of vendors for whom the same pricing schema is applicable, you create a vendor schema group and assign this to all those vendors. Similarly, the same calculation schema can be applicable for more than one purchasing organization; in this case, you can assign the purchasing organization schema group to all of these purchasing organizations.

   To define a schema group, you need to do the following:

   - Define a vendor schema group.
   - Define a purchasing organization schema group.

▶ Assign a purchasing organization schema group to the purchasing organization.

▶ Assign a vendor schema group in the vendor master record.

To define a vendor schema group, go to SAP IMG • MATERIALS MANAGEMENT • PURCHASING • CONDITIONS • DEFINE PRICE DETERMINATION PROCESS • DEFINE SCHEMA GROUP • SCHEMA GROUP: VENDOR (Figure 8.30).

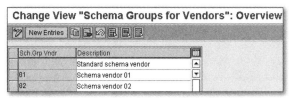

Figure 8.30 Define Schema Groups for Vendors

To define a purchasing organization schema group, go to SAP IMG • MATERIALS MANAGEMENT • PURCHASING • CONDITIONS • DEFINE PRICE DETERMINATION PROCESS • DEFINE SCHEMA GROUP • SCHEMA GROUPS FOR PURCHASING ORGANIZATIONS (Figure 8.31).

Figure 8.31 Define Schema Groups for Purchasing Organizations

To assign a purchasing organization schema group to a purchasing organization, go to SAP IMG • MATERIALS MANAGEMENT • PURCHASING • CONDITIONS • DEFINE PRICE DETERMINATION PROCESS • DEFINE SCHEMA GROUP • ASSIGNMENT OF SCHEMA GROUP TO PURCHASING ORGANIZATION (Figure 8.32).

Figure 8.32 Assign a Purchasing Organization Schema Group to a Purchasing Organization

When creating the vendor master record, assign the schema group to that vendor in the PURCHASING view via Transaction XK01 or Transaction MK01 (Figure 8.33).

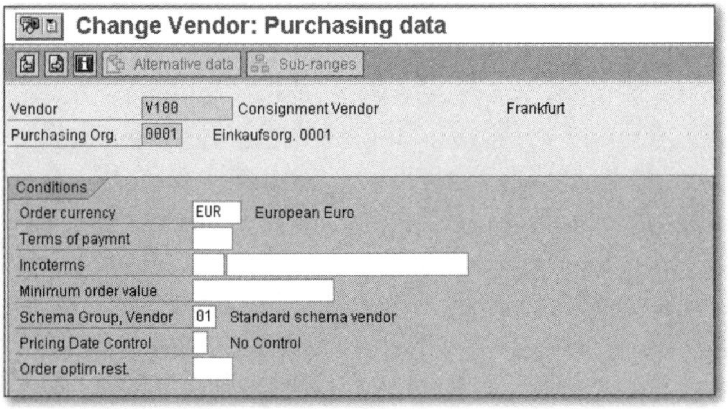

Figure 8.33 Assign a Vendor Schema Group to the Vendor Master

5. **Define the schema determination.**

   To define the schema determination, go to SAP IMG • MATERIALS MANAGEMENT • PURCHASING • CONDITIONS • DEFINE PRICE DETERMINATION PROCESS • DEFINE SCHEMA DETERMINATION • DETERMINE CALCULATION SCHEMA FOR STANDARD PURCHASE ORDERS. Here, you can define the calculation schema determination for standard POs and stock transport orders:

   ▶ **Standard POs**

   Click on DETERMINE CALCULATION SCHEMA FOR STANDARD PURCHASE ORDERS. Here you need to define the calculation schema for each purchasing organization schema group and vendor schema group combination as shown in Figure 8.34. Click on the NEW ENTRIES button, enter the purchasing organization schema group and vendor schema group, select the calculation schema group from the dropdown menu, and save.

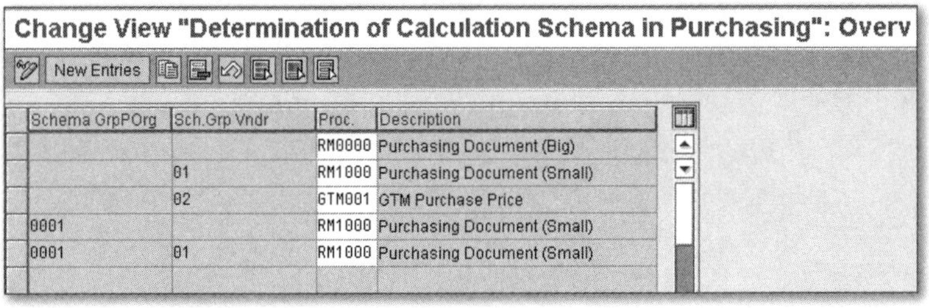

Schema GrpPOrg	Sch.Grp Vndr	Proc.	Description
		RM0000	Purchasing Document (Big)
	01	RM1000	Purchasing Document (Small)
	02	GTM001	GTM Purchase Price
0001		RM1000	Purchasing Document (Small)
0001	01	RM1000	Purchasing Document (Small)

Figure 8.34 Calculation Schema Determination

▶ **Stock transport orders**

Define the calculation schema for stock transport orders by following the same menu: SAP IMG • MATERIALS MANAGEMENT • PURCHASING • CONDITIONS • DEFINE PRICE DETERMINATION PROCESS • DEFINE SCHEMA DETERMINATION • SAP IMG • MATERIALS MANAGEMENT • PURCHASING • CONDITIONS • DEFINE PRICE DETERMINATION PROCESS • DEFINE SCHEMA DETERMINATION • DETERMINE CALCULATION SCHEMA FOR STANDARD PURCHASE ORDERS. Click on the NEW ENTRIES button, enter the purchasing organization schema group and document type, select the calculation schema, and save the entries. Here you can also define a supplying plant-specific calculation schema (if you have any) by selecting the supplying plant, or you can leave it blank. If left blank, it will be applicable for all of the plants.

8.3　Automatic Account Determination

Various transactions in MM are relevant for accounting, such as goods receipts, goods issues, and invoice receipts. In such cases, the system always creates an accounting document and posts the amount in the appropriate general ledger (G/L) accounts. G/L accounts are automatically determined with the help of *automatic account determination* settings.

8.3.1　Business Scenario

Consider, for example, a manufacturing enterprise that stores stock materials purchased from vendors. Whenever the material is received in a storage location with reference to a PO, the company wants its system to automatically determine and update the stock G/L account. Similarly, whenever an invoice is posted, the system should automatically determine the vendor G/L account and post the liability.

The SAP system provides automatic G/L account posting via the automatic account determination process. When you post a goods receipt against a PO, the system creates an accounting document (along with the material document) and G/L account postings are made. The system determines which G/L accounts should be debited and credited based on configuration settings for automatic account determination.

Before we discuss these configuration settings, let's cover the definitions of a few essential terms.

Valuation Area

A valuation area is an organizational unit that subdivides an enterprise for the purpose of uniform and complete valuation of material stocks. The valuation area can be at the company code or plant level. If the valuation area is at the plant level, each plant will have a valuation area assigned, and materials are valuated at the valuation area level. (For more information about valuation areas, see Chapter 7, Section 7.1.2.)

Chart of Accounts

A chart of accounts provides a framework for recording values to ensure an orderly rendering of accounting data. The G/L accounts it contains are used by one or more company codes. For each G/L account, the chart of accounts contains the account number, the account name, and technical information.

Valuation Class

A valuation class is used to determine the G/L account for the materials stock account. In automatic account determination, you must create valuation classes and assign them to material types. While creating material master records, you must select the appropriate valuation class in the ACCOUNTING view. The valuation class list in the material master record will depend on the material type. For example, in the standard SAP system, material type ROH (raw material) has three valuation classes: 3000, 3001, and 3002.

Transaction Key

Transaction keys are used to determine accounts or posting keys for line items that are automatically created by the system. They're defined in the system and can't be changed by the user.

Now that you understand the key terms in automatic account determination and how it will work in your business, we'll move on to describe the configuration and process steps involved.

8.3.2 Configuration with the Automatic Account Determination Wizard

Automatic account determination can be configured either with or without the automatic account determination wizard, a tool provided by SAP to help users with automatic account determination functionality. To configure automatic account determination with the help of the wizard, go to SAP IMG • MATERIALS MANAGEMENT • VALUATION AND ACCOUNT ASSIGNMENT • ACCOUNT DETERMINATION • ACCOUNT DETERMINATION WIZARD.

The wizard asks you a number of questions and, based on your answers, finds the correct settings and saves them in the corresponding SAP tables. With the exception of a few restrictions (these are documented in the wizard), the wizard undertakes the following steps:

1. Define valuation control.

2. Group valuation areas.

3. Define valuation classes.

4. Define account grouping for movement types.

5. Manage purchase accounts.

6. Configure automatic postings.

8.3.3 Configuration without the Automatic Account Determination Wizard

Account determination without the wizard enables you to create more complex customizations. In the sections that follow, we'll discuss each step involved in this configuration process.

Step 1: Define Valuation Control

To define valuation control, go to SAP IMG • MATERIALS MANAGEMENT • VALUATION AND ACCOUNT ASSIGNMENT • ACCOUNT DETERMINATION • ACCOUNT DETERMINATION WITHOUT WIZARD • DEFINE VALUATION CONTROL. For account determination, you can group together valuation areas by activating the valuation grouping code. This makes the configuration of automatic postings much easier. The valuation grouping code can be made active or inactive by choosing the respective radio button.

Step 2: Assign Valuation Grouping Codes to Valuation Areas

To assign valuation grouping codes to valuation areas, go to SAP IMG • MATERIALS MANAGEMENT • VALUATION AND ACCOUNT ASSIGNMENT • ACCOUNT DETERMINATION • ACCOUNT DETERMINATION WITHOUT WIZARD • GROUP TOGETHER VALUATION AREAS (Figure 8.35). The valuation grouping code makes it easier to set automatic account determination. Within the chart of accounts, you assign the same valuation grouping codes to the valuation areas you want to assign to the same account. As shown in Figure 8.35, valuation grouping code 0001 is assigned to valuation area 0001 and company code 0001. If another valuation area is using the same set of G/L accounts as valuation area 0001, you can assign valuation grouping code 0001 to that valuation area.

Change View "Acct Determination for Val. Areas": Overview					

Val. Area	CoCode	Company Name	Chrt/Accts	Val.Grpg Code	
0001	0001	SAP A.G.	INT	0001	
1000	0001	SAP A.G.	INT	0002	

Figure 8.35 Valuation Grouping Code

Step 3: Define Valuation Classes

In this step, you define the valuation classes allowed for material types. Define the account category reference and then the valuation class for each account category reference. After that, assign the account category reference to the material type.

As shown in Figure 8.36, account category references 0001 and 0002 are defined, and for each account category reference, one or more valuation classes are assigned. Account category reference 0001 is assigned to material type ROH, and valuation classes 3000, 3001, and 3002 are assigned to account category reference 0001. Consequently, valuation classes 3000, 3001, and 3002 are assigned to material type ROH. While creating the material master record for material type ROH, you can select any one of these valuation classes. Similarly, for material type HALB, you can select valuation classes 7900 or 7901.

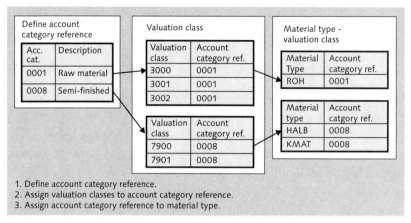

1. Define account category reference.
2. Assign valuation classes to account category reference.
3. Assign account category reference to material type.

Figure 8.36 Material Type: Valuation Class Assignment

To define which valuation classes are allowed for a material type, go to SAP IMG • MATERIALS MANAGEMENT • VALUATION AND ACCOUNT ASSIGNMENT • ACCOUNT DETERMINATION • ACCOUNT DETERMINATION WITHOUT WIZARD • DEFINE VALUATION CLASSES. In this screen, you'll see three options: ACCOUNT CATEGORY REFERENCE, VALUATION CLASS, and MATERIAL TYPE/ACCOUNT CATEGORY REFERENCE. Follow these steps:

1. Click on ACCOUNT CATEGORY REFERENCE.
   Define the code and description as shown in Figure 8.37. The account category reference is used to group valuation classes.

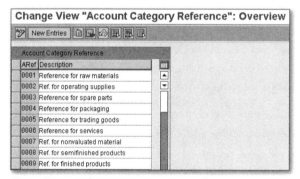

Figure 8.37 Define Account Category Reference

2. Click on VALUATION CLASS.
   In this step, you assign valuation classes to account category references, as shown in Figure 8.38.

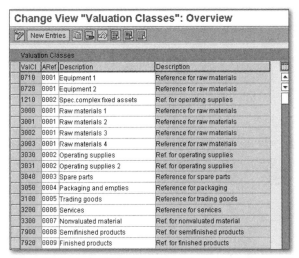

Figure 8.38 Assign Valuation Classes to Account Category References

3. Click on MATERIAL TYPE/ACCOUNT CATEGORY REFERENCE.

Assign material types to account category references, as shown in Figure 8.39.

Change View "Account Category Reference/Material Type": Overview

Account Category Reference/Material Type

MTyp	Material type descr.	ARef	Description
ABF	Waste	0007	Ref. for nonvaluated material
CH00	CH Contract Handling	0006	Reference for services
CONT	Kanban Container		
COUP	Coupons	0005	Reference for trading goods
DIEN	Service	0006	Reference for services
EPA	Equipment Package	0004	Reference for packaging
ERSA	Spare Parts	0003	Reference for spare parts
FERT	Finished Product	0009	Ref. for finished products
FGTR	Beverages	0005	Reference for trading goods
FHMI	Production Resource/Tool	0008	Ref. for semifinished products
FOOD	Foods (excl. perishables)	0005	Reference for trading goods
FRIP	Perishables	0005	Reference for trading goods
HALB	Semifinished Product	0008	Ref. for semifinished products
HAWA	Trading Goods	0005	Reference for trading goods

Figure 8.39 Assign Account Category Reference to Material Types

Step 4: Define Account Grouping for Movement Types

Now you assign an account grouping to movement types. The account grouping is a finer subdivision of the transaction/event keys for account determination. For example, during a goods movement, the offsetting entry for the inventory posting

(Transaction GBB) can be made to different accounts, depending on the movement type, as shown in Table 8.2.

Movement Type	Description	Account Grouping Code	Account
561	Initial entry of stock balance	BSA	399999
201	Goods issue to cost center	VBR	400000

Table 8.2 Account Grouping for Movement Types

The account grouping is provided for the following transactions:

▸ Transaction GBB (Offsetting Entry for Inventory Posting)

▸ Transaction PRD (Price Differences)

▸ Transaction KON (Consignment Liabilities)

> **Note**
> The account grouping in the standard system is only active for Transaction GBB.

To define account grouping for movement types, go to SAP IMG • MATERIALS MANAGEMENT • VALUATION AND ACCOUNT ASSIGNMENT • ACCOUNT DETERMINATION • ACCOUNT DETERMINATION WITHOUT WIZARD • DEFINE ACCOUNT GROUPING FOR MOVEMENT TYPES. Define the account grouping code, the movement type, and the transaction/event key combination as shown in Figure 8.40.

Step 5: Configure Automatic Posting

In this step, you enter the system settings for inventory management and invoice verification transactions that result in automatic posting to G/L accounts. To assign G/L accounts to transaction/event keys, go to SAP IMG • MATERIALS MANAGEMENT • VALUATION AND ACCOUNT ASSIGNMENT • ACCOUNT DETERMINATION • ACCOUNT DETERMINATION WITHOUT WIZARD • CONFIGURE AUTOMATIC POSTING.

Change View "Account Grouping": Overview

MvT	S	Val.Update	Qty update	Mvt	Cns	Val.strng	Cn	TEKey	Acct modif	C
101	Q	☐	☑	B	P	WE06	1	KBS		☑
101		☑	☐	B	A	WE06	1	KBS		☑
101		☑	☐	B	V	WE06	1	KBS		☑
101		☑	☑	B	A	WE06	1	KBS		☑
101		☑	☑	B	V	WE06	1	KBS		☑
101		☑	☑	F		WF01	2	GBB	AUF	☑
101		☑	☑	F		WF01	3	PRD	PRF	☐
101	E	☑	☑	B		WE01	3	PRD		☐
101	E	☑	☑	B	E	WE06	1	KBS		☑
101	E	☑	☑	B	P	WE06	1	KBS		☑
101	E	☑	☑	F		WF01	2	GBB	AUF	☑
101	E	☑	☑	F		WF01	3	PRD	PRF	☐
101	Q	☑	☑	B		WE01	3	PRD		☐
101	Q	☑	☑	B	P	WE06	1	KBS		☑
101	Q	☑	☑	F		WF01	2	GBB	AUF	☑
101	Q	☑	☑	F		WF01	3	PRD	PRF	☐
102		☐	☐	B	A	WE06	1	KBS		☑
102		☐	☐	B	P	WE06	1	KBS		☑

Figure 8.40 Account Grouping for Movement Types

To assign the G/L account, click on ACCOUNT ASSIGNMENT. You'll see a list of transaction keys; double-click on the key for which you want to set the G/L accounts. You need to define the valuation grouping code (also known as the *valuation modifier*), valuation class, and G/L account, as shown in Figure 8.41. You can then check your settings using the simulation function.

Maintain FI Configuration: Automatic Posting - Accounts

Chart of Accounts INT Sample chart of accounts
Transaction BSX Inventory posting

Account assignment

Valuation	Valuation cl	Account
0001	3000	300000
0001	3001	300010
0001	3030	303000
0001	3031	303500
0001	3040	304000
0001	3050	305000
0001	3100	792000
0001	7900	790000
0001	7920	792000

Figure 8.41 Account Assignment

8.3.4   Process Steps

Now, let's discuss the G/L account determination as they relate to goods receipt and goods issue postings.

Goods Receipt

Post a good receipt with reference to a PO via Transaction MIGO. Then display the goods receipt document and go to the Doc. info tab. Click on the FI Documents button; this will display a list of financial documents created for the goods receipt document (see Figure 8.42).

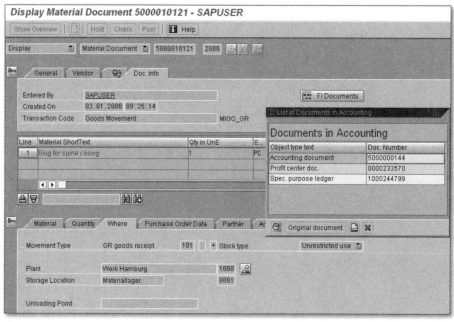

Figure 8.42   Accounting Documents List in a Goods Receipt

Select the accounting document to see the details of that accounting document (Figure 8.43). You can see the G/L account postings, which are determined based on the automatic account determination configuration. G/L account 300000 (inventory raw material stock account) is debited, and GR/IR account 191100 is credited.

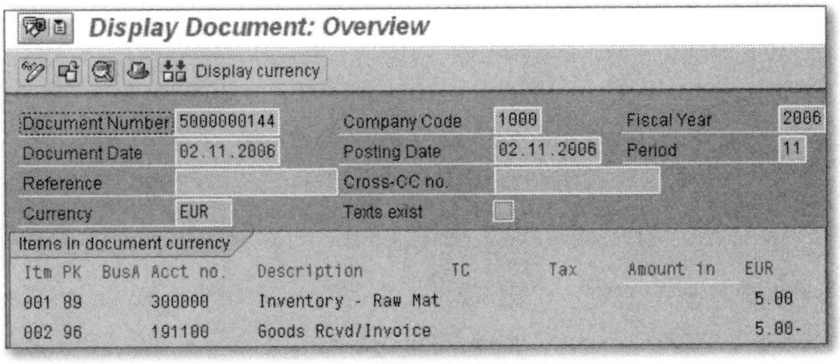

Figure 8.43 Accounting Document: Goods Receipt Transaction

Goods Issue

Similarly, when you issue goods to production, the respective G/L accounts are automatically determined. Go to Transaction MB1A or Transaction MIGO_GI, and use movement type 201 (goods issue to cost center). Select the cost center, plant, storage location, material, and quantity, and then post the transaction. Display the material document, and open the accounting document, as shown in Figure 8.44. Here, you can see that G/L account 300000 is credited, and account 400000 is debited.

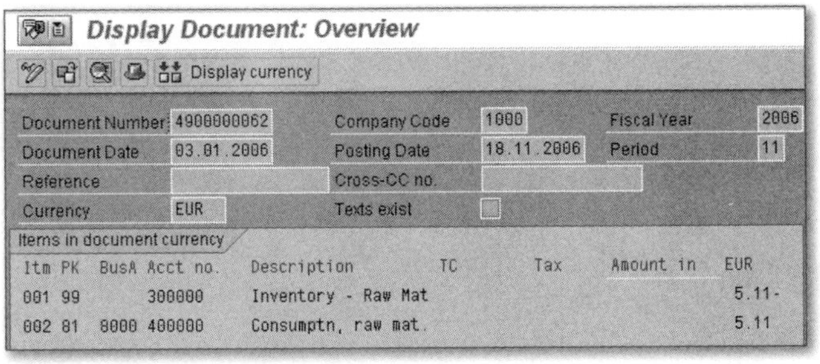

Figure 8.44 Accounting Document: Goods Issue to Cost Center

G/L account determination depends on various parameters such as plant, material, business transaction, and movement type. As shown in Figure 8.45, a goods issue to cost center transaction is posted, which automatically creates an accounting document with the appropriate G/L account postings. The following steps occur in the determination process:

1. Based on the business transaction, the system determines the value string. From there, system does the following:

▶ From the value string, the system determines the account modifier.

▶ From the value string, the system gets a list of transaction/event keys, as shown in Figure 8.45.

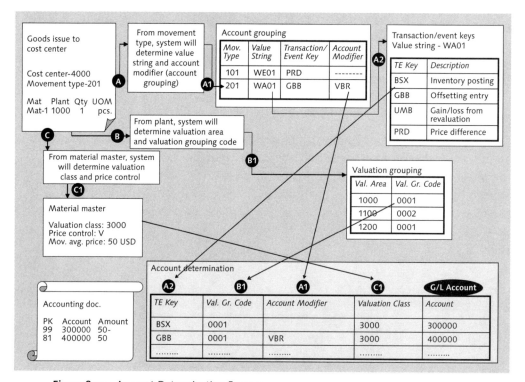

Figure 8.45 Account Determination Process

2. From the plant, the system determines the valuation area. (If you've defined the valuation area at the company code level, the system will determine the valuation area from the company code.)

3. From the valuation area, the system determines the valuation grouping code.

4. From the material master record, the system determines the valuation class, price control, and valuation price.

   After the system has determined the transaction key, account modifier, valuation grouping code, and valuation class, it will find the respective G/L account for the combination of these factors.

8.4   Document Type

You can define separate document types for each purchasing document category, such as PO, purchase requisition, RFQ, and so on (Figure 8.46).

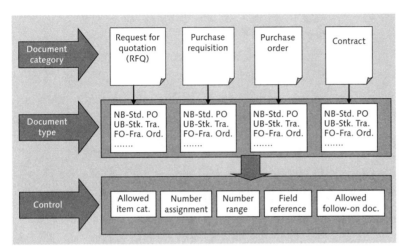

Figure 8.46   Document Types

The essential fields of document types are as follows:

► **Allowed item category**
You can define allowed item categories for document types.

► **Number assignment**
You can define number assignments for document types (internal or external numbers). Internal numbers are automatically assigned by the system when creating documents. External numbers are manually assigned by the user when creating documents.

► **Number range**
For each document type, you can assign number ranges for internal and external assignments. For internal number assignments, number ranges can be numeric only. For external number assignments, number ranges can be numeric or alphanumeric.

► **Field selection key**
You can define field selection keys for each document type. Field selection keys identify the field attributes such as hidden, display, optional, and mandatory.

► **Allowed follow-on documents**
You can define allowed follow-on documents for each document type.

Let's now discuss how document types can help you customize your business process in the SAP system.

8.4.1 Business Scenario

Consider a manufacturing enterprise that requires two different number ranges for stock material procurement to identify POs issued to local vendors and POs issued to overseas vendors (also known as import POs). In this case, document types will be very helpful. The SAP system includes preconfigured document types for each document category; however, you can create new document types based on your requirements.

Let us take an example of a company—TYRE International—who is a manufacturer of a wide range of car tires. The purchasing departments are broadly classified into central purchasing department and regional purchasing departments with clearly distinguished responsibilities. They also have a logistics department that takes care of import orders and in turn liaisons with external freight forwarders, customs clearing agents, and so on. The logistics department starts work only when it receives a copy of import POs from the purchasing department from either central or regional purchasing departments.

The management of this company wants a report on domestic and import purchases separately per purchasing department (represented as a purchasing organization in SAP).

The requirements in this example are:

► Classification of import and domestic POs

► Email output of import POs to the logistics department

These requirements can be met by having custom document types. To set this up for TYRE International, follow this procedure:

1. Create a DNB document type by copying standard document type NB for domestics POs.

2. Create an INB document type by copying standard document type NB for import POs.

3. For document type INB, in addition to vendor-specific output, set up email output, which goes to an internal email ID belonging to the logistics department.

4. Use an SAP standard report and/or develop a custom report to list domestic and import purchases based on document type DNB and INB, respectively.

In addition to the preceding example, there are many instances when customizing purchasing documents can be helpful; for example, adding custom fields, controlling authorizations, and so on. Another classic example would be to identify POs created by an external system through the interface in SAP.

8.4.2 Configuration Steps

You can configure document types for POs, purchase requisitions, RFQs, contracts, and scheduling agreements. The configuration steps for these documents are all quite similar; therefore, we'll focus only on the PO. You can follow the same steps for defining document types for other document categories.

1. **Define the document types.**

   To define document types for a PO, go to SAP IMG • PURCHASING • PURCHASE ORDER • DEFINE DOCUMENT TYPES. You can start either by clicking on the NEW ENTRIES button, or by copying an existing document type to save time.

   Enter the document type key, document type description, item interval, internal number range, external number range, and field selection key, as shown in Figure 8.47.

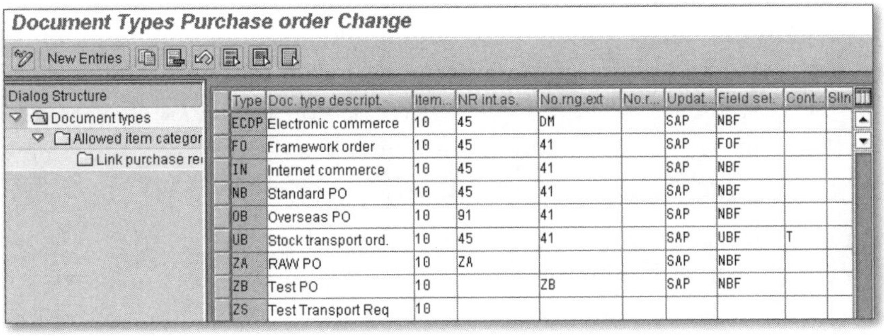

Document Types Purchase order Change

Type	Doc. type descript.	Item..	NR int.as.	No.rng.ext	No.r..	Updat.	Field sel.	Cont.	Sim
ECDP	Electronic commerce	10	45	DM		SAP	NBF		
FO	Framework order	10	45	41		SAP	FOF		
IN	Internet commerce	10	45	41		SAP	NBF		
NB	Standard PO	10	45	41		SAP	NBF		
OB	Overseas PO	10	91	41		SAP	NBF		
UB	Stock transport ord.	10	45	41		SAP	UBF	T	
ZA	RAW PO	10	ZA			SAP	NBF		
ZB	Test PO	10		ZB		SAP	NBF		
ZS	Test Transport Req	10							

Dialog Structure
- Document types
  - Allowed item categor
    - Link purchase re

Figure 8.47 Define Document Types for PO

To define allowed item categories, select DOCUMENT TYPES (in the left tree menu), and then double-click on ALLOWED ITEM CATEGORIES (again in the left tree menu; see Figure 8.48).

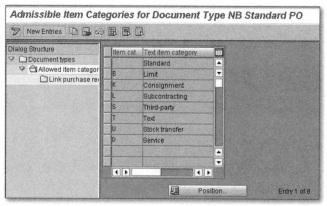

Figure 8.48 Allowed Item Categories for a Document Type

You can define allowed item categories based on the document type.

2. **Define a number range.**
   Every purchasing document type will have a number range, which can be internal, external, or both. To define the number range, go to SAP IMG • PURCHASING • PURCHASE ORDER • DEFINE DOCUMENT TYPES. Click on the CHANGE INTERVALS button. This will show you the existing number ranges; you can add a new number range by clicking on the INSERT NUMBER RANGE button (see Figure 8.49).

   Enter the number range key in the No column, and then make entries in FROM NUMBER and TO NUMBER. To make a number range external, select the EXTERNAL NUMBER RANGES checkbox; to make it internal, leave this checkbox unchecked.

3. **Assign a number range to the document type.**
   Number range intervals are assigned when defining document types, as you saw in step 1.

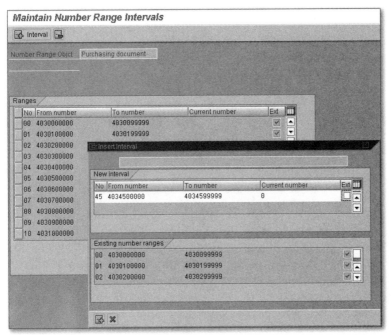

Figure 8.49 Define a Number Range Interval

8.4.3 Process Steps

When you create a purchasing document such as a PO, you need to select the document type. Based on the field selection key assigned to the document type, different fields of the PO will either be displayed, hidden, optional, or mandatory. The PO number will be created based on the number range assigned to the document type.

8.5 Version Management

You can control and manage purchasing document changes via SAP's version management functionality, which can be activated for both internal and external purchasing documents.

8.5.1 Business Scenario

Consider an enterprise that wants to track any changes made to POs. If changes are made on a PO, the new version of the PO should be issued to the vendor. This helps the company track the changes and also ensures that changes are being sent to the vendor with the new version of the PO.

SAP provides version management functionality to control and track changes in purchasing documents such as purchase requisitions, POs, contracts, scheduling agreements, and RFQs.

If version management is active for a document category and document type, the system will automatically create the first version at the time of document creation. Subsequent changes in the document will then create a new version of that document. As shown in Figure 8.50, a PO labeled "Version 0" is issued to the vendor by the purchasing department. However, the buyer then changes the order price, which updates the PO and creates Version 1. The revised PO is then sent to the vendor.

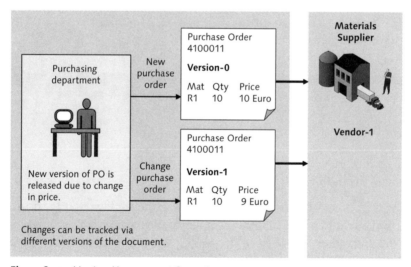

Figure 8.50 Version Management Scenario

In the following sections, we'll discuss the configuration and process steps involved in this process.

8.5.2 Configuration Steps

Follow these steps to configure version management:

1. **Set up version management.**

   There are two ways to do this, depending on whether you're working with internal or external documents. First, we'll look at internal documents (i.e., purchase requisitions).

   You can activate version management for a combination of document category and document type. After version management is active, changes made to a purchase requisition are managed in versions.

   To set up version management for purchase requisitions, go to SAP IMG • MATE-RIALS MANAGEMENT • PURCHASING • VERSION MANAGEMENT • SET UP VERSION MANAGEMENT FOR PURCHASE REQUISITION. You need to set up control data for version control, as shown in Figure 8.51.

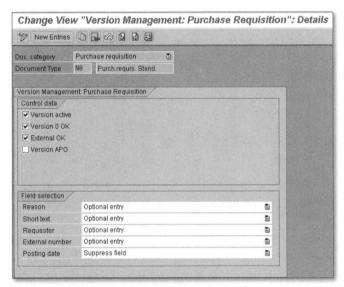

Figure 8.51 Version Management Setup for Purchase Requisitions

The following is a list and description of the important fields in this screen:

   ▶ VERSION ACTIVE

   This indicator enables the version control functionality for a particular document type.

▶ VERSION 0 OK
If this indicator is active, version 0 (a brand-new purchase requisition) will be automatically completed. If you haven't selected this indicator, version 0 must be manually flagged as completed.

▶ EXTERNAL OK
If this indicator is active, externally generated versions of purchase requisitions (e.g., those created via BAPI) will be completed automatically. If you haven't selected this indicator, the versions must be manually marked as completed.

▶ VERSION APO
If this indicator is active, version management for purchase requisitions transferred from an Advanced Planner and Optimizer (APO) system will be enabled. If you haven't selected this indicator, the system doesn't create a version.

▶ FIELD SELECTION
You can set up the field selection as DISPLAY, OPTIONAL ENTRY, REQUIRED, or SUPPRESS FIELD for the following fields: REASON, SHORT TEXT, REQUESTER, EXTERNAL NUMBER, and POSTING DATE. If not suppressed, these fields will be available on the VERSION DATA tab of the purchase requisition header.

External Purchasing Documents

We'll now discuss this same process (setting up version management) for external purchasing documents. In external purchasing documents, you can activate version management for a combination of purchasing organization, document category, and document type.

To set up version management for external purchasing documents, follow these steps:

1. **Configure version management.**
Go to SAP IMG • MATERIALS MANAGEMENT • PURCHASING • VERSION MANAGEMENT • SET UP VERSION MANAGEMENT FOR EXTERNAL PURCHASING DOCUMENTS.

A list of the document categories and document types will be displayed, as shown in Figure 8.52.

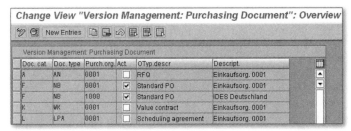

Figure 8.52 Version Management for External Purchasing Document

Click on the NEW ENTRIES button and enter the DOC. CATEGORY, DOCUMENT TYPE, and PURCHASING ORG. as shown in Figure 8.53. Then configure the control data as follows:

▶ VERSION ACTIVE
Select this to activate version management.

▶ VERSION 0 OK
If this indicator is active, a new purchasing document will automatically be created as version 0 and marked as completed. If you haven't selected the indicator, version 0 must be manually flagged as completed.

▶ FIELD SELECTION
You can set up field selection as DISPLAY, OPTIONAL ENTRY, REQUIRED, or SUPPRESSED FIELD for the following fields: REASON, SHORT TEXT, REQUESTER, EXTERNAL NUMBER, and POSTING DATE. If not suppressed, these fields will be available on the VERSION DATA tab of the purchasing document header.

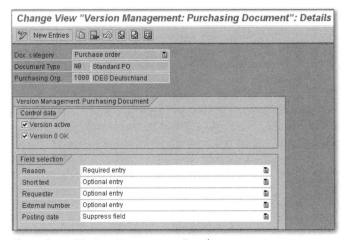

Figure 8.53 Version Management: Details

2. **Define reasons for changes.**

   In this step, you can define reasons for changes to both internal and external purchasing documents. To do so, go to SAP IMG • Materials Management • Purchasing • Version Management • Define Reasons for Change. Enter the reason code and description, as shown in Figure 8.54.

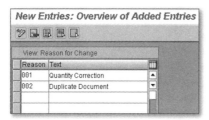

Figure 8.54   Define Reasons for Change

3. **Set up change displays.**

   In this step, you can define fields that should be displayed in the PO change history via the Display Changes button. This button is available on the Version Control tab of the document header.

   To set up change display, go to SAP IMG • Materials Management • Purchasing • Version Management • Set Up Change Displays. Click on the New Entries button, enter the document type, change the table name, and change the field name. Select the checkboxes No Output and Version, per your requirements. If No Output is selected, the corresponding field isn't included in the display. If Version is selected, the corresponding field won't be included in the change history that you can invoke via the Change icon on the Versions tab.

4. **Define version-relevant fields for purchase requisitions.**

   In this step, you can specify whether changes to a field are version-relevant. If a field is *version-relevant,* a change to that field causes a new version to be created. To define version-relevant fields, go to SAP IMG • Materials Management • Purchasing • Version Management • Version Relevant Fields of Purchase Requisitions. Click on the New Entries button and enter the document type, table name, and field name.

8.5.3 Process Steps

After you activate version management for a document category and document type, you can see the VERSIONS tab in the purchasing document header (Figure 8.55). Purchasing document output (messages such as printout, fax, email, etc.) will be triggered only if you set the COMPLETED indicator.

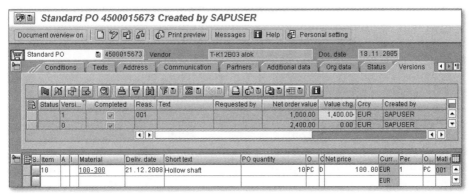

Figure 8.55 PO: Version Management

External purchase documents such as POs, RFQs, contracts, and scheduling agreements are sent to vendors in the form of printouts, faxes, EDI, or email. These outputs are called *messages* in the SAP system. Let's move on to learn how messages are configured in the system.

8.6 Message Determination

External purchasing documents generate output—or, in other words, a message. This message is information sent to a vendor using a variety of media such as printers, EDI, fax, or email (see Figure 8.56). The variety of media will depend on each vendor; that is, some may prefer faxes whereas others may prefer email, and so on. While generating output for a vendor, it's difficult for the user to remember the type of media acceptable to the vendor. For this reason, the SAP system provides message determination functionality where you can define the output media for vendors. The system then automatically proposes the output media during document creation.

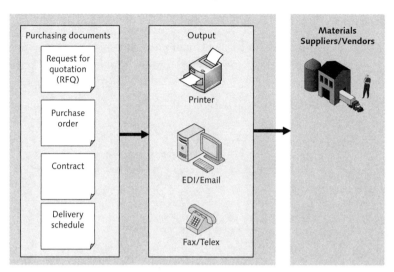

Figure 8.56 Output Messages for Purchasing Documents

8.6.1 Business Scenario

For example, consider an enterprise that wants the system to output messages upon creation of or changes to purchasing documents such as POs, contracts, and so on.

For each purchasing transaction, you can define whether the system should use message determination.

When you're not using message determination, the system can generate output for SAP-defined messages such as message NEU for POs. However, you can change the proposed parameters in the individual documents. For printout messages, the system needs to determine the printer. This is done via the following sequence:

▶ Printer defined for the purchasing group

▶ Printer defined in user parameter PRI

▶ Printer defined in user defaults

For messages *with* message determination, the SAP system uses the condition techniques discussed in Section 8.2. Messages are determined based on predefined criteria such as document type and vendor.

8.6.2 How Message Determination Works

Let's see how the system determines messages, using the help of an example (see Figure 8.57).

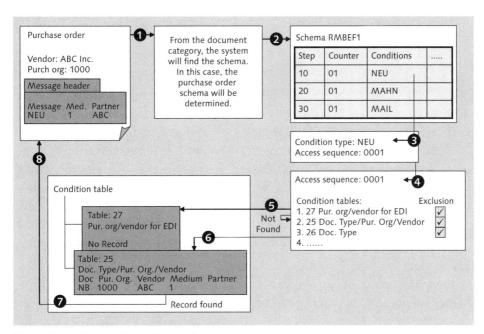

Figure 8.57 Message Determination Process

The PO is created with vendor ABC, purchasing organization 1000, and purchasing document type NB. Let's see how the message is determined for this PO:

1. **Determine the message schema.**
   The system determines the schema from the document category. In this example, the document category is PO, and the schema is RMBEF1. For each document category, the schema is defined in the system in Customizing (SAP IMG).

2. **Determine the condition type.**
   The calculation schema consists of various condition types listed in a sequence. In this example, condition type NEU is determined.

3. **Determine the access sequence and condition table.**
   The system determines the access sequence (0001) assigned to the condition type (NEU).

4. **Determine the condition record.**
   The system determines the condition tables assigned to access sequence 0001. A condition table consists of condition records in a sequence that defines priority. In this example, the system first determines condition table 27 and searches for a valid condition record in this table. Because the system doesn't find the condition record, it moves to the next condition table, which is condition table 25.

5. **Determine the next condition record.**
   Condition table 25 consists of condition records for the combination of document type, purchase organization, and vendor. In this example, the system determines the condition record for document type NB, purchase organization 1000, and vendor ABC. The condition record consists of medium, partner function, and partner. Medium 1 (printout) is found in this example. Partner is blank in the condition record; therefore, the output partner will be the PO vendor.

6. **Copy message details into the document.**
   The system copies all of the details such as medium, partner, and printer into the document. If required, you can change the print parameters for a specific document.

8.6.3 Configuration Steps

In this section we'll discuss message determination configuration for POs. Note that you can use the same configuration steps for all other external purchasing documents.

1. **Define the condition table.**
   In a condition table, you define the combination of fields for which you want to create message records. To define new condition tables or to check existing condition tables, go to SAP IMG • MATERIALS MANAGEMENT • PURCHASING • MESSAGES • OUTPUT CONTROL • CONDITION TABLE • DEFINE CONDITION TABLE FOR PURCHASE ORDER.

You can define a new table by copying an existing condition table. For example, condition table 025 has three fields assigned to it (Figure 8.58): PURCHASING DOC. TYPE, PURCH. ORGANIZATION, and VENDOR. The condition record is maintained for the combination of these selected fields. Condition records are maintained via Transaction MN06.

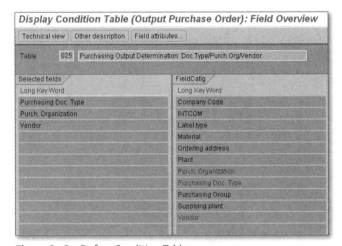

Figure 8.58 Define Condition Table

2. **Define the access sequence.**

   In this step, you define the access sequence. This is a search strategy by which the SAP system searches for valid message records. We recommend using the access sequence provided by the SAP system. To define the access sequence, go to SAP IMG • MATERIALS MANAGEMENT • PURCHASING • MESSAGES • OUTPUT CONTROL • ACCESS SEQUENCE • DEFINE ACCESS SEQUENCE FOR PURCHASE ORDER. You can define the access sequence by clicking on the NEW ENTRIES button or by copying an SAP-provided access sequence (Figure 8.59).

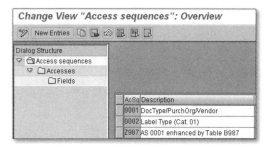

Figure 8.59 Define the Access Sequence

To make changes to the access sequence provided by the SAP system, select the sequence, and double-click on ACCESSES on the left tree menu. Here, you can define the access sequence number, table number, and EXCLUSIVE indicator, as shown in Figure 8.60.

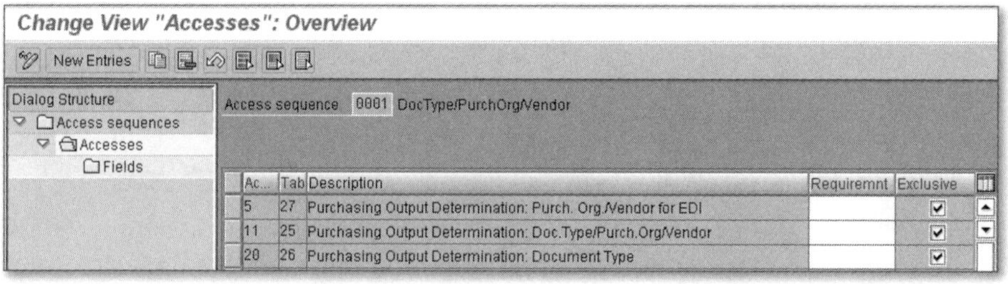

Figure 8.60 Define the Access Sequence: Condition Tables

3. **Define the message type.**

   In this step you define the message types for a PO. To define a message type, go to SAP IMG • MATERIALS MANAGEMENT • PURCHASING • MESSAGES • OUTPUT CONTROL • MESSAGE TYPES • DEFINE MESSAGE TYPES FOR PURCHASE ORDER. You can define a message type by clicking on the NEW ENTRIES button or by copying a standard message type provided by the SAP system (Figure 8.61).

   An access sequence is assigned to a message type, and you can define the processing routines. For different mediums of output type, you can define the FORM and FORM ROUTINE, as shown in Figure 8.62. Forms can be realigned per customer requirements, or you can create new forms.

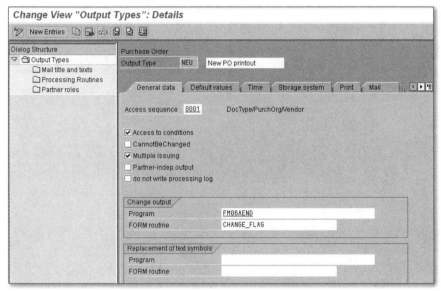

Figure 8.61 Define the Message Type

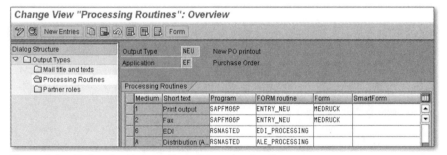

Figure 8.62 Define the Message Type: Processing Routines

4. **Define the message schema.**

   In this step, you define the message schema for purchasing documents. The allowed message types are stored in the message schema. To define message schemas, go to SAP IMG • MATERIALS MANAGEMENT • PURCHASING • MESSAGES • OUTPUT CONTROL • MESSAGE DETERMINATION SCHEMAS • DEFINE MESSAGE SCHEMA FOR PURCHASE ORDER. Define the sequence of the conditions for which you want the system to search for condition records (Figure 8.63). The defined schema needs to be assigned to a PO.

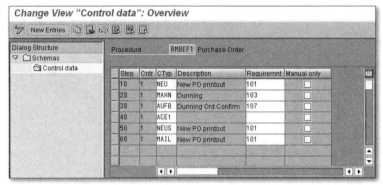

Figure 8.63 Define Message Schema

5. **Define partner roles.**

   In this step, you define the allowed partner roles for the message types. To do so, go to SAP IMG • Materials Management • Purchasing • Messages • Output Control • Partner Roles per Message Type • Define Partner Roles for Purchase Order. You can define the partner roles for each output type and medium type combination by clicking on the New Entries button (Figure 8.64).

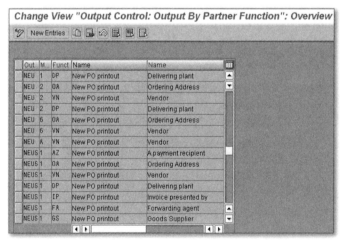

Figure 8.64 Define Partner Function

6. **Assign output devices to purchasing groups.**

In this step, you assign output devices to purchasing groups via SAP IMG •
MATERIALS MANAGEMENT • PURCHASING • MESSAGES • ASSIGN OUTPUT DEVICES
TO PURCHASING GROUPS. Assign the output device (such as a printer) to the
purchasing group, as shown in Figure 8.65.

Change View "Printer for Messages": Overview

PGr	Description	ODev	
000	Chef,H.	LP01	
001	Dietl,B.	LP01	
002	Harnisch,H.	LP01	
003	IDES USA	LP01	
004	Eiffel,J.	LP01	
005	Diller, M	LP01	
006	Sommer,St.	LP01	
007	Lux,L.	LP01	
008	Zuse,K.	LP01	
009	Müller,K.		

Figure 8.65 Assign Output Devices to Purchasing Groups

8.6.4 Process Steps

It's necessary to maintain the condition records for the condition tables configured
for message determination. To define condition records, go to Transaction MN04
and select the key combination for which you want to maintain the condition
records (Figure 8.66).

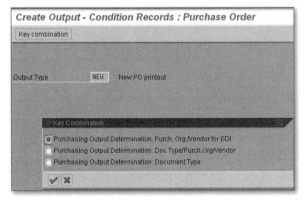

Figure 8.66 Maintain Condition Records: Select a Key Combination

For the selected key combination, enter the condition record, as shown in Figure 8.67. Fill in the VENDOR (number), PARTNER function, MEDIUM, and DATE/TIME fields. If the PARTNER field is left blank, the system will assign the ordering vendor to the output partner in the purchasing document. After you've maintained the condition records, the system will automatically determine the message condition in POs.

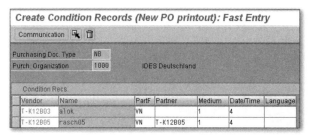

Figure 8.67 Maintain Condition Records

Create a PO via Transaction ME21N. Enter the vendor, purchasing organization, purchasing group, company code, and line item details. If you click on the MESSAGE button, you can see the message determined by the system (Figure 8.68). The printer is determined from the purchase group. Changes to the print parameters are made in a document.

Figure 8.68 Create PO Messages Tab

8.7 Serial Numbers in Purchasing

You can use a serial number functionality in purchasing. You can define the serial number during purchase requisition and PO creation.

Example

A car-manufacturing company in Germany procures various bearings for cars. For each bearing, the company wants to have unique serial numbers to differentiate the bearings from each other. This unique serial number also helps the company track if any future issue with bearing and replacements.

You can easily differentiate between them by serializing the materials, making it easier to request a specific piece of material.

You serialize the materials using the MAINTAIN SERIAL NUMBER popup, which you access on the DELIVERY SCHEDULE tab page in the PO or on the MATERIAL DATA tab page in the purchase requisition.

The following new features are available:

▶ **Serial number transfer**
When you create a sales order for third-party processing and assign serial numbers to its items, the created purchase requisition will contain these serial numbers. This purchase requisition is created in the background. When you create a PO with reference to a purchase requisition, the serial numbers are transferred automatically from the purchase requisition to the PO.

▶ **Schedule lines**
You can have more than one serial number per schedule line. If the PO has several schedule lines, the serialized numbers need to be assigned manually to the correct schedule line or created by the system by choosing CREATE SERIAL NUMBER AUTOMATICALLY in the MAINTAIN SERIAL NUMBER popup.

▶ **Base units of measure**
When serializing base units of measure (e.g., piece), the conversion of order unit of measure (e.g., kg) must result in a whole number at the schedule line level for POs and at the item level for purchase requisitions. For example, if the base unit of measure was 3 pieces, and the order unit was 2kg, each unit would be 0.66, which you can't serialize.

Note

You can't change the configuration of a purchase requisition or PO item if you're working with already-configured objects to which serial numbers are already assigned, and the original configuration in the material serial number isn't linked to these objects.

8.7.1 Configuration Steps

Now let's discuss the step-by-step procedure to configure the serial number for purchasing.

Step 1: Activate the Serial Number Functionality

First you need to activate the functionality in the switch framework by using Transaction SFW5. In the Switch Framework screen, select the function LOG_MM_SERNO (Serial Numbers in Purchasing with Integration in Inventory Management and Shipping), and from the main menu, click on the system settings. Click the Activate button, or press [Ctrl] + [F3]. It will give you an information message stating "Job started, click on OK." After the functionality is switched on, you can see the status message as "Business func. will remain switched on" as shown in Figure 8.69.

Name	Description	Planned Status	Depe	Docu	Relea	Software Component	Rele
LOG_MM_P2PSE_1	Procurement - SRM Integration	☐	🔀	ⓘ	ⓘ	SAP_APPL	604
LOG_MM_RL	Returnable Packaging Logistics	☐	🔀	ⓘ	ⓘ	ECC-DIMP	603
LOG_MM_SERNO	Serial Numbers in Purchasing with Integration in...	Business func. will remain switched on		ⓘ	ⓘ	SAP_APPL	604
LOG_PP_BATCH_HISTORY	Batch History	☐		ⓘ	ⓘ	SAP_APPL	604
LOG_PP_EWM_MAN	EWM Integration into Manufacturing	☐	🔀	ⓘ	ⓘ	SAP_APPL	604
LOG_PP_LMAN	Lean Manufacturing, Better MRP Evaluation (Sto...	☐		ⓘ	ⓘ		602
LOG_PP_LPO	SAP LPO Integration	☐		ⓘ	ⓘ	SAP_APPL	604
LOG_PP_MIS	Manufacturing Information System: Order Info Sy...	☐		ⓘ	ⓘ	SAP_APPL	603

Figure 8.69 Switch Framework—Switch on the Functionality

Step 2: Determine Serial Number Profile

In this step, you need to maintain the serial number profile. Go to SAP IMG • Materials Management • Purchasing • Serial Numbers • Determine Serial Number Profiles.

You can control the following in the serial number profile:

▶ The serialization transactions for the profile define the transactions for which serialization is possible.

▶ Serial number usage defines whether serialization is mandatory or optional.

▶ The equipment required function specifies whether a piece of equipment is required.

▶ The serial number profile can be allocated to different transactions with different parameterization.

▶ The equipment category distinguishes individual pieces of equipment according to their usage.

Click on NEW ENTRIES, or you can use the copy function to copy an existing profile. Enter the profile code and text, and then select the equipment category. You can create a new category by clicking on the CREATE button in the list option.

Select the appropriate option (such as NO STOCK CHECK or STOCK CHECK WITH WARN-ING OR ERROR) in STOCK CHECK FOR SERIAL NUMBERS. The STOCK CHECK indicator states whether the system should perform a stock check during serial number assignment. If your business requires this, it also establishes with what type of notification (warning or error) the system reacts in the event of stock inconsistencies with inventory management.

After entering these details, click on the SERIALIZING PROCEDURES option on the left side. Here you need to select the procedure (PROCD), usage (SERUSAGE), and equipment requirement (EQREQ) as shown in Figure 8.70.

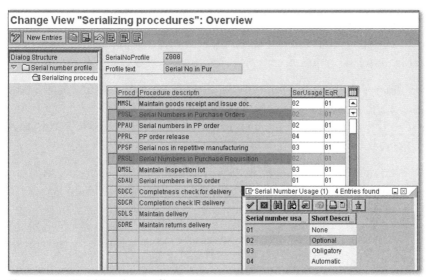

Figure 8.70 Serial Number Profile Creation

For purchase requisition, the serializing procedure is PPRL; for PO, it's POSL.

Let's now consider the significance of the usage indicator and equipment requirement:

▶ SERUSAGE
Determines one of the following for a business transaction:

  ▶ No serial numbers are assigned

  ▶ Serial numbers can be assigned

  ▶ Serial numbers must be assigned

  ▶ Serial numbers are assigned automatically

▶ EQREQ
Entry that determines whether or not an equipment master record should be created for each number when assigning serial numbers.

If you choose the DEFAULT: WITHOUT EQUIPMENT indicator, the user can later decide whether an equipment master record should still be created when they're assigning serial numbers in the dialog box.

If you choose the indicator WITH EQUIPMENT, this is binding for the user. The indicator can't be reset.

Step 3: Define the Serial Number in Purchasing Document Types

In this step, you need to define the serial numbers for the purchasing document types; that is, purchase requisition document types and PO document types.

To define the serial number in a purchase requisition, go to SAP IMG • MATERIALS MANAGEMENT • PURCHASING • PURCHASE REQUISITION • DEFINE DOCUMENT TYPES. And to define the serial number in a PO, go to SAP IMG • MATERIALS MANAGEMENT • PURCHASING • PURCHASE ORDER • DEFINE DOCUMENT TYPES.

Select the document type, and from the left side menu, click on SERIAL NUMBER PROFILES as shown in Figure 8.71. Here you need to select the serial number profile that you've created in previous step, and then save.

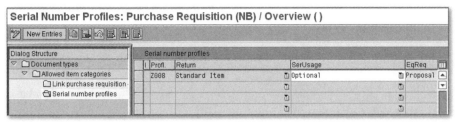

Figure 8.71 Assign the Serial Number Profile to the Purchasing Document Type

8.7.2 Process Steps

Let's discuss how you use serial numbers in purchasing in the following subsections.

Step 1: Create a Purchase Requisition

Create purchase requisition by using Transaction ME51N, and then entering the material number, vendor, and all other required fields. Click on the MATERIAL DATA tab. Click on the ASSIGN SERIAL NUMBERS button and enter the serial number for the material as shown in Figure 8.72. After entering the details, click OK and save the document.

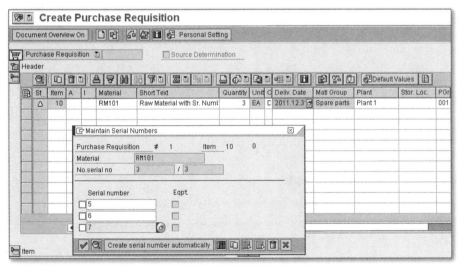

Figure 8.72 Serial Number Enter Screen in the Purchase Requisition

You can also choose an option to create serial numbers automatically; in this case, the system will automatically create the serial numbers for the material.

Step 2: Create a Purchase Order

You create a purchase order via Transaction ME21N, with reference to the purchase requisition, which you created in an earlier step. After you enter the details, you can see the SERIAL NUMBER button in the PO screen as shown in Figure 8.73. If you click on this button, you can see the serial number details of the items you've entered in the purchase requisition.

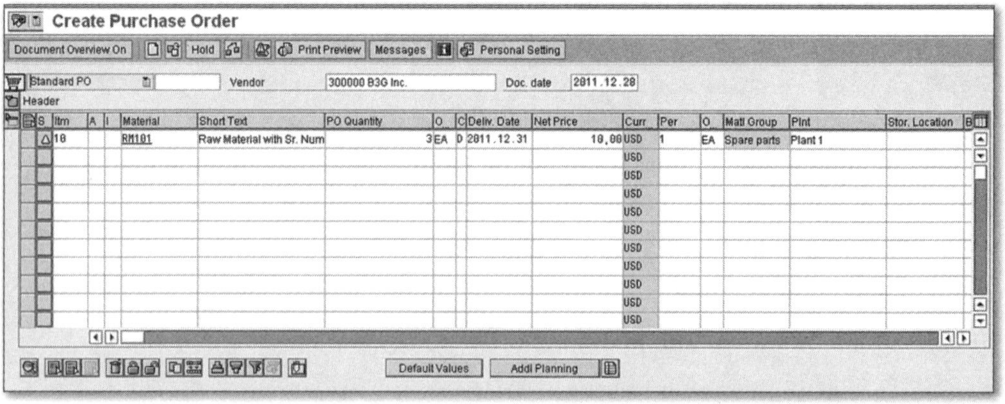

Figure 8.73 Purchase Order Creation with Serial Numbers

If you're creating a PO directly without reference to a purchase requisition, you can maintain the serial number in the PO. To enter the serial number in the PO, go to the item details DELIVERY SCHEDULE tab, click on the SERIAL NUMBER button, and enter the serial number.

Step 3: Post the Goods Receipt

To post the goods receipt, go to Transaction MIGO and enter the PO number that you created in an earlier step. In the item details, you can see the new tab named SERIAL NUMBERS as shown in Figure 8.74.

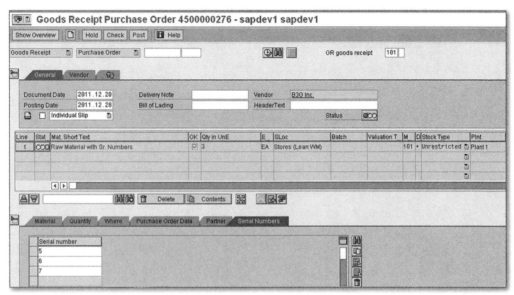

Figure 8.74 Goods Receipt with Serial Numbers

You can see the details of serial numbers via Transaction IQ03.

8.8 Public Templates in Purchase Orders and Requisitions

As of SAP EHP5 (SAP_APPL 605), business function Materials Management—Enhancements in Procurement (LOG_MM_CI_3), you can create purchase requisitions and POs more efficiently by using templates. This will save a lot of data entry time and also will reduce chances of errors. There are two types of templates:

▶ **User-specific template**
This is specific to a particular user. You can create your own template and save it for future use so that the next time, you can create purchase requisitions or POs with your own templates. These templates won't be available for other users.

▶ **Public template**
This is available to all users. If you create a template and set it as PUBLIC, it will be available for all users.

This function is available in the following transactions:

- ▶ Transaction ME21N: Create Purchase Order
- ▶ Transaction ME22N: Change Purchase Order
- ▶ Transaction ME51N: Create Purchase Requisition
- ▶ Transaction ME52N: Change Purchase Requisition

Next let's see how to create templates for POs.

8.8.1 Configuration Steps

Activate the business function LOG_MM_CI_3 via Transaction SFW5 (Switch Framework). You'll then see the template creation functionality activated in PO and purchase requisition transactions.

8.8.2 Process Steps

To create a template for a purchase order, follow these steps:

1. **Create a template.**
   Go to Transaction ME21N or Transaction ME22N (if you've already created a PO), enter the PO header details and line item details such as material, quantity, and so on. You can see the two new buttons in the screen as shown in Figure 8.75.

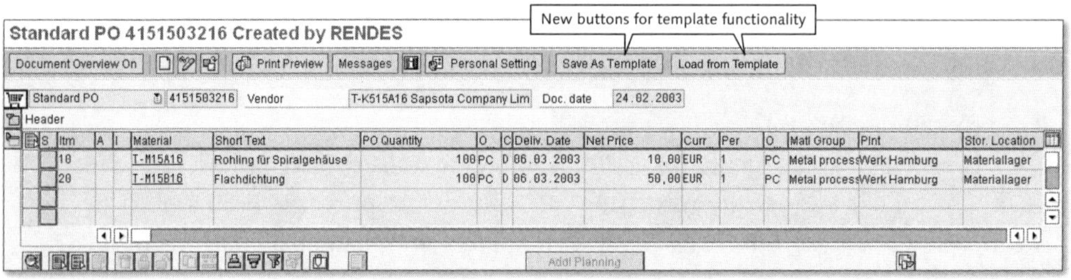

Figure 8.75 Template Functionality in Purchase Orders

Click on the SAVE AS TEMPLATE button, and a new screen appears as shown in Figure 8.76.

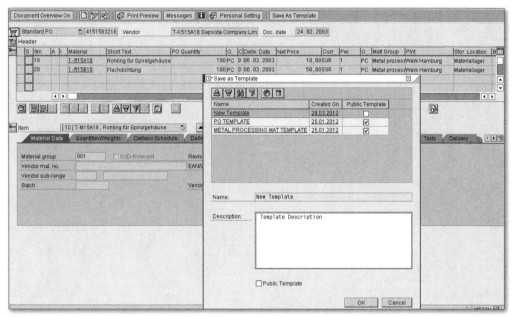

Figure 8.76 Creating a PO Template

Enter the template name and description. Select the PUBLIC TEMPLATE checkbox if you want this template to be made available for all users, and then click on OK. Your template has been saved.

2. **Create the PO via the template.**

Go to Transaction ME21N and click on the LOAD FROM TEMPLATE button. You'll get a list of your own templates and also all public templates, from which you can choose the appropriate template as shown in Figure 8.77. If you want the PO header data to be copied from the template, you can selct the LOAD WITH HEADER DATA checkbox, or you can leave it unchecked and click OK. An information pop-up window appears stating that the template data was copied. You can see that all of the data has been copied from the template, so you can now make the required changes and save the PO.

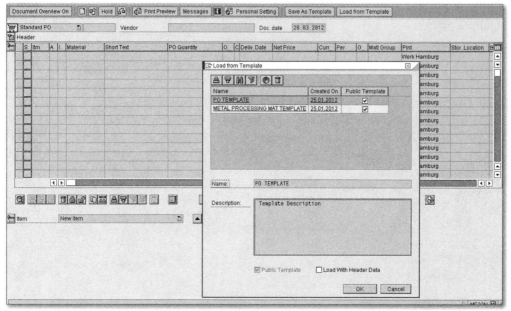

Figure 8.77   Creating POs via Templates

8.9   Blocking and Unblocking Purchase Orders

As of SAP EHP5 for SAP ERP 6.0 (SAP_APPL 605), business function Materials Management—Enhancements in Procurement (LOG_MM_CI_3), you can save the reasons for blocking a PO item in POs. This scenario helps you block a particular line item of the PO based on the specific reason.

8.9.1   Customizing Steps

Activate the business function LOG_MM_CI_3 via Transaction SFW5. After you activate this, you can see the new menu nodes in customization.

To customize the blocking reasons, go to SAP IMG • MATERIALS MANAGEMENT • PURCHASING • PURCHASE ORDER • DEFINE BLOCKING REASON. Define the blocking reasons as shown in Figure 8.78, click on the NEW button, and enter the two-digit reason code.

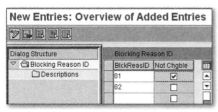

Figure 8.78 Blocking Reasons Creation

Click on DESCRIPTIONS in the left-hand menu. Enter the description as shown in Figure 8.79 and save.

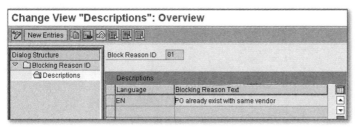

Figure 8.79 Blocking Reasons Description

8.9.2 Process Step

To use the blocking reasons functionality, go to Transaction ME21N to create a PO and enter the item details. Click on the BLOCK button, and in the line item details on the PURCHASE ORDER HISTORY tab, you can see the blocking reasons as shown in Figure 8.80. Select the blocking reason and save the PO.

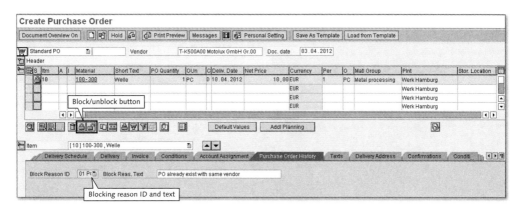

Figure 8.80 Create PO—Blocking Reasons

8.10 Summary

In this chapter, you learned the key configurations involved in MM release strategies, pricing procedures, automatic account determination, document types, version management, message determination, and serial numbers in purchasing.

In the next chapter, we'll discuss classification and variant configuration.

Classification is a powerful tool used to organize master data objects in a way that allows you to find them more easily, as well as enhance master data by adding additional information.

9   Material Classification

A *classification system* is an organized and structured way to arrange objects such as material and vendor master data. For example, a company may have several thousand materials; thus it becomes difficult to search for a specific material. A classification system is used to classify materials based on characteristics; with the help of this system, you can search for a material based on its characteristic values.

Such classification is used in almost all SAP components, including Materials Management (MM), Sales and Distribution (SD), Production Planning (PP), and others. This chapter will focus on material classification as it relates to MM, where it's used for release procedures and batch management.

In the following sections, we'll first provide an introduction to material classification and a review of key terms. We'll then cover the process and configuration steps required to configure this function.

9.1   Introduction to Material Classification

Material classification is used to find materials, as shown in Figure 9.1. One of the most useful aspects of classification is that it can be used to search for a specific material number. Figure 9.1 shows the process flow for searching for a material master record via the classification functionality, illustrating the search options via both class and characteristic values. To perform a search, click on the MATERIAL SEARCH button or press F4, and then enter or select the class name. A list of characteristics will be displayed for the selected class. Then, based on the values of the characteristics you enter, the system will search for the materials that are assigned these values.

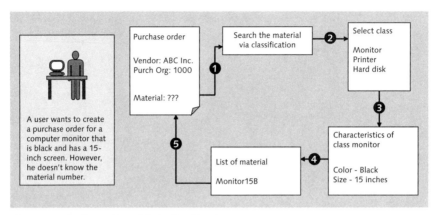

Figure 9.1 Finding a Material via Classification

Let's see how easily you can find a specific material master record from within thousands of master data records. Let's say you want to create a PO for a computer monitor that is black and has a 15-inch screen. Even if you don't know the material number for this type of monitor, you can search for it using the classification system. To do so, go to the transaction used to create POs (Transaction ME21N). Enter the vendor number and purchasing organization details. To find the material, press F4 or click on the SEARCH icon in the MATERIAL field (Figure 9.2).

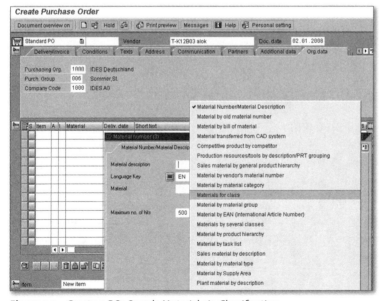

Figure 9.2 Create a PO: Search Material via Classification

In the material search options, select MATERIALS FOR CLASS. The system will then open the FIND OBJECTS IN CLASSES screen (Figure 9.3).

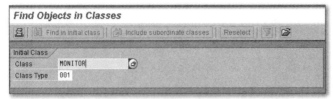

Figure 9.3 Finding an Object via Classification: Select Class

Enter the CLASS name, or select it from the dropdown list. Then, enter "001" (material class) as the CLASS TYPE. Press ⌊Enter⌋. The system will display the characteristics of the class; in this example, size and color. Select the size of the monitor and its color and click on the FIND button, as shown in Figure 9.4.

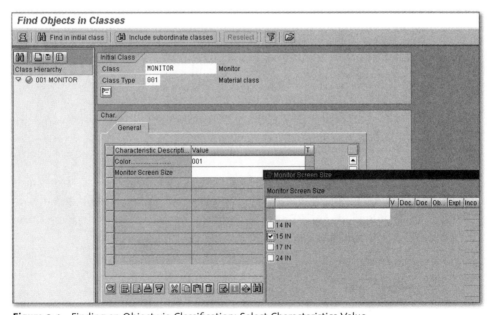

Figure 9.4 Finding an Object via Classification: Select Characteristics Value

The system will find the material number that has the selected characteristics (Figure 9.5). If you click on the material number, it will copy into the PO screen.

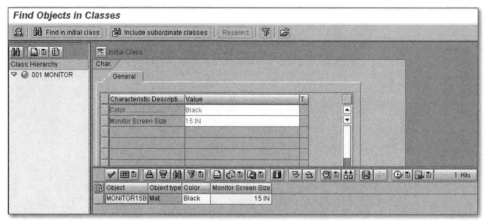

Figure 9.5 Finding an Object via Classification: Select Required Material

9.2 Key Terms of the Classification System

Before we discuss the technical configuration of material classification, you must have a good understanding of the different components involved in the process. The following key terms are essential to this subject:

▶ **Objects**
Objects consist of three different types—vendor, material, and batch—and are assigned to classes based on their characteristics.

▶ **Class type**
The class type has central control functions in class maintenance because it determines which object types you can assign to a class. Preconfigured class types are provided in the SAP system, but you can also create your own, if necessary. The following are examples of the standard class types:

▶ Material class type: 001

▶ Vendor class type: 010

▶ Release strategy: 023

▶ Variant classification: 300

> **Note**
>
> You can't change the class type after you've created a class.

▶ **Classes**

A class is a group of characteristics. For example, computer hardware trading companies define material classes for monitors, laser printers, and hard disk drives.

▶ **Characteristics**

Characteristics are properties of objects. In the case of material classification, the characteristics are material properties. For example, a computer monitor material class might have characteristics that include color and size.

▶ **Values**

Characteristics have their own values. For example, for a computer monitor class with a color characteristic and a size characteristic, the values of the former might be white and black, and the values of the latter might be 15 inches, 17 inches, and 21 inches.

9.3   Configuration Steps

Figure 9.6 illustrates the process flow for setting up a material classification system.

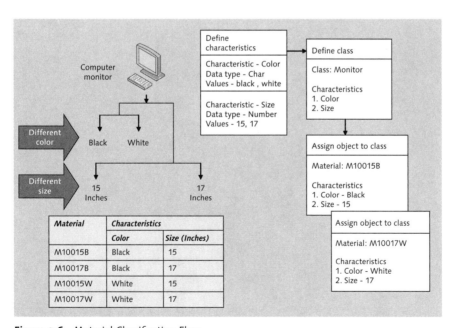

Figure 9.6 Material Classification Flow

First, define the characteristics and allowed values for each characteristic. Next, maintain classes and assign the characteristics to these classes. Finally, assign objects (such as materials) to the classes, and you use the characteristics to describe the objects.

In the following sections, we'll describe each of these steps in more detail.

9.3.1 Step 1: Define Characteristics

In the SAP system, characteristics and classes are both types of master data. You can define characteristics via the following menu path: SAP MENU • CROSS-APPLICATION COMPONENTS • CLASSIFICATION SYSTEM • MASTER DATA • CHARACTERISTICS. Alternatively, you can use Transaction CT04.

In the resulting screen, enter the CHARACTERISTIC name and click CREATE. Enter a DESCRIPTION and the CHARS GROUP, as shown in Figure 9.7. In the STATUS field, you have three options: IN PREPARATION, LOCKED, and RELEASED. A status of RELEASED means that the characteristic can be used; a status of LOCKED or IN PREPARATION means that it can't be used.

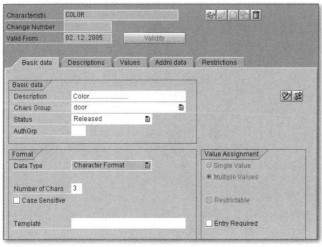

Figure 9.7 Define Characteristics: Basic Data Tab

In the FORMAT section, select the DATA TYPE, which is used to define the format of the characteristic's values. You can select any of the following predefined data types:

▶ CHARACTER FORMAT (CHAR)
Used for values that consist of a character string. For example, if one of the characteristics is color, it needs to be defined with CHARACTER FORMAT because its values are written as words (black, blue, white, etc.).

▶ NUMERIC FORMAT (NUM)
Used for numeric characteristic values.

▶ DATE FORMAT (DATE)
Used for characteristic values that represent a date.

▶ TIME FORMAT (TIME)
Used for characteristic values that represent a time.

▶ CURRENCY FORMAT (CURR)
Used for characteristic values that represent a currency.

In the VALUE ASSIGNMENT section, select either SINGLE VALUE or MULTIPLE VALUES. The SINGLE VALUE indicator specifies that only one value can be assigned to this characteristic; the MULTIPLE VALUES indicator is used when more than one value is possible.

Select the VALUES tab, and enter the possible values for this characteristic, as shown in Figure 9.8. The ADDITIONAL VALUES indicator allows you to enter characteristic values that aren't defined. After you've defined the values, save the characteristic.

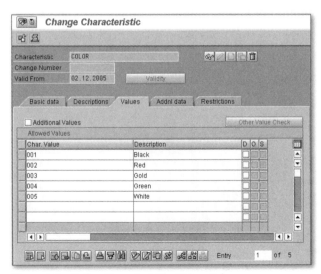

Figure 9.8 Define Characteristics: Values Tab

9.3.2 Step 2: Define Class

To define a class, go to SAP MENU • CROSS-APPLICATION COMPONENTS • CLASSIFICA-TION SYSTEM • MASTER DATA • CLASSES, or use Transaction CL02. Enter the CLASS TYPE as "001" (Material Class), and fill in the appropriate CLASS name. Then click on NEW (Figure 9.9). Enter a DESCRIPTION, and set the STATUS as RELEASED. Enter the validity dates.

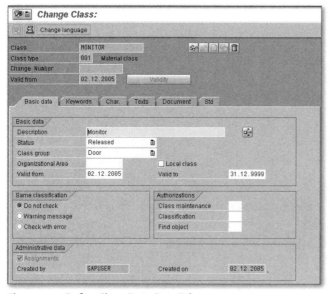

Figure 9.9 Define Class: Basic Data Tab

On the CHAR. tab, assign the characteristics to the class, as shown in Figure 9.10.

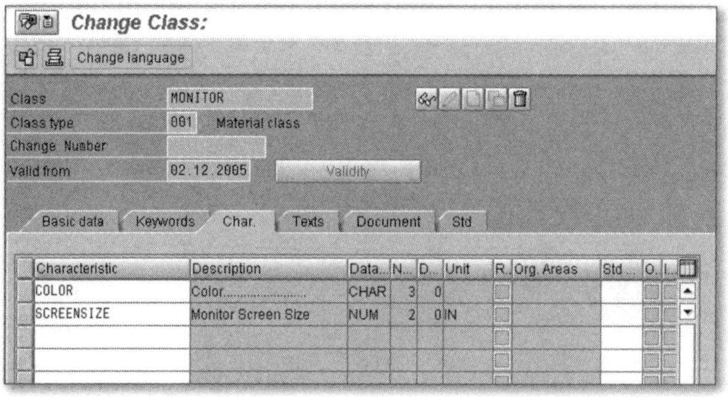

Figure 9.10 Define Class: Char. Tab

You've now defined the class and assigned characteristics to the class. You're ready to assign objects to the class.

9.3.3 Step 3: Assign Objects to Classes

To assign objects to classes, go to SAP MENU • CROSS-APPLICATION COMPONENTS • CLASSIFICATION SYSTEM • ASSIGNMENT • ASSIGN OBJECT TO CLASSES, or use Transaction CL20N. Enter the MATERIAL number and CLASS TYPE 001. Then enter the class in which you want this material to be assigned. The characteristics of the class will be displayed, as shown in Figure 9.11. Select the values for each of the characteristics.

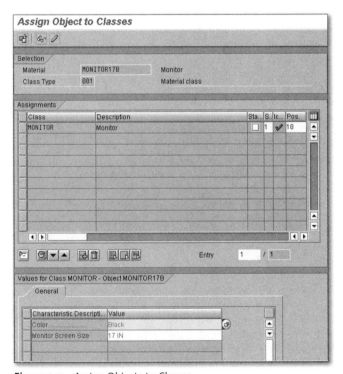

Figure 9.11 Assign Objects to Classes

You can classify a material while creating material master records via Transaction MM01. Enter the MATERIAL number, INDUSTRY TYPE, and MATERIAL TYPE to see a list of material views, as shown in Figure 9.12. In the VIEW section, select CLASSIFICATION. In this view, you'll get an option to select the class. After you've selected the class, display the list of characteristics. Enter the characteristic values and save the material master record.

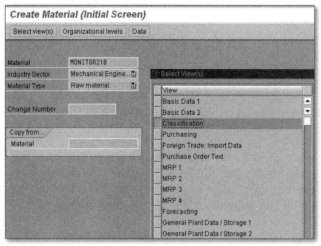

Figure 9.12 Create Material Master: Classification View

9.4 Summary

In this chapter, you learned about the key terms and configuration steps involved in material classification. Although it's a useful tool, remember that it can be used efficiently only when materials are properly classified.

In the next chapter we'll learn the importance of batch management in Materials Management in SAP. We'll also discuss the business requirements and step-by-step customization of batch management.

Batch management is a legal requirement that's used to track materials in your system. In this chapter, we'll discuss the unique characteristics of batch management and its industry application, as well as the customization options you have.

10 Batch Management

Batch management increases production, improves quality, reduces cycle times, and facilitates compliance for your company to meet most industry standards, such as ISO, FDA 21, CFR Part 11, and GAMP-5. However, to understand what batch management is, we need to break it down a bit more: Each company has technical requirements that remain the same for all production lots such as chemical composition or required viscosity. In the chemical industry, for example, when a material is produced using the same process order in a number of charges in a reactor, it's called a production lot, and the outcome of each production run is a batch. A batch is a consistent unit of a material that's defined in your SAP system with unique specifications. A batch represents a single subset of the total quantity of material that is held and produced during a production run. Many production runs can be used to produce a production lot.

The terms *batch* and *material* are interdependent. Consider the following structure:

1. All batch-reproducible criteria equals the criteria of the material, and not of the batch. In other words, the production criteria depends on the material, but not on the batch.

2. To identify a batch as a non-reproducible unit, the batch record should comprise the unique data applicable only to that respective batch.

3. Organizing master data in this unique manner enables the application of the same master data to various models of products, individually. Materials are only planned at the material level in the SAP ERP system.

Using a batch is also useful to recall the products from the market when the products are found to be faulty. It's common to read in the news that a company has recalled a product with a certain batch number.

> **Note**
>
> *Batch* is an abstract compression of the words "production of a batch." It represents the material being used in the process—at any given time during the process.

Let's look at the main reasons why batch management is useful for companies to implement:

- To be able to recall history in case of a problem
- To search by expiration date
- To follow compliance requirements of industry standards
- To manage the batch characteristics to suit a specific requirement for every industry—retail, aerospace, cosmetics, health, auto, food, pharmaceuticals, and so on—that can benefit from batch management

Business Scenario

Let's consider a pharmaceutical company that's facing complaints about the side effects from a particular drug it manufactures. In this scenario, the company recalls the whole batch of the same drug produced and shipped in a particular time period. After checking and analyzing the manufacturing process, it's revealed that other batches produced with the same process parameters have had no problems. Finally, the problem is identified as the poor quality material shipped by a particular vendor. The vendor stands responsible and asks the pharmaceutical company to return the faulty material.

In such scenarios, batch management can recall the entire supply chain—from procurement to production to stores and to supplies or shipping to the customers, as shown in Figure 10.1.

Next we'll discuss the implementation of batch management and its key elements.

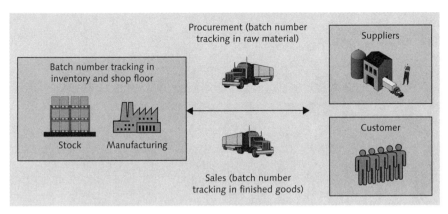

Figure 10.1 Batch Management in the Entire Supply Chain

10.1 Master Data in Batch Management

Your first step when working with batch management is to identify the material that needs to be batch managed, and then update the material master record by setting the batch management requirement. Let's go over the different processes and steps in the following sections.

10.1.1 Activate Batch Management in the Material Master

In the SAP system, batch master records always depend on material master records. Therefore, your first step is to define batch management requirements in the material master.

Go to Transaction MM01 (Create Material Master), enter all of the required details, and select the BATCH MANAGEMENT checkbox to state that the material has to be handled in batches. Each time there is a goods movement, be sure to update the batch number (see Figure 10.2).

The following material master records contain the indicator for batch management:

- Sales and Distribution
- General plant data
- Purchasing
- Work scheduling

- Storage 1
- Warehouse Management

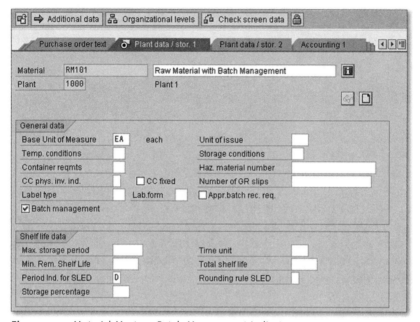

Figure 10.2 Material Master—Batch Management Indicator

All views are the same, and any change/updating that is done in one view appears in all views.

If there is a mismatch of subjected material and batch requirement, all stocks need to be posted out from the previous fiscal year, the previous period, and the current period. To do this, reset the indicator for batch requirement and repost the stock in batches into the system.

Similarly, you can cancel batch requirement for any material you don't want to be batch managed. If you have to reorganize the batch master records, you must reset the indicator to blank, post the required batch requirement, and then post the stock back into the SAP system by using Transaction MIGO.

10.1.2 Creating and Managing the Batch Master Record

As we've discussed, a batch is a partial quantity of a material in a company's existing stock that is managed separately from the other partial quantities of the same material. The information needed to manage the batch is stored in a data record called the *batch master record*. This record is identified by an alphanumeric batch number (see Section 10.2.4 for more information on how to create the batch master and number).

You can create a batch master record directly when you maintain master data. Otherwise, the system automatically generates the master record after you specify the batch number with the first goods movement for a batch. You can assign alternative number ranges to batch numbers externally or internally (for more details, see Section 10.3.2).

You can define the automatic creation of batch numbers in the system, whether for movement type or production and process orders. For instance, you can customize the system to automatically create unique batch numbers whenever goods are delivered by a particular vendor against a PO with movement type 101, depending on your business requirements. This means that every time goods type 101 is received, the unique batch number is created by the system automatically.

We'll discuss how batch numbers are created and at what level of the organization structure in the following subsections.

> **Example**
>
> Let's consider a scenario where your company has ordered a paint material (material master code RM101 – Paint) from two vendors: vendor A and vendor B. The material received from vendor A of quantity 4, against PO 4500000212, has to be recorded by creating a unique batch number to differentiate the same material from other stock quantity. Here, the batch number created is A101. When the same vendor ships the second lot of the same material, again quantity 4, against a PO 4500000215, the batch number created will be A102.
>
> The next lot of the same material is sent by vendor B, quantity 4, against a PO 4500000137, with A103 as the batch number. Although the total stock material for RM101 – Paint is 12, it has three batches. Whenever there is any issue in a material, you can refer back to the unique batch number, and subsequently every other detail too.

Figure 10.3 shows the material management of this scenario by batch number.

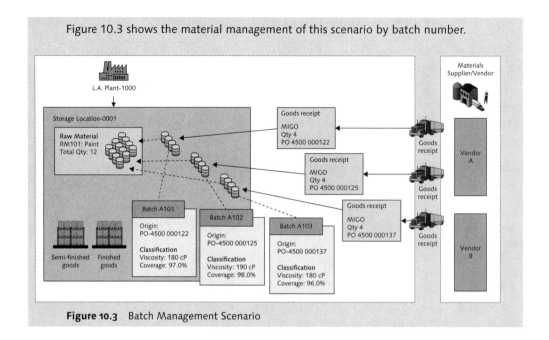

Figure 10.3 Batch Management Scenario

Batch Levels

The material number is unique at the client level, and you can use company or business criteria as benchmark to determine the uniqueness of the batch number. Use the following levels to determine that batch numbers are unique:

▶ **Plant and material combination level**
In this level, the plant and material combination have unique batch numbers. Remember, different material in the same plant can be assigned the same batch number, and the same material in different plants can also be assigned the same batch number. In this given context, the material is transferable from one plant to another, and although the batch number is the same, the specification of the destination batch will remain unaltered.

▶ **Material number level**
As the batch numbers are created at the material level, the same batch numbers can be used for other material as well. After you set the batch level as MATERIAL in the system, the following can happen:

  ▷ A material can have the same batch number even though the materials are in different plants with the same specifications.

▶ The same batch number can be reassigned for other materials with a different specification.

▶ **Client level**
The batch level is set at the client level, which is the highest level. The same batch number can't be used for different material or different plants. The batch number assigned is rather unique and can be assigned only once; thus, every material will always have a new or different batch number.

The default setting is the plant level. As mentioned earlier, this can be customized to the batch level you need. However, you need to keep in mind that while switching to a higher level is always possible, lowering your level is only possible from the client level to the material level. This is because the batch data is organized so that it has to be converted whenever switched to another batch level. This also affects the batch management status, so it must be maintained.

Figure 10.4 illustrates the uniqueness of the batch number based on different levels.

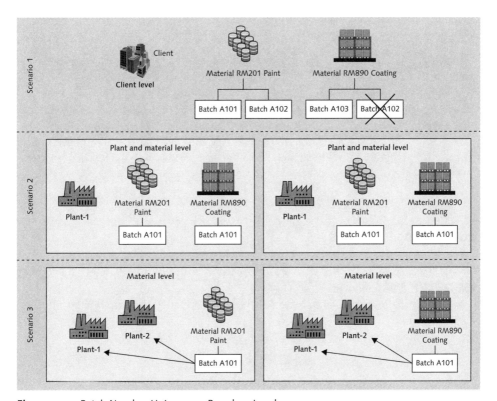

Figure 10.4 Batch Number Uniqueness Based on Levels

As you can see, there are two plants and two materials: plant 1 and plant 2, and RM201 Paint and RM890 Coating, respectively. When first maintained at the client level, in scenario 1, the batch number can't be repeated; batch number A102 thus can't be used by material RM890 Coating.

In scenario 2, you see the plant and material level. Here, for every plant and material combination within the same plant, a batch number is assigned.

And in scenario 3, you see the material level; different materials can have the same batch number.

10.1.3 Batch Classification

To differentiate batches of material depending on their individual properties, you can use characteristics to define the properties. For example, the paint industry uses color, coverage, and viscosity as characteristics to classify different batches. These characteristics are created in the SAP system and assigned to the materials. The same classification concept as in materials classification (Chapter 9), studied earlier, is applied in defining batch classification.

> **Example**
>
> A company that deals with various types of paints wants to capture the characteristics of paint: coverage, color, and viscosity. A class has to be created with three characteristics for coverage, color, and viscosity wavelength. This class has to be assigned to a material. Every time a new batch is created for the material, the characteristic values need to be entered. Figure 10.5 shows the material RM201 Paint with two characteristics—viscosity and coverage.

10.2 Process Steps

In this section we'll go over the step-by-step procedure of how batch management is used in the SAP system.

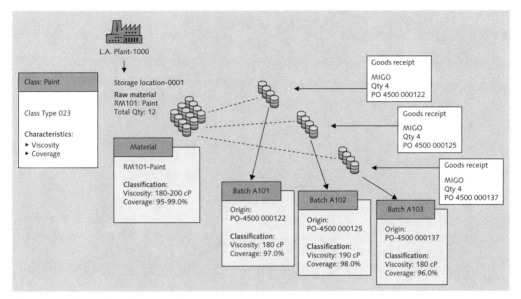

Figure 10.5 Batch Classification—Characteristics

10.2.1 Define Characteristics

First, create the various characteristics for your materials such as viscosity, density, color, and so on. We've already discussed the characteristics and classes in detail in Chapter 9, Sections 9.3.1 and 9.3.2, so we won't go into the same detail here. To create characteristics, go to SAP MENU • CROSS-APPLICATION COMPONENTS • CLASSIFICATION SYSTEM • MASTER DATA • CHARACTERISTICS. Alternatively, you can use Transaction CT04.

In the resulting screen, enter the CHARACTERISTIC name and click on CREATE. Enter a DESCRIPTION and the CHARS GROUP, as shown in Figure 10.6. In the STATUS field you have three options: IN PREPARATION, LOCKED, and RELEASED. A status of RELEASED means that the characteristic can be used; a status of LOCKED or IN PREPARATION means that it can't be used.

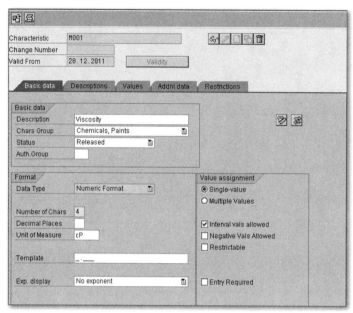

Figure 10.6 Define Characteristics

In the VALUE ASSIGNMENT section, select either SINGLE-VALUE or MULTIPLE VALUES. The SINGLE-VALUE indicator specifies that only one value can be assigned to this characteristic; the MULTIPLE VALUES indicator is used when more than one value is possible.

Select the VALUES tab and enter the possible values for this characteristic, as shown in Figure 10.7.

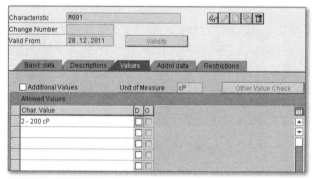

Figure 10.7 Characteristics Values

The ADDITIONAL VALUES indicator allows you to enter characteristic values that aren't defined. After you've defined the values, you can save the characteristic. In this example, we've taken the characteristic viscosity, and the value of viscosity can fall within the range of 2 to 200 cP.

Now that you've created characteristics, you need to assign the characteristics to the class, which is explained in the following section.

10.2.2 Define Class

A class represents a group of characteristics. Classes are defined based on the material classification such as a garment, oil and grease, or metals. To define a class, go to SAP MENU • CROSS-APPLICATION COMPONENTS • CLASSIFICATION SYSTEM • MASTER DATA • CLASSES, or use Transaction CL02. Enter the CLASS TYPE as "023" (Batch Class), and fill in the appropriate CLASS name. Then click on NEW (Figure 10.8). Enter a description, and set the STATUS as RELEASED. Enter the validity dates.

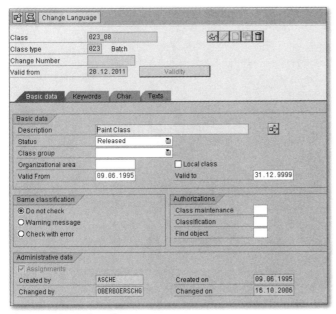

Figure 10.8 Define Class

On the CHAR. tab, assign the characteristics to the class, as shown in Figure 10.9. In this case, we've assigned four characteristics: VISCOSITY, DENSITY, WAVELENGTH, and DATE OF LAST GOODS RECEIPT.

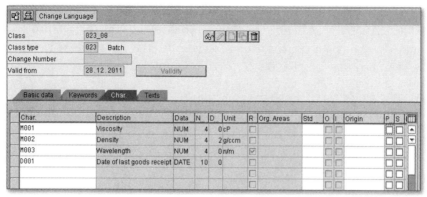

Figure 10.9 Assign Characteristics to Class

10.2.3 Create Material Master

After you've defined the class, you can create the material master via Transaction MM01. Select the BATCH MANAGEMENT checkbox in the PLANT DATA tab, and then in the CLASSIFICATION view, select the class to see all of its assigned characteristics as shown in Figure 10.10.

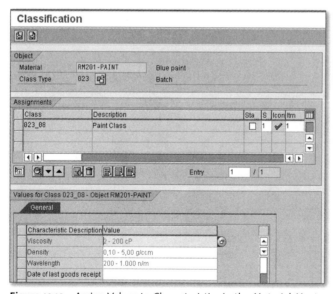

Figure 10.10 Assign Values to Characteristics in the Material Master

10.2.4 Create Batch Master

A batch master record is created manually in master data maintenance or automatically in the background by the system when you receive goods for the first time. To create batch master records, go to SAP MENU • LOGISTICS • CENTRAL FUNCTIONS • BATCH MANAGEMENT • BATCH CREATE, or use Transaction MSC1N.

> **Note**
>
> In SAP ERP, batch master records always take their information from the material master records.

Enter a material, plant, and storage location for which you want to create a batch master record. If you've defined the internal number range, the system will create the batch number automatically after you press Enter.

The data in a material master applies in general for all of the batches assigned to this master record. By contrast, a batch master record contains data that uniquely identifies the corresponding batch and characterizes the unit as one that can't be reproduced.

Various types of information are stored in the batch master record. Some can be updated manually, and some can be updated automatically. We'll discuss some of the relevant information on the tab pages in the following list:

▶ BASIC DATA 1

In this tab, you maintain the manufacturing date, shelf life expiry data, and so on.

In BATCH STATUS, you can select either UNRESTRICTED or BATCH RESTR. If a batch has the status RESTRICTED, when you post a goods receipt, the quantity of stock is posted in restricted-use stock and is treated like a blocked stock. If you set the status of a batch to UNRESTRICTED, the system transfers the total unrestricted-use stock to restricted-use stock and creates a material document.

In the TRADING DATA section, you can maintain the vendor number and vendor batch number details. If you don't maintain these, the system will automatically populate the details during goods receipt by pulling the data from the PO.

▶ BASIC DATA 2

In this tab, you can maintain the TEXTS and FREELY DEFINABLE DATE fields. There are six date fields. This is optional and only necessary if you want to use these dates somewhere in the process.

▶ CLASSIFICATION

In this tab, you can see the class that was assigned to a material during material master classification. You can enter the characteristics values here by clicking on the NEW button. After you click on the NEW button, all of you can enter the values of all of the characteristics listed based on the material class, as shown in Figure 10.11.

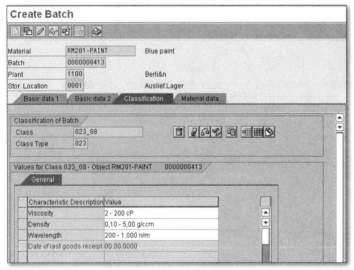

Figure 10.11 Batch Creation—Classification Tab

▶ MATERIAL DATA

In this tab, you can see the information from the material master record.

▶ CHANGES

All of the change history is updated and displayed in this tab. This tab won't appear when you're creating a batch for the first time, but you can see it when you go to change or display a transaction.

10.2.5   Post Goods Receipt

To receive goods without a PO via movement type 501, go to Transaction MIGO. Enter the material, whose batch master is already maintained. For example, after entering the material master RM201 – Paint, in the item details, you come across one more tab: BATCH. The batch number is automatically updated from the master record, created in the earlier step as shown in Figure 10.12.

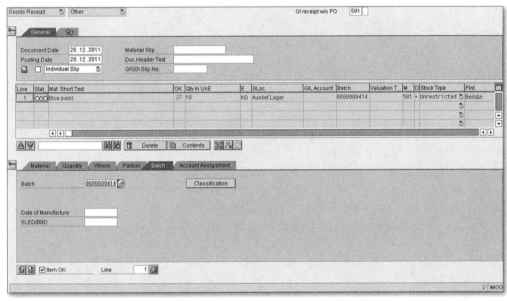

Figure 10.12   During Goods Receipt—Batch Details Tab

Click on the CLASSIFICATION button in the BATCH tab to enter the values of the characteristics. Because we've already defined the date of last goods receipt as one of the characteristics in this example, its value will be updated and appear automatically as today's date as shown in Figure 10.13. You can also maintain the shelf-life expiration date and save the goods receipt.

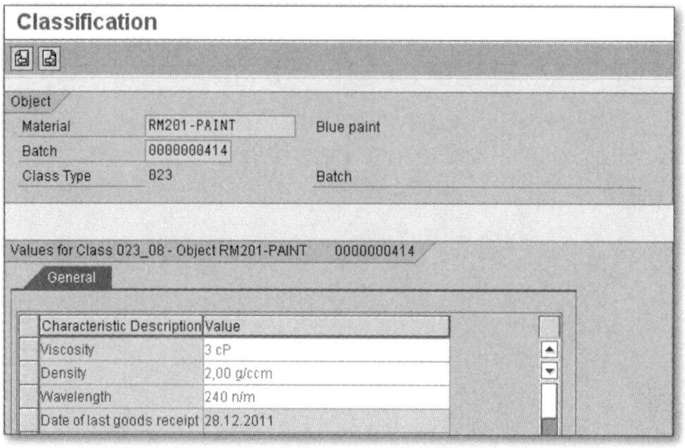

Figure 10.13 During Goods Receipt—Enter the Material Characteristics

10.2.6 Stock Overview

In the stock overview report, you can view how the stock is kept under different batches. Go to Transaction MMBE, enter the plant code and material number, and execute the report. You can see the stock overview with respective batch numbers, such as batch number 413, which was created using the batch master. Figure 10.14 shows the material MR291 – Paint, of quantity 10, received in the previous step.

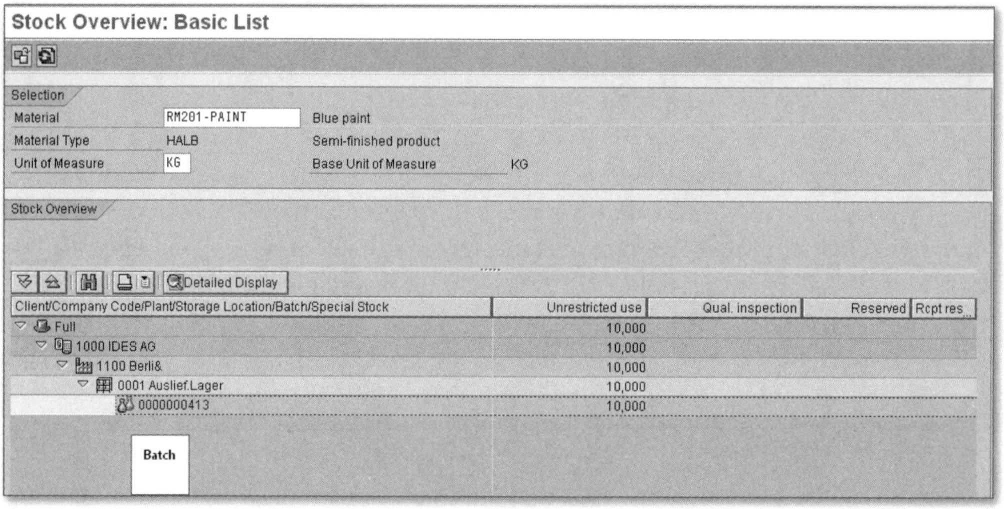

Figure 10.14 Stock Overview Report—Transaction MMBE

After you issue the material, and if there are multiple batches or the same material in stock, the system automatically lets you choose the batch number from the material to be issued. If you want to assign a batch number based on some strategy, the batch determination strategy should be configured. Details of configuration can be found in Section 10.3.

> **Tips & Tricks**
>
> You can use batch usage transactions to track the batches and for analysis. Transaction MB56 will give you the details of a batch where-used list. From SAP release 4.6C onward, SAP has provided the Batch Information Cockpit, which is a central tool for tracking batches.

10.2.7 Batch Information Cockpit

The Batch Information Cockpit has extensive analysis and editing options for batch management and facilitates a central access point. You can see the complete history of each batch; you can also view the where-used list of each batch.

Go to Transaction BMBC. Use various basic data as input on the selection screen such as material data, shelf-life data, stock data, or specification data stored in classification to search a specific material/batch. After you've entered the selection criteria, click on the EXECUTE button (or press F8), and you can see the batch details. The following existing batch functions are integrated into the Batch Information Cockpit:

▸ Batch master and batch where-used list

▸ Stock overview and minimum shelf-life evaluations

▸ Worklist

The batch management menu helps in accessing the Batch Information Cockpit; alternatively, you can call Transaction BMBC. In the Batch Information Cockpit, choose between a list display and a hierarchy display. Figure 10.15 shows the hierarchy display with two batches of material MR201 – PAINT.

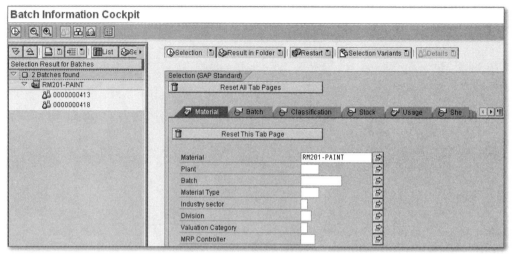

Figure 10.15 Batch Information Cockpit

You can also see the where-used list for a batch, as shown in Figure 10.16. Select the batch number from the left side by double-clicking, then click on the DETAILS button and select the USAGE option from the drop-down menu. This report helps you to track a particular batch master record.

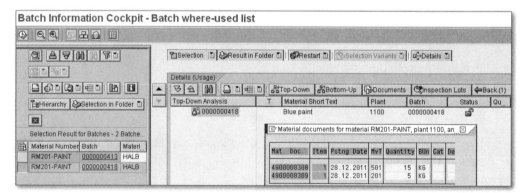

Figure 10.16 Batch Information Cockpit—Batch Where-Used List

10.3 Configuration Steps

Now that we've discussed the various concepts and key attributes of batch management, we'll explain how to configure batch management.

10.3.1 Define the Batch Level

As we discussed in Section 10.1.2, the batch level can be defined at three different levels, but by default is defined at the plant level. To define the batch level, go to SAP IMG • LOGISTICS - GENERAL • BATCH MANAGEMENT • SPECIFY BATCH LEVEL AND ACTIVATE STATUS MANAGEMENT. The screen in Figure 10.17 displays, where you define the settings per your business requirements.

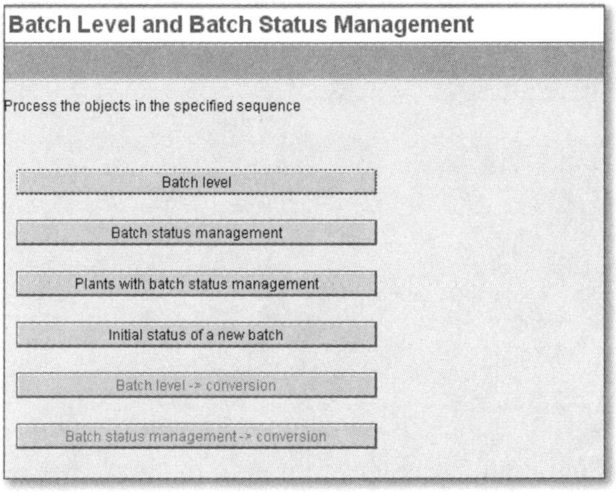

Batch Level and Batch Status Management

Process the objects in the specified sequence

Batch level

Batch status management

Plants with batch status management

Initial status of a new batch

Batch level -> conversion

Batch status management -> conversion

Figure 10.17 Define Batch Levels and Activate Status Management

The following list describes each option:

► BATCH LEVEL
  Choose the level to maintain the unique batch number, as shown in Figure 10.18, and then save.

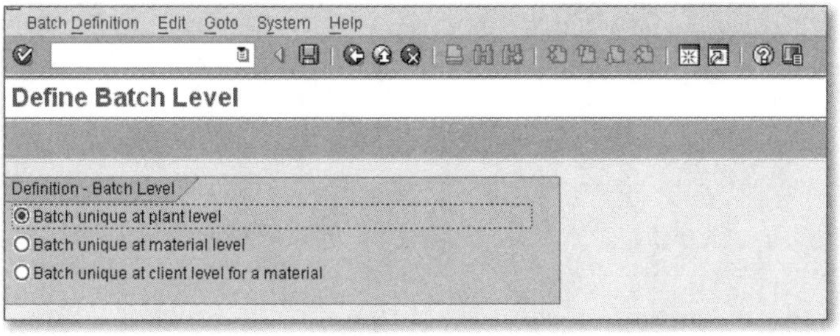

Batch Definition   Edit   Goto   System   Help

Define Batch Level

Definition - Batch Level
◉ Batch unique at plant level
○ Batch unique at material level
○ Batch unique at client level for a material

Figure 10.18 Define Batch Level

439

▶ BATCH STATUS MANAGEMENT

To activate batch management status in the client, select the ACTIVE checkbox, and then save.

▶ PLANTS WITH BATCH STATUS MANAGEMENT

Set the BATCH STATUS MANAGEMENT indicator in the resulting list for those plants where batch status management has to be active, as shown in Figure 10.19. Select the checkbox and save.

Figure 10.19 Batch Status Management Activation at Plant Level

▶ INITIAL STATUS OF A NEW BATCH

Specify which initial new batches are to be assigned for each material type, as shown in Figure 10.20. Check the INITIAL STATUS box.

Material Type	Material type description	Initial Status	
0003	Packaging	☐	
0005	Finished product	☐	
0006	Trading goods	☐	
9999	Finished product	☑	
ABF	Waste	☐	
AEM	Samples	☐	
BLG	BLG Empties External	☐	
BLGA	BLGAEmpties Fixed assets	☐	
CBAU	Compatible Unit	☐	
CH00	CH Contract Handling	☐	
COMP	Prod. alloc., purchased	☐	
CONT	KANBAN Container	☐	
CONU	Container non-value	☐	
COUP	Coupons	☐	
DIEN	Service	☐	
DOCU	documentary batch	☐	
EPA	Equipment Package	☐	

Figure 10.20 Initial Status of New Batch for Material Types

10.3.2 Batch Number Assignment

In this step, you define the batch number range and assignments. Go to SAP IMG • LOGISTICS - GENERAL • BATCH MANAGEMENT • BATCH NUMBER ASSIGNMENT • ACTIVATE INTERNAL BATCH NUMBER ASSIGNMENT.

In the resulting screen, select the ACTIVE radio button to activate the internal batch number assignment.

You can also define whether internal batch number assignment is allowed for goods receipts that have an account assignment as shown in Figure 10.21 via SAP IMG • LOGISTICS - GENERAL • BATCH MANAGEMENT • BATCH NUMBER ASSIGNMENT • INTERNAL BATCH NUMBER ASSIGNMENT FOR ASSIGNED GOODS RECEIPT.

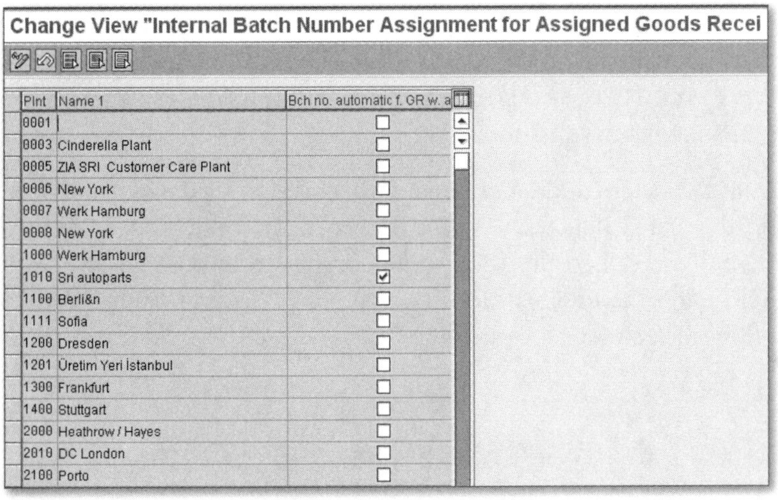

Change View "Internal Batch Number Assignment for Assigned Goods Recei

Plnt	Name 1	Bch no. automatic f. GR w. a
0001		☐
0003	Cinderella Plant	☐
0005	ZIA SRI Customer Care Plant	☐
0006	New York	☐
0007	Werk Hamburg	☐
0008	New York	☐
1000	Werk Hamburg	☐
1010	Sri autoparts	☑
1100	Berli&n	☐
1111	Sofia	☐
1200	Dresden	☐
1201	Üretim Yeri İstanbul	☐
1300	Frankfurt	☐
1400	Stuttgart	☐
2000	Heathrow / Hayes	☐
2010	DC London	☐
2100	Porto	☐

Figure 10.21 Internal Batch Number Assignment Activation for Plant

In the next step, define the number ranges for internal batch number assignment. Go to SAP IMG • LOGISTICS - GENERAL • BATCH MANAGEMENT • BATCH NUMBER ASSIGNMENT • MAINTAIN INTERNAL BATCH NUMBER ASSIGNMENT RANGE.

In Figure 10.22, you can see the number range object BATCH_CLT, and in Figure 10.23, the number range 01 from 0000000001 to 9999999999 has been defined.

Number Range Object: Display

Change Documents

Object	BATCH_CLT	Number range object has intervals
Short text	Client batch number	
Long text	Client-level batch number	

Interval characteristics

To-year flag	☐
Number length domain	CHAR6
No interval rolling	☐

Customizing specifications

Number range transaction	
Warning %	10,0
Main memory buffering	☑ No. of numbers in buffer 1

Figure 10.22 Number Range Assignment

Similar to the internal batch number assignment, you can assign a number range for external number assignment. Go to SAP IMG • Logistics - General • Batch Management • Batch Number Assignment • Maintain Number Range for External Batch Number Assignment.

You can maintain the external number range by clicking on the Number Ranges button and then the change Intervals button. Here, you can see the already-defined number range, and you can create a new number range by clicking on the Inset Interval button. Enter the number range number (No.), From number, and To number, and then click on Save (Figure 10.23).

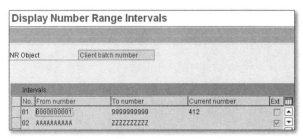

Display Number Range Intervals

NR Object	Client batch number

Intervals

No.	From number	To number	Current number	Ext	
01	0000000001	9999999999	412	☐	▲
02	AAAAAAAAAA	ZZZZZZZZZZ		☑	▼

Figure 10.23 External Number Range Interval

▶ EXI_SAPLVO1Z_001

This exit is used to replace the number range object and/or interval proposed with your own number range object by the system and/or interval. It's also used to stop the system from assigning an internal number based on the material or plant. This exit can be used to stop the dialog box from appearing.

▶ EXIT_SAPLVO1Z_002

This exit helps assign your own number or even change the number assigned by the system.

10.3.3 Creation of New Batches

As we've seen, batches can be created manually and automatically by the system. In this step, we'll show you how to define how the new batches will be created for movement types and for process/production orders.

To define the new batch creation for process/production orders, go to SAP IMG • Logistics - General • Batch Management • Creation of New Batches • Define Batch Creation for Production Order/Process Order.

In this step, you can make specific settings in batch management for the existing production control profiles. Choose the production control profile for which you want to make settings, and select the required option (as shown in Figure 10.24) for automatic batch creation:

▶ Automatic batch creation at order creation

▶ Automatic batch creation at order release

▶ No automatic batch creation in production/process order

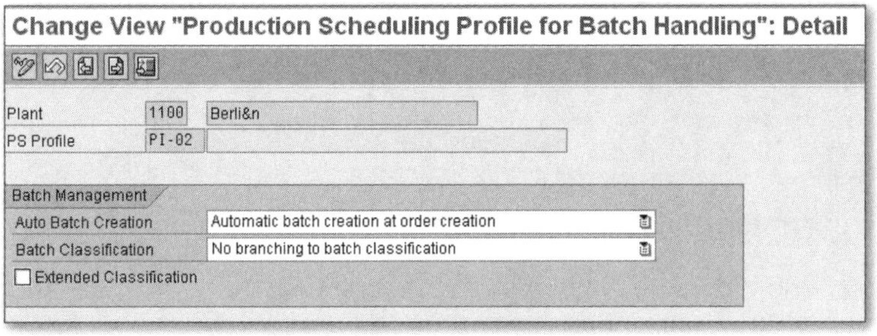

Figure 10.24 Define Batch Creation for Production Orders

Then select the batch classification option in BATCH CLASSIFICATION field.

You can also define the new batch creation settings for movement types. Go to SAP IMG • LOGISTICS - GENERAL • BATCH MANAGEMENT • CREATION OF NEW BATCHES • DEFINE BATCH CREATION FOR GOODS MOVEMENTS.

For instance, when batch numbers aren't determined by the system automatically, you may want to issue a batch number for goods receipt on a purchase order (movement type 101) manually. To achieve this, choose the AUTOMATIC/MANUAL WITHOUT CHECK option for movement 101, as shown in Figure 10.25.

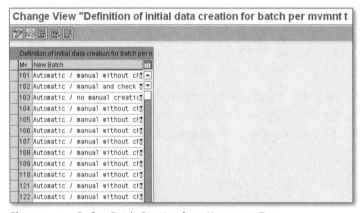

Figure 10.25 Define Batch Creation for a Movement Type

For each material type, you can also define whether a new batch can be created via the batch master transaction (Transaction MSC1N). To do so, go to SAP IMG • LOGISTICS - GENERAL • BATCH MANAGEMENT • CREATION OF NEW BATCHES • DEFINE INITIAL CREATION OF DATA FOR BATCH MASTER TRANSACTIONS.

If you want to assign the batch numbers only automatically by the system and don't opt for assigning manually, especially for the finished products, then choose option AUTOMATIC/NO MANUAL CREATION FOR MATERIAL TYPE FERT.

10.3.4 Batch Determination

In a real-world scenario, you'll be receiving one material in a number of batches, and this will be kept in storage location stock or in warehouse storage bins. When you want to issue the material to production, you need to have a strategy to choose the batch. You can define the strategy in the system, where the system determines and offers up the right batch to pick. This process is called *batch determination*. Batch determination uses the condition technique. (We've seen the same technique in the automatic price determination process in Chapter 8, Section 8.2.)

Strategy records of the respective application determine batch determination. Different strategy records in the system have to be created for different purposes such as goods issue to production, goods issue to customer, and so on. Batch determination can be used in the goods movement, production/process order, sales order/ delivery, and transfer order functions.

Customizations for each application such as production, sales, and stock transfers are stored in search procedures, which run the batch determination. After the batch determination procedure is running, the system automatically accesses the corresponding entry of the application, which further locates the relevant entries in Customizing.

Figure 10.26 shows how the system searches the batch number.

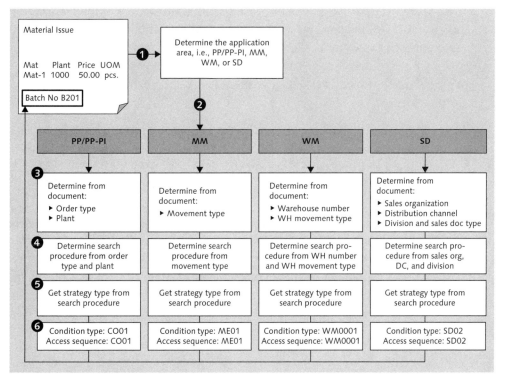

Figure 10.26 Batch Determination Flow

In any transaction, the system will first determine the application area—PP (Production Planning) and PP-PI (Production Planning Process Integration), MM, WM (Warehouse Management), or SD (Sales and Distribution)—and then determine the search procedures, which are assigned based on different combinations (❶, ❷). In the case of PP& PP-PI combination, the system will determine the order type and plant from the transaction and then find a search procedure (❸, ❹). For MM, the system will find a search procedure based on movement type. And in case of SD, the search procedure will be based on sales organization, distribution channel, division, and sales document type.

The search procedure helps the system determine the search type (❺). The search type helps to identify the condition type and condition tables (❻). The system will find the appropriate batch number based on the access sequence system.

To customize the batch determination, follow the steps in the next subsection.

Step 1: Define Condition Tables

Go to SAP IMG • Logistics - General • Batch Management • Batch Determination and Batch Check • Condition Tables. You'll see options to define condition tables for each application area; that is, inventory management, production order, process order, Sales and Distribution, and Warehouse Management separately. We'll discuss the inventory management area here, but you can use the same steps for the others.

In the SAP menu, click on the Define Inventory Management Condition Table option. You'll get a new screen with Create, Change, and Display options. To create a new condition table, click on the Create Condition Table for Batch Determination (IM), enter the condition table number, and choose the fields from the field catalog. Then click on the Generate button, and the system will create the condition table. You can also edit the already-created tables by choosing the Change Condition Table for Batch Determination (IM) option. You'll see a screen with only a Condition table field; enter the condition table and press Enter. You'll get a screen as shown in Figure 10.27. Here you can select the fields for the condition table from the Field Catalogue. You can define the condition tables for each application area in the same way.

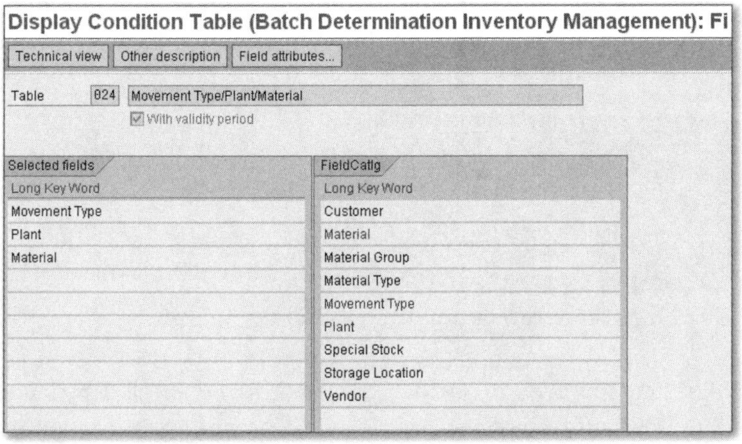

Figure 10.27 Define Condition Table for Batch Determination

The standard delivery contains the following condition tables for batch determination in inventory management:

- 020: Movement type
- 021: Movement type/plant
- 022: Movement type/material
- 023: Plant/material
- 024: Movement type/plant/material
- 025: Plant

Step 2: Define the Access Sequence:

Now define the access sequence for each application area as mentioned in the previous steps. Go to SAP IMG • LOGISTICS - GENERAL • BATCH MANAGEMENT • BATCH DETERMINATION AND BATCH CHECK • ACCESS SEQUENCES.

Figure 10.28 shows the access sequence for inventory management. Similarly, you can define the access sequence for other application areas. Select the access sequence and click on the EDIT button. You can define the sequence of tables you want the system to follow. For example, in Figure 10.28 the system will first search the MOVEMENT TYPE/PLANT/MATERIALS combination, then the PLANT/MATERIAL combination, and so on.

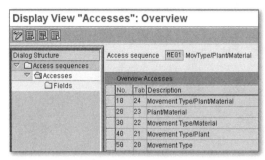

Figure 10.28 Define the Access Sequence for Batch Determination

In the standard SAP system for inventory management, access sequences ME01 and ME02 are defined. In the standard system for production orders, access sequences CO01 and CO02 are defined. And in the standard system for Sales and Distribution, access sequences SD01, SD02, and SD03 are defined. It's recommended to use the same access sequence and then make changes in the condition table sequences to meet your unique requirements.

Step 3: Define Strategy Types

Define the strategy types for each application area by going to SAP IMG • LOGISTICS - GENERAL • BATCH MANAGEMENT • BATCH DETERMINATION AND BATCH CHECK • STRATEGY TYPES.

Click on the NEW button or copy the standard strategy type provided by SAP. It's recommended to copy the standard strategy type, then make the required changes, and save the new strategy type. Figure 10.29 shows the strategy types for batch determination in inventory management.

In the standard SAP system for inventory management, strategy types ME01 and ME02 are defined.

Step 4: Define the Batch Search Procedure

In this IMG activity, you define search procedures for batch determination in inventory management. Go to SAP IMG • LOGISTICS - GENERAL • BATCH MANAGEMENT • BATCH DETERMINATION AND BATCH CHECK • BATCH SEARCH PROCEDURE DEFINITION (see Figure 10.30).

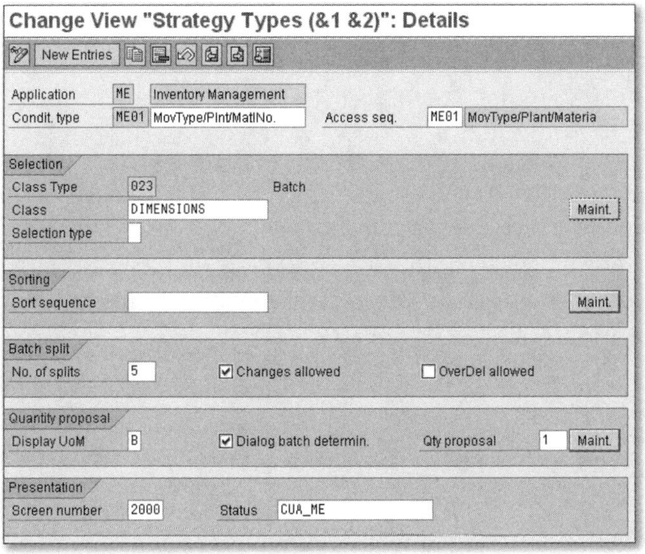

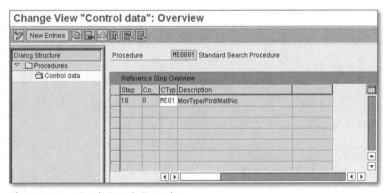

Figure 10.29 Define Strategy Types

Figure 10.30 Batch Search Procedure

Click on the NEW button to define the search procedure, or define it by copying the SAP-provided search procedure. It's recommended to copy the standard procedure (so that you don't miss any required settings), make the required changes, and save the entries.

All strategy types used for a particular goods movement are included in a search procedure. The standard SAP system contains search procedure ME0001.

Step 5: Batch Search Procedure Allocation

In this step, allocate the search procedure to different combinations for each application area. Go to SAP IMG • Logistics - General • Batch Management • Batch Determination and Batch Check • Batch Search Procedure Allocation and Check Activation.

For MM, you need to assign search strategy to movement types as shown in Figure 10.31. So for a particular movement type, this search strategy will help to search the batch. For example, goods issues to cost centers have the movement type 201, and search strategy Z00001 is assigned in Figure 10.31.

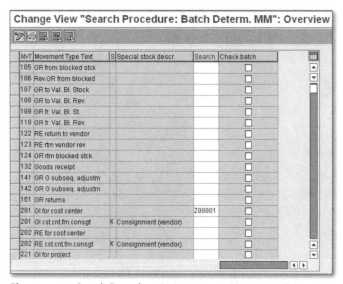

MvT	Movement Type Text	S	Special stock descr.	Search	Check batch	
105	GR from blocked stck				☐	
106	Rev.GR from blocked				☐	
107	GR to Val. Bl. Stock				☐	
108	GR to Val. Bl. Rev.				☐	
109	GR fr. Val. Bl. St.				☐	
110	GR fr. Val. Bl. Rev.				☐	
122	RE return to vendor				☐	
123	RE rtrn vendor rev.				☐	
124	GR rtrn blocked stck				☐	
132	Goods receipt				☐	
141	GR G subseq. adjustm				☐	
142	GR G subseq. adjustm				☐	
161	GR returns				☐	
201	GI for cost center			Z00001	☐	
201	GI cst.cnt.fm.consgt	K	Consignment (vendor)		☐	
202	RE for cost center				☐	
202	RE cst.cnt.fm.consgt	K	Consignment (vendor)		☐	
221	GI for project				☐	

Figure 10.31   Search Procedure Assignment to Movement Type

For SD, you need to assign the search procedure to the combination of sales organization, DC, division, and sales document type.

Step 6: Maintain Condition Records

As a last step, you need to maintain the condition records. For the condition tables that have been defined in the access sequence, you need to maintain the condition records. These records will be picked by the system for automatic batch determination. Go to the SAP Easy Access Menu and choose Logistics • Central Functions • Batch Management • Batch Determination • Batch Search Strategy • For

INVENTORY MANAGEMENT • CREATE, or use Transaction MBC1 to create condition records.

Select the strategy that you've defined in the earlier configuration steps (in this case, ME01), and select the movement type and plant combination. Enter the material number and movement type as shown in Figure 10.32.

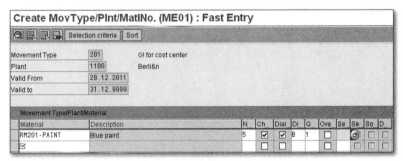

Figure 10.32 Maintain Condition Records for Batch Determination

10.4 Summary

In this chapter, we discussed the importance of batch management and how it works in SAP. We also covered the step-by-step configuration of batch management. You can now design the batch management requirement for your client and also configure it from end to end.

In the next chapter, we'll study material requirements planning (MRP), the types of MRP, and client requirement-based implementation.

This chapter provides an overview of the material requirements planning (MRP) process, the prerequisites of its execution, and insight into various MRP procedures and consumption-based planning (CBP) procedures.

11   Material Requirements Planning

Material requirements planning (MRP) is all about planning the requirements a business will have for materials, as suggested by the name. We can define materials as direct and indirect materials, which are input to various processes that can be executed from different locations. You can plan manually (without MRP in SAP) for the demand of certain materials and their supply only in very small volume situations. When there's an increase in the volume of materials, processes, and locations, things can get complicated. To manage the requirements planning, you need a complex system setup.

SAP provides different tools to manage such scenarios with MRP. In this chapter, you'll learn how MRP in SAP helps businesses calculate the materials requirement planning based on the actual demand or forecast demand and helps create the requirements in the form of purchase requisitions, internal orders, or stock transport orders. The application of proper MRP leads to improved efficiency, optimum inventory levels, reduced lead times, and overall cost savings. In this chapter, you'll learn about various MRP types and how MRP can be customized to meet business-specific requirements.

Let's take an example of a leading automobile company, with business dealings in more than 100 countries. Each model of car requires more than 1,000 components, and the company has more than 16 manufacturing plant and 4,000 service centers. The company needs to perform materials requirement planning based on the model of car and the demand in each country. The company also needs to check the available stocks in various storage locations and decide whether to buy materials or transfer materials from one plant to another.

In such scenarios, MRP is very useful because the system runs the materials requirement planning based on the actual demand or forecast demand and creates the requirements in the form of purchase requisitions, internal orders, or stock transport orders. Now that you know the benefits of MRP, let's learn more about it.

11.1   Introduction to MRP

Let's use another real-world example to help understand the MRP requirements. For example, consider a global automobile company—ABC Inc.—that's setting up its operations in India. (As per industry standards, they've classified their materials with ABC classification where A is more important material and used in production as a main component, B is of medium importance, and C has low importance and less valuable materials.) To begin with, it sets up only an assembly line and decides to procure "C" components locally and import "A" components from the global market.

The market research analysis provides a target of producing 100 semi-luxury cars and 50 luxury cars during its first year. The following parameters are important to take into consideration while planning:

▶ Expected demand is a total of 150 cars: 100 semi-luxury cars and 50 luxury cars.

▶ A few parts will be locally procured, such as horns, tires, seat covers, and so on, and a few others, such as the engine, will be imported.

▶ The lead time for local procurement and importing of components may vary. So, is the quantity requirement dependent on the type of cars?

▶ Some parts could fit for both types of cars, such as the engine, while the wheels could vary for both.

These parameters change to suit variations in business demand. The factors to be considered are as follows:

▶ During the festival seasons, sales are likely to go up as indicated by market research.

▶ Raw material shortage in the rubber industry is leading to a reduction in the quantity of tire production.

- To boost sales, the marketing department decides to launch only limited-edition models with added features. This causes changes in configuration and later in assembly/procurement functions.

- The company's limited edition model is a huge success, and the demands are revised from 150 to 200, during the midyear of operation. This also means that the prediction has gone up by 66.67% for the remaining midyear.

- To keep up with the demand-supply ratio, the company decides to locally manufacture the spare parts and subsequently start local manufacturing, too.

Many factors influence the business decision and later on the planning function. In such a scenario, MRP is the best solution. Based on the historical data forecast, demand can be proposed by MRP, and overall planning can be more accurate. SAP offers two different planning types: MRP and CBP (consumption-based planning). We'll take a look at these in later sections.

Consumption-Based Planning

Consumption-based planning (CBP) uses the various statistical procedures or the forecast to decide future requirements, so it is dependent on past consumption values. CBP procedures are nothing but simple planning procedures. They are used to plan material requirements based on historical data, forecast procedures, and set targets. Therefore, CBP is used in the production plants area and in areas without in-house production to plan for operating supplies and planning (both class B parts and class C parts).

Note

The master production schedule isn't the same as the procedure in CBP, which means that the net requirements calculation isn't triggered by planned dependent or independent requirements. Rather, the calculation is triggered when stock levels fall below a predefined reorder point or by a forecast requirements calculation based on past consumption values.

Both MRP and CBP ensure material availability as their main function, such as timely procurement of materials in respective quantities, either for in-house production or for third-party sales. Table 11.1 shows the key differentiating factors between MRP and CBP.

MRP	CBP
Usually used for class A materials; that is, finished products, important assembly groups, and components.	Usually used for class B and C materials and operating supplies.
Mostly relevant for in-house production; that is, part of the SAP Production Planning (PP) component.	Mostly used for external procurement; that is, part of the SAP Materials Management (MM) component.
Based on current and future requirements of a material.	Based on historical data; that is, past consumption records of a material.
While planning, external requirements such as sales orders, planned independent requirements (PIR), and reservations, as well as the dependent requirements that a BOM explosion creates, are considered (measured).	While planning, external requirements such as sales orders, planned independent requirements, and reservations are generally not relevant. However, these can be considered only with the reorder point planning procedure.

Table 11.1 Differences Between MRP and CBP

11.2 Planning Procedures in MRP

There are three procedures in MRP/CBP; each using different statistical methods. The nature of planning required by an individual business or client can determine any of these planning procedures:

▶ Reorder-point planning

▶ Forecast-based planning

▶ Time-phased planning

Now that you have a better understanding of what MRP is, we'll go over the steps for setting it up in your system and working with the planning process, as shown in Figure 11.1.

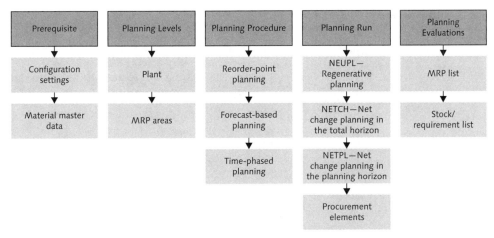

Figure 11.1 Various Elements of the Planning Process

In the following sections, we'll go through each of the planning process illustrated here, step by step.

11.3 Prerequisites

Before getting started with MRP, you need to determine the basic considerations for CBP for your business. In all situations, the following must be done in the system before performing the configuration settings:

▶ While working with forecast requirements, the consumption pattern should reflect only low random fluctuations and should be moderately linear or constant.

▶ Inventory management should be updated and efficient.

In the following subsections, we'll go over how to configure the prerequisites.

11.3.1 Configuration Settings

Let's take an example from an automobile company. Say you want to plan for a gear-assembly unit, which is used in cars. You have a manufacturing plant in Frankfurt, Germany. In this scenario, you need to activate the Frankfurt plant for MRP, define the plant parameters, and maintain the MRP data in the materials master (gear assembly unit). To configure MRP, follow these steps:

1. **Activate MRP.**

   Follow the menu path SAP IMG • Materials Management • Consumption Based Planning • Planning • Activate Materials Requirements Planning.

   Select the Activate requirements planning checkbox to activate the MRP for a plant, as shown in Figure 11.2. As you can see, some plants aren't checked for MRP, which means these plants aren't activated for an MRP run.

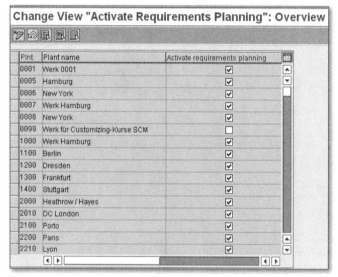

Figure 11.2 Activate MRP for a Plant

2. **Maintain the plant parameters.**

   Follow the menu path SAP IMG • Materials Management • Consumption Based Planning • Plant Parameters • Carry out Overall Maintenance of Plant Parameters.

   After you've decided which plant to maintain, you need to select the plant parameters in the screen shown in Figure 11.3. Enter the plant number and click on the Maintain button.

   You'll now see a screen where you can maintain various parameters as shown in Figure 11.4.

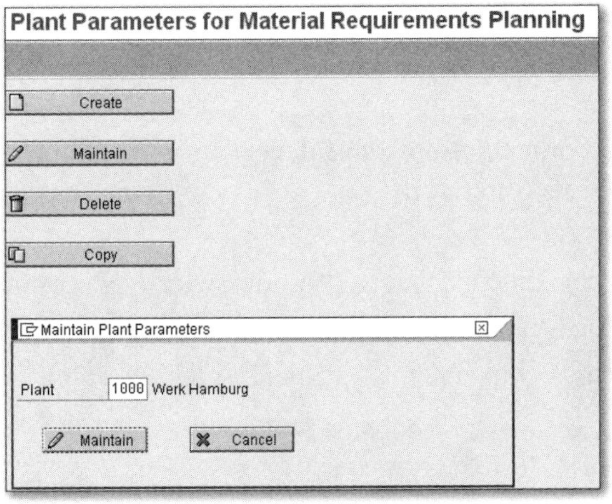

Plant Parameters for Material Requirements Planning

Create

Maintain

Delete

Copy

Maintain Plant Parameters

Plant   1000 Werk Hamburg

Maintain   Cancel

Figure 11.3 Plant Parameters for MRP

Maintain Plant Parameters

Plant   1000 Werk Hamburg

Environment

Number Ranges   Maintained

Master Data

MRP Controllers   Maintained

Special Procurement   Maintained

Floats   Maintained

Planned Orders

Conversion PlOrd->PReq   Maintained

Availability Dep Req   Maintained

Reporting

Runtime Statistics   Maintained

Period Grouping   Maintained

Planning Run

External Procurement   Maintained

Rescheduling   Maintained

Planning Horizon   Maintained

Available Stocks   Maintained

Error Handling   Maintained

Item Numbers   Maintained

Start in Past   Initial

Performance

Aggregation: MRP List   Initial

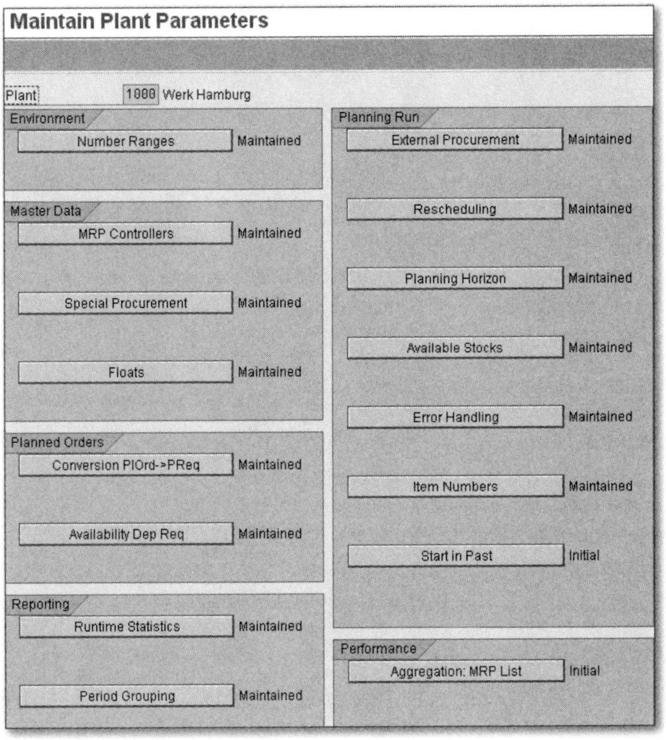

Figure 11.4 Plant Parameters for MRP

Depending on the requirements of your business scenario, you need to maintain the plant parameters as follows:

- ▶ Number Ranges
  Number ranges for planned orders, reservations/dependent requirements, purchase requisitions, MRP lists, and so on.

- ▶ Master Data
  Master data such as MRP Controllers, Special Procurement, and Floats.

- ▶ Planned Orders
  Procurement elements such as conversion of planned orders to purchase requisitions.

- ▶ Planning Run
  Relevant to planning runs, such as External Rescheduling, Planning Horizon, Available Stocks, and so on.

Similar to plant parameters, you can also maintain parameters in MRP groups.

11.3.2 MRP Groups

An MRP group is an organizational object that's used to assign certain control parameters for MRP to a group of materials. For instance, in plant P1, there are M1, M2, and M3 materials. The plant parameters that are being maintained for plant P1 apply automatically to M1, M2, and M3. And if the MRP group is maintained and assigned only to material M3, then M1 and M2 will be planned depending on the planning parameters maintained for the plant, and M3 will be planned based on the planning parameters set in the MRP group.

Thus, planning parameters maintained for the MRP group always have a priority over plant parameters.

The menu path to maintain MRP groups and their corresponding parameters is SAP IMG • Materials Management • Consumption Based Planning • MRP Groups • Carry out Overall Maintenance of Plant Parameters.

Various parameters can be maintained such as Planning Horizon, Scheduling/ Document Type, and Planning Run values for the MRP group as shown in Figure 11.5.

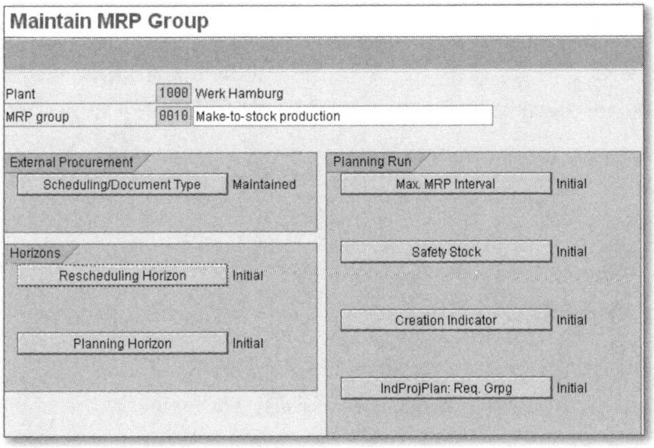

Figure 11.5 Maintain the MRP Group

You can customize the MRP group as the default in the material master. The menu path is SPRO • MATERIALS MANAGEMENT • CONSUMPTION BASED PLANNING • MRP GROUPS • DEFINE MRP GROUPS FOR EACH MATERIAL TYPE.

As shown in Figure 11.6, you can define the default MRP group for every material type and plant. In this example, MRP group 0031 is assigned for materials type FERT (Finished Product) and plant 0005. Similarly, group 0081 is assigned for plant 1300 MRP. By default, this will assign the MRP parameters for all of the materials created for these plants with materials type FERT.

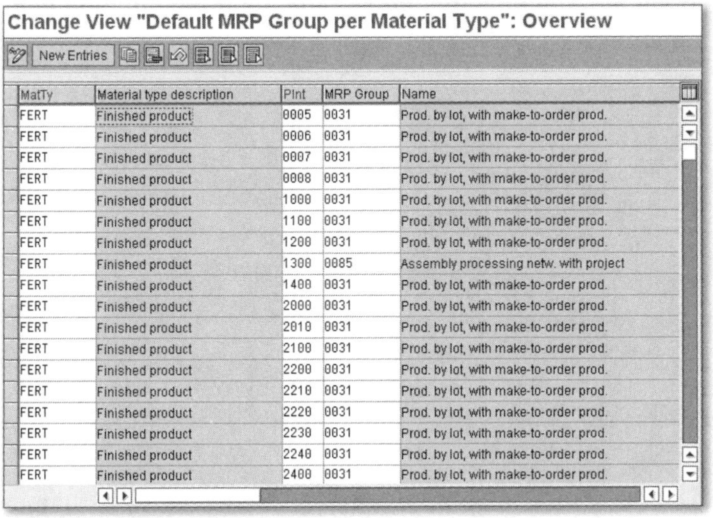
Change View "Default MRP Group per Material Type": Overview

New Entries

MatTy	Material type description	Plnt	MRP Group	Name
FERT	Finished product	0005	0031	Prod. by lot, with make-to-order prod.
FERT	Finished product	0006	0031	Prod. by lot, with make-to-order prod.
FERT	Finished product	0007	0031	Prod. by lot, with make-to-order prod.
FERT	Finished product	0008	0031	Prod. by lot, with make-to-order prod.
FERT	Finished product	1000	0031	Prod. by lot, with make-to-order prod.
FERT	Finished product	1100	0031	Prod. by lot, with make-to-order prod.
FERT	Finished product	1200	0031	Prod. by lot, with make-to-order prod.
FERT	Finished product	1300	0085	Assembly processing netw. with project
FERT	Finished product	1400	0031	Prod. by lot, with make-to-order prod.
FERT	Finished product	2000	0031	Prod. by lot, with make-to-order prod.
FERT	Finished product	2010	0031	Prod. by lot, with make-to-order prod.
FERT	Finished product	2100	0031	Prod. by lot, with make-to-order prod.
FERT	Finished product	2200	0031	Prod. by lot, with make-to-order prod.
FERT	Finished product	2210	0031	Prod. by lot, with make-to-order prod.
FERT	Finished product	2220	0031	Prod. by lot, with make-to-order prod.
FERT	Finished product	2230	0031	Prod. by lot, with make-to-order prod.
FERT	Finished product	2240	0031	Prod. by lot, with make-to-order prod.
FERT	Finished product	2400	0031	Prod. by lot, with make-to-order prod.

Figure 11.6 Define the Default MRP Group for Material Type

11.3.3 MRP Data in the Material Master

You need to maintain the MRP data in the material master, which is grouped under different views. In the material master, MRP data falls into the following categories:

- General data
- Data specific to MRP procedures
- Data specific to scheduling
- Data specific to lot-size calculation

The data fields are grouped into four views: MRP 1, MRP 2, MRP 3, and MRP 4. Among these, MRP 4 data is maintained at the storage location level and the plant level, whereas all other MRP views are maintained at the plant level. Figure 11.7 (Transaction MM01) shows the different views and fields to maintain. Let's go over what you need to maintain in each view:

1. Go to Transaction MM01 and select all of the four MRP views. In the MRP 1 view, you can maintain the general data, lot-sizing data, and MRP procedures.

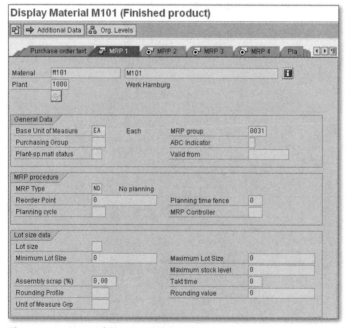

Figure 11.7 Material Master—MRP 1 View

2. Use the MRP 2 view to maintain procurement, scheduling, and net requirements calculation data.

3. In the MRP 3 view, you can maintain forecast requirements, planning parameters, and availability check requirements.

4. In the MRP 4 view, maintain the dependent requirements (BOM), repetitive manufacturing, and so on.

Some of the fields that need to be maintained for MRP aren't dependent on the material master, so they are common for groups of materials with similar properties.

11.3.4 MRP Profile

SAP allows you to customize your own MRP profile to help update these common parameters/fields for many materials without any difficulty, depending on your business scenarios. Using an MRP profile makes maintenance and administration of MRP data in the material master an easier task. Use Transaction MMD1 to create an MRP profile, or access the SAP Easy Access Menu and choose LOGISTICS • MATERIALS MANAGEMENT • MATERIAL MASTER • PROFILE • MRP PROFILE • CREATE. Here you can select the fixed value, select the default value checkboxes for the MRP profile, and click on SAVE.

You can specify which fields you want to display in your MRP profile, as shown in Figure 11.8:

▶ FIXED VAL. column
If you select the FIXED VAL. checkbox, then the system will always copy the value from the MRP profile to the material master. It cannot be changed in the material master.

▶ DEFAULT VALUE column
If you select this checkbox, the system will copy the value of the field from the MRP profile to the material master, but it can be changed in the material master.

After selecting the fixed value and default value indicators for different fields, click on the DATA SCREEN 1 button, which will show you the fields which you have selected as default and fixed. Enter the values for the each field here, which will be copied into the material master.

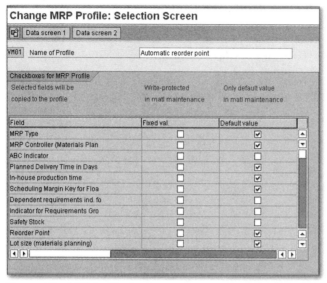

Figure 11.8 MRP Profile Creation

Whenever you make a change to an MRP profile, the system automatically creates a background job (PROFILE), which will update the changes to all allocated materials. You can define the start time of the PROFILE job in Customizing by following the menu path SPRO • LOGISTICS GENERAL • MATERIAL MASTER • TOOLS • DEFINE START TIMES OF BACKGROUND JOBS.

> **Note**
>
> Here are some helpful tips when working with MRP profiles:
>
> ▶ When you change an MRP profile, only the fixed values of the new MRP profile will be changed.
>
> ▶ The materials assigned to a particular MRP profile are listed via Transaction MMD7.

Restrict Materials

You can restrict how materials are used by setting the material status at the client level and/or plant level in the material master. This also means that with the material status, a certain material can have various messages for a particular plant. For instance, for the material requirements function you can set (1) no message, (2) warning message, or (3) error message to appear when the following processes are carried out:

- Independent requirement created
- Forecasting run carried out
- MRP relevance
- Long-term planning

At the client level and/or plant level, the material status is maintained. This also means that with the material status, a certain material can have various messages for a particular plant.

SAP Tools

You've seen how the MRP profiles can be created and how easily you can set MRP-related parameters in the material master. Similarly, forecast profiles can also be used to maintain forecast data in the material master.

11.4 Planning Levels (MRP Areas)

In general, MRP is executed at the plant level. While planning, all of the materials in the particular plant are considered. An option is provided to either plan storage location stock independently or eliminate the stock from MRP consideration. You need to choose the latter option only if your business doesn't want to include any of the storage location stock in the planning run. In a similar manner, planning can be executed for every MRP area, meaning that many storage locations can be put together to structure one MRP area.

The menu path to define MRP areas is SAP IMG • MATERIALS MANAGEMENT • CONSUMPTION BASED PLANNING • MASTER DATA • MRP AREAS • DEFINE MRP AREAS (see Figure 11.9).

There are three different types of MRP areas, as shown in the DIALOG STRUCTURE on the left side of Figure 11.9:

- PLANT
  The plant MRP area will have a plant together with all its storage locations and stock with subcontractors. The plant MRP area is created automatically when you convert the existing planning file entries to planning file entries for MRP areas.

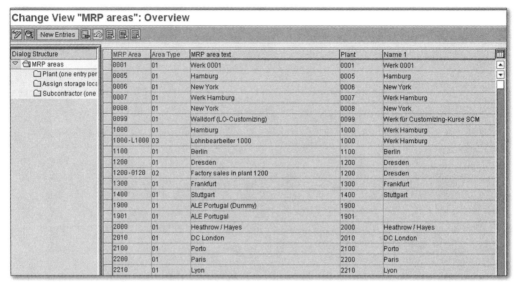

Figure 11.9 MRP Area

- ▸ ASSIGN STORAGE LOCATION
  This area is defined by designating the storage locations.

- ▸ SUBCONTRACTOR
  This area is defined by assigning the subcontractor, which further covers all of the materials given for this subcontractor.

MRP Area

Keep these important key points in mind when working with an MRP area:

- ▸ MRP areas facilitate planning of materials that belong to specific storage locations and/or subcontractors.

- ▸ Planning parameters can be set specific to each MRP area. This complements the purpose of creating MRP areas. Thus, materials belonging to MRP areas will be planned according to the planning parameters set for the MRP area they belong to.

- ▸ MRP areas are optional.

11.5   Planning Procedures in Consumption-Based Planning

There are three procedures in CBP, and each uses different statistical methods. The nature of a business's planning will determine which of these planning procedures is best to use:

▶ **Reorder-point planning**
In reorder point procedures, procurement is triggered when the sum of the plant stock and firmed receipts falls under the reorder point.

▶ **Forecast-based planning**
Forecast-based planning is also dependent on material consumption. Similar to the reorder point procedure, forecast-based planning functions use historical values and forecast values. The integrated forecasting program determines the future requirement. Unlike in the reorder point procedure, the values here form the basis of the planning run. The forecast requirements are the forecast values that have a direct effect on MRP.

▶ **Time-phased planning**
If it's routine for a vendor to deliver a material on a particular day of the week, it makes sense to plan to buy this material on that particular day and adopt this cycle.

You can plan your material master data around any of these planning procedures.

As we'll discuss next, the MRP type determines which planning procedure is to be used and which parameters/fields in the material master will be mandatory versus optional.

11.5.1   MRP Type

It's important to understand MRP types, such as PD for MRP, ND for no planning, VB for reorder planning, and so on, before we get into details of each of the preceding MRP procedures. MRP types are defined in customizing via SPRO • MATERIALS MANAGEMENT • CONSUMPTION BASED PLANNING • MASTER DATA • CHECK MRP TYPES (see Figure 11.10 and Figure 11.11). Here, you can define and change the settings for standard MRP types to suit the requirement as provided by SAP.

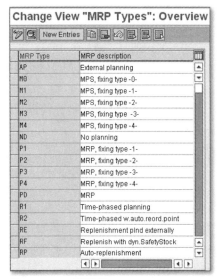

Figure 11.10 MRP Types

You can select any MRP type in Figure 11.10 and click on the Details button to see the various controlling elements as shown in Figure 11.11.

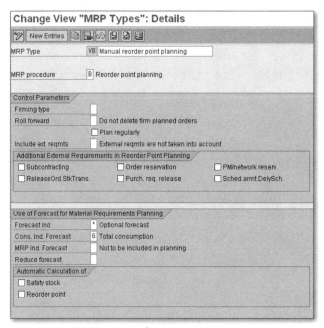

Figure 11.11 MRP Types Configurations Screen

You can configure the various parameters for each of the MRP types; however, SAP-provided MRP types have prerequisite settings and mostly meet the requirements. Following are the various parameters:

▶ MRP procedures such as reorder point planning, materials requirement planning, no MRP, forecast-based planning, time-phased planning, and master production scheduling

▶ Control parameters such as firming type and roll forward

▶ Forecast-related parameters such as the forecast indicator and the automatic calculation of safety stock and reorder point

11.5.2 Lot Size Calculation

Lot size is the measure of how much quantity of a material should be ordered/planned/produced. You'll define the lot size and lot-sizing procedure in the system depending on your requirements for planning materials. The planning of a material is at times constrained due to costs associated with procurement, transportation and storage, and so on. For example, if a material such as butter is bought in advance, this will reduce the procurement and transportation cost but increase the storage cost. So it's very important for the business to know how much to order and when to order. Calculating the appropriate lot size helps in achieving these objectives.

In the lot size calculation, there are different groups of procedures, as explained here:

▶ **Static lot-sizing procedure**
The replenishment quantity is calculated based on the quantities you enter here. This suits certain types of products such as spare parts. In general, spare parts are purchased only in required quantities. Following are the various static lot-sizing procedures:

   ▶ **Lot-for-lot order quantity**
   Set indicator EX in the MRP 1 view of the material master. Lot-for-lot quantity means the exact requirement quantity becomes a lot.

   ▶ **Fixed lot size**
   Set indicator FX in the MRP 1 view in the material master. (*Order Quantity = Quantity Set in Material Master*)

If the quantity set in the material master falls short of the requirements, then several lots are planned on the same day to match the requirements.

▶ **Replenishment up to maximum stock level**
Set the indicator HB in the MRP 1 view of the material master. (*Order Quantity = [Maximum Stock Level – Current Stock – Existing Fixed Receipts]*)

▶ **Periodic lot-sizing procedure**
A *lot* is formed by the system, by grouping the requirement quantities dependent on a time frame. However, this procedure suits only the forecast-based planning procedure in CBP. This is good for direct materials and indirect materials if the safety stock is maintained enough to fulfill the requirement during the time frame in which it is delivered. This saves a lot of transportation costs, as requirements are combined during the time frame.

▶ **Optimizing lot-sizing procedure**
A *lot* is created by grouping requirements from several periods put together, and by referring the maintained optimum cost ratio, lot size independent costs, and storage costs. Price/quantity scales are excluded. It's useful for direct materials. Unlike the static and periodic lot-sizing procedures, optimum lot-sizing procedures focus on reducing the cost involved in stock keeping, setup, and order costs.

Moreover, lot size calculations can be restricted with the help of the following fields:

▶ ROUNDING VALUE
Used to round up the order quantity. This is useful, for example, if materials are always delivered in lots of 12 or in full pallets.

▶ ROUNDING PROFILE
Has a threshold and a rounding value. If the requirement quantity exceeds the threshold value, then it's rounded up per the rounding value; otherwise, it remains unchanged.

▶ MINIMUM/MAXIMUM LOT SIZE
Refers to the minimum and maximum procurement/order quantities per lot.

You define lot-sizing procedures in Customizing via SAP IMG • MATERIALS MANAGEMENT • CONSUMPTION BASED PLANNING • PLANNING • LOT-SIZE CALCULATION • DEFINE LOT SIZING PROCEDURE as shown in Figure 11.12. As you can see, various lot-sizing procedures are defined. LOT SIZES 2D, 2W, and 3D are based on the number of days, which means any requirements generated during this time frame will be combined as one lot. Similarly, you can see lot sizing procedure EX – LOT-FOR-LOT ORDER QUANTITY; in this case, the requirement quantity itself is a lot.

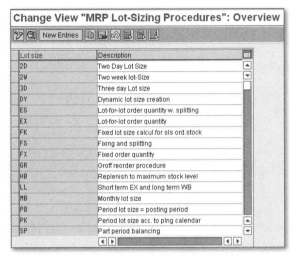

Figure 11.12   Lot-Sizing Procedures

Now we have a basis to understand the different planning procedures, as discussed in the following subsections.

11.5.3   Planning Procedure Type 1: Reorder Point Planning

The reorder point is the stage at which the materials need to be ordered. The expected average material requirements during the replenishment lead time should be covered by the reorder point. The safety stock is part of the reorder level because it covers both surplus material consumption within the replenishment lead time and any new requirements that could be caused by delayed delivery.

The following values are important for defining the reorder point (define these fields in the material master via Transaction MM01):

▶ SAFETY STOCK

▶ AVERAGE CONSUMPTION

▶ REPLENISHMENT LEAD TIME

The following values are important for defining the safety stock:

▶ Past consumption values or future requirements

▶ Vendor/production delivery timelines

► Service level to be achieved

► Forecast error; that is, the deviation from the expected requirements

To help manage the reorder point planning, maintain the following in the material master MRP views:

► **Manual reorder point planning**
Both the reorder level and the safety stock level are defined manually in the appropriate material master.

► **Automatic reorder point planning**
The integrated forecasting program determines both the reorder level and the safety level. Historical or past consumption data are used by the system to predict future requirements. These forecast values are used by the system to work out the reorder level and the safety stock level. It takes the service level, specified by the MRP controller, and the material's replenishment lead time and transfers them into the material master.

Note

The reorder level and the safety stock level are constantly modified to the present consumption and delivery situation, depending on the forecast that is carried out at regular intervals. This ensures that the stock levels are kept low.

Prerequisites

Let's how consider how to set reorder point planning in the system:

► For reorder point planning in the material master, set the MRP type (MRP 1 view).

► Enter or let the system calculate automatically in the material master. Enter the values for the reorder point (MRP 1 view) and for the safety stock (MRP 2 view).

Process Flow

Let's discuss how the reorder point process is carried out in the system to help you understand the reorder point, safety stock point, and replenishment lead time. Follow Figure 11.13. You can see that the reorder point is set at quantity 50, which means at this point, you raise the PO. Until the material is delivered, your stock levels will be going further down, and materials should arrive at the safety stock level (which is set at a quantity of 10). This safety stock quantity 10 is available in case of emergency when due to some reason, materials could not come on time or some urgent requirements come from production. After the stock is received from the vendor again, the stock level will go up.

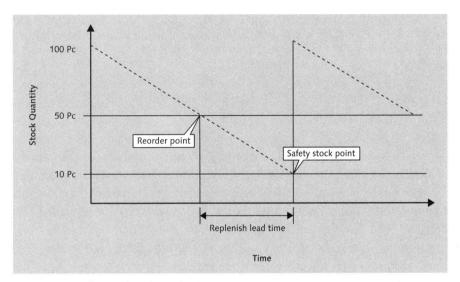

Figure 11.13 Safety Stock and Reorder Point

The following list details the process steps that the system follows:

1. In inventory management, continuous monitoring of available stock is carried out within the reorder point. This also means that the system is tracking all of the material issues and receipts.

2. The net requirements are then calculated by the system. The available stock at the plant level (safety stock included) and the firmed receipts, already planned (POs, firmed purchase requisitions, production orders, etc.) are compared with the reorder point by the system. If the reorder point is greater than the sum of the stock plus receipts, then it indicates that a material shortage exists.

3. Based on the lot-sizing procedure, the system calculates the procurement quantity in the material master.

4. The system then schedules the procurement proposal, including the dates of to send the PO, when the production should begin, by what date the goods will be delivered by the vendor, and by when the goods need to be kept ready.

Remember these important points when performing reorder point planning:

▶ The system supports the lot-sizing procedures—fixed lot size and replenish up to maximum stock level—in reorder point planning.

▶ If you use period or optimum lot-sizing procedures for reorder point materials, you must use the forecasting functions to calculate future requirements. The forecast values are then considered as requirements.

Reorder Point Planning with External Requirements

In reorder point planning, entries are created in the planning file. Only when the stock levels fall below the reorder point will the system perform the net requirements calculation. To help avoid overplanning, dependent requirements, sales orders, reservations, and so on aren't generally included in the net requirements calculations. These future requirements are already taken care off or planned by the reorder level. The system, however, displays sales orders, manual reservations, dependent reservations, and the like to ensure that the MRP controller is informed of current issues. However, if there is a business requirement to include such external requirement in the net requirements calculations, there is an option available in Customizing.

To enable this, set the EXTERNAL REQUIREMENTS indicator in Customizing via the path SAP IMG • MATERIALS MANAGEMENT • CONSUMPTION BASED PLANNING • MASTER DATA • CHECK MRP TYPES. To take external requirements into account, select the MRP type for the reorder point procedure.

Customizing

During the replenishment lead time, sales orders and manual reservations are incorporated in planning. While customizing, you can also enter settings for the MRP type:

▶ While planning, the sales order and manual reservations are included during the whole horizon and the replenishment lead time.

▶ Apart from manual reservations and sales orders, many other requirements are taken into account in MRP.

▶ As you can see in Figure 11.14, for materials type VB – MANUAL REORDER POINT PLANNING, MRP PROCEDURE B – REORDER POINT PLANNING is selected. You can select the INCLUDE EXT. REQMTS option and choose from EXTERNAL REQMTS ARE NOT TAKEN, EXTERNAL REQMTS IN TOTAL HORIZON, and EXTERNAL REQMTS WITHIN REPLENISHMENT LEAD TIME.

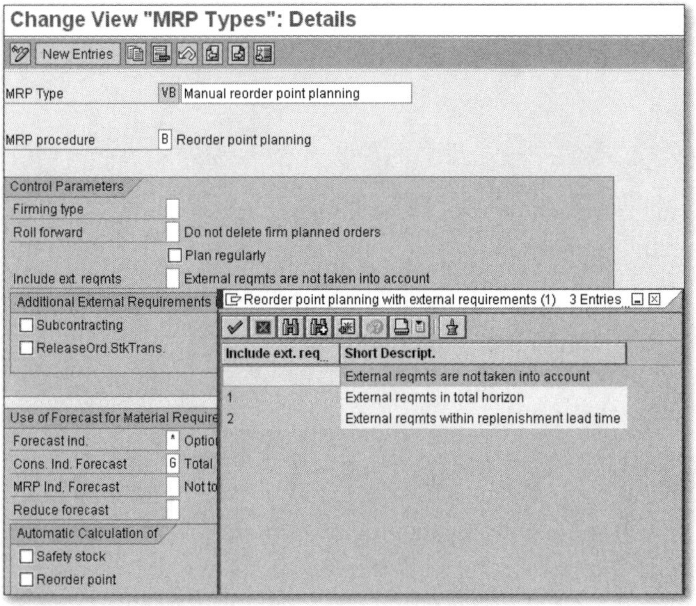

Figure 11.14 External Requirements in MRP Types

11.5.4 Planning Procedure Type 2: Forecast-Based Planning

Forecast-based planning creates estimates based on past consumption values. Forecast values and future requirements are determined using an integrated forecasting program, which is executed at regular intervals, offering the benefit that automatically determined requirements are constantly adapted to go with present consumption needs. The forecast requirement quantity is reduced to ensure that it isn't included in the planning run again. Forecast requirements can be reduced by doing the following:

▶ **Reducing forecast requirements by consumption**
The system reduces future forecast requirements if the current month consumption is higher than the forecast requirements.

▶ **Reducing current forecast requirements by consumption**
The system doesn't reduce the future forecast requirements in the current month if the consumption is higher than the forecast requirements.

▶ **Average reduction of the forecast requirements**
The actual consumption isn't considered, and the reduction of the forecast requirements is dependent on the daily average consumption.

The formula

forecast requirement / number of workdays in the forecast period

is used by the system to calculate the average daily requirement in the first place. Then the forecast requirements are reduced by the quantity applying the following formula:

number of workdays worked × average daily requirements

Period Pattern and Forecast Periods

You can specify the period pattern for the forecast for every material such as daily, weekly, monthly, or per accounting period. You can also specify the number of periods to be included in the forecast separately for each material. At times, the forecast planning pattern won't be sufficiently precise for planning purposes; in such cases, it can be defined that the forecast requirements be divided to a better quality pattern for planning per material. The numbers of forecast periods are also to be considered during requirements planning.

Tips & Tricks

During a monthly forecast, set the requirement date in the material master to the first working day of the month because in planning, it is considered that the total requirement be available at the start of the period. You can also split this into daily or weekly requirements.

Prerequisites

To use forecast-based planning, ensure that the following settings are defined in the system:

▶ Set an MRP type for forecast-based planning in the material master (MRP 1 view).

▶ Define MRP types in Customizing for MRP in the IMG activity CHECK MRP TYPES.

Process Flow

Let's understand the process flow of how the system calculates the forecast demand and how the overall planning is run:

1. The net requirements are calculated by the system by copying the requirement quantities, brought out in the forecast requirements planning run. In this calculation, every period is checked to ensure that the forecast requirements are taken into account by available stock, by planned receipts, or by production. If there is a material shortage, the system generates a procurement proposal.

2. The quantity in the procurement proposal is calculated by the system based on the lot-sizing procedure specified in the material master. Depending on the same procedure, the forecast requirements are put together as one lot.

3. For every given procurement proposal, the date to be converted into a purchase or production order is calculated by the system.

Various forecast models can be used depending on the business scenario. Let's look at the various forecast models.

11.5.5   Forecast Models

Analysis of consumption values results in certain patterns. The predefined forecast models correlate to these patterns, which are explained here:

1. **Constant**
   A constant consumption flow is applied when consumption values differ very little from a steady mean value. For instance, in the FMCG sector, most products are in the constant model, such as soaps, creams, toothpastes, and so on. You can see in Figure 11.15 that the demand is always between 50 and 75 pieces throughout the period, which means the demand isn't varying and is in the constant zone.

2. **Trend**
   Consumption values rise or fall regularly over a long duration with minimum deviations. For example, because there is rapid growth in technology, most products in electronics industries have a shorter lifecycle. Innovative products sell quickly in the market. For instance, touch screens in mobile phones boomed the short-term sales. You can follow Figure 11.15 to understand the trend model. When the trend is constantly moving upward, the demand is continuing to increase over time.

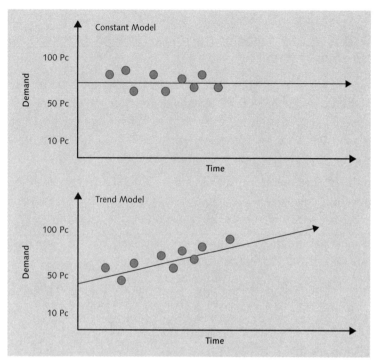

Figure 11.15 Forecast Model: Constant Model and Trend Model

3. **Seasonal**

   A seasonal consumption flow features periodically appearing low or peak values, differing greatly from a stable mean value. For instance, most products in garment industries are brought in line with seasonal consumption, such as winter parkas, uniforms, and so on. Figure 11.16 shows the seasonal model. You can see the demand is going up and down over time, but overall the trend is constant—neither upward nor downward.

4. **Seasonal Trend**

   A continuous increase or decrease of the mean value is the characterization of a seasonal trend consumption model. For instance, many products in the cosmetic sector again follow seasonal trends; that is, winter care lotions and creams sell huge with the oncoming winter season, and decline after the season is over. Figure 11.16 shows the difference between the seasonal and seasonal trend models. The seasonal trend model has an upward trend, which means the demand is varying in each season, but overall the demand is increasing from season to season.

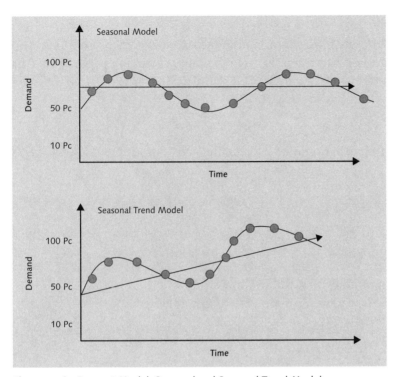

Figure 11.16 Forecast Model: Seasonal and Seasonal Trend Model

The irregular consumption flow trend is chosen in the material master when none of the previously mentioned patterns are detected in past consumption series. In a forecast model in the material master, there are three options to choose from concerning irregular flow:

▶ **Manual model selection by MRP controller**
When you're sure about the model of the materials, you can select the model manually.

▶ **Automatic model selection**
When you want the system to choose the most appropriate model based on the past data, use this option.

▶ **Manual model selection with additional system check**
When you want manual selection with some additional checks, use this option.

Forecast Run

A forecast run is executed while the forecast-based planning procedure is used. This run results in forecast values coming from the forecast model and historical data being added with the appropriate parameters in a material master. The forecast run is carried out in the following ways:

- ▶ Individual forecast (Transaction MP30)

- ▶ Total forecast (Transaction MP38 for online and Transaction MPBT for background)

Note

Different MRP procedures supporting the forecast have different effects, when a forecast is run:

- ▶ In the automatic reorder point planning procedure, the forecast run automatically determines the safety level and the reorder level.

- ▶ In forecast-based planning, the safety stock level is calculated, and the results of the forecast are pasted into MRP.

In both cases, the basis for forecasting is the statistical total consumption fields of the material master data.

11.5.6 Planning Procedure Type 3: Time-Phased Planning

The time-phased planning technique in MM provides the planning file with an MRP date. The date is first set when the material master is created and later resets every time after it runs. It gives the date of material planning for specific intervals (weekly, monthly, etc.), which is calculated based on the planning cycle data in the material planning.

In real-world scenarios, the distributors supply materials to retailers once every month, or biweekly. In this case, the retailer needs to plan their requirements until the next delivery date. Based on the plan, the retailer will buy the required quantity of each material from the distributor. Time-phased planning is executed using CBP or MRP to do one of the following:

- ▶ Use material forecast to create requirements when you want to carry out time-phased planning with CBP techniques. By using CBP, the forecast requirements are only included in the calculation of the net requirement. To reduce forecast requirements, choose the same setting as forecast-based planning in Customizing.

▶ With time-phased planning using MRP, all MRP-relevant requirements are included in the calculation of net requirements. However, the TIME-PHASED WITH REQUIREMENTS indicator should be selected in the MRP type. If need be, also consider the forecast requirements in this process.

Prerequisites

In the material master, follow these steps:

1. Go to the MRP 1 view and enter an MRP TYPE for time-phased planning, and the PLANNING CYCLE in the form of a planning calendar.

2. Go to the MRP 1 view and define a PLANNED DELIVERY TIME.

3. Go to the MRP 1 view and enter LOT-FOR-LOT ORDER QUANTITY as the MRP lot size.

4. Define the MRP type in Customizing for MRP in the IMG activity and select CHECK MRP TYPES.

Process Flow

The system will take these process steps:

1. When the plan is run, the system uses the MRP date record in the planning file to actually see which materials are really to be planned. Then the plan date is estimated using the planning cycle.

2. The system calculates requirements and determines a time break/interval. This interval considers the material needed to cover all requirements until the next MRP date and the delivery time as well.

   The requirements are calculated according to the following formula:

   Forecast requirements – other requirements in the interval (interval = planning cycle + purchasing processing time + planned delivery time + goods receipt processing time) + safety stock

   The periods requirements lying totally within the interval in question are to be considered while calculating the requirements; otherwise, the system only considers a part of it, rather than fully.

> **Note**
>
> The planned delivery time is decided based on the calendar days, the goods receipt processing time, and the purchasing processing time.

3. In the net requirements calculation, the requirements calculated in the interval by stock and firmed receipts are reduced by the system. The leftover quantity equals the shortage quantity.

4. If you use lot-for-lot, a procurement proposal is created by the system. This proposal is for the amount of shortage quantity. And if you've chosen any other lot-sizing procedure, it will determine the quantity in the order proposal.

> **Note**
>
> While calculating, the system accepts that the firmed receipts are in the interval in question. It doesn't matter whether the firmed receipts are available at the start or end of the interval, meaning that a shortage might exist for some time, which is acceptable.

Time-Phased Planning Process with Reorder Point Planning

You can combine time-phased planning with reorder point planning.

The prerequisites for this combination are the following:

▸ Set the MRP TYPE for time-phased planning in the material master (MRP 1 view).

▸ Define a reorder point, or a forecast automatically calculates it. Enter the same in the material master (MRP 1 view).

The material is planned with the recorded MRP date. It's also planned in case the stock falls lower than the recorder level. In such a case, the system automatically sets the NET CHANGE PLANNING indicator in the planning file, ensuring that the material will be included in the next run.

The interval starting from the time the stock falls below the reorder level to the available date of the next regular MRP is calculated and used for the requirement calculation. The ordered quantity should cover this interval. The material is planned as always in the next MRP date.

11.6   Planning Run

We've now gone through the various planning procedures and techniques. After you select the appropriate planning procedure, you need to run the planning. Planning can be run in the system for the following combinations:

- For a plant, several plants, an MRP area, several MRP areas, or a combination of these (total planning)
- For a single material or product group (single-item planning)

The following functions are provided:

- Total planning
- Single-item, single-level planning
- Multi-level, single-item planning
- Interactive planning
- Multi-level, make-to-order production
- Individual project planning

Total planning and single-item planning are executed only on a single level in CBP. Transaction MD01 is used to execute total planning, whereas Transaction MD03 is used for single-level planning of a single item.

11.6.1   Planning File

All materials that are relevant for the planning run are contained in a planning file by the system. All materials are automatically included in the planning file after you create the material master with MRP views and valid MRP types, except the materials that are defined as ND/No MRP.

The planning run and scope of planning are controlled by the planning file. The following changes trigger an entry in the planning file:

- Changes in stock/requirements
- Addition of purchase requisitions, POs, sales orders, reservations, and forecasts
- Posting and reversal of goods receipt/goods issue documents

You create a planning file manual entry with Transaction MD20. After the planning file is created, use Transaction MDRE to check the consistency of the planning file entry. To display the planning file entries, go to Transaction MD21. You'll get a selection screen as shown in Figure 11.17. Enter MATERIAL, MRP AREA, or PLNT. You can also choose the various selection criteria to filer the records.

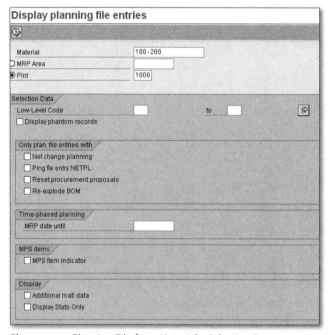

Figure 11.17 Planning File for a Material—Selection Screen

Click on the EXECUTE button to generate the report shown in Figure 11.18.

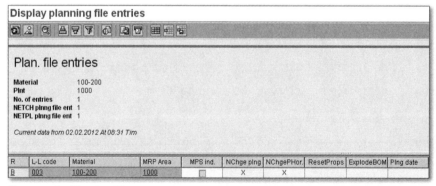

Figure 11.18 Planning File

By using certain control parameters, you can determine the manner in which the planning run will be executed.

11.6.2 Planning Horizon

The planning horizon is the time period in workdays, for which you want to plan materials and purchasing. This can be set per MRP group or per plant.

Planning horizons are defined in Customizing via the menu path SPRO • MATERIALS MANAGEMENT • CONSUMPTION BASED PLANNING • PLANT PARAMETERS • CARRY OUT OVERALL MAINTENANCE OF PLANT PARAMETERS.

11.6.3 Control Parameters for the Planning Run

The control parameters that you need to set, depending on your individual business scenario, include the following:

▶ **Planning run type/processing key**
You can choose whether all materials are to be planned or only those with MRP-relevant changes. There are three processing keys or planning run types available (see Table 11.2):

  ▶ **Regenerative planning (processing key: NEUPL)**
  All materials entered in the planning file will be planned by the system. Indicators NETCH and NETPL are reset. The disadvantage is that a lot of the burden is put on the system because every material is considered in planning.

  ▶ **Net change planning in total horizon (processing key: NETCH)**
  Only materials marked with the NETCH indicator are planned by the system in the planning file. Changes falling past the planning horizon that are MRP-relevant are noted in the planning file.

  ▶ **Net change planning in planning horizon (processing key: NETPL)**
  The system marks the materials marked with the NETPL indicator in the planning file. All materials will be planned that have undergone MRP-relevant changes within the planning horizon.

Planning Run	Processing Key	Materials in Scope
Regenerative planning	NEUPL	All materials in planning file
Net change planning in total horizon	NETCH	Only materials in planning file with NETCH indicator
Net change planning in planning horizon	NETPL	Only materials in planning file with NETPL indicator

Table 11.2 Planning Run Types

The creation indicators for purchase requisitions are:

– Planned orders only

– Purchase requisitions only

– Purchase requisitions within the opening period and planned orders outside of the opening period

The creation indicators for scheduling lines are:

– No schedule lines

– Only schedule lines

– Schedule lines within the opening period and purchase requisitions outside of the opening period

The creation indicators for MRP lists are:

– No MRP lists

– Always MRP lists

– MRP lists only in certain exceptional situations that are documented in exception messages

▶ **Planning mode**
Determines the system's dealing with procurement proposals such as planned orders, scheduling agreement lines, and purchase requisitions from the previous planning run and the next planning run (not totally firm yet). In the planning file, this is set as the planning mode for a material. The planning mode in the initial screen of the planning run can overrule the planning mode set in the planning file for a material. The planning mode with the highest numeric value takes priority for planning a particular material. So, planning mode 2 takes

priority over planning mode 1. Planning mode 3 takes priority over planning mode 1 and planning mode 2. The following options are available:

▶ Adapt existing planning data (planning mode 1)

▶ Re-explode BOM after change to BOM (planning mode 2)

▶ Delete planning data and recreate procurement proposals (planning mode 3)

▶ **Scheduling**

The SCHEDULING indicator in the initial screen of the planning run determines how the planned orders for materials produced in-house should be scheduled. The indicator is applicable to all planned orders—new, changed, or with BOM re-exploded. The following options are available:

▶ Determination of basic dates (scheduling option 1)

▶ Lead time scheduling (scheduling option 2)

In CBP, the determination of basic dates is normally used because it deals with materials that are procured externally.

We've now discussed the various controlling elements you can select during your planning run. Transaction MD03 is used for single-item, single-level planning as shown in Figure 11.19. You can see that planning is being run for material 100-200 and plant 1000 with various control parameters.

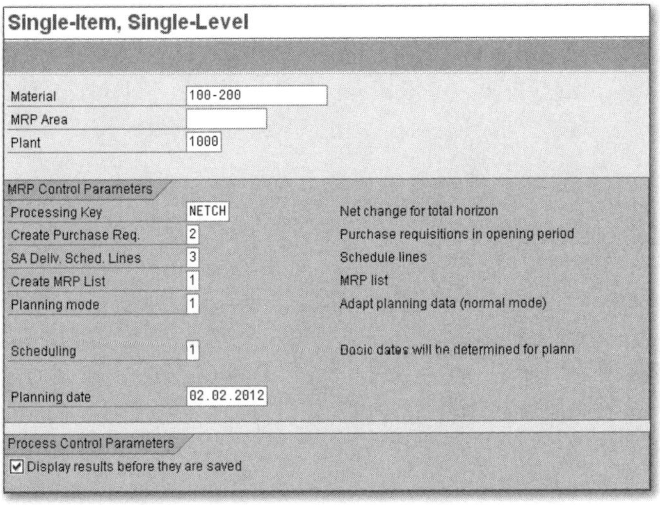

Single-Item, Single-Level		
Material	100-200	
MRP Area		
Plant	1000	
MRP Control Parameters		
Processing Key	NETCH	Net change for total horizon
Create Purchase Req.	2	Purchase requisitions in opening period
SA Deliv. Sched. Lines	3	Schedule lines
Create MRP List	1	MRP list
Planning mode	1	Adapt planning data (normal mode)
Scheduling	1	Basic dates will be determined for plann
Planning date	02.02.2012	
Process Control Parameters		
☑ Display results before they are saved		

Figure 11.19 Planning Run—Transaction MD03

11.6.4 Planning Execution

After you've customized MRP based on your business requirements, you need to execute the planning run so that the system will plan the materials requirements and create the internal orders or purchase requisistions based on the settings. You can execute planning in online mode or in background via background jobs. Three options are available:

▶ **Carry out total planning online**
To carry out overall planning, go to the SAP Easy Access Menu and choose SAP MENU • LOGISTICS • MATERIALS MANAGEMENT • MATERIAL REQUIREMENTS PLAN-NING (MRP) • MRP. Choose PLANNING • TOTAL PLANNING • ONLINE (Transaction MD01). The system executes both total planning for the selected plant and for the scope of the planning defined. The MRP areas or the individual plants are automatically planned in the defined sequence.

▶ **Execute total planning in background mode**
Choose PLANNING • TOTAL PLANNING • AS BACKGROUND JOB (Transaction MDBT). If SCHEDULE ONCE is chosen, the planning run is executed on the specified date and with defined control parameters in the variant. To repeat total planning at constant intervals, choose SCHEDULE PERIODICALLY.

▶ **Carrying out single-item, single-level planning**
As the name suggests, the planning applies only to one individual material. Single-level, however, means that the level directly below the material is only planned because the BOM hasn't exploded. Choose PLANNING • SINGLE-ITEM PLANNING, SINGLE-LEVEL. Single-level, single-item planning is carried out for the material selected.

11.7 Planning Evaluations

After you execute the MRP run, planning files will be created. The system will propose how much quantity of a material is required and when it is required. You can see these planning evaluations in the system. The following evaluations are available for evaluating the planning results in CBP:

▶ MRP list

▶ Current stock/requirements list

The evaluations of CBP are found by starting from the MATERIALS MANAGEMENT node and choosing MATERIALS PLANNING • MRP.

11.7.1 MRP List and Stock/Requirements List

After the planning run is executed, you need to view the results of the planning run to take further actions; that is, create POs, productions orders, and so on. You need to view the MRP list and stock requirement list to see the planning results. Let's discuss each one of these in detail.

MRP List

While the planning run is executed, the system creates MRP lists based on the indicator that's set. These lists provide the material planning result. The stock/requirements situation is always displayed by the MRP list, at the time of the last planning run. A work basis is also contained for the MRP controller. Changes aren't effective if done after the planning date. Thus, the list remains fixed.

MRP lists have to be either deleted manually or updated by new lists from a consecutive planning run until they're stored in the system. You can access your MRP lists via Transaction MD05. Enter the material and plant for which you want to see the planning result, and press Enter. The system will display the list as shown in Figure 11.20.

Figure 11.20 MRP List

Converting Planned Orders

The planning run creates planned orders, which can be firmed by converting them into production orders for in-house production and external procurement of purchase requisitions. You have two different options to convert the internal orders into purchase requisitions: individually or collectively.

- **Individual conversion**

  SAP EASY ACCESS MENU • LOGISTICS • MATERIALS MANAGEMENT • MATERIALS REQUIREMENTS PLANNING • MRP • PLANNED ORDER • CONVERT TO PURCHASE REQUISITION • INDIVIDUAL CONVERSION.

- **Collective conversion**

  When you want to convert a planned order into a purchase requisition collectively, choose this option. In this case, the same material required in the multiple planned order will be converted into one requisition.

  SAP EASY ACCESS MENU • LOGISTICS • MATERIALS MANAGEMENT • MATERIALS REQUIREMENTS PLANNING • MRP • PLANNED ORDER • CONVERT TO PURCHASE REQUISITION • COLLECTIVE CONVERSION.

Stock/Requirements List

After the planning run is executed, you can see the stock positions and requirements via the stock/requirements list. The most up-to-date stock and requirements situation is displayed in the stock/requirements list. You can view the stock/requirements list via Transaction MD04 as shown in Figure 11.21. You can see the available stock by date and various requirements by different dates. You can also see the AVAILABLE QTY column, which shows the available stock quantity on a particular date based on the requirements.

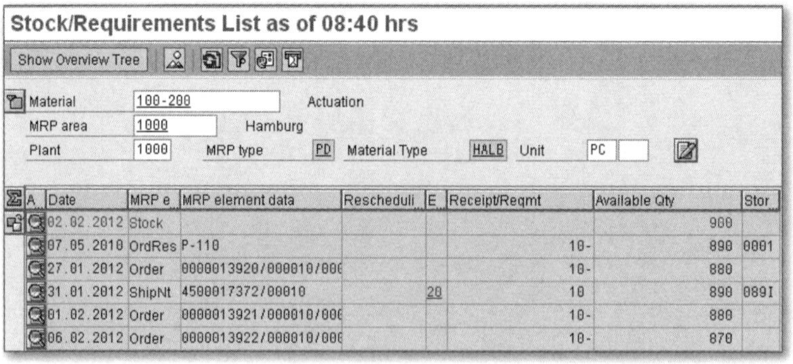

Figure 11.21 Stock/Requirements List

The distinguishing factor between the MRP list and the stock/requirements list is that every time the stock/requirements list is listed, the system chooses the MRP elements and shows the most updated situation. The current availability situation of material is thus always shown. Modifications made after the planning date are directly displayed, making the list dynamic.

Stock/requirements lists are never saved in a fixed state, so it is always subject to change. The list exists only in the working memory.

11.7.2 Navigation Profile

A navigation profile contains transaction calls for the direct-called transactions from the current stock/requirements list or the MRP list. Navigation profiles enable you to navigate faster and more flexibly between transactions. You can define a navigation profile in Customizing via SPRO • MATERIALS MANAGEMENT • CONSUMPTION BASED PLANNING • EVALUATION • DEFINE NAVIGATION PROFILE.

Define the profile by clicking the NEW ENTRIES button. To define the profile by copying an existing profile, select the profile and click on the COPY button. Enter the profile name and description, then click on GENERAL TRANSACTION CALLS from the left-side menu (Figure 11.22). Select the transaction codes with the required sequence and save.

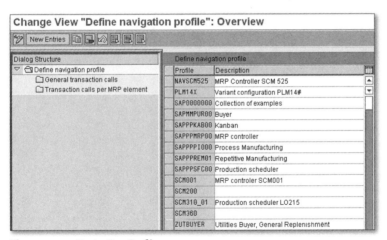

Figure 11.22 Navigation Profile

You can assign the navigation profile from the SAP Easy Access menu under the menu path ENVIRONMENT • NAVIGATION PROFILE • ASSIGN or under SETTINGS. The system then offers transactions suitable for the users, without the user having to define the jumps.

11.7.3   Exception Messages

You can use exception messages to highlight the situations that need attention from the MRP controller (planner) during the planning run. Exception messages may indicate the following:

▶ New order proposals created by MRP

▶ Date in the past (start, finish, or opening dates)

▶ Problems during BOM explosion

▶ Problems during scheduling

▶ Rescheduling

You can define exception messages in Customizing via the menu path SPRO • MATERIALS MANAGEMENT • CONSUMPTION BASED PLANNING • EVALUATION • EXCEPTION MESSAGES • DEFINE AND GROUP EXCEPTION MESSAGES. You can see the list of exception messages in Figure 11.23. For example, exception message 96 indicates that stock has fallen below the safety stock level.

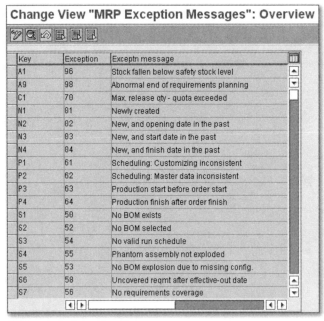

Figure 11.23   Exception Messages

Select the exception message and click CHANGE; you'll get another screen where you can make the following selections:

▶ EXCEPTION MESSAGE PRIORITY
You can select the priority of the exception message from the dropdown list. Priority determines which exception message is displayed in the MRP list, if there is more than one.

▶ NO EXCEPTION MESSAGE
You can select the exception message checkbox only if you don't want the exceptions to be created during the planning run for an MRP element.

▶ CREATE MRP LIST
You can select this checkbox for creation of the MRP list depending on the exception messages in order of appearance.

▶ SELECTION GROUP
You can select the exception group. Various exception messages are grouped together for selection.

11.8 Summary

In this chapter, you learned about various MRP procedures, configuration steps, and process steps. You're now able to configure MRP procedures based on your individual business requirements. You can also set up an MRP run in background jobs based on your requirements.

In the next chapter, we'll discuss enhancements in the area of Materials Management in SAP.

Although SAP is highly configurable, at times your business's specific requirements might not be achievable through standard configuration. Such requirements can be achieved through enhancement development, which is the topic of this chapter.

12   Enhancements in Materials Management

In our experience, we've found that functional consultants oftentimes don't know about the different enhancement objects and components that can help provide the real customization for different clients and businesses. In this chapter, we'll provide an overview of ABAP components to get you familiar with the many technical elements, design a unique interface with enhancements, and give you the ability to direct a technical team and give options to your clients. Because this book is meant for functional and not technical consultants, we won't delve into great depths.

First, let's understand the SAP system architecture before going through the development objects.

12.1   System Architecture

SAP has been evolving since its start to provide the best in technology. At present, SAP NetWeaver is the latest platform that also supports Service-Oriented Architecture (SOA). The three-tier architecture (client/server) available in SAP R/3 is extended in SAP NetWeaver. The three layers are presentation, application, and database as illustrated in Figure 12.1 and described here:

► **Database layer**
All data, such as programs, transactional data, and so on, are stored in the database layer, which is the lowest-level layer. Any of the relational databases (RDBMS) such as Oracle, SQL, Max DB, and so on can be used with the SAP system.

▶ **Application layer**

The application layer is the middle-level layer. In this layer, all business logic resides in the form of programs. For programming, SAP uses the ABAP language.

▶ **Presentation layer**

The presentation layer is a user interface (UI) layer, accessible for the users to transact. It forms the topmost level.

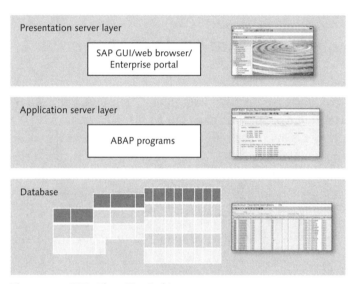

Figure 12.1 SAP—Three-Tier Architecture

This highly scalable architecture has its technical distribution of software independent of its hardware's physical location. The layer can be installed vertically, on top of the other in one computer, or each layer on another computer. The application servers and presentation can be divided by any number of computers.

Let's go through an example to understand how the three layers integrate. Transaction ME21N (presentation layer) is called by the user/purchaser to create a purchase order (PO). In turn, the PO screen is sent to the presentation layer by calling the PO creation program in the application layer. When the purchaser saves after keying the data in the PO creation screen, the data flows into respective PO tables such as EKPO, EKKO, and so on. But only after relevant validations and verification will the data flow. This validation and verification is conducted by the program stored in the application layer. This is illustrated in Figure 12.2.

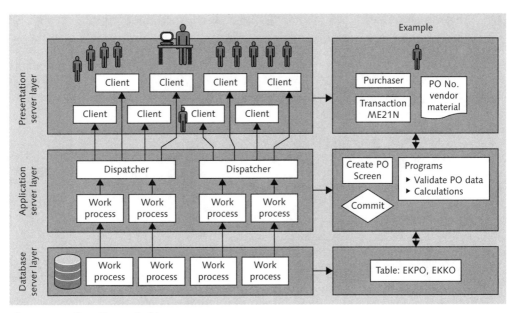

Figure 12.2 Client/Server Architecture

Now let's discuss the various types of development objects.

12.2   Introduction to Development Objects

Let's run through a business scenario of an implementation project using ASAP methodology. Figure 12.3 provides a very high-level overview of ASAP methodology.

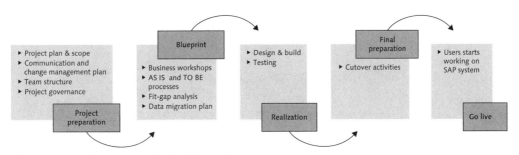

Figure 12.3 Implementation Methodology—Phases

Consider you're in the blue-printing phase where "AS IS" and "TO BE" processes are documented. During the fit-gap analysis, you come across various requirements that can't be achieved with standard configurations such as reports, interfacing with legacy systems, and so on.

Such requirements needs to development. In general, all technical developments in ABAP are classified as RICEFW/FRICEW, which are acronyms for a category of technical development as described in Table 12.1.

R	Reports (Reports, SQVI/Query, BI/BO reports)
I	Interface (ALE/IDOC, RFC)
C	Conversions (BDC, LSMW)
E	Enhancement (BAPI/BAdI)
F	Forms (SAP Scripts, smart forms, Web Dynpro—Adobe)
W	Workflow (workflow and new BRF)

Table 12.1 RICEFW/FRICEW

In the following sections, we'll go through an overview of each of these development objects.

12.3 Reports

Output of data in a required format is a report. Many standard reports are provided by SAP, which are easily found in the SAP Easy Access menu by clicking INFORMATION SYSTEMS.

Most of your reporting requirements will be met through the standard reports provided by SAP. Reports that are required and don't exist in the SAP system can be developed by using reporting tools or through technical development (ABAP). Let's see the various reporting tools available in SAP:

▶ **SAP Query**
This tool creates queries to get data and output the same in a particular format. To fetch data, SAP Query uses InfoSet. When using the InfoSet Query, an InfoSet provides a view of a reported dataset. The InfoSet determines the tables and fields being referred to.

▶ **InfoSet Query**

This is a tool to set up a SAP Query. They are also used to quickly retrieve data from an InfoSet, without creating a query from an InfoSet. InfoSet always forms the base for every query, as queries are a collection of data in InfoSet. Note that queries are created, either for a specific function or for a specific user group. Queries allocated to a particular group are accessed by all users of a particular user group.

▶ **QuickView**

You can define the QuickView reports and can view them via Transaction SQVI. This helps you display information from various data sources. To create a Quick-View, you won't require an InfoSet; rather the data can be selected from a table, logical database, and a table join.

Each user can define his own specific QuickViews that are only displayed for that user. They can't be copied, and are user specific. You can compile an SAP Query from a QuickView. However, the condition is that the QuickView uses a functional area from the standard system as a data source. The query is then visible to the user group.

To create a query report, go to Transaction SQ01 as shown in Figure 12.4. Click on the CREATE button. From this transaction, you can also create InfoSet Query and QuickViewer reports, or you can use Transaction SQVI.

Query from User Group /GRC/APPL: Initial Screen

Query area   Global Area (Cross-client)

Query | Change | Create

Quick Viewer | InfoSet Query | Display | Description

Queries of user group /GRC/APPL : GRC Integration (SAP_APPL)

Name	Title	InfoSet	Logical Database	Table/View/Join	InfoSet Title
CO_OM_CA_10_Q1	Cost Center: Plan/Budget vs. Actual Value	/GRC/CO_OM_CCA_10		/GRC/CO_OM_CCA_10	Cost Center: Plan/Budget vs. Actual Value
CO_OM_CA_20_Q1	Overhead Cost Controlling: Posting Reversals	/GRC/CO_OM_CCA_20		/GRC/CO_OM_CCA_20	Overhead Cost Controlling: Posting Reversals
CO_OM_OP_10_Q1	Internal Orders: Plan/Budget vs. Actual Value	/GRC/CO_OM_OPA_10		/GRC/CO_OM_OPA_10	Internal Orders: Plan/Budget vs. Actual Value
CO_OM_PR_10_Q1	Projects: Plan/Budget vs. Actual Value	/GRC/CO_OM_PRO_10		/GRC/CO_OM_PRO_10	Projects: Plan/Budget vs. Acture Value
FI_AP_20_Q1	Onetime Vendor credit notes percentage of total purchases	/GRC/FI_AP_20		/GRC/GRC_S_FI_AP_20	Onetime vendor Purchase Percentage
FI_AP_21_Q1	Vendor credit note percentage of total sales	/GRC/FI_AP_21		/GRC/GRC_S_FI_AP_21	Vendor Credit Notes Percentage
FI_AR_10_Q1	Customer credit note percentage of total sales	/GRC/FI_AR_10		/GRC/GRC_S_FI_AP_21	Customer Credit Notes Percentage
FI_AR_AR_10_Q1	Accounts Receivable: DSO calculated by company code	/GRC/FI_AR_AR_10		/GRC/FI_AR_AR_10	Accounts Receivable: DSO calculated by company code
FI_AR_AR_11_Q1	Accounts Receivable: DSO calculated by country	/GRC/FI_AR_AR_11		/GRC/FI_AR_AR_11	Accounts Receivable: DSO calculated by country
FI_BL_PT_10_Q1	Overdue payments	/GRC/FI_BL_PT_10		/GRC/FI_BL_PT_10	Overdue payments
FSCM_CM_10_Q1	Cash Mgt: Cash Position	/GRC/FSCM_CM_10		/GRC/FSCM_CM_20	Cash Mgt: Cash Position
FSCM_CM_20_Q1	Cash Mgt: Liquidity Forecast	/GRC/FSCM_CM_20		/GRC/FSCM_CM_20	Cash Mgt: Liquidity Forecast

Figure 12.4 Query Creation—Transaction SQ01

▶ **Your own ABAP program**

If the requirements couldn't be achieved via any of the preceding tools, then writing your own ABAP program helps deliver a custom report. There are two types of reports: the List, which has very minimal features, and the ALV, which has more features. An ALV report has broad functionality, similar to Microsoft Excel. It lets you hide, reformat, and emphasize list items; add graphic elements; and overall make an ABAP list into a very powerful communication tool. The different types of ALV reports are Simple, Grid Control, Blocked List, Hierarchical, Graphical List, and Interactive.

Table 12.2 shows the merits and demerits of all of the reporting tools.

Reporting Tool	Purpose	Advantages	Limitations
Standard reports	Provision of solutions for the most common reporting requirements	▶ Use immediately (an off-the-shelf report) ▶ No development effort required	▶ Limited flexibility ▶ You can't choose output fields arbitrarily
InfoSet Query	Intuitively operable, general SAP reporting tool for creating your own reports	▶ Clear interface ▶ Very easy to operate ▶ No programming effort required ▶ Integrates with SAP Query, so queries can also be processed with SAP Query	▶ InfoSets and user groups need to be defined in SAP Query to be able to use the InfoSet Query ▶ Not possible to display multiple row lists
SAP Query	General SAP reporting tool for creating your own reports, InfoSets, and queries	▶ Very flexible ▶ No programming effort required ▶ Queries can be made available in the SAP Easy Access Menu ▶ Provides extensive options for aggregating data, performing calculations, and for graphical display	Requires a higher training investment

Table 12.2 Reporting Tools Comparison

Reporting Tool	Purpose	Advantages	Limitations
		▶ Allows the display of multi-row lists ▶ Allows you to define a basic list, multiple statistics, and ranked lists for each query	
Your own ABAP programs	Implement the customer's own requirements	▶ Entire scope of the ABAP language can be leveraged ▶ The ABAP Workbench provides an easy-to-use development environment	Programmer has full freedom to write code, which sometimes can lead to damage such as runtime errors and incorrect data retrieval

Table 12.2 Reporting Tools Comparison (Cont.)

Business Example

Let's consider a few real-world examples to better understand when a customized report is required.

A leading FMCG (fast-moving consumer products) company with operations located worldwide wanted to see the report of materials that are above the reorder point along with the available quantity and open quantity, as well as the materials falling below the reorder point. There is no such standard report available in SAP that provides the required information in a single report, so it was developed using ABAP.

A requirement for this business is to see the following fields in the report:

▶ Plant

▶ Material No.

▶ Material Description

▶ Material Group

▶ Reorder Point

▶ Unrestricted Stock

▶ UOM

- ▶ Open PO Quantity
- ▶ PO No.
- ▶ PO Date
- ▶ Vendor

This report was developed with the selection option as shown in Figure 12.5. The user can select Stock Below ReOrder Level or Stock Above ReOrder Level for a particular plant or range of plants, material or range of materials, and material group or range of material groups.

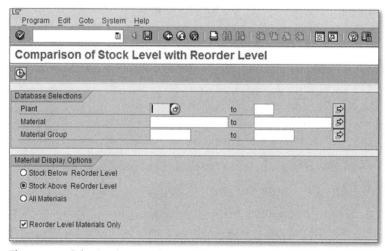

Figure 12.5 Selection Screen—Custom Report

After the report is executed, it will display the list of data based on the selection criteria as shown in Figure 12.6.

Comparison of Stock Level with Reorder Level

SAFETY STOCK REPORT

Date:12.01.2012

Plant	Material	Material Description	Matl Group	Unrestr.	Reorder Pt	Purch.Doc.	Item	Doc. Date	Open Qty	OUn	Vendor	Vendor Name
2030	E101-111-2222-3333	Test Material for Output Excisable AAAAA	REPAIRABL	225	100	4510000023	10	03.07.2010	95	EA	400010	Test Vendor for ZDOM00 AAAAAAA
				225	100	4510000024	10	03.07.2010	184	EA	400010	Test Vendor for ZDOM00 AAAAAAA
				225	100	4520000002	10	06.08.2010	100	EA	400005	MB & C0
	E888-666-2222-3333	Test Material for Output Non Excisable B		125	100	4510000023	20	03.07.2010	95	EA	400010	Test Vendor for ZDOM00 AAAAAAA
				125	100	4510000024	20	03.07.2010	74	EA	400010	Test Vendor for ZDOM00 AAAAAAA
				125	100	4510000032	10	05.07.2010	1,000,000	EA	400010	Test Vendor for ZDOM00 AAAAAAA
				125	100	4510000033	10	05.07.2010	10	EA	400010	Test Vendor for ZDOM00 AAAAAAA

Figure 12.6 Custom Report Display

When you're faced with reporting requirements, always check if there is a standard SAP report to suit the requirement first. Otherwise, you need to develop a custom report with an ABAP consultant.

In the next section, we'll discuss the interface.

12.4 Interface

An *interface* is used when two systems are integrated to let data flow in electronic form. For example, a well-known postal company located in the United States has multiple SAP and non-SAP systems being used for business. The company's system landscape is shown in Figure 12.7.

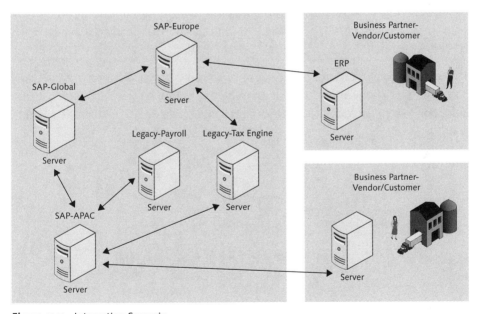

Figure 12.7 Integration Scenario

The company has two regional SAP instances and one global SAP instance. One SAP instance's users are based in Asia-Pacific regions (APAC), while the other is used for business in Europe. The global SAP system is the group reporting system, which is also being used for North America. For financial consolidation, the data from the

APAC system and Europe system should flow in to the global system. SAP-to-SAP integration will make this happen. For tax calculations and payroll, the company uses a non-SAP system, which is further integrated with SAP systems.

A few of the company's business partners' systems are also integrated with its SAP systems. The PO received by the vendor is in electronic format. When vendor sends the order confirmation, it comes to SAP automatically and also updates the PO confirmation status.

As you can see in Figure 12.7, there could be requirements to integrate SAP-to-SAP systems or SAP to non-SAP systems within or outside your company.

The upcoming subsections provide an overview of the various integration technologies provided by SAP. They also explain the application area of each technology in the communication process.

The order of technologies described also mirrors the order in which they were developed; right from ABAP-based communication and data exchange technologies, such as IDocs, RFC, BAPI, to globally applicable Internet formats such as HTTP, HTTPS, XML, and SOAP.

There are various tools and techniques are available for system integrations, and based on your client or business's requirements, you need to select the most suitable tool. We've listed the tool/techniques available in SAP for integration here:

- Classical SAP technologies (ABAP)
  - RFC
  - ALE/EDI
  - IDoc Interface
  - BAPI
- Communication between ABAP and non-ABAP technologies
  - SAP Business Connector
  - SAP Java Connector
  - SAP Java Resource Adapter
  - SAP .NET Connector
  - Internet Communication Framework

- SOAP Runtime for SAP Web AS
- Web Service Technologies in SAP Web AS

12.4.1 Technical Terminology—Synchronous and Asynchronous Communications

Synchronous and asynchronous communication are the two types of communication between two systems. Let's go over each type.

Synchronous Communication

The communication using a single function cell is called *synchronous* communication. The receiving system should also be active and accept the call or the message sent for any further processing. This is the prerequisite for synchronous communication. Synchronous communication has the following advantages and disadvantages:

- **Advantage**
  Function calls requiring the immediate return of data back to the sender system will find synchronous communication helpful.

  Example: With account assignment, create a PO in the sender system. Before saving the PO, carry out a budget check in central accounting.

- **Disadvantage**
  Can only be used after both the systems are checked to be active and can be contacted; otherwise, a serious disruption of processes can be expected. Problems arise especially if the receiving system isn't available for longer periods because of maintenance; for instance, a system upgrade.

Asynchronous Communication

For *asynchronous* communication, a function call can be dispatched from the sender, even without the availability of the receiving system because the receiving system is capable of receiving and processing the calls even at a later time. At such times, the function call waits in the outbound queue of the sending system. From here, the calls are repeated at regular intervals until the receiving system can process them. Asynchronous communication has the following advantages and disadvantages:

- **Advantage**
  The non-availability of the receiving system for a long duration—for reasons such as upgrading, during the time of a function call—still doesn't stop the

processing of the data because it's stored in the interim to be processed at a later time.

Example: Suppose a PO is being sent to a vendor system; the availability of the receiving system can't be influenced by the sending system. Until the vendor is available, the PO can be sent over and over again.

▶ **Disadvantage**
Processes requiring an immediate response to the sender system can't be achieved with this method.

12.4.2 Classical SAP Technologies (ABAP)

In this section, we'll provide an overview of the key ABAP technologies for communication. You can use these technologies to communicate between SAP systems, as well as between SAP and non-SAP systems. In MM, you might have a scenario where your vendor's non-SAP system needs to be integrated with your SAP system. In this case POs, PO confirmations, shipping notifications, and so on will flow between the SAP and non-SAP system.

Whenever you have customizing requirements in the MM area, you need to work with technical consultants to design the integration. The main communication techniques are RFC, ALE, EDI, BAPI, and IDoc. Let's delve into the overview of these techniques.

RFC (Remote Function Call)

The standard SAP interface for communication between SAP systems is the Remote Function Call (RFC), which calls a function to be carried out in a remote system. Following are the types of RFCs:

▶ **Synchronous RFC (sRFC)**
Synchronous RFC is the first version of RFC. It executes the function call depending on the synchronous communication, which means that when the call is made, both the systems involved should be available.

▶ **Transactional RFC (tRFC; previously known as asynchronous RFC)**
Asynchronous communication method performs the called function module only once in the RFC server. When the RFC client program is executing a tRFC, the remote system need not be available. The called RFC function and the corresponding data is stored by the tRFC component, in the SAP database with a unique transaction ID (TID). When the call is in line while the receiving system

is down, the call waits in the local queue. Without checking if the remote call was successful, the calling dialog program can proceed.

tRFCs have the following characteristics:

▶ tRFCs are executed in the order in which they are called.

▶ tRFCs are executed in the same program context in the target system.

▶ tRFCs run as a single transaction; they are either committed or rolled back as a unit.

If you want to maintain the transactional sequence of the calls, it's better to implement tRFC.

However, there are some disadvantages to using tRFC:

▶ All LUWs are processed independently by tRFC. However, performance is reduced significantly in both send and target systems, due to the number of tRFC processes activated.

▶ The sequence of LUWs described in the application can't be kept. Ensuring the execution of transactions in the defined sequence by the application won't be possible. The only thing that can be ensured is that all LUWs described in the application will be transferred at some point soon.

▶ **Queued RFC (qRFC)**
To guarantee the specified order of the multiple LUWs processing, tRFC can be serialized using inbound and outbound queues. This is called qRFC.

qRFC is thus an extension of tRFC, except that it has no predecessors in the participating queues. Depending on the sequence defined in various application programs, it transfers an LUW.

If you want to guarantee that several transactions are processed in a predefined order, you should implement qRFC.

ALE/EDI

EDI (Electronic Data Interchange) and ALE (Application Link Enabling) are used to exchange business data between different systems. These communications require an IDoc interface, which is the general exchange format of the communicating system. IDocs are sent using various methods, such as RFCs or files.

Application Link Enabling (ALE)

To communicate from one system to one or more other systems, mostly internal, you can use ALE to distribute data. The integration of business processes across several SAP or non-SAP systems is enabled by ALE.

Electronic Data Interchange (EDI)

Use EDI when you want to exchange business application documents with an external partner system, such as a customer or a vendor. The EDI messages are sent in IDoc format by the SAP system to an EDI subsystem. This is shown in Figure 12.8, where the messages are transformed to a universal EDI standard (UN/EDIFACT or ANXSI/X12), enabling communication with non-SAP systems. The two partners involved in the EDI application process scenario are the sender and the recipient of an EDI message.

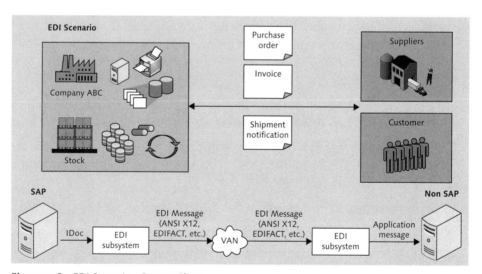

Figure 12.8 EDI Scenario—Process Flow

IDoc Interface/ALE

Business data is exchanged with an external system by the IDoc interface. The IDoc interface has the definition of a data structure, with the processing logic for this data structure. IDoc is the data structure and is the exchange format common to every communicating system. You can use IDocs to specify exception handling in the SAP Business Workflow, without the data already having to exist as SAP application documents.

The IDoc carries the data from the source system to the destination system. For example, a PO from an SAP system can be sent to your vendor in the IDoc format via middleware, and this can create the sales order in the vendor system automatically. You need to use the IDoc interface in the following scenarios:

▶ Electronic Data Exchange (EDI)

▶ Connect to other business application systems (e.g., PC applications, external SAP Business Workflow tools) by IDoc

▶ Application Link Enabling (ALE)

BAPI (Business Application Programming Interface)

BAPIs are stored in the SAP BusinessObjects Repository (BOR). They're specific methods (programs) for SAP BusinessObjects and carry out specific business tasks. For example, if you have two SAP instances used for the United States and Europe, respectively, then during intercompany purchases, the PO generated in the US system can create a sales order in the Europe instance by using a BAPI.

In the SAP system's ABAP Workbench Function Builder BAPIs are stored as RFC-capable function modules. BAPIs comprise standard business interfaces, enabling external applications with the aid of SAP BusinessObjects to access SAP processes, data, and functions.

To access SAP business objects, client programs using BAPIs can be part of the same SAP system (e.g., a .NET application), part of an HTTP Gateway, or part of another SAP system.

To activate a business process in another system by using a BAPI, you use the synchronous communication methods RFC because you want the data to return to the sending system.

Additional IDoc interfaces are generated for the BAPIs. BAPIs and ALE are used for asynchronous communication.

Communication between ABAP and Non-ABAP Technologies

A great number of different systems are now capable of exchanging business data at short notice. Using the central structures of Internet technologies such as HTTP, HTTPS, XML, and SOAP, business systems are able to communicate with each other.

However, to attain this goal it becomes obligatory to transform the proprietary structures of a system into the Internet standards. A range of components are provided by SAP to translate the ABAP standards (RFC, IDoc, BAPI) into the communication formats of the Internet.

Communication between different systems (SAP to non-SAP) uses the components in the following list. Any of these communication techniques can be used depending on the target (non-SAP) system's programming language.

▶ **SAP Business Connector (SAP BC)**
Enables the extension of business processes across the Internet and the incorporation of non-SAP products with an open and non-proprietary technology. With the SAP ERP server, the SAP Business Connector covers bi-directional, synchronous, and asynchronous communication.

▶ **SAP Java Connector (SAP JCo)**
SAP Java Connector, a middleware component, enables the development of SAP-compatible components and applications in Java. It also supports communication, in both directions: inbound calls—Java calls ABAP—and outbound calls—ABAP calls Java—with the SAP ERP server. SAP JCo can be implemented with web server applications and with desktop applications. SAP JCo, an integrated component, is used in these applications:

  ▶ SAP Business Connector, with external Java applications, for communication

  ▶ SAP Web Application Server, for connecting the integrated J2EE server with the ABAP environment

SAP JCo can also be implemented as a standalone component. For instance, for individual online (web) applications, SAP JCo establishes communication with the SAP system.

▶ **SAP Java Resource Adapter (SAP JRA)**
SAP Java Resource Adapter, a J2EE-compatible connector for SAP systems,

enables the integration of SAP systems (ABAP) with external SAP J2EE application servers. The standard J2EE interfaces for SAP JCo are implemented by SAP JRA. This simplifies the communication between heterogeneously distributed SAP J2EE landscapes and ABAP application servers.

You can also use SAP JRA to call remote functions by executing RFCs using TCP/IP in an ABAP system.

▶ **SAP .NET Connector**
The SAP .NET Connector, a development environment, enables the communication between the Microsoft .NET platform and SAP systems. This connector supports RFCs, and Web services allows you to write different applications such as web forms, Windows forms, or console applications in Microsoft Visual Studio.Net. You can use all common programming languages, including Visual Basic. NET, C#, and Managed C++ with the SAP .NET Connector.

▶ **Internet Communication Framework (ICF)**
ICF, an integrated component of the SAP Web AS, provides an environment for handling HTTP requests in the ABAP work processes of an SAP system. These HTTP requests with ICF as a client or as a server can be processed by the SAP Web AS.

▶ **SOAP Runtime for SAP Web AS**
You can create and use web services based on SOAP (Simple Object Access Protocol), which is enabled by the SOAP framework.

▶ **Web service technologies in SAP Web AS**
Using SOAP and Web Services Description Language (WSDL) technologies, the Web AS can do the following:

  ▶ Offer existing functions — BAPIs, IDocs, EJBs — as web services

  ▶ Enable any Web service provider to process web services

SOAP is an XML-based protocol for exchanging information in a decentralized, distributed environment.

WSDL is an XML format.

Note

Universal Description, Discovery, and Integration (UDDI) is a protocol to simplify finding particular services. It also simplifies the corresponding companies over the Internet.

12.4.3 Example

Here we'll go over a few examples that are generally used to transfer data with vendors in large companies.

- **Inbound Interface Examples**

  - **PO confirmation**
    Most large customers are integrated with their vendor systems. The vendor sends the company the confirmation of the PO electronically. This confirmation is processed in the SAP system, and the PO is updated with the confirmed quantity and delivery dates.

  - **Purchase invoice**
    Many large vendors send the invoices electronically, which in turn posts the purchase invoice automatically in their SAP system.

- **Outbound Interface Examples**

  - **PO**
    Most large companies send the PO to their vendors electronically. This saves time and money, and avoids data entry errors.

  - **Standard IDoc types**
    The required integration for the commonly used documents is provided by SAP; for example, IDoc type "Order" is used for POs.

12.5 Conversion

Conversions are used to migrate legacy system data to the SAP system. This is commonly used during implementation and roll-out projects. Conversions also migrate the historical data stored in legacy systems to the newly implemented SAP system. Migrating historical data helps with business continuity. This historical data is usually master data such as materials, customers and so on. The transactional data is usually open POs, open G/Ls, and so on.

Conversions can be objects generated through Legacy System Migration Workbench (LSMW) or a technical development ABAP program.

SAP offers various techniques for data migration:

► **BAPIs as interfaces**

With BAPIs as interfaces to the SAP system, the same technology is used by the LSMW, as with the permanent data transfer via ALE between SAP systems or between SAP systems and non-SAP systems. The data needs to be loaded in IDoc format, with unique IDoc numbers in the file. When the task is run, the IDocs in the specified input files are read and then transferred to the BAPI.

► **IDoc**

IDoc loading is almost the same as BAPI loading. However, the difference is that the IDoc type and the ALE inbound processing aren't generated from a BAPI but rather have to be programmed by the concerned application itself.

► **Batch input**

A standard technique for transferring large sets of data into the SAP system is batch input. The transaction flow is realized by simulation, and the data is transferred as if it were entered online. All relevant checks of the transaction are executed, ensuring that the data is consistent. The batch input process is divided into two steps:

  ► A batch input session is created to transfer the data containing all relevant data.

  ► The batch input session is processed, and the contained data is transferred into the SAP system.

The batch input technique is used by the majority of SAP standard data-transfer programs. This data-transfer program creates a batch input session to be processed later. These batch input sessions can be processed in various ways:

  ► In the foreground

  ► In the background

  ► During processing, with error display

> **Note**
>
> If you want to test the data transfer, you should process batch input sessions in the foreground or use the error display. Process the sessions in the background if you want to execute the data transfer or test its performance.

► **Direct input (DINP)**

Before transferring data directly into the SAP system, the data from the data transfer file undergoes the same checks as with the online transaction in direct output. There are two types of direct input programs: direct-input programs supported by Transaction BMV0 and direct-input programs *not* supported by Transaction BMV0. These programs always provide error handling.

For those programs supported by Transaction BMV0, there are two ways to trigger direct input:

▶ **Start the program directly**
Because the system doesn't generate error logs, nor is it possible to restart the system during an error, the program is suitable only for testing purposes.

▶ **Direct input in the background (Transaction BMV0)**
Here you can restart processing only if the program terminates or with an occurrence of a logical error, such as when a material goes missing. Although the system can restart, it can't be ensured that the data can be posted to the database again. The program is only reset to where it stopped. However, you can post or correct later any errors that occurred. Direct input places only a small load on the system, which can be an added advantage.

Example

Often, you'll come across the requirement to upload material master and vendor master records from the legacy systems during implementation or rollouts. If the data volume is huge, and a large number of fields needs to be uploaded, it's recommended to use ABAP programs.

We'll discuss enhancements in the next section.

12.6   Enhancements

To meet company-specific requirements, you may need to enhance/modify the standard SAP process by adding an additional field, additional validations, and or enhancing the business logic. These can be achieved through enhancements. SAP NetWeaver 7.0 and onward provides the Enhancement Framework to unify all possible ways of modifying or enhancing SAP products (more precisely, Repository objects of the SAP NetWeaver Application Server ABAP), which go beyond the scope of Customizing. You would need ABAP consultants to develop these enhancements. But at the same time, you need to work with ABAP consultants to explain the business requirements and also test the scenario to ensure that it's developed per your requirements. The Enhancement Builder is the corresponding tool integrated in the ABAP Workbench.

The following can be handled as enhancements:

▶ Modifying a Repository object

▶ Replacing a Repository object with an identically named object

▶ Enhancing a Repository object at a predefined position

▶ Using a foreign object

There are various tools and techniques that can be used to enhance an SAP system. User exits are one very old technique used by SAP, and are still in use today.

SAP has also introduced the Enhancement Framework for any new enhancements in standard SAP programs.

The following basic technologies can be used through the Enhancement Framework:

▶ ABAP source code enhancements

▶ Function module enhancements

▶ Global class enhancements

▶ BAdIs

The BAdI is the most commonly used enhancement technique. SAP has provided various BAdIs for various transactions such as enhancement in POs, enhancement in goods receipts, and so on. Based on the Customizing requirement, you need to work with an ABAP consultant to find the appropriate BAdI. Some important BAdIs for MM are provided in the appendix. Let's discuss BAdIs in a little more detail.

12.6.1 BAdIs

BAdIs are important elements for enhancement spots in the Enhancement Framework. They are directly processed in the Enhancement Builder.

BAdIs are the basis for object plug-ins. Without making any modifications, they enhance the functions in ABAP programs. In the interface, the BAdIs create the enhancement options, which can be implemented later in an external system or the same system.

BAdIs make a remarkable difference between the definition and individual implementations with every enhancement. A BAdI definition is generally created in an SAP ERP system. The calling points in ABAP programs together form explicit enhancement options in such programs.

The BAdI definition contains a BAdI interface, which is a set of selection filters and a few settings. The settings influence the runtime behavior later on. A BAdI interface forms a part or the entire interface of an object plug-in.

The term *BAdI implementation* is used in the Enhancement Framework for an enhancement implementation element. This consists of implementing the BAdI class, implementing the BAdI interface, and imposing conditions on the filters specified in the respective definition of a BAdI. These help with the selection of the BAdI implementation.

The calling points of a BAdI are defined through the ABAP statements `GET BADI` and `CALL BADI`. In the Enhancement Framework, these calling points form the enhancement spot elements from the explicit enhancement option.

The above options should be well understood and correlated to the business requirements by a functional consultant. Let's consider an example now.

12.6.2 Example

A unique requirement needs to be filled by a well-known FMCG company. When the PO is created, the company wants the system to look into any open PO with an existing same material. If the open PO exists for the same material, then a pop-up message needs to appear automatically to the user that reads: "PO already exists. Do you still want to create new PO?"

Based on this message, the user will know that an already-existing open PO is available for the same vendor and material combination. The user will change the PO quantity, rather than create a new PO. This is only possible by enhancing the PO program and is not achievable with standard SAP.

12.7 Forms

Forms are nothing but the technical development made for business forms, which are used for printing a particular document, such as the invoice, check prints, POs, delivery notes, picking lists, and so on. Various features are supported by these developments, such as maintaining the records of company logos and colors, placing headers and footers data in tabular format, and so on. It also prints labels and barcodes. There are three different techniques in SAP to develop the forms:

- **SAP scripts**
  In building forms, this is the oldest available technique. Although it consumes more time to develop the form and also isn't easy to develop, many SAP-delivered forms are the products built in to SAP scripts. Only SAP scripts can be customized here, and some features, such as colors and different page formats in the same form, are not supported.

- **SAP Smart Forms**
  This method features the technique to build forms faster and in a developer-friendly way. SAP Smart Forms can have colored layouts and multiple page formatting on the same form.

  SAP Smart Forms have the following advantages:

  - User friendly and easy to use GUI

  - Easy development and maintenance of forms with less programming effort

  - Separate data retrieval and form logic

  - Web-publishing capability using a generated XML output

  - Allows graphics as part of the form or as background

  - Easy migration from SAP scripts to SAP Smart Forms

> **Note**
>
> Because SAP Smart Forms are connected to the transport system, you can easily test your forms and then transfer them subsequently to your production system.

- **SAP Interactive Forms by Adobe**
  In developing forms, this is the latest technology, with support from SAP ERP 6.0 onward and in collaboration with SAP and Adobe. Static and interactive forms are developed with this tool, where the outputs are generated in PDF documents. The static PDF forms resist any changes, while the interactive PDF form lets the user interact with the PDF document.

Example

Most companies maintain their own format of POs, invoices, and so on with their company logos. The formats differ from company to company, so form development is required to create documents unique to each company.

12.8   Workflow

In every organizational department, there are approval processes; for example, in the purchasing department, the PO has to go through many different levels of approval depending on the price of the PO. Apart from this, many criteria, such as cost center, material group, plant, and purchasing organization, are also affected by workflow.

In a broader sense, workflow stands for the approval process (e.g., a PO is approved by the department head, vice president, etc. based on the value of the PO). The approval process has many features and is paperless, which reduces the lead time in a paper-based approval process.

With the recent developments, SAP offers two categories of workflows:

▸ SAP Business Workflow (application controlled workflows)

▸ SAP Business Rule Framework (BRF) (process controlled workflows)

Workflow templates are provided by the SAP Business Workflow. These workflow templates drive and control the approval process. BRFs are used to define the triggering events and expressions, serving as start conditions for various process levels.

SAP provides a release strategy to map such approval processes. As discussed in Chapter 8, some limitations to release strategies include that there is no substitution functionality or delegation functionality. All such functionalities are covered in SAP Business Workflow. Workflow and release strategies are used for cross-application business processes and are not just limited to purchasing documents.

Example

Consider a large company in Europe that manufactures paper. They have a requirement that all purchase orders are to be approved by different positions person based on the PO value, plant, purchasing organization, and document type. They've used SAP Business Workflow for this requirement. While saving the PO, the system will check for the approval requirements; if approval is required, the system will determine who is the actor (person) who is suppose to approve this PO based on the value, plant, and purchasing organization. If the PO value is between 10,000 and 50,000 Euro, the plant manager needs to approve the PO. The system will determine the plant manager's name from the HR organization structure and send the email for approval.

12.9 Summary

In this chapter, we briefly discussed the different technical developments classified as RICEFW—Report || Interface || Conversion || Enhancement || Forms || Workflow. Based on your business requirements, you can work along with technical consultants to customize the processes by using these development objects.

Now let's move on to the next chapter to review what you've learned in this book.

13   Conclusion

Materials Management (MM) is the heart of supply chain management, which makes this book essential for SAP components such as Warehouse Management (WM), Quality Management (QM), Sales and Distribution (SD), and Production Planning (PP). In the following sections, we'll review what you've learned in each chapter of this book.

Chapter 1

Chapter 1 explained the concept of ERP and discussed how the SAP system is integrated with various different functional areas of an enterprise. This is an important topic because SAP system architecture and landscape knowledge are very important for SAP consultants and SAP users.

Chapter 2

Organizational structure is the key for successful SAP system implementation. This chapter explained a variety of possible organizational structures, as well as the step-by-step procedures used to configure them. The organizational elements discussed in this chapter—including client, company code, plant, storage location, and purchasing organization—are fundamental concepts essential to understanding MM. You can now define and customize the organization structure based on business requirements.

Chapter 3

This chapter described the different types of master data, including material master data, vendor master data, info records, and source lists. Material master data is the most important of these because it's used by almost all of the functional areas of the SAP system. You can customize the materials types, number ranges, vendor account groups, and so on based on your client's business requirements.

Chapter 4

Procurement processes are extremely important for MM consultants and users. This chapter explained most of the procurement processes used in the industry. Each section covered the process and configuration steps for its respective procurement process. Efficient procurement processes save a lot of money for your client by establishing competitive prices, lower transportation costs, and material handling costs.

Chapter 5

Inventory management is a key element for the success of any company. You need to keep minimum stock levels while ensuring materials are always available on a needs basis. Inventory management is important not only for MM but also for Financial Accounting (FI), Production Planning (PP), and material requirements planning (MRP). This chapter described the importance of movement types in stock keeping as well as in account determination. It also explained various physical inventory management processes and how to configure physical inventory.

Chapter 6

This chapter described the various processes in invoice verification, including the account postings for each of these processes. Invoice verification is important from both a Purchasing and FI perspective because it generates liability and facilitates vendor payment. We have also seen various scenarios and how invoicing can be customized to meet business-specific requirements.

Chapter 7

MM is tightly integrated with FI, and this chapter explained the importance of stock valuation and its methods. This chapter also covered split valuation and discussed how you can use this functionality to meet customer requirements.

Chapter 8

This chapter covered various major customizing areas. Release strategies, pricing procedures, automatic account determination, document types, version management, and message determination are all very important aspects of MM. This chapter introduced these topics and provided detailed configuration steps.

Chapter 9

This chapter described the concept of material classification, which is used to search for materials and is a very important feature for enterprises with large numbers of material master records. The topics discussed included how to define characteristics and classes, and how to assign objects.

Chapter 10

Batch management is an important requirement mainly in the pharmaceuticals and foods processing industries. This chapter covered the end-to-end configuration of batch management and also how batch management works in SAP.

Chapter 11

We described the various types of MRP and also covered the various scenarios where these MRP types are used. In this chapter, we also discussed the configuration of consumption-based planning (CBP). Accurate planning helps reduce the overall total cost of ownership (TCO). It reduces the stock levels to optimum levels and also ensures material availability.

Chapter 12

This is very important chapter, especially for those who are not familiar with ABAP or those who don't have a programming background. This chapter covered the various types of development objects in SAP and also provided examples of each of the development object.

Appendices

In Appendix A, you can find a list of important transaction codes. Refer to these tables to find the transaction code for the required transaction such as PO creation, material master creation, and so on.

In Appendix B, you can find a list of important tables used in Materials Management in SAP. These tables will be helpful if you're working with SAP technical consultants to customize an SAP system (enhancements) and you need to find appropriate tables to fetch the required data.

In Appendix C, you can find a list of important BAdIs that you need for enhancements requirements. You can also learn how to search for the required BAdIs in the SAP ERP system.

Appendices

A Important Transaction Codes

A.1 Material Master and Service Master

Transaction Code	Description
MM01	Create Material
MM02	Change Material
MM03	Display Material
MM06	Flag for Deletion
AC03	Service Master
AC06	Service List
MMNR	Define Number Range for Material Master

Table A.1 Material Master Transaction Codes

A.2 Vendor Master

Transaction Code	Description
MK01	Create Vendor—Purchasing
MK02	Change Vendor—Purchasing
MK03	Display Vendor—Purchasing
XK01	Create Vendor—Centrally
XK02	Change Vendor—Centrally
XK03	Display Vendor—Centrally
XK05	Block Vendor—Centrally
XK06	Flat for Deletion—Centrally
XKN1	Define Number Range for Vendor Accounts

Table A.2 Vendor Master Transaction Codes

A.3 Other Master Records

Transaction Code	Description
ME11	Create Info Record
ME12	Change Info Record
ME13	Display Info Record
ME15	Flag for Deletion—Info Records
MEMASSIN	Mass Maintenance—Info Records
ME01	Maintain Source List
ME03	Display Source List
ME07	Delete Info Record
MEQ1	Maintain Quota Arrangement
MEQ3	Display Quota Arrangement
OMEO	Define Number Range for Purchasing Info Records

Table A.3 Info Records, Source List, and Quota Arrangement Transaction Codes

A.4 Inventory Management

Transaction Code	Description
MMBE	Stock Overview
MB51	Material Document List
MIGO	Goods Movement (Receipts/Issues/Transfers)
MIGO_GI	Goods Issue
MIGO_GR	Goods Receipt
MIGO_TR	Transfer Posting
MIGO_GS	Subcontracting—Subsequent Adjustment
MBST	Cancel/Reverse Material Document
MBRL	Return Delivery
MB90	Process Output—Messages

Table A.4 Inventory Management—Material Movements Transaction Codes

A.5   Materials Requirement Planning (MRP)

Transaction	Description
MD01	Carry Out Total Planning Online
MD03	Carry Out Single-Item, Single-Level Planning
MDBT	Carry Out Total Planning in Background Mode
MD05	Display MRP List
MD06	Access Collective Display of MRP List
MDLD	Print MRP List
MD04	Display Current Stock/Requirements List
MD07	Display Collective Display of Current Stock/Requirements List
MD11	Create Planned Order
MD12	Change Planned Order
MD13	Display Planned Order (Individual)
MD16	Access Planned Order (Collective Display)
MD14	Convert Planned Order to Purchase Requisition (Individual Conversion)
MD15	Convert Planned Order to Purchase Requisition (Collective Conversion)
MD20	Create Planning File Entry
MD21	Display Planning File Entry
MDAB	Set Up Planning File Entries
MDRE	Consistency Check of Planning File Entries

Table A.5   MRP relavant Transaction Codes

A.6   Physical Inventory

Transaction Code	Description
MI01	Create Physical Inventory Document
MI02	Change Physical Inventory Document
MI03	Display Physical Inventory Document
MI04	Enter Inventory Count
MI05	Change Inventory Count
MI06	Display Inventory Count
MI09	Enter Inventory Count without Reference to Document
MI11	Recount

Table A.6 Inventory Management—Physical Inventory Transaction Codes

A.7   Purchasing and Invoicing Transactions

Transaction Code	Description
ME51N	Create Purchase Requisition
ME52N	Change Purchase Requisition
ME53N	Display Purchase Requisition
ME59N	Automatic Creation of PO
ME41	Create RFQ
ME42	Change RFQ
ME43	Display RFQ
ME47	Maintain Quotation
ME48	Display Quotation
ME49	Price Comparison—Quotations
ME21N	Create PO

Table A.7 Purchasing Transaction Codes

Transaction Code	Description
ME22N	Change PO
ME23N	Display PO
ME29N	Individual Release PO
ME28	Collective Release PO
ME31K	Create Contract
ME32K	Change Contract
ME33K	Display Contract
ME31L	Create Scheduling Agreement
ME32L	Change Scheduling Agreement
ME33L	Display Scheduling Agreement
ME38	Maintain Delivery Schedule
ME81N	Maintain Service Entry Sheet
MIRO	Enter Invoice
MIR7	Park Invoice
MIRA	Enter Invoice Verification in Background
MIR4	Display Invoice Document
MRRL	ERS Settlement
MRKO	Consignment and Pipeline Settlement
MRIS	Invoicing Plan Settlement
MR11	GR/IR Account Maintenance
MR21	Material Price Change
MR22	Debit/Credit Material

Table A.7 Purchasing Transaction Codes (Cont.)

Transaction Code	Description
OX10	Define Plant (Copy, Check and Delete)
OX14	Define Valuation Level
OX09	Maintain Storage Location
OX08	Define Purchase Organization
OX17	Assigning Plant to Purchasing Organization
OX18	Assigning Plant to Company Code
OMS2	Define Material Types

Table A.8 MM Configuration Transaction Codes

A.8 ALE/IDoc Transactions

Transaction Code	Description
WEDI	Main Menu for EDI Transactions
BALE	Main Menu for ALE Transactions
SWLD	Main Menu for Workflow Transactions
SALE	Main Menu for ALE Configurations
NACE	Main Menu for Message Control Configurations

Table A.9 Main Menu Transaction Codes

Transaction Code	Description
SE11	Data Dictionary
WE02	IDoc Display
WE05	IDoc List
WE07	IDoc Statistics
WE19	Test Tool for IDoc

Table A.10 Transaction Codes for Technical Areas

Transaction Code	Description
WE12	Convert and Outbound IDoc to Inbound IDoc
WE16	Process an Incoming IDoc
WE17	Process an Incoming Status File
BD64	Maintain ALE Distribution Model
ST22	Dump Analysis
SM21	System Log
SM12	Locked Entries

Table A.10 Transaction Codes for Technical Areas (Cont.)

B Important Tables

B.1 Material Master Tables

Table	Description
MARA	General Data
MAKT	Short Texts, Descriptions
MARM	Conversion Factors
MVKE	Sales Org, Distribution Channel
MLAN	Sales Data, Tax Indicator, Tax
MARC	Classification
MBEW	Plant Planning Data
MLGN	Valuation Data
MLGT	Warehouse Management Inventory Data
MVER	Warehouse Management Storage Type
MARD	Consumption Data
MCHB	Storage Location Data with Stock Balances

Table B.1 Material Master Tables

B.2 Other Important Tables

Table	Description
EINA	Purchasing Info Record—General Data
EINE	Purchasing Info Record—Purchasing Organization Data
EBAN	Purchase Requisition

Table B.2 MM Tables

Table	Description
EBKN	Purchase Requisition Account Assignment
EKAB	Release Documentation
EKBE	History per Purchasing Document
EKET	Scheduling Agreement Schedule Lines
EKKN	Account Assignment in Purchasing Document
EKKO	Purchasing Document Header
EKPO	Purchasing Document Item
IKPF	Header—Physical Inventory Document
ISEG	Physical Inventory Document Items
LFA1	Vendor Master General Data
LFB1	Vendor Master Company Code Data
NRIV	Number Range Intervals
T161T	Texts for Purchasing Document Types
T023	Material Groups
T024	Purchasing Groups

Table B.2 MM Tables (Cont.)

C   BAdIs

You can access the list of BAdIs via the IMG menu SAP CUSTOMIZING IMPLEMEN-
TATION GUIDE • MATERIALS MANAGEMENT • PURCHASING • BUSINESS ADD-INS FOR
PURCHASING.

You can see the list of BAdIs related to Purchasing as shown in Figure C.1.

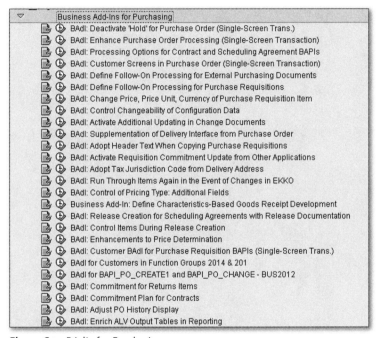

Figure C.1   BAdIs for Purchasing

Similarly, you can find the BAdIs for External Service Management, Inventory
Management, and Physical Inventory & Logistics Invoice Verification. Some of the
most important BAdIs are listed in Table C.1.

BAdI	Description
ME_PROCESS_PO_CUST	BAdI: Enhance Purchase Order Processing (Single-Screen Transaction)
ME_PROCESS_OUT_CUST	BAdI: Processing Options for Contract and Scheduling Agreement BAPIs
ME_PURCHDOC_POSTED	BAdI: Define Follow-On Processing for External Purchasing Documents
ME_REQ_POSTED	BAdI: Define Follow-On Processing for Purchase Requisitions
MM_EDI_DESADV_IN	BAdI: Supplementation of Delivery Interface from Purchase Order
ME_PO_PRICING_CUST	BAdI: Enhancements to Price Determination
MRM_ERS_HDAT_MODIFY	BAdI: Change Document Header Data in ERS
MRM_PARTNER_CHECK	BAdI: Check Partner Data in Purchase Order
MRM_DOWNPAYMENT	BAdI: Down Payments
MRM_RETENTIONS	BAdI: Default Values and Input Parameters for Retention
MRM_INVOICE_UPDATE	BAdI: Checks when Saving and Deleting Invoices
MB_INSMK_WIP_CHANGE	BAdI: Stock Transfer of a WIP Batch

Table C.1 Important BAdIs

You can also find the BAdIs via Transaction SE84 (ABAP Developement Workbench) as shown in Figure C.2.

You can select the area to search for a BAdI in the APPLICATION COMPONENT field. For example, if you're searching a BAdI for the Purchasing area, select MM-PUR in the APPLICATION COMPONENT field.

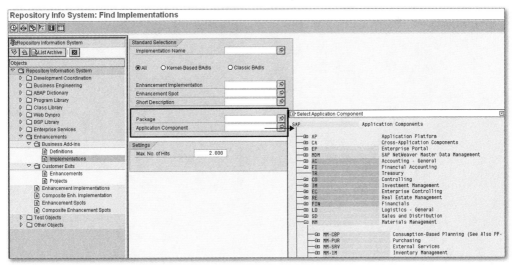

Figure C.2 Searching BAdIs via Transaction SE84

D   The Author

Akash Agrawal has more than 15 years of experience in SAP Supply Chain Management in the continuous process chemical, batch process, discrete manufacturing (telecom & media), utilities, and banking and retail industries.

He's worked extensively on SAP system support, rollouts, and upgrade and implementation projects and has managed large global SAP projects in both the United States and Europe. His experience includes working with SAP 4.0B, SAP 4.6C, SAP 4.7 Enterprise Edition, SAP ECC 5.0, SAP ECC 6.0, SAP SRM 5.0, SAP IS Utilities, and other SAP ERP products.

Akash is a frequent lecturer and visiting faculty member in some of the world's top business schools, and he speaks on the topics of SCM, ERP, and Production & Operations Management.

Akash has received many awards such as the best SAP Architect Award from IBM and the best Quality and Delivery Award. He is an engineer and has an MBA from a premier educational institution. Akash can be reached at *akash2k@gmail.com*.

Index

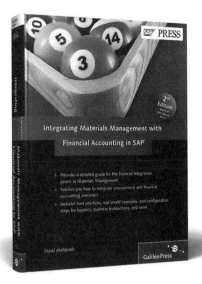

Explains the key financial integration points in Materials Management

Teaches you how to integrate procurement and financial accounting processes

Includes best practices, real-world examples, and configuration steps for logistics, business transactions, and more

Faisal Mahboob

Integrating Materials Management with Financial Accounting in SAP

If you are an SAP super user or a consultant involved in a complex Materials Management and Financial Accounting integration project, this is the book you've been looking for. Explore the complex relationship between MM and FI and the key integration points. Maximize the potential of an integrated MM system solution with a focus on account and controlling postings as related to FI compliance and its impact on MM functional design and configuration. Offering a practical, straightforward approach with real-world examples, trouble-shooting techniques, step-by-step descriptions, this title allows you to capitalize on the strengths of the powerful MM solution and the FI module to create a smooth and efficient procurement process.

approx. 500 pp., 2. edition, 79,95 Euro / US$ 79.95, ISBN 978-1-59229-426-8, Oct 2012

>> www.sap-press.com

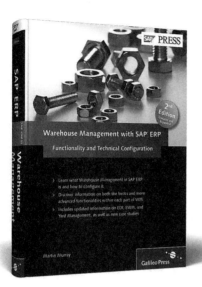

Learn what Warehouse Management in SAP ERP is and how to configure it

Discover information on both the basics and more advanced functionalities within each part of WM

Includes updated information on EDI, EWM, and Yard Management, as well as new case studies

Martin Murray

Warehouse Management with SAP ERP: Functionality and Technical Configuration

This book provides a expanded, comprehensive overview of the various functionalities and configurations needed for SAP WM. This book is the ultimate reference for anyone looking for WM information, dealing with everything from the very basic key elements through standard WM function, such as stock placement and stock removal, to more advance technology such as RFID and EWM. This new edition includes new chapters on EWM, Yard Management, and EDI. This is your one-stop guide to help you to understand and master SAP WM, and work more efficiently.

581 pp., 2. edition 2012, 79,95 Euro / US$ 79.95
ISBN 978-1-59229-409-1

Workshops for custom enhancement of the SAP standard

Examples for purchasing, inventory management, logistics invoice verification, and much more

More than 130 User Exits and BAdIs at a glance

Jürgen Schwaninger

ABAP Development for Materials Management in SAP: User Exits and BAdIs

Find the solution to your user exit problems with "ABAP Programming for SAP Materials Management: User Exits and BAdIs." This book offers helpful advice and insider knowledge to the user exits and Business Add-Ins that are used the most in Materials Management projects. As a developer's guide, you will find basic programming principles, programming examples for the most important user exits and BAdIs, and a systematic, complete description of all exits.

270 pp., 2011, 69,95 Euro / US$ 84.95
ISBN 978-1-59229-373-5

>> www.sap-press.com

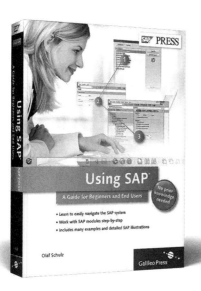

Learn to easily navigate the SAP system

Work with SAP modules step-by-step

Includes many examples and detailed SAP illustrations

Olaf Schulz

Using SAP:
A Guide for Beginners and End Users

This book helps end users and beginners get started in SAP ERP and provides readers with the basic knowledge they need for their daily work. Readers will get to know the essentials of working with the SAP system, learn about the SAP systems' structures and functions, and discover how SAP connects to critical business processes. Whether this book is used as an exercise book or as a reference book, readers will find what they need to help them become more comfortable with SAP ERP.

388 pp., 39,95 Euro / US$ 39.95
ISBN 978-1-59229-408-4

>> www.sap-press.com

Interested in reading more?

Please visit our website for all
new book releases from SAP PRESS.

www.sap-press.com